Cultural Management and Policy in Latin America

This book represents an important milestone in the agenda for diversity and equity for the cultural management discipline. Henze and Escribal carry out an excellent exercise to make visible the research agendas, approaches, and contributions to the discipline, putting emphasis on the importance of the social, political, and cultural context in which they develop. Decolonising cultural management education is definitely a new priority for the field.

Javier J. Hernández Acosta, *Universidad del Sagrado Corazón,*
Puerto Rico

Cultural rights are fundamental for everyone, everywhere. Solidarity among cultural management professionals is vital to defend the free development of culture and secure its working for citizens in all circumstances. This timely book contributes by offering insights into practices in Latin America and to ideals which are relevant around the world.

Dr. Johan Kolsteeg, *Faculty of Arts, Department of Arts, Culture and*
Media Studies, University of Groningen, The Netherlands

Each territory develops its own systems to attend its local specificities. In cultural management this is not different. This important book provides greater knowledge about current issues at stake in Latin America and the creative solutions provided. It is a highly valuable contribution to spread the 'tecnologias' of this region and inspire researchers and practitioners in the field in and outside Latin America.

Karine Legrand, *Culture Programme Coordinator,*
Goethe-Institut Sao Palo, Brazil

Cultural Management and Policy in Latin America provides in-depth insights into the education and training of cultural managers, their practice, and the specific challenges they are confronted with from an interdisciplinary and comparative perspective. The book takes a particular focus on the effects of neoliberalism on cultural practices across the region, and questions how cultural managers in Latin America deal not only with contemporary political challenges but also with the omnipresent legacy of colonialism. In doing so, it unpacks the methods, formats, and narratives they employ.

The book reflects on the topics that researchers and practitioners in Latin America are currently investigating, the literature and frames of reference they draw upon, and how they interact both within the region and beyond. The volume provides those who operate as researchers, scholars, practitioners, and students of cultural management and policy with a comprehensive resource on international cultural management that aims to overcome Western-centric methods and theories.

Raphaela Henze is Professor of Cultural Management at Heilbronn University, Germany.

Federico Escribal is Professor of Cultural Management at the National University for the Arts, Argentina.

Routledge Research in the Creative and Cultural Industries

Series Editor: Ruth Rentschler

This series brings together book-length original research in cultural and creative industries from a range of perspectives. Charting developments in contemporary cultural and creative industries thinking around the world, the series aims to shape the research agenda to reflect the expanding significance of the creative sector in a globalised world.

For more information about this series, please visit: www.routledge.com/Routledge-Research-in-the-Creative-and-Cultural-Industries/book-series/RRCCI

Cultural Management and Policy in Latin America

Edited by
Raphaela Henze and Federico Escribal

Routledge
Taylor & Francis Group

LONDON AND NEW YORK

First published 2021
by Routledge
2 Park Square, Milton Park, Abingdon, Oxon OX14 4RN

and by Routledge
52 Vanderbilt Avenue, New York, NY 10017

Routledge is an imprint of the Taylor & Francis Group, an informa business

British Library Cataloguing-in-Publication Data
A catalogue record for this book is available from the British Library

Library of Congress Cataloging-in-Publication Data
Names: Henze, Raphaela, editor. | Escribal, Federico, editor.
Title: Cultural management and policy in Latin America / edited by
Raphaela Henze, Federico Escribal.
Description: Milton Park, Abingdon, Oxon ; New York, NY : Routledge,
2021. | Includes bibliographical references and index.
Identifiers: LCCN 2020053232 (print) | LCCN 2020053233 (ebook)
Subjects: LCSH: International business enterprises--Management--Social
aspects--Latin America. | Management--Latin America. | Corporate
culture--Latin America.
Classification: LCC HD62.4 .C8528 2021 (print) | LCC HD62.4 (ebook) |
DDC 306.098--dc23
LC record available at https://lccn.loc.gov/2020053232
LC ebook record available at https://lccn.loc.gov/2020053233

ISBN: 978-0-367-62269-5 (hbk)
ISBN: 978-0-367-62391-3 (pbk)
ISBN: 978-1-003-10923-5 (ebk)

Typeset in Times New Roman
by Deanta Global Publishing Services, Chennai, India

Contents

Illustrations

Figures

Tables

Contributors

Editors

Raphaela Henze is Professor of Cultural Management at Heilbronn University (Germany) and co-investigator of the Arts & Humanities Research Council-funded, international and interdisciplinary Network Brokering Intercultural Exchange (www.managingculture.net). Prior to joining Heilbronn University, Raphaela worked in several senior management positions in universities, ministries, and foundations. Her main research focus is on the impacts of globalisation and internationalisation on cultural management, international cultural management and policy, participatory cultural projects, and empowerment processes.

Raphaela studied Law at Humboldt-University Berlin and Paris X-Nanterre in France, received her PhD from Ruhr University Bochum, was a postdoc in the Law, Media & Culture Project at Yale Law School, USA, as well as at the National Institute for Educational Policy Research (NIER) in Tokyo, Japan. She holds an MBA from the University of London.

Federico Escribal is a cultural manager specialised in cultural policy, diversity, and cultural rights. Federico teaches at the National University of the Arts (Argentina) and serves as academic director of a co-learning institutional space on Cultural Management at the National University of La Plata (Argentina), and was a guest professor at the Universidad Nacional de Colombia. Between 2006 and 2007, he directed a School of Arts and Crafts in Sao Tome and Principe (Africa). Between 2011 and 2015, he served as National Director for Cultural Rights and Diversity Promotion, completing almost ten years in Argentina´s National Ministry of Culture. He was manager of the local vocational training system in the government of the city of Buenos Aires and is currently an adviser to the national Cabinet of Ministers.

Contributors

Bianca Araújo holds a PhD in Cultural Management from the Federal University of Bahia (Brazil) and at the University of South Australia as a visiting student. She holds a master's and a bachelor's degree in Performing Arts. Bianca has more than 20 years of experience in arts management and production.

Carlos Yáñez Canal is a professor and researcher at the National University of Colombia. He is the author of numerous books, articles, research papers, and a frequent keynote speaker at conferences in the field of culture and identities. Carlos has been a visiting professor at universities in North America, Europe, and South America. As a teacher and researcher, he has received various distinctions and awards nationally and internationally.

Norma Muñoz del Campo is an associate professor at the Universidad de Santiago de Chile and member of the Public Policies Department at the faculty of Administration and Economics. Her main research focus is in the fields of political sociology and analysis of public policies. Norma analyses the institutional reforms that took place in Chile from the transition to democracy to the present day from perspectives that integrate neo-institutionalist studies and cognitive approaches. She was a visiting professor at Sciences Po Paris (Fellow Caf-Sciences Po 2016–2017) and at the Centre d'Études et des Recherches de Science Administrative et Politiques, CERSA, Paris II, Assas, France.

Aarón Hernández Farfán is a Mexican actor and director. Since 1993 he has been working in theatre, TV, and film production. Aarón has worked at UNAM, Centro Cultural Helénico, INBA, and in several independent groups. He represented Mexico in the 2016 International Forum on Cultural Management and Cultural Policy organised by the Goethe-Institut and the Munich Kulturreferat.

Cláudia Leitão is a professor at the Ceará State University (UECE) (Brazil). She holds a PhD in Sociology from Sorbonne and a master's degree in Law from USP. Claudia was Secretary of Culture of Ceará, and Secretary of Creative Economy at the Ministry of Culture in Brazil. She is a consultant for the UNESCO 2030 agenda for sustainable development.

Cristina Peregrina Leyva is a cultural manager based in Tijuana, Mexico. Cristina did her bachelor's degree in Cultural Management at the Western Institute of Technology and Higher Education Guadalajara, Mexico. She has experience in the non-profit and private sector in Tijuana and Guadalajara. She has worked in both cities in collaboration with national governmental institutions as well as within the international cooperation area of the Mexican Embassy in Morocco as an intern. She was awarded the Orange Tulip Scholarship 2020 for studies at the Faculty of Arts at the University of Groningen (the Netherlands).

Vanessa de Britto Maluf is a cultural manager specialised in management and planning of development cooperation interventions, cultural public policies, and public spaces. Since 2017 she has been the project consultant for the Ibero-American cooperation programme Ibermuseums as well as consultant for the International Adviser of the Brazilian Institute of Museums and the General Director of Cultural and Artistic Promotion of the Ministry of Culture and Tourism of Bolivia. Furthermore, she is an adviser to the Cinemateca Bolivia Foundation.

Mario Hernan Mejia is a professor, researcher, and cultural manager. He has been the director of the Museum for National Identity of Honduras (2006–2013) and consultant for the United Nations Development Programme (UNDP) when preparing the Human Development Report of Honduras in 2003 Culture, Means and End for Development'. Mario is UNESCO Consultant on Cultural Policy for Central America specialised in economy and culture as well as heritage management. Some of the consultancies carried out for this organisation are 'Estudio sobre Indicadores Culturales en Centroamérica' (2005), 'Las políticas culturales en Honduras: análisis y perspectivas para su desarrollo' (2004), 'Actualización de Políticas Culturales en Panamá' (2006), 'Estudio-Inventario del Patrimonio Inmaterial en Honduras' (2003). For six years, he held the position of Director of Planning and Management Evaluation in the Secretariat of State in Culture, Arts and Sports of Honduras where he coordinated a training programme in cultural management for the National Network of Houses of Culture.

Cinthya Moizo holds a degree in Cultural Management from the Faculty of Culture, CLAEH University (Uruguay) as well as a diploma in Cultural Management from Fundación ITAÚ. Cinthya attended the international postgraduate course in Management and Politics in Culture and Communication at FLACSO Argentina. She serves as the Director of Culture at the Departmental Government of Paysandú (Uruguay) and as Professor of Cultural Management at the Faculty of Culture at the University of Paysandú.

Beth Ponte is a Brazilian arts manager, researcher, and independent consultant. She is an associate researcher at the Observatory of Creative Economy in Bahia/Brazil (OBEC-BA) and member of the Board of the Brazilian Association of Social Organisations of Culture (ABRAOSC). She is author and curator of the project Quality for Culture, developed during her time as German Chancellor Fellow (2018/2019) of the Alexander von Humboldt Foundation and guest researcher at KMM Hamburg, Germany.

Suelen Silva holds a bachelor's degree in Social Sciences (Amazonia University/Brazil), a master's in Anthropology (Federal University of Pará/Brazil, CNPQ scholarship) and specialisations in management and cultural policies (Universitat de Girona/Spain and Itaú Cultural/Brazil) as well as in community-based cultural policies (Facultad Latinoamericana de Ciencias Sociales/Argentina, Ibercultura-Viva scholarship). She has researched about the social significance of artistic and cultural practices (such as handicraft and theatre) by minority groups, published articles, and edited a book on 'June Birds', a traditional theatre-performance in the Brazilian Amazon region. She has also designed and managed programmes with a decolonial approach in one of the most active cultural centres in the north of Brazil and has worked on several cultural projects as a freelance executive producer. Suelen was selected as a German Chancellor Fellow of the Alexander von Humboldt Foundation in the Programme for Prospective Leaders (2018/2019) with a project about decentralisation and management of arts and cultural organisations in Germany.

Danilo Urbanavicius is a cultural manager who graduated from CLAEH University in Montevideo, Uruguay. He is a member of the audience research team of the SODRE National Ballet and develops projects in the performing arts in public and private institutions.

Paloma Carpio Valdeavellano is a Peruvian stage designer, communicator, and cultural manager. She holds a master's degree in Human Development from the Pontificia Universidad Católica and teaches at both the Pontificia Universidad Católica del Perú and the Universidad Científica del Sur. She has served in the public sector, being responsible for the Cultura Viva Comunitaria programme of the Municipality of Lima and the Puntos de Cultura within the Peruvian National Ministry of Culture.

Paola de la Vega Velastegui is a professor and researcher in the Literature and Cultural Studies Department at the Universidad Andina Simón Bolívar (Ecuador).

Mariano Martín Zamorano holds a PhD in Culture and Heritage Management from the University of Barcelona (UB). His thesis, 'The Dispute over External Representation in Contemporary Cultural Policies: The Case of the Cultural Paradiplomacy of Catalonia', received the International Mention (2015). He holds a master's in Cultural Management (UB) and a bachelor's and a professor's degree in Visual Arts from the National University of Cuyo, Argentina. Mariano also received a bachelor's degree in Art History at the same university. He specialised in public cultural policies at both national and international levels. He has more than ten years' experience in the design, coordination, and development of scientific projects, participating in more than 12 funded scientific investigations. These projects have been funded by the National University of Cuyo, the Spanish Agency for International Cooperation for Development (AECID), the European Union Agency for Fundamental Rights (FRA), and the European Commission (H2020), among other institutions. Mariano has been visiting scholar at the Department of Arts Administration, Education and Policy of the Ohio State University (2012), associate professor at the UB (2017), and he currently teaches on three different postgraduate programmes in Cultural Diplomacy, Policies and Management at the University Oberta de Cataluna (UOC) and the UB. Since 2010, he is a member of the Centre for the Study of Culture, Politics and Society (CECUPS).

Acknowledgements

We would like to thank the Würth Foundation for their generous support that allowed us to translate the majority of texts within this volume from either Spanish or Portuguese into English. Translation is of enormous importance for the mutual exchange that we would like to foster but unfortunately, still heavily underfunded. Furthermore, we owe a thank you to Simon Colledge from Colledge Associates who went out of his way proofreading these texts, as none have been written by a native speaker.

A thank you goes to all members and friends of the Brokering Intercultural Exchange Network (www.managingculture.net). Your support, willingness to share and for mutual learning, as well as your positivity has been inspiring to us over the last years. We strongly encourage our readers to join this international and interdisciplinary discourse.

Abbreviations

AAAE	Association of Arts Administration Educators
ABGC	Brazilian Association of Cultural Management
ACMC	Arts and Cultural Management Conference
ADN	Nationalist Democratic Action (Bolivia)
AECID	Spanish Agency for International Development Cooperation
AGEXPORT	Guatemalan Export Agency
ALACP	Latin American Articulation Culture and Politics
ANCER	The Asia Pacific Network for Cultural Education and Research
ARN	Colorado Party
BCE	Central Bank of Ecuador
CAB	Andrés Bello Convention.
CAN	Andean Community of Nations
CCE	Spanish Cultural Centre
CCEc	Ecuatorian Cultural Centre
CECC	Central American Educational and Cultural Coordinator
CEPAL	Economic Commission for Latin America
CERC	Centre of Cultural Studies and Resources of the Barcelona Provincial Council
CLACSO	Latin American Social Sciences Council
CNCA	Chilean National Council for Culture and the Arts
CONACULTA	National Council for Culture and the Arts of Mexico
CONCULTURA	National Council for Culture and the Arts of El Salvador
CPE	State Political Constitution
CPI	Corruption Perceptions Index
CSC	Culture Satellite Account
CSCU	Satellite Culture Account for Uruguay
EC	European Community
ECLAC	Economic Commission for Latin America and the Caribbean
ENCATC	European Network on Cultural Management and Policy
ERICarts	European Association of Cultural Researchers e.V.

FEFCA	Fund for the Promotion of Training and Artistic Creation
FIC	Cultural Incentive Funds
F-ODM	Millennium Development Goals Achievement Fund
FONCA	Mexican National Fund for Culture and the Arts
FONCULTURA	National Culture Fund of Ecuador
FONDART	National Fund for Cultural Development and the Arts of Chile
GDP	Gross Domestic Product
HIVOS Fund	Humanist Institute for Cooperation and Development
IBC	Bolivian Cultural Institute
IBERFORMAT	Ibero-American Network of Cultural Management Training Units
ICI	Intercultural Coexistence Index
IETM	International Network for Contemporary Performing Arts
IFAI	Mexican Federal Institute of Access to Information and Data Protection
IMCINE	Mexican Film Institute
IMM	Department of Culture of the Municipality of Montevideo
INAC	Panamanian National Institute of Culture
INAH	Mexican National Institute of Anthropology and History
INBAL	Mexican National Institute of Fine Arts
INC	Nicaraguan National Institute of Culture
INEGI	Mexican National Institute of Statistics and Geography
KMM Hamburg	Institut für Kultur – und Medienmanagement of Hamburg
MARACA	Central American Network of Community Art
MAS/IPSP	Movement to Socialism – Political Instrument for the Sovereignty of the Peoples
MCD	Ministry of Culture and Sports of Guatemala
MCJ	Ministry of Culture and Youth of Costa Rica
MCT	Ministry of Culture and Tourism
MEC	Ministry of Education and Culture
MIR	Revolutionary Leftist Movement (Bolivia)
MNR	Revolutionary Nationalist Movement (Bolivia)
MORENA	National Regeneration Movement (México)
NEMO	Trans Europe Halles, Network of European Museum Organisations
NGO	Non-Governmental Organisation.
NR	Revolutionary Nationalism (Bolivia)
ODS	Sustainable Development Goals
OEI	Organisation of Ibero-American States
ONE	Orchestra Network for Europe
ONU	United Nations
PCB	Bolivian Communist Party
PIB	Gross Domestic Product
PNC	National Culture Plan

PNUD	United Nations Development Programme
PRAHC	Integral Rehabilitation Programme for Historical Areas in Cochabamba
PRI	Institutional Revolutionary Party (Mexico)
PSOE	Spanish Socialist Workers' Party
QEIIACNZ	The Queen Elizabeth the Second Arts Council of New Zealand
RLATS	Latin American Network of Art and Social Transformation
SCN	Secretariat of Culture of the Argentine Nation
SCNB	National Culture System of Brazil
SEGIB	Ibero-American Secretariat General
SENACULT	National Secretariat of Culture (Bolivia)
SEP	Secretariat of Public Education of México
SICA	Central American Integration System
UCLAEH	Faculty of Culture of the University CLAEH
UCR	University of Costa Rica
UdeG	University of Guadalajara
UDELAR	University of Uruguay
UDP	Democratic and Popular Movement (Bolivia)
UNAH	National Autonomous University of Honduras
UNAM	National Autonomous University of Mexico
UNCTAD	United Nations Conference on Trade and Development
UNESCO	United Nations Educational, Scientific, and Cultural Organisation
UN-HABITAT	The United Nations Programme for Human Settlements
UPSA	University of Santa Cruz de la Sierra

Introduction

Raphaela Henze and Federico Escribal

This book is, in part, the result of the work of the Brokering Intercultural Exchange Network[1] that was founded in 2016 to bring international and interdisciplinary researchers and practitioners together to explore the role of cultural managers as intercultural brokers in our context of globalisation, internationalisation, and global migration. What started in Europe with a specific focus on community arts and empowerment soon raised interest in various parts of the world and it is through this network and the "Winter School Brokering Intercultural Exchange within Societies'" that our collaboration came about. Aware that content from Latin America is under-represented in cultural management and policy research and discourse, we were inspired to work on a publication that provides an in-depth insight into cultural management and policy in various Latin American countries.

Our objective is, inter alia, to review the education and training of cultural managers, their practice, and the specific challenges they are confronted by from an interdisciplinary and comparative perspective. What have been and remain the effects of neoliberalism on cultural practices across the region? How do cultural managers in Latin America deal not only with contemporary political challenges but also with the omnipresent legacy of colonialism? Which methods, formats, and narratives do they employ – of these, which have functioned effectively, which have failed, and for what reasons? The book explores the topics that researchers in Latin America are currently investigating, the literature and frames of reference they draw upon, and how they interact both within the region and beyond. What role does intercultural and international exchange play?

We hope to broaden the existing knowledge base by experiencing epistemologies, methodologies, and literature that are still relatively unknown outside (and, due to a weak infrastructure for collaboration, sometimes even within) the region. We are convinced that a greater degree of exchange will offer new, creative, and alternative cultural experiences to the benefit of the discipline as a whole (Cowan, 2002, p. 6; Dewey & Wyszomirski, 2004; Durrer & Henze, 2020, p. 10).

Working on two different continents with only a limited amount of knowledge on the respective political, historical, and social backgrounds and potential political biases, while confronted by a pandemic that had a particularly strong impact on many Latin American countries and that prevented further in-person exchange, proved challenging. This book project represents a learning process in many regards, and we are glad to share our insights.

Defining the geographical scope

The majority of countries covered in this volume are located in South America, and this was our primary focus when we approached potential contributors, which proved for a variety of reasons, among them a sometimes relatively low command of English and a lack of networks, relatively difficult. Having been in contact with colleagues from Puerto Rico, Honduras, Mexico, and Guatemala and recognising that many authors referred to colleagues based in and resources derived from Central America, because of common characteristics and similar challenges to the rest of the region, it was decided to broaden the scope of our research. One of the challenges this produced was how to refer to the region. Prior to European colonisation, the "territoriality" did not advance to the point of understanding the region as a whole. Consequently, there were no nominal frameworks for it. The closest one is possibly *abya yala*, a name that comes from the *Kuna* people of modern-day Panama, which means *land of life* (López-Hernández, 2004, p. 4). While common in indigenous activism – and progressively used in the academic field by the decolonial current (Walsh, 2014; Escobar, 2016) – most of the population of the region is completely unaware of its existence and meaning. The same applies to other indigenous nominations which represent visions that are not in accordance with the idea of the continent,[2] and whose use is assumed as an ideological position by those who argue that the names "America" (or even more so the expression "New World", no longer in use) would be specific to the European colonisers and, therefore, a component of the perpetuation of their domination. The same applies to the term "Latin America". This is a problematic geographical construction that might somehow define the geographic scope of this book but is inscribed in the colonial register as a term developed when France tried to influence the region in pursuit of its own interests (Stavenhagen, 2001, p. 13). France was competing with Great Britain for more political and economic influence in the region after most of the countries had achieved their independence (Selser, 1994). Despite its frequent use, particularly in publications about the region, but produced from outside it, the term is controversial (Escobar, 2018; Mignolo, 2005; Cupples et al., 2019, p. 1). Furthermore, the question can be asked whether the borders of Latin America even extend into the United States along with the diaspora of migrants inhabiting transnational labour circuits (Postero, 2019, p. 43)? A question that reappeared frequently and is discussed in several texts within this book (Henze; Escribal, this volume) is whether the populations share sufficient common ground to make it a meaningful research object for the field of cultural management and policy. We are convinced that they do and have decided to use the term "Latin America" although we are well aware of its shortcomings. This decision was not taken lightly. The term "South and Central America", while less politically charged, would have excluded Mexico which is located in North America and which we consider an important reference point and resource.

Cultural management and cultural policy

The historical and geopolitical but also social, economic, and, obviously, political particularities condition the practice of managing culture in each country. These conditions differ in the various countries within the region, despite some evident commonalities, among them colonialism that plays an integral part in many contributions. That there is, therefore, no "Latin American cultural management model" as Zamorano et al. explained in 2014 (Zamorano, Ulldemolins & Klein, 2014) can be proved by the contributions to this volume. However, despite the recognition of all these differences, intellectuals such as Beatriz Sarlo, Sergio Miceli, Guillermo Bonfil Batalla, Nestor Garcia Canclini, and Jose Joaquin Brunner have for at least four decades thought about ways to deal with common and current challenges through cultural policies seeking to effect social change. The main political leaders of the regional independence movements, Simon Bolivar and Jose de San Martín, as well as later intellectuals like José Martí and Manuel Ugarte, also understood that the political path to sovereignty is regional integration and were aware of the role that culture in addition to cultural policy plays in such a process. "Cultural policy" will be understood as described by Santillan Guemes as

> a set of interventions, strategies and actions that different governmental, non-governmental, private, community-based institutions, etc. implement with the purpose of orienting their meaning towards the achievement of certain development objectives, satisfying the strictly "cultural", symbolic and expressive needs and aspirations of society at its different levels (socio-economic), modalities (gender, age classes, native peoples, ethnic minorities, etc.) and environments. Its mission is, therefore, focused on making decisions regarding how to operate and dynamically set in play (manage) the cultural elements (material, organisational, knowledge, symbolic, and emotional) of a community, society, region or nation in order to fulfil the objectives in question which are never politically neutral.
>
> (2009)

At the beginning of the 1980s, the challenge was to consolidate the recently recovered democracy by creating a citizenship culture that could provide the democratic efforts with civil support. Citizen participation and the occupation of public space were identified as key components for strengthening democratisation efforts (Mejia Arango, 2009; Logiódice, 2012) as well as addressing the deep inequalities that persist structurally in the region (Grimson, 2011). It seems to be exactly these efforts and approaches that are of particular interest to cultural management and policy researchers in the so-called West that are interested in finding new ways of engaging heterogeneous audiences and empowering (marginalised) communities.

With populism on the rise in many Western societies (Henze, 2017), the interest in the experiences of colleagues that deal with various forms of populism (from both sides of the political spectrum) for decades appears to be growing.

Within Latin America, cultural management is increasingly questioned as a category, imposed – once again – by interests from outside the region, particularly because of its intertwining with the introduction of neoliberalism in the 1990s and the strong Spanish influence (de la Vega Valestegui; Moizo & Urbanavicius; Escribal, this volume). This hegemony of cultural management allegedly made invisible and interrupted other disciplinary approaches based on alternative theoretical frameworks that had long existed in the region. The two most relevant in this regard are socio-cultural animation and cultural promotion. The first was defined, again extra-regionally, as "the set of social practices that aim to stimulate the initiative and participation of communities in the process of their own development and in the global dynamics of socio-political life in which they are integrated" (UNESCO, 1982) and had a considerable development both in Spain and in Latin America until the eruption of cultural management as a narrative in the 1990s.[3] Although its major field of application was in non-formal adult education, many of the professional practices now covered by the framework of cultural management were at that time recognised within the scope of socio-cultural animation which "can be better described as a movement than as a theory or body of doctrine" (Simpson, 1989). As for cultural promotion, this differs from socio-cultural animation as it prioritises the transforming ability of the members of a community themselves, questioning the "missionary" tendency of external agents, considering them to be unaware of the subtleties and particularities of each culture in each territory. Its theoretical framework – enunciated by the Argentinean anthropologist Adolfo Colombres[4] – is shaped by the work of the Mexican Guillermo Bonfil Batalla and his *Theory of Cultural Control*, in which he identifies the political centrality of reinforcing the capability of each community to define which elements of foreign cultures to incorporate (and which not to incorporate) and how to do so (Bonfil Batalla, 1982). What became known relatively recently as Community Engagement and Empowerment in North America and Europe is obviously closely related to this decade-old cultural practice within Latin America.

However, despite understandable scepticism towards and ongoing debates about concepts coined and formed outside the region, cultural management gained ground in the field in Latin America (Escribal, this volume). It is a kind of common leverage point for practices within the public or private sector that share similar challenges, among them centralism, low prioritisation by political systems that privilege the instrumental dimension of culture (Chaui, 2008), modest budgets as well as fragile and constantly changing institutional frameworks (Carpio Valdeavellano; de la Vega Valestegui; Peregrina & Hernandez Farfan, this volume). A further challenge for the sector in the region, but also beyond it, is the increasing difficulty of funding projects that produce and circulate contents that are of social relevance but not necessarily economically exploitable (Srnicek, 2017; Yudice, 2019). This goes hand in hand with culture regarded as an important contributor to development processes (Escobar, 2011; Yudice, 2019). The theory of the Orange Economy (Buitrago & Dugue, 2013), promoted by the Inter-American Development Bank (IDB), that focuses strongly on the copy-rights-based industries,[5] is therefore prevailing in the region. It is criticised for putting the economic potential of arts and culture exclusively in focus without much regard to social aspects of arts, culture, and particularly heritage. As such, it represents a commercial-oriented privatisation of identities (Arango, 2020). Those in the field that believe in arts and culture as a means of social transformation, with a focus on reducing inequalities, adopt interculturality as their theoretical framework (Walsh, Mignolo & Linera, 2006).

Unsurprisingly, there is no obvious and easy one-size-fits-all solution for the challenges shared by the majority of the countries in Latin America. However, as many of the contributions within this volume show, there seems to be a common set of concerns, which is not reflected in cultural management curricula, shaped again by Western, particularly Spanish, influences. The growing professionalisation of the sector (with the exception of Bolivia, where education available in the field is close to non-existent) is criticised for its strong focus on economic aspects. There is also a shared sensitivity concerning the common colonial legacy as well as the desire to construct new and authentic paradigms and narratives for the region.

As can be seen throughout this book, attention must be paid to the various processes that are boiling on the margins of institutional systems. In the absence of predictability of public cultural policies, transformations are often driven by political movements with a strong foundation in arts and culture, but not so in party politics (de la Vega Valestegui; de Britto Maluf, this volume). Actually, anyone who wants to understand how bottom-up struggles for a better world are enacted, fought, and how they play out, should have a closer look at these social movements in Latin America (Cupples et al., 2019, p. 3): the most prominent ones being the *Madres* and *Abuela de Plaza de Mayo*, the Confederation of Workers in the Popular Economy (CTEP), the feminist movement in Argentina, the Grupo de Apoyo Mutuo in Guatemala, CONAIE of the indigenous peoples in Ecuador, or Landless Workers' Movement (Movimento dos Trabalhadores Rurais Sem Terra [MST]) and Fora do Eixo in Brasil, to name only a few.

Contents

This collection is divided into two sections. The first part gives a comparative overview of cultural management and policy within the region sometimes informed by experiences gained though international exchanges. The second provides insights into cultural management and policy in particular countries. Each author contributed from her own vantage point. The particular viewpoints are shaped not only by the different national and local contexts but also by the respective disciplines as well as professions the contributors come from. Many of them are in the early stages of their respective careers in either academia or practice. Despite the focus on a specific region, we need to be mindful of the already described diverse historical, social, and political backgrounds. Questions that we asked collectively are approached individually, and we as editors do not necessarily always agree.

The collection begins with discussions by Henze, Ponte, Araujo & Leitao, Meija, and Yañez-Canal of cultural management and policy in Latin America in general. Henze starts with the observation that Latin American narratives and epistemology are under-represented in many Western discourses. She not only focuses on the various reasons for this marginalisation but strives to find ways to establish mutual learning processes between the so-called West and South, being convinced that Europe, in particular, can learn from the experiences with unequal societies and de-colonialisation processes.

In her contribution, Ponte focuses particularly on Ibero-American relations from a post-colonial perspective. She identifies the potential for the Latin America-Europe dialectic to succeed in shifting away from the roles assigned by history and strengthened by stereotypes, and to build a new relationship in facing current challenges. Understanding cultural management as a profession linked to history, and recognising the cultural diversity of the region, she proposes avoiding false dichotomies and reductionisms in order to re-think international cultural exchange from novel and fairer perspectives.

Similar to Ponte, Araujo and Leitao argue for an emancipation of cultural management in the region that, despite its particular cultural richness, still prosecutes the management and production as well as policies models developed in the North (Europe and America). They draw on experiences from Oceania that has several similarities with South America in that both are young compared to Europe, and Europeans have colonised them in the past. They discuss social and sustainable development, the interdependence between North and South and reflect on another epistemology to understand the dynamics between the hemispheres. Araujo and Leitao propose an advance in the dialogue between the "souths" to improve the international exchange between places that demonstrate many similarities and can collaborate to promote a new epistemology of sustainability.

Mejía provides a comprehensive overview of the institutional and legal frameworks governing culture in Central America. He examines the significance assigned to culture in each country of the region, in order to understand how this is reflected in institutional structures as well as in theoretical-methodological approaches. He also reviews cultural management training, taking into account the new social mandates for cultural policies as well as the changes resulting from globalisation and the impact of the COVID-19 pandemic.

National identity, the market, cultural rights, cultural diversity, and the aesthetisation of life are topics Yañez-Canal puts into the focus of interviews he conducted with renowned professionals in the field of cultural management in the region. The chapter provides a sample of the different perspectives on the sensitive dimensions of cultural management throughout the continent, while identifying a certain tendency to homologate cultural management with arts management (as it is the more common concept within the Anglo-Saxon sphere), and to over-emphasise the administration of cultural institutions. Finally, he presents the tension between an end-based rationale that prevails in the practice of the profession and the theory developed by various cultural managers involved in the management of cultural collectives or artist networks.

The second section includes those texts that deal with cultural management and the analysis of its dimensions based on concrete national experiences and examples. In his contribution, Escribal analyses cultural management as a discourse that crosses and intervenes in the cultural sector in Argentina, stimulating certain political discussions that have not yet been resolved regarding the relationship between culture and politics, the social function of the arts and, particularly, the issue of cultural citizenship. Following what Ponte presents in her contribution in relation to the monocultural assimilationist model, he shows that it was specifically effective in conjunction with the cultural centralism around the city of Buenos Aires. Escribal asks whether cultural management will be capable of transforming the public approach to cultural diversity within the Latin American context of heterogeneous and unequal societies.

Zamorano explains the context within which cultural management takes place in Paraguay, which, despite promising growth rates over the last couple of years, is still one of the poorest and most unequal nations within the region. He explores the work of several cultural initiatives that have been implemented since the democratic transition in a country that features a vibrant cultural heritage, but whose cultural policies are still interventionist and patronising. Using empirical research that spans a decade, Zamorano shows how cultural management is progressing, for instance, by increased training offers and integrating community-based practices.

Muñoz del Campo examines cultural management in Chile from the perspective of public action and questions the skills and knowledge required for the training of professionals in the sector. To her, the recent institutional development of Chilean public cultural policy determined educational offerings and, as such, the professional profiles of those in the field. Outlining the regional as well as international influences on this development in the cultural management sector, she distinguishes a tension between a technocratic orientation of cultural managers' profiles, and one based on learning through practice. Like many others in this volume, Muñoz del Campo argues that the concept of cultural management, that is still very much associated with economic concerns, needs to broaden its focus in order to have more impact in the respective countries of the region.

The arrival of cultural management in Ecuador is analysed by de la Vega Valestegui, who critically reflects on the Spanish geopolitical strategy towards Latin America. Considering that its inclusion in the agenda of the cultural sector undermined bottom-up cultural processes, as well as epistemologies and knowledge originating in the social margins typical for the Ecuadorian cultural scene, she describes the Hispanic motivations for unleashing this process, as well as the political and historical context in which it occurred. She observes the failure of the Ecuadorian political system to address cultural rights beyond folklorist rhetoric and problematises the processes of monocultural and nation-based identity building. From a decolonial perspective, she argues for placing Andean epistemologies at the centre of the discipline and prioritising forms of community organisations.

In her contribution, Silva focuses on the bureaucratic apparatus that Brazil has established in order to meet the challenges cultural policy is facing. She explores the meanings assigned to culture by the State as well as the typology used in cultural management today. Different nominal frameworks are distinguished, areas of work described, skills and knowledge required for the profession are analysed and linked to the evaluation of current training programmes. Understanding cultural management as "a field seeking definitions", she explores cultural managers' self-perceptions, and concludes that there is a wide register of practices currently on the margins of the professional field that deserve to be included in it in an organic way in order to achieve mutual enhancement.

Moizo and Urbanavicius give a brief account of Uruguay's history – which showcases the strong impact of European culture – in order to explain how cultural management developed in the smallest country in the region. After describing the institutional and normative framework in which professional practice and cultural policies are developed, they describe the educational history of the profession and emphasise the adoption of economic-based perspectives for culture. Understanding that the development of a robust creative industries-based economy requires sustained public investment over time, they describe certain oscillations in relation to the state's commitment in this regard which correspond to changes in the government's political orientation.

Carpio examines the fragility of public cultural institutions in Peru and presents the activities of relevant non-public cultural groups and organisations, putting them into the necessary historical as well as political context. As a critical dimension of a nation that has experienced instability and, more recently, political violence that has left obvious marks on the country's socio-demographic and symbolic structure, culture does not seem to be able to break out of the restricted zone to which it was confined by the colonial conformation of the Peruvian nation. Carpio perceives the possibility that the national reflection around the global pandemic crisis will allow a social appropriation of the political agenda of culture to advance in order to build an alternative to the one currently displayed.

Cultural management in Bolivia is analysed from the standpoint that culture, as well as its management, is ideologically charged and in dispute. De Britto Maluf reports the most relevant experiences regarding the role that both artists and cultural managers play in the cultural sector and in Bolivian public life dating back to the mid-20th century. From there, she examines the impact of cultural institutions, artists, and cultural managers on Bolivia's political and social transformations occurring in the first years of the 21st century, unleashed by the election of the first indigenous president in the continent's history, Evo Morales. De Britto Maluf pays special attention to how political movements grounded in the arts and culture shape and influence the discussions about what constitutes Bolivian culture and its management.

Mexico, the only country presented in this volume located in North America, shares a rich, fascinating, and complex history that far exceeds the five hundred years that have elapsed since the beginning of European colonisation. Despite strong centralism within its capital, Mexico features an enormous heterogeneity with many cultural differences within the country. Tijuana, a city close to the US-American border, has a specific context and is very distinct from, for example, the city of Merida that is located in the south-east, with strong roots in the Mayan culture and tradition. Peregrina Leyva and Hernandez Farfán explore the antecedents of cultural management and policy as it is understood in Mexico today. They analyse the way in which politics enabled or hindered advancements in the field of cultural policies by raising questions about a certain tendency towards corporatisation and the reproduction of clientelist logics that are not uncommon in the region. With a framework strongly focused on cultural rights, they analyse the challenges that cultural management faces in the light of a significant change of political direction, unprecedented in Mexico's contemporary history, with the election of the leftist government of Andrés Manuel López Obrador in 2018.

We are aware that many voices are still missing, and we sincerely hope that this book will be a starting point for more mutual discourse in the future. While we are starting from different vantage points, there is a growing recognition of our individual and professional place in how perceptions and realities of cultural rights are shaped through global exchange. This exchange needs funding possibilities as well as tools to deal with language barriers but, most of all, an awareness of power imbalances and asymmetries and the will to overcome them by learning from each another. For us, this book has been a first step into this direction and we strongly encourage our readers to join in.

Notes

1 www.managingculture.net.
2 Such as, for example, with the terms *mayab*, used by the Mayas of the Yucatan peninsula, and *Tawantinsuyo*, used by the Incas – the Mesoamerican civilisation with the largest territorial expansion of the period.
3 For more insights into socio-cultural animation, see the work of the Argentinian author Ezequiel Ander-Egg, unfortunately only accessible in Spanish (Ander-Egg, 2002).
4 It is important to note that both Ander-Egg and Colombres developed a central part of their work in exile, being targeted by the Argentinian dictatorship that lasted from 1976 to 1982. The persecution of intellectuals and artists throughout the region may also have contributed to their political commitment with the consolidation of democracy in the 1980s.
5 Defined by the Economic Commission for Latin America and the Caribbean (ECLAC) as publishing, film, TV, radio, phonographic, mobile contents, independent audiovisual production, web contents, electronic games, and content produced for digital convergence (cross-media).

References

Ander-Egg, E. (2002). *La práctica de la animación sociocultural y el léxico del animador*, Lima: Fondo Editorial PUCP.
Arango, F. (2020). Pandemia cultural. *Le Monde Diplomatique Colombia*, (203), 8–9.
Bonfil Batalla, G. (1982). Lo propio y lo ajeno. Una aproximación al problema del control cultural. In: Colombres, A. (Comp.), *La cultura popular*, México: Ediciones Coyoacán, pp. 1–7.
Buitrago, F. & Duque, I. (2013). *The Orange Economy. An Infinite Opportunity*, Washington / Bogotá: Inter-American Development Bank.

Carpio Valdeavellano, P. (this volume). Cultural management in Peru: the role of the ministry of culture in challenging times. In: Henze, R. & Escribal, F. (Eds.), *Cultural Management and Policy in Latin America*, Abingdon & New York: Routledge, pp. 230–246.

Chaui, M. (2008). *Cultura y democracia*, Cuadernos de Pensamiento Crítico Latinoamericano, Vol. 8.

Cowan, T. (2002). *Creative Destruction: How Globalisation Is Changing the World's Cultures*, Princeton, NJ: Princeton University Press.

Cupples, J., Prieto, M. & Palomino-Schalscha, M. (2019). Latin American development. Editors' introduction. In: Cupples, J., Palomino-Schalscha, M. & Prieto, M. (Eds.), *The Routledge Handbook of Latin American Development*, New York: Routledge, pp. 1–11.

de Britto Maluf, V. (this volume). Cultural management in Mexico: from precariousness to development. In: Henze, R. & Escribal, F. (Eds.), *Cultural Management and Policy in Latin America*, Abingdon & New York: Routledge, pp. 198–214.

de la Vega Velástegui, P. (this volume). Cultural management in Ecuador: genealogy and power relations within the constitution of a field. In: Henze, R. & Escribal, F. (Eds.), *Cultural Management and Policy in Latin America*, Abingdon & New York: Routledge, pp. 143–162.

Dewey, P. & Wyszomirski, M. (2004). *International Issues in Cultural Policy and Administration: A Conceptual Framework for Higher Education. International Conference on Cultural Policy Research.* Montreal, QC, http://neumann.hec.ca/iccpr/PDF_Texts/Dewey_Wyszomirski.pdf (Accessed October 27, 2020).

Durrer, V. & Henze, R. (2020). Introduction. In: Durrer, V. & Henze, R. (Eds.), Managing Culture. Reflecting on Exchange in Global Times, Cham: Palgrave Macmillan, pp. 1–21.

Escobar, A. (2012) "Más allá del desarrollo: Postdesarrollo y transiciones hacia el pluriverso", *Revista de Antropologia Social*. doi: 10.5209/rev_RASO.2012.v21.40049.

Escobar, A. (2016). Desde abajo, por la izquierda y con la Tierra: La diferencia de Abya Yala/Afro/Latino-América. In: Rescatar la esperanza. Más allá del neoliberalismo y el progresismo. Barcelona: EntrePueblos, pp. 337–369. https://www.entrepueblos.org/wp-content/uploads/2016/11/RescatarEsperanza_web.pdf (Accessed October 20, 2020).

Escobar, A. (2018). *Otro posible es posible: Caminando hacia las transiciones desde Abya Yala/Afro/Latino-America.* Bogota: Ediciones desde abajo.

Escribal, F. (this volume). Cultural management in Argentina: political agenda and challenges for practitioners and researchers. In: Henze, R. & Escribal, F. (Eds.), *Cultural Management and Policy in Latin America*, Abingdon & New York: Routledge, pp. 87–105.

Grimson, A. (2011). *Los límites de la cultura. Crítica de las teorías de la identidad*, Buenos Aires: Siglo XXI Editores.

Henze, R. (2017). Why we have to overcome paternalism in times of populism. In: Dragisevic-Sesic, M. (Ed.), *Cultural Diplomacy: Arts, Festivals and Geopolitics*, Belgrade: Ministry of Culture of the Republic of Serbia, pp. 73–87.

Henze, R. (this volume). Thinking cultural management from the South. New frames for the "western" discourse informed by Latin America. In: Henze, R. & Escribal, F. (Eds.), *Cultural Management and Policy in Latin America*, Abingdon & New York: Routledge, pp. 3–21.

Logiódice, M. J. (2012). Políticas culturales, la conformación de un campo disciplinar. Sentidos y prácticas en las opciones de políticas. Documentos y Aportes en

Administración Pública y Gestión Estatal, 18, pp. 59–87. http://www.scielo.org.ar/pdf/ daapge/n18/n18a03.pdf (Accessed May 28, 2017).

López-Hernández, M. (2004). *Encuentros en los senderos de Abya Yala*. Quito: Editorial Abya Yala.

Mejia Arango, J. L. (2009). Apuntes sobre las políticas culturales en América Latina (1987–2009), *Pensamiento Iberoamericano*, 4, pp. 105–129.

Mignolo, W. (2005). *The Idea of Latin America*, Malden, MA: Wiley-Blackwell.

Moizo, C. & Urbanavicius, D. (this volume). Cultural management in Uruguay: a country synonymous with a river. In: Henze, R. & Escribal, F. (Eds.), *Cultural Management and Policy in Latin America*, Abingdon & New York: Routledge, pp. 184–197.

Peregrina, C. & Hernández Farfán, A. (this volume). Cultural management in Mexico: from precariousness to development. In: Henze, R. & Escribal, F. (Eds.), *Cultural Management and Policy in Latin America*, Abingdon & New York: Routledge, pp. 215–229.

Postero, N. (2019). Indigenous development in Latin America. In: Cupples, J., Palomino-Schalscha, M. & Prieto, M. (Eds.), *The Routledge Handbook of Latin American Development*, New York: Routledge, pp. 43–53.

Santillan Guemes, R. (2009). Políticas culturales, cultura y gestión cultural, *RGC [revista gestión cultural]*, 1, pp. 1–16. http://rgcediciones.com.ar/1548-2/.

Selser, G. (1994). Cronología de las intervenciones extranjeras en América Latina: 1849–1898, México: UNAM.

Simpson, J. (1989). Sociocultural animation. In: Titmus, C. J. (Ed.), *Lifelong Education for Adults. An International Handbook. Advances in Education*, Amsterdam: Pergamon, pp. 54–57.

Srnicek, N. (2017). *Platform Capitalism*, Hoboken, New Jersey: John Wiley & Sons.

Stavenhagen, R. (2001). La diversidad cultural en el desarrollo de las Américas. Los pueblos indígenas y los estados nacionales en Hispanoamerica, *Serie de Estudios Culturales*, 8, p. 48.

UNESCO (1982), "Mexico City declaration on cultural policies", World Conference on Cultural Policies, Mexico City, 26 July-6 August.

Walsh, C. (2014). Pedagogías decoloniales caminando y preguntando: Notas a Paulo Freire desde Abya Yala. Entramados: educación y sociedad, 1, pp. 17–30.

Walsh, C./ Mignolo, W. & Linera, A. G. (2006). Interculturalidad, descolonización del estado y del conocimiento, p. 1ra edn. Buenos Aires: Del Signo.

Yudice, G. (2019). Culture and development in Latin America. In: Cupples, J., Palomino-Schalscha, M. & Prieto, M. (Eds.), *The Routledge Handbook of Latin American Development*, New York: Routledge, pp. 29–42.

Zamorano, M. M., Ulldemolins, J. R. & Klein, R. (2014). ¿Hacia un modelo sudamericano de política cultural? Singularidades y convergencias en Uruguay, Paraguay y Chile en el Siglo XXI, *European Review of Latin American and Caribbean Studies|Revista Europea de Estudios Latinoamericanos y Del Caribe*, 96(96), pp. 5–34.

Part I

Cultural management and policy in Latin America

1 Thinking cultural management from the South

New frames for the "Western" discourse informed by Latin America

Raphaela Henze

Introduction

The motivation for undertaking this entire book project was sparked by the recognition that narratives and epistemology originating in Latin America are missing in many of the ongoing discourses in cultural management in Europe and beyond. However, many European researchers are surely acquainted with the seminal work of Paulo Freire in addition to those of Augusto Boal, and Antanas Mockus. Admittedly, these somewhat dated works were precisely the entrance points when I started to explore cultural management and policy in Latin America, convinced that solutions to some of the pressing challenges that Europe faces cannot be solved in Europe alone (Henze, 2017). New tools and epistemologies are required throughout the so-called West to produce new frames of understanding that are informed by the experiences of the Global South (Shome, 2019, p. 197).

Interest in the Global South is not new. Scholars such as Connell, Comaroff, De Sousa Santos, Hall, Spivak, Mbeme, Nigam, Banerjee, and Prashad have already been arguing for "going South" and making visible marginalised narratives and epistemology for some time (Shome, 2019, p. 197). In Europe, and particularly Germany, this interest appears to be centred on a variety of African countries but not on those in Latin America (Bonet, Negrier & Zamorano, 2019, p. 30). Goethe-Instituts are dispersed across 98 countries but are only present in nine countries in Latin America.

This interest on the part of German and other European cultural management and policy scholars in Africa might be explained inter alia by the colonial legacy and the huge momentum that postcolonial theory and thought gained in the 1950s and 1960s. Many are not aware that precursors already existed in Mexico, Haiti, and Cuba in the 19th century (Henze, Teissl & Oswald, 2020). Although few young people, unfortunately, know, Germany has a colonial history particularly in Africa and Asia but – unlike Spain and Portugal – not in South America. Indeed, particular Spanish scholars have not only an interest in but, as can be seen from many of the contributions to this book (de la Vega; Valestegui; Escribal), for a variety of reasons, also a huge influence on cultural management as well as policy in many Latin American countries (Bonet & Schargorodsky, 2019). Interestingly, albeit not unexpectedly, this influence still seems to lack reciprocity.

Authors from the Global South rarely feature in literature lists in the Global North and West (Gutierrez, Grant & Colbert, 2016, p.7; Jacobsen, 2018; Henze, 2020, p. 54; Morato & Zamorano, 2018, p. 566; Silva, this volume).

In the interests of clarity with regard to definitions, Latin America (as well as Africa) is often considered to constitute the Global South per se. From a geographical perspective, the term "South" is obviously correctly applied at least to South America. However, that of "Global" is more problematic because of its political overtones. The vast and, in numerous ways, heterogeneous region of South and Central America has, as explained by Shome (2019, p. 198), both the Global North (which can be understood to denote spheres of economic and geopolitical power) as well as the Global South (signifying, among others, spheres of dispossession, the eradication of certain indigenous populations and as such violations of human rights). In essence, the Global South is not necessarily a space but a condition, and there are several conditions e.g., environmental or health issues where a couple of countries, among them the United States, are Global South albeit being geographically located in the West (Henze, 2017). My personal interest in cultural management and policy in Latin America was only to a certain extent driven by research on postcolonialism, although this represents an omnipresent issue inseparable from cultural management topics, particularly in this region. However, it was more the desire to include thus-far hidden voices in the international discourse (Durrer & Henze, 2018), as well as the vague notion that the concept of "cultural agent" differs from that of "cultural manager" which prevails in the West (Sommer, 2006, p. 3). There is an assumption that cultural agents deal with topics increasingly urgent in the Western hemisphere. I am, therefore, less interested in cultural diplomacy issues that have been extensively explored by Bonet & Schargorodsky (2019) but more in the work of those that undertake and facilitate creative work sometimes supported, many times hindered, by politics. Interestingly, I found the terms "cultural agent" and "cultural manager" being used synonymously by many authors in this publication. Neither researchers nor practitioners provided a compelling explanation of the difference between the two. This could relate to the vagueness and lack of autonomy of cultural management as a profession and field of action in Latin America as often described in this book.

I encountered a couple of other terms employed interchangeably; most prominent among them "cultural animator" and "cultural promoter" which are relatively unknown in the European cultural management discourse. Mariscal Orozco (2019, p. 165) explains that these different forms of naming the role, have to do not only with the shaping of political, institutional, and ideological contexts where they arise and operate, but also with the different areas of performance and the cultural fields within which the practice is carried out. As such, I am convinced that further discourse is required on the different concepts expressed by the various terms employed to refer to arts and culture-related work in Latin America, hoping that this will provide those in the 'West' with new perspectives on, and knowledge of, the profession of cultural manager. With Handel Wright (1998), I agree that it is time to de-centre Birmingham and locate it way more South.

In a world in which more and more people are losing access to academic institutions and conventional forms of education, cultural studies as well as, obviously, cultural management can and should operate both within and outside academia as already noted by Stuart Hall (1992, p. 11). Consequently, I have focused to a greater extent on community-based, production-oriented, popular education forms of study in the hope of finding them in Latin America. This hope was sparked by the abovementioned works of Freire, Boal, and Mockus, but also by the more recent ones by Sommer and Hernandez-Acosta. The latter describes the cultural agent as an individual who explores creative processes based on social interventions that contribute to dealing with social challenges such as violence in Colombia, Guatemala, and Mexico, corruption in Argentina and Peru, ethnic diversity in Mexico and Chile and inequality in Brazil to name only a few of the many challenges (Hernandez-Acosta, 2013, p. 134).

Lessons to be learned

I was particularly intrigued to learn more on:

a) How cultural management is exercised in those geographically extensive and frequently heterogeneous countries such as Brazil, Bolivia, and Mexico with a multiplicity of indigenous ethnic groups and Afro-descendant populations.
b) Whether nationalism in the different forms that can be experienced in Venezuela, Columbia, Chile, and Brazil, for instance, is a factor to be considered in relation to the framework of cultural management and policy in South and Central America. While nationalism in Brazil under the current president, Jair Bolsonaro, is interventionist and repressive, the interventions to which the cultural sector has been and remains subject to in Venezuela might actually result more from issues of class than from those of nationalism (Kozak Rovera, 2015).
c) The role that the colonial legacy, common to all countries in the region, continues to play and which if any decolonialisation efforts are undertaken within cultural organisations or by various groups and initiatives that seem to be to a vast extent predominately "white" as Silva explains is the case in Brazil (Silva, 2020, p. 21). Within this context, a specific focus was placed on indigenous populations whose situation only started to be taken into consideration in the cultural policy of many Latin American countries at the end of the 20th century.[1]
d) The frames of reference in cultural management education within the region.
e) Whether there is anything like a Latin American cultural management that unites the work of those in the region and whether cultural managers within Latin America are somehow connected and network.

At the beginning of 2018, I was contacted by the Goethe-Institut in Sao Paulo and asked to support the establishment of a network of cultural managers in South America because of my experience as co-founder of the international and interdisciplinary Brokering Intercultural Exchange Network. An initial attempt in this direction, launched by the Goethe-Institut in Santiago de Chile a couple of years ago, had failed. The kick-off session took place in September 2019 at the Goethe-Institut in Sao Paulo with cultural managers from Brazil, Peru, Chile, Uruguay, and Argentina present. COVID 19, that hit many South American countries severely, unfortunately interrupted the process, which foresaw some more meetings in different parts of South America. Nevertheless, I began to work on this book project and, by doing so, getting in touch with numerous researchers and practitioners from the region, despite a range of challenges, among them language barriers. Furthermore, I was in the fortunate position of gathering even more young and aspiring cultural managers from Argentina, Brazil, Mexico, and Columbia in the Winter School "Brokering Intercultural Exchange within Societies", a three-days intensive course for international masters and doctoral students organised annually in Berlin. Previous visits to Argentina, Mexico, and Chile provided further insights. Despite this background, I am obviously not an expert in Latin America but stay an outsider who remains in the spheres of the Global North with all its attached geopolitical privileges. It is from this perspective that I write and take the reader on a personal journey to explore the origins, references, and current challenges associated with cultural management and policy in the region.

Lessons learned

a) The danger of the "single" story

Approaching Latin America from the outset as a single entity is problematic, maybe even wrong from the beginning. The danger of the "single" story (Adichie, 2009) is inherent within it. With 20 million square kilometres, Latin America is twice as large as Europe and features not only a range of vegetation and climates but also countries with very different political systems and a variety of different ethnicities (Arauja & Leitao, this volume). Considering language as a unifying factor proves equally shortsighted. South America was divided between Spain and Portugal by the Treaty of Tordesillas in 1494 which resulted in Spanish being adopted as the official language in most of the South American countries, whereas Portuguese is spoken in Brazil. Apart from these two dominant languages, which are, despite their linguistic roots, more different from one another than is sometimes believed to be the case, an enormous range of indigenous languages is spoken and in many countries such as Bolivia and Peru recognised as official languages and protected. However, Amerindian languages have suffered gradual processes of subordination and have become the basis for social and political discrimination against their speakers (Godenzzi, 2006, p. 148).

There is a reason why this book is not entitled *Latin American Cultural Management and Policy*: there is – despite similarities like the discontinuity of political regimes and socio-economic transformations that framed cultural policy – nothing like this (Zamorano, Ulldemolins & Klein, 2014, p. 8; Morato & Zamorano, 2018), as there is – despite some unifying factors and historical commonalities – also no European or African cultural management. The contexts within the region are too different and complex, notwithstanding historical and political animosities between several countries. This was one of the obvious outcomes of the first gathering in the frame of establishing a network in the region. Many of the participating cultural managers were preoccupied with what they conceived to be unique situations in their respective countries. Their approaches to cultural management were due to the diversity of the sector as such as well as the heterogeneity of their backgrounds different. Several, therefore, doubted the benefit and transferability of lessons learned from other contexts, whereas others saw huge potential in networks of artists and organisations (Gleich, 2015). The value of (cultural) networks that is omnipresent in Europe and has already been widely researched (Pehn, 1999; Cvjeticanin, 2011; Suteu 1999; Laaksonen, 2016; Henze, 2018), seems yet to reach out to colleagues in Latin America where despite the successful Cultura Viva Communitaria (CVC) Network,[2] cultural networks remain relatively weak (Gleich, 2015).

While it is impossible to identify a Latin American cultural management and policy, there are a few factors that were repeatedly referred to by colleagues from the region and that seem to be issues that many of them face regardless of their respective home-countries.

b)   The interdependence of arts and policy

As mentioned above, numerous cultural managers have to deal with political interference in their work, but, despite this difficult relationship, they strive for recognition from their respective governments. The reasons for this are clearly related to a combination of the need for funding, labour rights (Escribal, this volume), and legitimacy (Morato & Zamorano, 2018, p. 574). When it comes to funding, resources are scarce in many of these heavily indebted nations and sometimes come with strings attached (Hernandez Farfan, 2017) that force artists to emigrate as, for instance, in Guatemala (Gleich, 2015). In a couple of countries in the region, corruption exacerbates the situation. Apart from Uruguay, which occupied 23rd position in the 2018 Corruption Perceptions Index (CPI) Ranking, the vast majority of South and Central American countries were placed in the lower half of this index with Venezuela ranking 168 out of 180. However, many cultural managers and artists become involved in cultural policy, not only out of necessity, but because they believe that institutions can and should change. Numerous texts contain reminiscences of popular figures, often ones from an artistic background, who have served in ministries and governments and succeeded in advancing the cultural sector, often unfortunately only for brief periods in history. This politicisation of the sector and the struggle to develop or maintain institutions that serve the arts and culture, both within and beyond capital cities, render artistic productions accessible to diverse audiences, rather than merely being bodies that further enhance the power of those in government or the foreign policy agendas of Spain or, to a lesser extent, Portugal as has been described in several texts within this volume.

The recovery of culture as a democratic expression, the beginnings of post-dictatorial institutionalisation, and different processes of re-organisation marked all of Latin America in the 1990s and 2000s (Zamorano, Ulldemolins & Klein, 2014, p. 10). In the postcolonial context, the fact that institutions built on Western (frequently French) models have never matched the prevailing realities exacerbated the situation. Peregrina Leyva and Hernandez Farfan (this volume) write "our governmental models have a European heritage, as do our academic institutions, but our socio-economic reality differs considerably". These socio-economic realities should be briefly described because they are required as background with regard to access to culture and cultural consumption. The Iberian colonial policies led to an uneven distribution of land and insecure property rights which, in turn, contributed to persistent economic and political inequality until the 19th and 20th centuries. Despite some improvements in the majority of South American countries in recent years, 30.7 per cent of their populations still live in poverty. In fact, 61 million people experience extreme poverty and 220 million people in the region subsist on less than $10 a day (Ray, 2018). Land and territory are particularly important factors, not only when it comes to wealth creation, but also with regard to the rights of indigenous populations that have been expelled from their land with profound and devastating consequences, inter alia, for their cultural identities.

The understandable desire for a Ministry of Culture that is neutral and independent of government and ruling parties has frequently been expressed. In countries like Brazil, this is unfortunately wishful thinking, whereas the neighbouring country of Uruguay appears to have adopted this approach. The strength of its institutions as well as its democratic tradition seemed to have helped Uruguay to assume something of a vanguard role in the region that was evidenced, among other ways, by its handling of the Covid-19 pandemic. Apart from Uruguay, where there is a deeply rooted trust in public organisations, the confidence in government bodies in the region remains low (Ebert, 2020).

Not only institutions, language, European gender orders, and religion are legacies of the colonial past, racism deeply rooted in countries such as Brazil and Mexico needs to be mentioned in this context as well (Thome de Sousa, 2020; Silva, 2020, p. 21). Race and racial identity were established as instruments of basic social classification (Quijano, 2000, p. 534). While the indigenous population in Brazil was almost wiped out and represents only 0.4 per cent of the contemporary society, blacks – just over half of the total population – are systematically oppressed. Seventy-five per cent of those killed by the police, 64 per cent of prison inmates, and 75 per cent of the poorest are black. Every 23 minutes, a young black man is killed in Brazil (Thome de Sousa, 2020). The struggles of indigenous populations and marginal communities are key concerns raised by many contributors to this book (Silva; de Britto Maluf). With Quijano (2000, p. 551) it should be stressed that the Aztecs, Mayas, Chimus, Aymaras, Incas, Chibchas, to name but a few, have been merged into a single identity. The same happened with those forcefully brought from Africa as slaves: Ashantis, Yorubas, Zulus, Congos, Bacongos, among others. In the span of three hundred years, all of

them became blacks. Peoples were dispossessed of their own and singular historical identities. Their new racial identity, colonial and negative, involved the plundering of their place in the history of the cultural production of humanity. Escribal
(2020, p. 36), therefore, describes the main function of cultural management in
the region as a means of returning indigenous cultures, history, and identities to
the core of daily social reflection.

Several contributors to this volume have emphasised that the centralisation
(comparable to French and Portuguese administrative systems) is highly problematic. In Brazil, Ecuador, and Mexico the vast majority of public money is being
spent in the capital on some flagship institutions with touristic value, leaving more
rural areas without any support for their cultural scene. In Peru, one of the fast-
est growing global tourist destinations, a significant proportion of already scare
resources is being invested in cultural heritage infrastructure and crafts of touristic
interest. The preservation of the enormous wealth of cultural heritage represents
an increasing concern in the cultural sector across the whole of Latin America and
educational institutions have launched specific offerings to educate experts in this
field such as the PhD Programme on Regional Planning and Scientific Dimensions
of Heritage Protection at the Autonomous University of Oaxaca in Mexico. These
public investments, at times less directed at the cultural heritage site as such and
more so at tourist infrastructures, have notorious and, occasionally, devastating
consequences as in the case of Machu Picchu. The same applies to the destruction
of unique natural ecosystems to enable the construction of tourist complexes in
Brazil, Costa Rica, and the Dominican Republic. This, to a certain extent understandable but in many cases shortsighted focus on promoting tourism common
to several countries in Africa, has obvious pitfalls, particularly when it comes
to sustainability and, as has recently become apparent, the volatility of the tourism sector per se.[3] As often within globalisation, an overwhelming proportion
of the profits generated by this form of exploitation ends up in the pockets of
Western shareholders. By way of example, the New York Stock Exchange-listed
Belmond Ltd. owns the Belmond Sanctuary Lodge, the only hotel located within
the Macchu Picchu citadel. In addition, it controls 50 per cent of Peru Rail, the
only legal means of transportation to Aguascalientes.

The growing focus on eco-ethno-tourism could have even more devastating
effects on cultural production. For instance, the marketing of local cultures which
are presented through dubious stereotypes and over-simplifications of ethnic
groups portrayed in an easy-to-digest folkloristic manner that has little or nothing in common with ethnic characteristics or traditions is a classic example of
this phenomenon (Henze, 2017, p. 19; Dallen & Nyaupane, 2009; Postero, 2019,
p. 49). Flamenco, Mexican Muralism, and Brazilian Carnival in particular among
others run this risk.

However, in Bolivia and Ecuador, legal and constitutional reforms have
granted "rights" to nature (Shome, 2019, p. 212). In Bolivia, these take the form
of the "Mother Earth law" (Mother Earth, Pachamama, as the source of all life).
The underlying assumption is that Earth (including the seas, oceans, forests, etc.)
is not a resource to be exploited, but a dynamic life system that is interconnected

with all other living organisms (Shome, 2019, p. 212). The Bolivian law enshrines the right of nature not to be "affected by mega-infrastructure and development projects that affect the balance of ecosystems and the local inhabitant communities" (Dodington, 2011). In Ecuador and Bolivia, the rights of nature, including its regeneration, are now codified within the Constitution (Shome, 2019, p. 212). Development should be driven by "buen vivir", an indigenous form of sustainable life, that protects not only nature but also society (Postero, 2019, p. 49).[4] I am not aware of any Western country, where the sustainability and anti-climate change movements are huge, that grants similar rights to nature.

In the 1980s and 1990s, an economic understanding of culture emerged at the state level that was and remains, in large part, oriented towards the cultural and creative industries, especially those that profit financially from the exploitation of copyrights (Yudice, 2018). Creative city clusters have been established in Buenos Aires, Rio de Janeiro, and Mexico City (Yudice, 2019, p. 37) leaving other less marketable sectors, particularly those focusing on social impact and value, even further behind. Due to marginal funding for both culture and education in several countries within the region, many cultural managers and artists are concerned about potential audiences (Gleich, 2015). Culture has been alienated from the daily life of many for a particular time, not only because they lack the financial or educational means to participate, but also because community knowledge was devalued and cultural practices were considered as folkloristic, vernacular, or superstitious by elites that used culture as an instrument of differentiation, despite political ideas of forming nation states being based on cultural identities and integration.

c) Colonial influence in cultural management education and research up to the present

One of the main challenges in many Latin American countries is the education quality and social inequity (Küper, 2005, p. 24). Despite initiatives, mostly supported by foreign development aid, like the bi-lingual education programme for indigenous children in the Andean Highlands of Ecuador and Peru (Küper, 2005, p. 27), the education level still depends largely on social status and economic background. Violent protests by students in Chile and Peru in 2011 raised public awareness of how under-financed and, consequently, ailing the education systems are. Student protests were again on the rise in May 2020 when students in 170 cities in Brazil protested against budget cuts by the government of far-right Jair Bolsonaro. Despite some initiatives by universities that have introduced special quota policies and established scholarship programmes, those particularly disadvantaged in this regard are indigenous and black populations (Mato, 2019, p. 214).[5]

When it comes to the international discourse, particularly in cultural management and policy, the fact that many researchers and practitioners in Latin America find expressing themselves in English challenging represents a major factor in their marginalisation (Morato & Zamorano, 2018, p. 566). The Annual English proficiency test proves that the situation is improving slightly over the years. Whereas in 2014 not a single South American country belonged to the group classed as possessing a very high or high proficiency in English, in 2020 Argentina made it to the fourth to last place on the high proficiency list. All other countries of the region can be found in the moderate, low (Brazil, Peru), or even very low (Venezuela) categories (EF EPI, 2020). The majority of the articles contained in this book had to be translated in order to produce a volume specifically targeting non-Spanish or Portuguese speaking readers in the so-called West. As important as translation is, particularly in science and research, it unfortunately remains under-funded (Henze, 2020, p. 53). It should be noted that this applies to texts being translated into English in order to make content available for readers able to read English. However, this is not a one-way street. Equally important is the translation of texts into other languages and even dialects in order to allow for a mutual and multi-directional exchange (Henze, 2020, p. 53). Many of those that we miss in international discourses still find it difficult to develop an international knowledge base due to their lack of competence in English (Zheng, 2019; Henze, 2020, p. 53). If you have a closer look at the bibliography of the authors in this book, you will in many cases almost exclusively find references in Spanish or Portuguese written largely by authors from the region or featuring prominently academics from Spain. In part, this can be explained by the fact that the chapters are intended to present the peculiarities of the respective country, albeit not comprehensively. If the references of this article are surveyed closely, the reverse will, to some extent, be true. The references written in Spanish have been laboriously translated using artificial intelligence with all of its inherent challenges. This one-sidedness of the literature and narratives is what I came to refer to as the Ethnocentrism of our frames of reference (Henze, 2020).[6] In a study dating from 2015, I found that cultural managers in German-speaking countries tend to prefer to work with colleagues from precisely this group of countries with very similar approaches and the unifying German language (Henze, 2017, p. 48). Although in Europe networks such as the European network on cultural management and policy (ENCATC), The European Institute for Comparative Cultural Research (ERICarts), or ones with an even broader outreach, including Brokering Intercultural Exchange exist, this does not mean that all those involved in cultural management are international in scope.

As almost everywhere, where cultural management constitutes a comparatively young discipline, as is the case in Latin America, the primary resource consists of the experiences conditioned by the political provisions and social, cultural, economic, ideological, and environmental issues of practitioners who subsequently became academics (Mariscal Orozco, 2019, p. 162). As explained by Chavarrea Contreras & Valdes Vergara (2019, p. 207), practices and experiences that constitute cultural management draw on a heritage that spans a wide range of experiences in the cultural development of the region. However, there is one important caveat that needs to be made and that was mentioned in many of the texts within this volume (Silva; de la Vega Valestegui): it is the strong influence that particularly Spanish scholars had and still have on the cultural management discipline in Latin America. This connection is for a variety of reasons, among them colonial ties and language, not surprising but the strength of this influence is noteworthy. Bonet and Schargorodsky (2019) locate the Spanish efforts within the context of cultural diplomacy and policy. Nevertheless, they do not always appear welcome. De la Vega Valestegui (this volume) refers to the Barcelona connection and it is apparent that she aims for more independence of these influences in order to develop a knowledge base for the discipline that is based on more authentic experiences, taking the regional situation and particularly issues of colonialism more fully into account. Escribal (2020, p. 38) underlines the fact that the northern-Atlantic authors he was supposed to read during his years of studying cultural management in Argentina, operate from a perspective that equates culture with the arts and reflect on institutional frameworks that are very different from those of the region. In addition, if Western art is understood as universal, there is very little room for thinking about diversity in terms located outside the central position that those in Latin America, due to historical and colonial conditions, do not hold.

While it is impossible to define a Latin American cultural management due to all the factors mentioned, it seems as if there are three dimensions that form part of it that require further explanation. Fauré Polloni (2019, p. 139) describes these dimensions of cultural management education as knowledge, its character as social practice, and its political objective – its relationship with power. In Latin America, cultural management is, in fact, still largely thought of as, and assumed to be, an interdisciplinary field of professionalisation (Licona Calpe, 2019, p. 19; Mariscal Orozco, 2019, p. 177) where knowledge is better understood as know-how (Sepulveda Contreras, 2019, p. 78). Martinell (2007, p. 27), one of the most prominent figures in the field, states,

> Cultural management cannot be defined as a science, nor can it be considered within its own epistemological framework, but as the result of a social en-cargo that professionalizes a considerable number of people in response to the needs of a complex society. This gives it a very important multidisciplinary perspective that we should not forget, but it demands that the sector itself makes the necessary approaches to build a theoretical and conceptual framework in accordance with the needs of this function.

In many Western countries, the focus has been specifically on these theoretical and conceptual frameworks driven by the desire to make cultural management a fully accepted academic discipline during the last 30 years. The dimension of social practice is one that is relatively recent in cultural management research in Europe. The strong focus on this in Latin America might, in part, as Faure Polloni points out (2019), be explained by the unequal societies across the continent where access to formal education was and, in many cases remains, the preserve of elites. Many forms of non-formal or informal education developed particularly under the auspices of socialist or communist ideologies and culture and those in the arts played an important role. Literary and choral societies, cultural and social centres, as well as book fairs, flourished in Mexico, Cuba, Peru, Brazil, and Argentina. However, the conflict with politics has been constant and fierce as described in most of the chapters in this book. When globalisation forced countries to walk down the aisle of transnational capitalism and "development" with (institutional) models sought in France, the UK, and the United States, this second dimension was surely no longer a prime priority of many governments that focused – if at all – more on those aspects of the cultural sector that were economically exploitable and/or saw culture as a foundational element for this kind of development which has become, according to Escobar (2011), the "magic formula" and which left behind, in particular, indigenous peoples, Afro-descendants, mixed-race peoples, and rural communities which were even considered by some a cause of underdevelopment (Yudice, 2019, p. 29). For many in the field, particularly those with a stronger focus on societal issues and, especially, inequities, cultural management came to be associated with exactly these market-oriented, neoliberal approaches by the State and, therefore, experienced a certain and understandable rejection. To many authors, especially in this publication, it is precisely in the scenario of globalisation and neoliberalism that collective identity and the strengthening of local communities based on a collective and social memory become increasingly important in order to initiate empowerment processes.

The continually developing discipline of cultural management, deemed to have been imported from Europe (Chavarrea Contreras & Valdes Vergara, 2019, p. 209) where its origins in increasing the efficiency and effectiveness of cultural organisations are clearly observable, is understandably subject to question and reflection in Latin America (Licona Calpe, 2019, p. 22).

Despite challenges like visa issues and limited funding (Silva, 2020, p. 18), several colleagues in Latin America have taken the opportunity to gain experience abroad. Due to the long lack of any formal education in cultural management in many of the countries within the region, this constituted an understandable step with Spain being the logical choice due to attractive programmes, the provision of financial support, and the availability of Spanish language courses. However, as is evident from the professional profiles of the contributors to this volume, the Netherlands, France, Germany, Australia, and Sao Tome and Principe are attractive destinations, particularly to the younger generation who also seems to experience fewer language barriers than the previous one.

d) Decolonialisation

Approximately 200 years after many countries within the region achieved independence, the effects of colonialism are, unsurprisingly, still evident.[7] Racism and the marginalisation of indigenous populations and the destruction of cultural identities and even entire cultures are only a few of them that have been mentioned already.

Against this background, role models were sought. Rather than returning to the century-old societies and cultures within the region that were, to an overwhelming extent, wiped out and stripped of their objectified intellectual legacy by the colonisers (Quijano, 2000, p. 541), these were found in North America and Europe (Escobar, 2011) and, when it came to public administration, particularly in France which is still reflected in many organisations and public entities in the region today. Latin America – the term coined in France for propaganda purposes (Stavenhagen, 2001, p. 13) and controversial for a variety of reasons within the region (Henze & Escribal, this volume) – has experienced civil uprisings, guerrilla movements, dictatorships, swings to the left (known as the Pink Tide) and since 2010 political shifts to the right and struggles until today with the economic influence that specifically the United States exercises over many countries in the region, particularly through institutions such as the World Bank and the International Monetary Fund (IMF). The Washington Consensus could be regarded as the most influential set of policy objectives informing neoliberalism in Latin America (Ruttenberg, 2019, p. 113). The work of these Bretton Woods institutions has been criticised as neo-colonialism by such influential figures as economist and Nobel prize winner Joseph Stiglitz, who, like many others, does not believe in the "one-size-fits all" solution that these institutions apply, despite the very different, and in many cases, equally complex contexts (Stiglitz, 2003; Escobar, 2011). The drastic impact of their "Structural Adjustment Programmes" particularly on rural populations, whose agricultural products were replaced by cheap imports, are widely documented (Postero, 2019, p. 47). At the beginning of the 21st century, this led to socio-political change founded on a widespread anti-neoliberal sentiment based on the anti-imperialist legacies of Simon Bolivar and Jose Marti (Ruttenberg, 2019, p. 115).

With both colonialism and neo-colonialism, those involved in cultural management have plenty on their agenda when it comes to the topic of decolonialisation. The discussions and, more specifically, actions around this inevitably involve more than debates on how to display artefacts with colonial history, as appears to be one of the predominant concerns within this context for German museums. It is precisely the century-old social function, attributed to what we came to call cultural management more recently, that seems to make the difference and that is of particular interest to cultural managers outside the region. That the context briefly described above is only to a certain extent generalisable to the entire region is what sets the way culture is managed apart and leads to the development of skills and practices that are essential to survival for those in the field, yet which might not be regarded as something special or noteworthy. However, it is exactly this that should be brought into sharper focus. How to do cultural management in precarious as well as politically complex conditions within unequal societies? Costa (2015, p. 81) writes: "Specialized in crisis management, Brazilian museums can contribute greatly to the global debate on the social functions of museums".[8] This is precisely the reason why the voices of, for example, Brazilian museum managers and curators need to be heard since it is not only crisis management that they can teach us. A closer look at the work of the National Museum of Brazil is important even if the contexts of colonised and colonisers are, obviously, incomparable.

To Brazil's indigenous peoples, devastated by colonization and genocide, and for African Brazilians, whose ancestors were brought to the country in chains, the museum was a concrete link to their history and a resource for building a better future. There, it was believed, indigenous and black cultural history would be protected and employed in the creation of these peoples' own museums which are now beginning to proliferate in Brazil. The National Museum and its researchers were seen as allies in these projects, helping traditionally oppressed Brazilian peoples to safeguard their heritage and construct a better world for their children. Working with indigenous groups, the museum's anthropology department produced videos and CDs documenting cultural practices together with African Brazilian and indigenous religious music. The museum trained indigenous museologists, and video producers, working with them to build Native heritage centres. The museum's ethnologists helped Native and African Brazilian groups document, map, and survey their lands. Its linguists worked to recover and teach lost or almost-lost languages and dialects.

(de Sousa Lima, 2018)

Cultural managers' work with indigenous communities ranges from heritage protection to a broad understanding of diverse cultural activities, which include social policies. One of the critical strategies has been the training of indigenous cultural managers by indigenous bottom-up organisations.[9] However, these activities, as well as the deconstruction process mainly being developed within academia, have often been deluded by cultural policies that are still or again based on national rationales.

Conclusion

This research was a learning process. I did not find answers to all the questions I had. I might have had exaggerated expectations and hoped for easy answers. There are certainly lessons to be learned but, equally, no easy-fix solutions exist that can be transferred to contexts that are so different as the Latin American one is from the European. It might be more important to work out these differences than trying hard to find unifying factors and this applies not only to Europe and Latin America but to every single country because – as we have seen – there is (and can be) no typical Latin American or European cultural management. Fundamentally, it appears to be the question of how to define cultural identity within a specific context and for a particular community that we all struggle with, having in mind that it is not about one national identity but about a myriad of identities – a question that is even more difficult to answer within the described context of post- and neo-colonialism that sets Latin America firmly apart from Europe.

Several of the discussions within the region sound familiar, for example, the difficulties that many of those active in the arts and culture have with the term "management" and the hesitation to use it because it seems to overemphasise economic aspects (Henze, 2013). In Europe, cultural management as a discipline emerged during the last century when the state decided that cultural organisations should be made more effective and efficient in order not to further burden the taxpayer (Henze, 2013). It is, therefore, unsurprising that the discussions within the discipline centred predominantly on such topics as finance, marketing, organisational structures, and audience development, for instance. The social dimension of the arts sometimes reflected in such terms and concepts as Cultural Work or Cultural Mediation was, for a long period, not a prime priority of those within cultural management and, particularly, not within academia. Indeed, it is this dimension that seemed to have played a more important role in the work of all those in arts and culture in Latin America for decades. The reasons for this are manifold and surely relate to unequal societies composed of many diverse ethnicities and based on the deeply rooted and well-founded distrust of everything that relates to the State and its organisations in many countries. Geopolitical challenges, as well as rapidly changing governments and policies, have rendered the establishment of the discipline relatively difficult. Due to Spain's ongoing economic and political interest in the region, its narratives and epistemology have played a dominant role in cultural management up to the present day (de la Vega Valestegui, this volume). However, colleagues in the region are deeply conscious of the importance of authenticity and strive to develop their own knowledge bases.

Despite numerous challenges, the sector seems to be opening up slowly but surely to international references and discourses. I am convinced that we will see more of the younger generation of cultural managers as well as researchers making their voices heard in the near future and I look forward to this. However, it will be particularly incumbent upon those in the so-called West to work on overcoming power imbalances and asymmetries. Invitations to debate these issues are surely a first step but do not in themselves help to overcome them (Durrer & Henze, 2018). We need to find ways, opportunities, and funding for mutual exchange and projects as well as for translations. There is a wealth of important literature from and about the region that is only available in Spanish (Morato & Zamorano, 2018). Furthermore, I personally believe that cultural managers as well as researchers in Latin America would profit from a professional network that would represent them in the international arena such as, e.g., ENCATC, Association of Arts Administration Educators (AAAE), Asia Pacific Network for Cultural Education and Research (ANCER), and the Arterial network are doing it for their respective regions. Keenly aware of the problems associated with role models and, even more so, best practices (Mattocks, 2017), I nevertheless believe that the African Arterial Network, representing an entire and extremely diverse continent, can serve as a kind of reference point. The initiative for establishing such a network has been taken by the Goethe-Institut twice in recent years. From my brief involvement in this process in 2019, I believe that it is up to those working within this sector to take this further. Although never expressed openly by participants of the kick-off meeting in Sao Paulo, there is this sentiment that the involvement of a European institution does not make sense. Inspired by CVC, I think it is cultural organisations such as Itau Cultural in Sao Paulo that are undertaking inspiring work and are keen to reach out beyond the region or to those in academia to consolidate the voices that are yet to be heard internationally and gather and provide more data on the cultural sector that is missing so far. I am convinced that many Western cultural managers and researchers would greatly welcome the opportunity to hear, read, and learn more about developments in the field in Latin America. The invitation, at least, is on the table.

Notes

1 The widespread indigenous protests of 1992 marking the occasion of the quincentenary of Columbus' first incursion into the Americas represented for many Latin Americans the first occasion on which they were confronted with the demands of indigenous peoples (di Giminiani, 2019, p. 226).
2 A network of community cultural initiatives throughout Latin America whose origins can be traced back to December 2009 in Mar de la Plata where several civil society organisations and leaders of cultural organisations and movements from half a dozen countries met at the First International Congress of Culture for Social Transformation organised by the Cultural Institute of the Province of Buenos Aires in collaboration with the Federal Investment Council. The network proves the success of bottom-up efforts of local community cultural organisations that joined forces and defended cultural rights through capacity-building initiatives in cultural management and policy (Yudice, 2019, p. 38).
3 According to the World Travel and Tourism Council (WTTC) report 2018, tourism accounted for 3.8 per cent of the GPD of Peru in 2017.
4 Ruttenberg (2019, p. 116) brings awareness to the limitations because both countries continue to pursue post-neoliberal policy objectives reliant upon extractive resources industries fuelling economic growth as foreseen in the neoliberal growth-for-development paradigm.
5 Even when indigenous or African-descendant peoples enter universities, they rarely find their histories, knowledge, and languages reflected in the curricula (Mato, 2019).
6 On the important notion that translated texts serve as expressions of power, see amongst others Tymoczko & Gentzler, 2002.
7 Puerto Rico and French Guiana still being colonised by the United States and France, respectively.
8 The horrible conditions many Brazilian museums – collecting treasures of incalculable value – are in, became obvious when the National Museum of Brazil in Rio de Janeiro (established as the Royal Museum in 1818 and as such the first space for public education) burned to the ground in September 2018.
9 Indigenous cinema FICWALLMAPU developed by the Mapuche community in Chile: https://www.mapuexpress.org/2018/10/25/en-osorno-exhibiran-cine-indigena-para-ninosas/ Wichilhenay: a project aimed at promoting the art and crafts of the Wichi community in the north of Argentina: https://formar.cultura.gob.ar/comunidad/u/wichilhenay/; and the indigenous association MBORAYHU PORÃ from Areguá, Paraguay, dedicated to the protection of Guarani heritage: https://www.facebook.com/mborayhupora/ to name but three of the numerous examples. Mato (2019) has written extensively about indigenous and Afro-descendant higher education initiatives.

References

Adichie, C. (2009). The danger of a single story. https://www.ted.com/talks/chimamanda_ngozi_adichie_the_danger_of_a_single_story?language=de (Accessed October 6, 2020).

Araújo, B. & Leitão, C. (this volume). Thinking of the South as if there were no north: an exercise in culture-based imagination. In: Henze, R. & Escribal, F. (Eds.), *Cultural Management and Policy in South and Central America*, Abingdon & New York: Routledge, pp. 34–52.

Bonet, L.& Schargorodsky, H. (2019). The challenges of cultural relations between the European Union and Latin America and the Caribbean, Quaderns Gescènic. Col·lecció Quaderns de Cultura n. 5.

Bonet, L., Negrier, E. & Zamorano, M. (2019). Cultural policy and diplomacy in the euro-Latin American and Caribbean relationships: genesis, discourse, praxis and prospective. In: Bonet, L.% Schargorodsky, H. (Eds.), *The Challenges of Cultural Relations between the European Union and Latin America and the Caribbean*, Rustica Catalan: Quaderns Gescènic. Col·Lecció Quaderns De Cultura n. 5, pp. 23–49.

Chavarría Contreras, R. & Valdés Vergara, J. (2019). Aproximaciones y provocaciones en torno a la emergencia de la Gestión Cultural en las postrimerías del Siglo XX latinoamericano. In: Chavarría Contreras, R., Fauré Polloni, D., Mariscal Orozco, J. L., Rucker, U. & Yáñez Canal, C. (Eds.). *Conceptos Clave De La Gestión Cultural Enfoques Desde Latinoamérica volumen I*, Santiago de Chile: Ariadna ediciones, pp. 207–226.

Costa, M. (2015). Southern landscape, Brazilian scene, and museum action, ICOFOM Study Series [En ligne], 43a http://journals.openedition.org/iss/577 (Accessed September 30, 2020).

Cvjeticanin, B. (2011). Networks: the evolving aspects of culture in the 21st century, Cluturelink.Org; http://www.culturelink.org/publics/joint/clinkconf/Cvjeticanin_Networks.pdF (Accessed October 6, 2020).

Dallen, J. T. & Nyaupane, G. P. (2009). *Cultural Heritage and Tourism in the Developing World: A Regional Perspective*, Routledge, London, New York.

de Britto Maluf, V. (this volume). Cultural management in Bolivia: journey through history. In: Henze, R. & Escribal, F. (Eds.), *Cultural Management and Policy in South and Central America*, Abingdon & New York: Routledge, pp. 198–214.

de la Vega Valestegui, P. (this volume). Cultural management in Ecuador: genealogy and power relations within the constitution of a field. In: Henze, R. & Ecsribal, F. (Eds.), *Cultural Management and Policy in South and Central America*, Abingdon & New York: Routledge, pp. 143–162.

de Sousa Lima, A. C. (2018). The destruction of Brazil's National Museum poses a threat to ethnic minorities, *Washington Post*, https://www.washingtonpost.com/news/global-opinions/wp/2018/09/08/the-destruction-of-brazils-national-museum-poses-a-threat-to-ethnic-minorities/ (Accessed October 5, 2020).

di Giminiani, P. (2019). Indigenous activism in Latin America. In: Cupples, J., Palomino-Schalscha, M. & Prieto, M. (Eds.), *The Routledge Handbook of Latin American Development*, Routledge, Milton Park, pp. 225–235.

Dodington, N. (2011). The nature-rights movement or the "law of mother earth'" *The Expanded Environment*, June 2, 2011, http://www.expandedenvironment.org/the-naturerights-movement-or-the-law-of-mother-earth/ (Accessed October 5, 2020).

Durrer, V. & Henze, R. (2018). Leaving comfort zones, arts management quarterly, leaving comfort zones, *Cultural Inequalities*, 129(June), p. 3.

EF English Proficiency Index https://www.ef.com/wwen/epi/

Ebert, M. (2020). In Uruguay von Krise keine Spur. https://www.tagesschau.de/ausland/uruguay-coronakrise-pandemie-101.html (Accessed October 5, 2020).

Escobar, A. (2011). *Encountering development: the making and unmaking of the third world*, Princeton, New Jersey: Princeton University Press.

Escribal, F. (2020). Reflections from an African experience. From Buenos Aires to Diogo Vaz, Arts, *Management Quarterly*, 133, pp. 36–41.

Escribal, F. (this volume). Cultural management in Argentina: political agenda and challenges for practitioners and researchers. In: Henze, R. & Ecsribal, F. (Eds.) *Cultural Management and Policy in South and Central America*, Abingdon & New York: Routledge, pp. 87–105.

Fauré Polloni, D. (2019). Educación (Popular) y Gestión Cultural (Comunitaria): Aportes para entender su relación desde una perspectiva nuestroamericana. In: Chavarría Contreras, R., Fauré Polloni, D., Mariscal Orozco, J. L./,Rucker, U. & Yáñez Canal, C. (Eds.). *CONCEPTOS CLAVE DE LA GESTIÓN CULTURAL ENFOQUES DESDE LATINOAMÉRICA Volumen I*, Santiago de Chile: Ariadna Ediciones, pp. 129–150.

Gleich, C. (2015). Culture and Politics in Ecuador. Where culture is limited to the cities. https://www.artsmanagement.net/Articles/Series-on-Central-and-Southern-America-Culture-and-Politics-in-Ecuador,3676 (Accessed October 5, 2020).

Godenzzi, J. C. (2006). The discourse of diversity: language, ethnicity, and interculturality in Latin America. In: Sommer, D. (Ed.), *Cultural Agency in the Americas*, Duke University Press, Durham, London, pp. 146–166.

Hall, S. (1992). Race, culture and communications: looking backward and forward at cultural studies, *Rethinking Marxism a Journal of Economics, Culture, and Society*, 5(1), pp. 10–18.

Handel Wright, K. (1998). Dare we de-centre Birmingham?: troubling the "origin" and trajectories of cultural studies, *European Journal of Cultural Studies*, 1(1), pp. 33–56.

Henze, R. (2013). Kunst und management – Zwei Seiten einer Medaille. In: Henze, R. (Ed.), *Kultur und Management*, Springer, Wiesbaden, pp. 183–197.

Henze, R. (2017). *Introduction to International Arts Management*, Springer VS, Wiesbaden.

Henze, R. (2018). Netzwerke – Potenziale für die Zukunft, *KM-Magazin, No. 132*, April 2018, pp. 60–64.

Henze, R. (2020). More than just lost in translation: the ethnocentrism of our frames of reference and the underestimated potential of multilingualism. In: Durrer, V. & Henze, R. (Eds.), *Managing Culture: Reflecting on Exchange In Global*, Palgrave Macmillan, Cham, pp. 51–80.

Henze, R., Teissl, V. & Oswald, K. (2020). Underneath our thoughts. An introduction into Postcolonoal Concepts and the Cultural Sector. In: Henze, R., Teissl, V. & Oswald, K. (Eds). *Postcolonial Cultural Management, Arts Management Quarterly, No. 135*, Arts Management Network, Weimar, pp. 14–25.

Hernandez-Acosta, J. (2013). Differences in cultural policy and its implications for Arts management: case of Puerto Rico, *The Journal of Arts Management, Law and Society*, 43(3), pp. 125–138.

Hernandez Farfan, A. (2017). The Mexican arts sector. Good connections are more important than artistic quality. https://www.artsmanagement.net/Articles/Series-on-Central-and-Southern-America-In-Mexico-good-connections-are-more-important-than-artistic-quality,3803 (Accessed October 5, 2020).

Jacobsen, U. C. (2018). Language in art and cultural management, arts management quarterly. Leaving comfort zones, *Cultural Inequalities*, 129(June), pp. 17–23.

Kozak Rovera, G. (2015). Revolución Bolivariana: políticas culturales en la Venezuela socialista de Hugo Chávez (1999–2013), cuadernos de literatura Vol. XiX n. 37 enero-Junio 2015, pp. 38–56.

Küper, W. (2005) Education for all in Südamerika fünf Jahre nach Dakar. Die Situation in Peru, ZEP: Zeitschrift für internationale Bildungsforschung und Entwicklungspädagogik 28 (2005), pp. 24–28.

Laaksonen, A. (2016). D'Art 49: International Culture Networks. IFACCA. Sydney http://media.ifacca.org/files/DArt49_International_Culture_Networks.pdf (Accessed October 6, 2020).

Licona Calpe, W. (2019). *La administración estratégica de las culturas.* In: Chavarría Contreras, R., Fauré Polloni, D., Mariscal Orozco, J. L., Rucker, U. & Yáñez Canal, C. (Eds.). *Conceptos Clave de la gestion Cultural enfoques desde Latinomerica Volumen I*, Ariadna Ediciones, pp. 19–42.

Mariscal Orozco, M. (2019). Gestión Cultural. Aproximaciones empírico – teóricas, In: Mariscal Orozco, M. & Rucker, U. (Eds), *Conceptos clave de la gestion cultural. Enfoque desdo latinoamerica. Vol. II.* Santiago de Chile: Ariadna Ediciones, pp. 162–186.

Martinell, A. & Elisenda, B. (2007). Seminario internacional: La formación en Gestión y Políticas culturales para la Diversidad Cultural y el Desarrollo, Girona, España, Documenta Universitaria, UdeG Publicaciones.

Mato, D. (2019). Intercultural universities and modes of learning, In: Cupples, J., Palomino-Schalscha, M. & Prieto, M. (Eds.). *The Routledge Handbook of Latin American Development*, Routledge, Milton Park, pp. 213–224.

Mattocks, K. (2017). Just describing is not enough: policy learning, transfer, and the limits of best practices, *The Journal of Arts Management, Law, and Society*, 48(2), pp. 85–97.

Morato, A. R. & Zamorano, M. M. (2018). Introduction: cultural policies in Ibero-America at the beginning of the XXI century, *International Journal of Cultural Policy*, 24(5), pp. 565–576.

Pehn, G. (1999). *Networking Culture. The Role of European Cultural Networks*, Council of Europe Publishing, Strasbourg.

Peregrina Leyva, C. & Hernandez Farfan, A. (this volume). Cultural management in Mexico: from precariousness to development. In: Henze, R. & Escribal, F. (Eds.), *Cultural Management and Policy in South and Central America*, Routledge.

Postero, N. (2019). Indigenous development in Latin, America, In: Cupples, J., Palomino-Schalscha, M. & Prieto, M. (Eds.), *The Routledge Handbook of Latin American Development*, Routledge, Milton Park, pp. 43–53.

Quijano, A. (2000). Coloniality of power, Eurocentrism, and Latin America. *Nepantla: Views from South*, 1(3), pp. 533–580.

Ray, J. S. (2018). 10 important Facts about Poverty in South America. https://borgenprojec t.org/facts-about-poverty-in-south-america/ (Accessed October 6, 2020).

Ruiz-Guitierrez, J., Grant, P. & Colbert, F. (2016). Arts and culture management Arts management in developing countries: a Latin American perspective, *International Journal of Arts Management*, 18, pp. 6–17.

Ruttenberg, T. (2019). Post-neoliberalism in Latin America. In: Cupples, J., Palomino-Schalscha, M. & Prieto, M. (Eds.), *The Routledge Handbook of Latin American Development*, Routledge, Milton Park, pp. 111–120.

Sepúlveda Contreras, M. (2019). Saberes y Conocimientos. Aproximaciones desde la gestión cultural en América Latina. In: Mariscal Orozco, M. & Rucker, U. (Eds.), *Conceptos clave de la gestion cultural. Enfoque desdo latinoamerica. Vol. II*, Santiago de Chile: Ariadna Ediciones, pp. 78–95.

Shome, R. (2019). Thinking culture and cultural studies – from/of the global south, *Communication and Critical/Cultural Studies*, 16(3), pp. 196–218.

Silva, S. (2020). Reflections on cultural mobility through a post-colonial lens. From the (so-called) South to the North, Arts, *Management Quarterly*, 133, pp. 17–24.

Silva, S. (this volume). Cultural management in Brazil: persistence in times of uncertainty. In: Henze, R. & Ecsribal, F. (Eds.) *Cultural Management and Policy in South and Central America*, Abingdon & New York: Routledge, pp. 163–183.

Sommer, D. (2006). *Cultural Agency in the Americas*, Durham, NC: Duke University Press.

Stavenhagen, R. (2001). La diversidad cultural en el desarrollo de las Américas. Los pueblos indígenas y los estados nacionales en Hispanoamerica, *Serie de Estudios Culturales*, 8, 1–81.

Stiglitz, J. (2003). *Globalization and Its Discontents*, Norton, New York.

Suteu, C. (1999). *Networking Culture: The Role of European Cultural Networks*, Council of Europe Publishing, Strasbourg.

Thome de Sousa, F. (2020). Plötzlich Person of Colour. https://www.zeit.de/kultur/202 0-08/brasilien-person-of-color-weiss-sein-rassismus-10nach8 (Accessed October 5, 2020).

Tymoczko, M. & Gentzler, E. (2002). *Translation and Power*, University of Massachusetts Press, Amhurst.

Yudice, G. (2018). Innovations in cultural policy and development in Latin America, *International Journal of Cultural Policy*, 24(5), pp. 647–663.

Yudice, G. (2019). Culture and development in Latin America. In: Cupples, J., Palomino-Schalscha, M. & Prieto, M. (Eds.), *The Routledge Handbook of Latin American Development*, Routledge, Milton Park, pp. 29–42.

Zamorano, M., Ulldemolins, J. and Klein, R. (2014). ¿Hacia un modelo sudamericano de política cultural? Singularidades y convergencias en Uruguay, Paraguay y Chile en el Siglo XXI, European Review of Latin American and Caribbean Studies,*European Review of Latin American and Caribbean Studies | revista europea de estudios latinoamericanos y del caribe* 96 (April), pp. 5–34.

Zheng, J. (2019). *Cultural Management: Evolution and Education in the World*, Chung Hwa Book Co. (H.K.) Ltd., Hong Kong.

2 Cultural management in Latin America and Europe

Between the ashes and the flame

Beth Ponte

Introduction

At 3:00 p.m. on August 19, 2019, the sky darkened in the city of São Paulo, in southeastern Brazil, in a phenomenon that impressed the 12 million inhabitants of South America's most populous metropolis. The cause was related to fires in large tracts of the Amazon rainforest in the state of Rondônia, in northern Brazil, and in parts of Bolivia. The smoke particles travelled more than 2,500 kilometres and, combined with a cold coastal front, turned the day into night in the city that is also the richest in Latin America. Much more than a rare meteorological phenomenon and a warning of the growing environmental crisis that threatens the Amazon forest, this event carried with it an immense symbology. It highlighted the deceptive distance that separates urban Brazil from its countryside and, above all, that historically separated Brazil itself from its South American neighbours.

On the perspective of international relations in the field of cultural management, paradoxically, Brazil often sees itself as closer to Europe. It is no coincidence that, for many professionals who have the chance to engage themselves in international exchange, the main experiences have taken place in Europe. This cannot be explained only by the existence of more exchange opportunities coming from the European continent. It is a feedback loop. The urban development of Brazil was concentrated for centuries on the Atlantic coast and turned its back on continental America. Likewise, most of the cultural managers of the major cities of Brazil with access to formal education and training (and it is important to make this differentiation) still develop themselves professionally "turning their backs" on the Latin American countries (Araujo & Leitao; Escribal; Moizo & Urbanavicius; Carpio Valdeavellano, this volume). They look beyond the Atlantic, draw inspiration from European institutions and cultural policies, prioritise English or French as a second language, and build more academic bridges with Ibero-American (Portuguese and Spanish) universities than with their own neighbours.

Even though Brazil is geographically closer to other South American countries (and this is also relative, when considering the dimensions of our continent compared to Europe), we have indeed, remarkable differences in our languages and in our history. Over the centuries we were somehow convinced that these differences were greater than our similarities. However, today we begin to understand that what brings us closer is much greater than what separates us. This requires us to continuously ask ourselves what makes this distance between Latin American countries (or even between the so-called Global South) seem and feel greater than it really is or could be as well as to reflect on the impacts it has on the way Latin American and European cultural managers see themselves and work together.

Beyond dualities: The plurality of Europe and Latin America

Thinking and writing about Latin America is not something trivial or simple to most of the Brazilians. It is already challenging to understand Brazil's own diversity and even more to see the country, socially and culturally, as a member of Latin America and close to it much beyond the geographical perspective. As Santini (2017) states, "thinking about Latin America is a complex task". Accepting the complexity that comes from the diversity of countries, contexts, and actors is the first condition to talk about with regard to cultural management on the continent. It is necessary to escape the almost natural impulse to label and try to understand where the real convergences and divergences reside. There are different Latin Americas, as well as different Europes. On similarities and differences within Latin America, Santini (2017) explains:

> Reality confronts us with a heterogeneous continent, unequal in terms of its levels of development, with different national spaces and perspectives, and with acute internal contradictions between our countries and our peoples. However, we can investigate what are the unifying elements of a history common to our entire America. They, by the way, exist. Historical, political, and cultural issues that unite us, a linguistic unit that covers almost all the countries of the region, but above all common political, social, and cultural problems that encourage the search for an overview. Latin American unity is, above all, a political project that gives direction and substance to a discourse, to a historical construction in development.

Brazil occupies a peculiar space in the Latin American environment. It is like a strange and giant brother, who has walked, by external impositions and by his own choices, a different trajectory from his neighbouring countries. Brazil has been invaded and colonised by Portugal for more than three centuries, and therefore, unlike all our Latin American neighbours, Brazilians speak Portuguese and not Spanish. But the historical differences are even deeper, as the processes of independence, which were quite distinct on the continent, illustrate.

The countries of the so-called "Spanish America", which today make up Central and most of South America, conquered their autonomy through the wars of independence against the Spanish Kingdom, in successive battles between the years 1808 and 1833 and became republics. Brazil, in turn, had its independence proclaimed in a coup of Portuguese Emperor Dom. Pedro I against Portugal in 1822, becoming an "independent empire" until the year 1889, when it finally adopted the republican regime. Only a year before, 1888, Brazil abolished slavery, taking with it the vexatious post of the last country in the West to forbid it. Over four centuries, Brazil has received around 4.8 million enslaved Africans, more than double the 1.5 million destined for Spanish America.

This basic information is key to understanding the history of the continent's development, its diversity, and its social relations. Relations that to this day are marked by racism not only against black people but also against indigenous communities. As Galeano (1976, p. 223) said, "development is a journey with more castaways than sailors". Much of Latin America's development came at an extremely high price, which included the reduction of the continent's cultural and linguistic diversity due to the extermination of significant portions of the population.

Cultural management, as a profession and as a social function, is related to history. It is related to the degree of awareness we have about our history, our representations, and their consequences. The growth of the decolonial discourse is calling cultural organisations on both sides of the Atlantic to position themselves and make themselves accountable around this historical debate.

To contemplate diversity, in any field of knowledge, it is necessary to identify and avoid false dichotomies. Reductionism is seductive because it is simple, but it is also a two-way street. We commonly find in Europe an imaginary of the Latin American cultural sector linked mainly to indigenous and black traditions, to what has been called folklore, to community experiences, and artistic projects with a social character. On the other hand, the cultural sector in Europe is also reduced to a certain conservatism, to the hegemony of canonical artistic languages (e.g., opera, orchestras, theatre, ballet) and to large and consolidated cultural institutions (especially museums). This shows that the reductive meanings around the concept of "tradition" are at the core of the usual understanding of cultural practices coming from Latin America and Europe.

These visions are stereotyped, meaning that they are not entirely false, but are surely deceiving. The most important factor is that they exist, if not in our own colleagues in the cultural field, certainly, in a considerable part of the public that consumes the cultural experiences that we enable. The reductionism in it ignores, for instance, that there is still much conservatism in Latin America´s cultural management, as well as a lot of innovation and social engagement in European projects and institutions. If not recognised and challenged, these views can influence how we cooperate, produce, and work.

Our work as cultural agents, from any side of the ocean, is also to deconstruct these reductions while rethinking the meaning, the origins, and the importance of traditions in our present world. In this sense, it is always valuable to remember the phrase attributed to the composer Gustav Mahler (1861–1911) who said that "tradition is not worshipping the ashes but passing on the flame". There are ashes and flames on both sides of the Atlantic.

Narratives, identities, and cultural cooperation

Argentine writer Jorge Luís Borges said in a 1992 interview, quoted by Santini (2017), that "the only Europeans are us, the Latin Americans, who see Europe as a whole of which we feel heirs, while no one in Europe feels European, but Spanish, French, Swedish or German". Behind the irony of the statement, there was truth in it both in terms of the overvaluation of the "European heritage" in Latin America as well as the feeling of a Europe fragmented between different nationalities and identities. The two phenomena, however, have undergone major changes over the last 30 years. It is important to understand these changes, which are a backdrop of cultural management on both continents today. European influence may be more visible in Argentina, the country that received the second largest contingent of European immigrants in the world, behind only the United States (Moya 2006), but it is not exclusive to that country. The direct relationship of economic dominance changed after the independence of the old colonies, but the European cultural and intellectual influence remained strong and was decisive for the construction of Latin America's cultural identity. As Calabre (2013) explains:

> During the independence process, the construction of a new cultural identity was undertaken, seconding, or even rejecting, the black, indigenous, and mixed, bias in the new societies. These new identities were based on European culture and civilisation. The creation and strengthening of cultural institutions such as historical museums, national libraries, national theaters, or even the construction of monuments, the institution of national ephemeris, as well as the search for local values in literature, music, theater, are some of the facts that mark the action of Latin American governments in the nineteenth century. The whole process was aimed to satisfy a political and economic elite, preserving strict ties with European origins. On the other hand, these countries, at that same time, maintained very high levels of illiteracy and social exclusion – of black, indigenous, mixed-race and poor immigrants' populations.

Both Europe and Latin America were marked in the 1990s by changes in their continental narratives in both politics and academia. The signing of the Maastricht Treaty in 1993 marked a new moment with the creation of the European Union. Two years earlier, in 1991, in the city of Guadalajara, Mexico, the first Ibero-American Summit of Heads of State and Government took place and recognised in its Final Declaration a common Ibero-American space. From the late 1990s on, researches by Latin American intellectuals on decoloniality (Quijano, 2000; Lander, 2000; Escobar, 2005; Quintero, 2010) paved the way for the review of Latin American historical and cultural narratives, making the concept of decolonisation transcend the academic environment and be part of the social and cultural debate.

However, the narrative of the "European cultural identity", after the 1993 milestone, was followed by massive economic investment. In the cultural area, this can be observed through the creation of large investment programmes such as Creative Europe and initiatives such as the European Capital of Culture, Erasmus Programme, European Collections, among others. European identity is also visible in strengthening trans-European cultural associativism, resulting in highly active entities, many of which are financially supported by the European Union. Among these initiatives are International Network for Contemporary Performing Arts (IETM), Trans Europe Halles, Network of European Museum Organisations (NEMO), Orchestra Network for Europe (ONE), European Network of Cultural Management and Policy (ENCATC), among others. These entities play an important role in facilitating the exchange, the network, and the capacity building within the European cultural ecosystem.

This movement also influenced research, training, and professionalisation within the sector, followed by the creation of dozens of postgraduate courses in cultural management and of agencies and offices specialised in research. In the context of training, students benefit from the existence of a common European area that facilitates international exchange. A recent example of this is the Arts and Cultural Management Conference (ACMC), created in 2018 and managed by arts management students from different countries in Europe.

Latin America also had a significant increase in the offer of courses and training in cultural management but does not so far have such stable networks of exchange among professionals. According to Santini (2017), several networks were created between the end of the 1990s and the first decade of the 21st century, such as the Latin American Network of Art and Social Transformation (RLATS), Latin American Community Theatre Network, Central American Network of Community Art (MARACA), Latin American Articulation Culture and Politics (ALACP), among others. Some of these initiatives received grants from foundations and international cooperation agencies, such as the Avina Foundation, the Hivos Foundation, or the Ford Foundation, in funding programmes that were discontinued.

The interruption of funding from international foundations, the difficulties of travelling inside the continent due to the distances and costs, and the political instability in several countries may explain why many Latin American cultural networks have been dissolved. However, new autonomous initiatives continue to emerge, such as the Network of Latin American and Caribbean Memory Sites, the Network of Contemporary Latin American Art Workers, the Network of Women Workers of Cultures and The Arts, and the Network and the Latin American Observatory of Cultural Management. They are mostly still more informal initiatives than associations comparable to those in Europe, but even with their limitations, they have been contributing to the development of the Latin American cultural ecosystem.

In addition, the history of fragmentation and colonisation, followed by military dictatorships in several countries between the 1960s and 1980s, can also be listed as reasons why Latin America has not built such solid networks of cultural cooperation. However, it is interesting to note that some of the most structured cultural development and cooperation programmes in Latin America are promoted by Ibero-American organisations, especially the Ibero-American General Secretariat (SEGIB) and the Organisation of Ibero-American States for Education, Science and Culture (OEI). The two organisations are the most responsible organisations for support programmes targeted to different sectors, such as *IberMidias, Iberescena, Ibermuseums, Ibermúsicas*, and more recently *IberCultura Viva*.[1]

The construction of a post-colonial Ibero-American space is also part of a narrative strategy, which served primarily economic purposes and was built over a colonial mindset. The narrative that has led to the creation of Ibero-American cooperation bodies can have its roots traced back to the foundation of the first Ibero-American Union in 1885, which aimed to strengthen the social, economic, artistic, and political relations of Spain, Portugal and their former colonies. According to Gomes (2014), "the ´economic union´ was pursued without forgetting the ´intellectual union´, even advocating an authentic ´intellectual solidarity´, through the extension and intensification of teaching, exchange of scientific ideas and educational methods, and the signing of treaties of literary property". "Intellectual solidarity" on a one-way street, of course.

Therefore, while we must encourage the programmes resulting from Ibero-American cooperation, we also need to look at these initiatives with decolonial lenses. Even with all the advances in the discourse, practices, and cultural diplomacy, cultural agents are still vulnerable to the pitfalls of duality. I have personally heard a cultural leader say that Brazil was "the best invention of Portugal" at a diplomatic event in Lisbon. It shows that cooperation practices can change, but colonial logic can remain the same. Besides avoiding colonial mindsets, we must incentivise cultural cooperation through flows of knowledge that travel in both directions between continents.

The programmes should also create ways to support autonomous Latin American networks. A positive example of new Ibero-American approaches is the IberCultura Viva programme, one of the most genuine experiences of Latin American cooperation. In 2004, the Cultura Viva/Pontos de Cultura Program was created in Brazil, which inspired similar programmes in Argentina (2011), Peru (2012), Costa Rica (2015) and Uruguay (2017). These experiences led to the creation of IberCultura Viva, a technical and financial cooperation programme to strengthen the community cultural policies of currently ten Latin American countries (Argentina, Brazil, Chile, Colombia, Costa Rica, El Salvador, Ecuador, Mexico, Peru, Uruguay) and Spain.

Unlike most other "Iber" programmes, the Cultura Viva programme was genuinely born in Latin America. It is not only an investment programme, but a mix between social technology and public policy to support small cultural initiatives, reaching regions and communities on the fringes of traditional public policies. It is something that can create the basis for stronger cooperation between different parts of Latin America, beyond large urban centres and the most consolidated cultural industries. It is also an experience that can inspire other European countries in the democratisation of their cultural investments.

Touching points: Words and relationships

The past helps us understand the differences between European and Latin American "cultural ecosystems" (Holden, 2015). However, the present reveals similarities in the challenges faced by the two continents to build a desirable future.

The growing urbanisation and financial capitalism today unite the urban centres of Europe and Latin America. Currently, 80% of the continent's population – about 450 million people – live in cities, slightly higher than 75% of Europe's urban population. In some Latin American countries, this percentage is even higher: Argentina has an urban population of 91.8%, Chile 87.5%, and Brazil 86.5%. Of the 33 megacities in the world, five are in Latin America (Mexico City, São Paulo, Rio de Janeiro, Buenos Aires, and Lima) and, after Brexit, only one in the European Union (Paris). Urban development poses some common challenges to both continents regarding gentrification, migration flows, and mobility.

However, if the phenomenon of urbanisation unites us, the social inequality that comes with it is something that profoundly separates Latin America from Europe. We can take some numbers of São Paulo as an example of the Latin American urban paradox. In 2017, the city's Gross Domestic Product (GDP) (approx. USD 211 million) was five times greater than Bolivia's GDP or the equivalent to 109% of the sum of the GDP of all the capitals of the North, Northeast, and South regions of Brazil. At the same time, São Paulo, as well as Rio de Janeiro, has one of the highest unemployment rates, the lowest rate of primary education, and the highest income inequality in the Americas.

Some of the largest and richest cultural organisations in Brazil are in these two cities and the two urban centres concentrate about 900,000 professionals employed in creative enterprises (not including IT and advertising sectors). Although large arts institutions in São Paulo or Rio de Janeiro do not represent most Brazilian cultural landscape, they are responsible for some of the main cultural exchange projects between Europe and Brazil.

Thus, we can notice somehow much more similarities than differences in the institutionalised cultural landscape of large urban centres in Europe and Latin America. Large cultural institutions on both continents are much closer than far away in terms of work skills, or management and communication strategies. Innovation and conservatism are also present in the cultural leadership of both continents.

However, the similarities between large European and Brazilian organisations have their limits and the most visible of them lies at the exit door. In large Brazilian capitals – and certainly in most Latin American capitals – we have access to products and cultural experiences that equal or exceed much of what is presented in Europe. In these cities, it is possible to visit world-class exhibitions, to listen to great orchestras in good concert halls, or to attend innovative performances of the highest technical degree and artistic quality. But many of these experiences are not within reach of the working class that makes the economy of these cities work. A large portion of the audiences of these cultural events does not use public transportation, especially at night, for fear of violence. Often, there are dozens of homeless people sleeping on the sidewalks of the great cultural facilities. Or you can visit a museum of excellence that may have to fire its entire staff because it has not received government subsidies in months. The list goes on.

Many of the large cultural organisations in urban centres in Brazil are fruits of what de la Vega Velástegui (2020) calls "incomplete modernising projects". This idea recalls the concept of "peripheral modernisation" developed by the Brazilian economist and former Minister of Culture (1986–1988) Celso Furtado. Perhaps this is the saddest legacy in our history, this eternal anachronism between the colonial past and the future of global development. In the big cities in Latin America, we developed and nurtured "sophisticated consumption patterns without corresponding progress" (Furtado, 1974) either in the social and or in the material (capital) spheres. In the cultural field, as in several others, it feels like as we had access to some of the results, without having been given the conditions to build and live the development process fully. Theoretically, we have guaranteed cultural rights, but not all of them and especially not to all of us. In the words of Mejia (2012):

> This is the big problem we are facing at the moment and the outstanding theme of Latin America: the rights have been presented without strong states that can guarantee them. [...] We do not have a State that guarantees cultural rights derived from our constitutions and that works to make them effective; the State is weak and unable to abolish social differences. It is difficult to think of human development without a guarantee of human and cultural rights. [...] The reality of Latin America then faces a great crossroads.

The weight of the colonial past and its current consequences – poverty and social inequality, urban violence, and a strong patrimonialism, etc. – impose a reality that cannot be ignored by Latin American cultural managers. This background profoundly affects the management of cultural organisations. Therefore, it should have a central role in the premises that guide its strategies and its role in society.

In relation to other challenges, the cultural sectors of Europe and Latin America are at some similar crossroads, even if in different positions or starting points. We can identify on both sides of the Atlantic some recurring concepts that represent common challenges in the world of cultural management. These are concepts such as diversity (of gender, race, and social class among audiences, artists, and leaders); audience development and participation; cultural leadership; sustainability (financial, social, and environmental) and decolonisation, to name but a few. As Buber (1984) said, "the predominant words do not mean things, but indicate relationships". The cultural sectors of Europe and Latin America relate differently to each of these concepts but produce specific answers and solutions that can generate mutual learning. Regarding audiences and participation, for example, while European orchestras deal with the ageing of their audiences, we deal with immense potential for new audiences that, however, do not have access to music education. While Europe deals with the international migration issues, Latin America faces old challenges with rural migration, social inclusion, and the recognition of our black and indigenous cultures, as well as the emerging urban peripheric cultures. The challenges of diversity in its different spheres, as well as the development of new, more horizontal, and innovative leadership practices, are present in the cultural sector of both continents.

In the big picture, the recent prominence of these concepts has a common background: the need to review the structures of power. We are all at a great crossroads today. On the one hand, the growing conflict between the new and old forms of power (Heimans & Timms, 2018) and its effects on politics and economics. On the other, the urgency of issues such as antiracism, feminism, the revision of the colonial past, and the confrontation of social inequality. The cultural sector both in Latin America and Europe affects and is affected by these same agendas.

Besides these issues, we have another rising challenge, which the cultural sector on both continents cannot ignore: the crisis of democratic regimes and even more problems ahead after it: the newest major health and economic crisis resulting from the COVID-19 pandemic that began in 2020. Faced with these common challenges, cultural managers will need to review their roles and ask themselves difficult but necessary questions. Reflecting on the perspectives of the Ecuadorian cultural sector, de la Vega Velástegui (2020) raises some global and central questions about the relevance and future of the cultural sector in these new times:

> in times of post-crisis, culture played different roles in Latin American countries, serving government projects of different political tendencies, which reduced culture to its usefulness for social consensus and reconciliation, or for economic recovery, as well as for the deepening of cultural nationalisms, now extremely dangerous with anti-immigrant movements. What will be the "value and usefulness" of culture in authoritarian, populist, extractive economies, (in) weakening public spirit and labor precariousness? How important will culture be when it is no longer, at least for a long time, directly linked to tourism and economic spectacles of great economical return?

The threat to democratic values and the consequences of the COVID-19 pandemic are added to existing environmental and global challenges (de la Vega Velástegui, this volume). Perhaps this is the ideal time to understand the future of the cultural sector as a common cause and to create new forms of cooperation between continents that help us "globalize the fight but localize the action" (Aguilar & Burgos, 2020).

Conclusion: Reimagining culture to build the future

Despite the differences, Latin America and Europe have many common challenges ahead and can use these commonalities to exchange experiences and learn together.

What the European experience shows us is that the construction and maintenance of continental identity narratives must be sustained by massive investments in the different links of the cultural chain. Investment in the training of artists and managers, cultural infrastructure, and initiatives of associativism, research, and innovation in the sector have helped strengthen the European cultural ecosystem. This should serve as an example for Latin American cultural policies. On the other hand, the Latin American experience points to new ways of relating culture to social changes and problems, focusing on the local and on the community – lessons that can be precious to a post-pandemic world.

The emergence of decolonial thinking and its consequences shows that if we do not have the power to change the past, we have the possibility and obligation to review our narratives. This is the first step towards the change of power structures and the construction of a better future. Imagination, an asset of the cultural sector, plays an important role in this process and should be taken more seriously. The cultural sector can boost and benefit from future building processes that involve imagination. It would be interesting if the cultural sector, along with other sectors of society, took part more widely in the creation of what Porto (2019) calls "capsules of imagination":

> If every order of reality is the fruit of an imagination that has won, imagining should be taken seriously as a dimension of life. To imagine what can be and what it is not. To imagine what and how it could be. The generating principle of all creation and all destruction is imagination. Good ideas must overcome bad ideas. (...) Capsules of imagination should be encouraged in all art actions, in science, in schools, in temples, wherever there is any dimension that deals with human subjectivity.

To move forward, we should imagine what does not yet exist as well as to reimagine existing practices and structures that need to be updated. Some recent experiences with which I have had contact both in Latin America and in Europe point to interesting paths and deserve to be highlighted. The IberCultura Viva programme, already mentioned, has contributed to thinking about decentralised policies and cultural investments with a local focus. The conference "The Museum Reimagined" held annually by Fundacion Typa,[2] from Argentina, is a great forum of new ideas on the social role of museums in the present and in the future. The Die Vielen movement,[3] created in Germany in 2018, shows new ways of articulating the cultural sector to respond to the advance of the right-wing ideology. The project "Reshape Network" brings together arts organisations from Europe and the South Mediterranean to jointly create innovative organisational models and reflect on concrete answers to crucial challenges of contemporary art practices.[4] The Culture of Solidarity Fund, an initiative of the European Cultural Foundation, supports imaginative cultural initiatives that, during the global pandemic crisis reinforce European solidarity and the idea of Europe as a shared public space.[5]

We also should imagine new ways of understanding the complex and essential role of culture in our societies. An interesting example is the Intercultural Coexistence Index (ICI). The index seeks to highlight cultural factors that favour or hinder coexistence in the same territory, with an emphasis on relations between different social groups and considering the differences in opportunities for sustainable development. It was inspired by the work of Chilean researcher María Paulina Soto Labbé and carried out with the collaboration of researchers and international experts from different countries in Latin America and abroad, supported by the Itaú Cultural Observatory, in Brazil.

These examples and many others not cited indicate that the debate on cooperation and cultural management between Latin America and Europe goes far beyond the dichotomy and stereotypes of the "new world" and the "old continent". The central issue should be to identify practices and learnings to guide the development of a cultural management that is relevant to its time, to its societies, and their challenges. The evergoing mission is to discard the ashes, renew the flames, and keep passing it on.

Notes

1 More information at http://iberculturaviva.org/.
2 More information at https://elmuseoreimaginado.com/.
3 More information at https://www.dievielen.de/.
4 More information at https://reshape.network/.
5 More information at www.culturalfoundation.eu.

References

Aguilar, A. M. & Burgos, M. J. (2020). Narrativas y aprendizajes en disputa. *Revista Gestión Cultural*. Politicas Culturales y Covid19: el desvelamiento de una crisis. July. pp. 53–73. http://rgcediciones.com.ar/narrativas-y-aprendizajes-en-disputa/.

Araújo, B. & Leitao, C. (this volume). Thinking of the South as if there were no north: an exercise in culture-based imagination. In: Henze, R. & Escribal, F. (Eds.), *Cultural Management and Policy in Latin America*. Abingdon & New York: Routledge, pp. 34–52.

Buber, M. (1984). *Yo y tu*. Buenos Aires: Ediciones Nueva Vision.

Calabre, L. (2013). História das políticas culturais na América Latina: um estudo comparativo de Brasil, Argentina, México e Colômbia. *Revista Escritos. Year 7. Nº7*. Rio de Janeiro: Fundação Casa de Rui Barbosa.

Escobar, A. (2005). *Más allá del tercer Mundo. Globalización y diferencia*. Bogotá: Colombian Institute of Anthropology and History & University of Cauca.

Escribal, F. (this volume). Cultural management in Argentina: political agenda and challenges for practitioners and researchers. In: Henze, R. & Escribal, F. (Eds.), *Cultural Management and Policy in Latin America*. Abingdon & New York: Routledge, pp. 87–105.

Furtado, C. (1974). *O mito do desenvolvimento econômico*. Rio de Janeiro: Paz e Terra.

Galeano, E. (1976). *As Veias Abertas Da América Latina*. Rio de Janeiro: Paz e Terra.

Gomes, N. (2014). *A politica de Portugal para a Ibero-America. A partir de 1991*. Thesis for a PhD in International Relations. New University of Lisbon.

Heimans, J. & Timms, H. (2018). *New Power: Why Outsiders Are Winning, Institutions Are Failing, and How the Rest of Us Can Keep up in the Age of Mass Participation*. London: Palgrave MacMillan.

Holden, J. (2015). *The Ecology of Culture: A Report Commissioned by the Arts and Humanities*. London: Research Council's Cultural Value Project.

Lander, E. (2000). *La colonialidad del saber: Eurocentrismo y ciencias sociales. Perspectivas latinoamericanas*. Buenos Aires: CLACSO.

Mejía, J. (2012). ¿Derechos sin estado? Tres momentos de la institucionalidad cultural en América Latina. *8th Euro-American Campus for Cultural Cooperation "Cultural cooperation in the face of the new processes of human development"*, November 28–30, Cuenca (Ecuador).

Moizo, C. & Urbanavicius, D. (this volume). Cultural management in Uruguay: a country synonymous with a river. In: Henze, R. & Escribal, F. (Eds.), *Cultural Management and Policy in Latin America*. Abingdon & New York: Routledge, pp. 184–197.

Moya, J. (2006). A continent of immigrants: postcolonial shifts in the western hemisphere. *Hispanic American Historical Review*, 86(1), pp. 1–28.

Porto, M. (2019). *Imaginação: Reinventando a cultura*. São Paulo: Ed. Pólen.

Quijano, A. (2000). Colonialidad del poder, eurocentrismo y América Latina. In: Lander, E. (Ed.). *La colonialidad del saber: Eurocentrismo y ciencias sociales. Perspectivas latinoamericanas*. Buenos Aires: CLACSO. pp. 203–241.

Quintero, P. (2010). Notas sobre la teoría de la colonialidad del poder y la estructuración de la sociedad en América Latina. *Papeles de Trabajo*, 19, pp. 3–18.

Santillan Guemes, R. (2009). *Políticas Culturales, Cultura Y Gestión Cultural*. Buenos Aires: RGC Ediciones. http://rgcediciones.com.ar/1548-2/ (Accessed July 5, 2020).

Santini, A. (2017). Cultura Viva Comunitaria: políticas culturales en Brasil y América Latina. Caseros: RGC Libros, 1a ed.

de la Vega Velástegui, P. (2020). Ecuador: Politicas Culturales y Covid19. El desvelamiento de una crisis. *Revista Gestión Cultural*, Políticas Culturales y Covid-19 en América del Sur. pp. 73–83. http://rgcediciones.com.ar/ecuador-politicas-culturales-y-covid-19-el-desvelamiento-de-una-crisis/.

——— (this volume). Cultural management in Ecuador: genealogy and power relations within the constitution of a field. In: Henze, R. & Escribal, F. (Eds.), *Cultural Management and Policy in Latin America*. Abingdon & New York: Routledge, pp. 143–162.

3 Thinking of the South as if there were no North

An exercise in culture-based imagination

Bianca Araújo and Cláudia Leitão

South America: Diversity or identity?

One of the authors of this chapter remembers vividly her experience as an exchange student in California, USA. When the Brazilian student was introduced by her host mother to a neighbour, the latter immediately commented that living in Central America, speaking Spanish, and being in direct contact with all the enchanting animals of the Amazon forest must be exciting. It took a while to explain to her that, given its geographical size, Brazil would not fit into Central America, that Brazilians speak Portuguese as opposed to Spanish, and that more than half of the country's population had never even been to the Amazon. She became increasingly frustrated, while her host mother found it difficult to accept that everything she believed to be true of Brazil (or any other country south of the United States) bore scant resemblance to reality. Even with the passage of 23 years, and irrespective of whatever our current location, we still find ourselves obliged to correct the same old misconceptions.

Even though Brazil constitutes the largest South American country, it is the only one whose official language is Portuguese. Moreover, several dialects of "Portuguese" exist which feature a wide range of accents and different words signifying the same object or concept depending on the state or region within Brazil. The same is true of the Spanish spoken across that continent with several accents and forms of speech, depending on the country or region, being discernible. Thus, a general consensus prevails that no "single Brazil" exists just as there is no "one South America" (Henze and Escribal, this volume). In reality, Brazil is composed of many Brazils. Likewise, there are many more distinctive influences and cultures in South America. Consequently, studying the continent, its cultures, and policies involves understanding a myriad of cultural encounters, combinations, and exchanges between vastly different peoples that converge to form multiple identities and nationalities (Loureiro, 2015).

If the performing arts in early Egypt represented a means through which the wishes and orders of the pharaoh were disseminated (Berthold, 1972), similarly, during the first half of the 20th century, cultural policies in South America were designed to satisfy government demands and to disseminate their particular concepts of nationality (Rubim, 2007b; Williams, 2001). Several countries in South

America developed projects and systems to achieve the ideals of progress and modernisation together with their attempts to engender the unity of each nation on assumed "standardized" cultural bases (Londoño, 2017). Arts and culture were elements employed to build a national identity for certain countries in South America: an identity proposed by governments influenced by their aspirations in this regard. In Brazil, an official cultural policy emerged between 1930 and 1945 during the era of the Getúlio Vargas government (Barbalho, 2007; Rubim, 2007a). At that time, the apparent strategy was to overcome regional fragmentation and construct a sense of identity in terms of the "Brazilian nation" (Mota & Moreira, 2019) or *brazilness*. Popular music, for instance, played the role of a "political propaganda weapon" not only in Brazil (e.g. Samba and, subsequently, the Bossa Nova, created at the end of the 1950s as a successor to Samba), but also in other countries such as Argentina and Uruguay, and received financial support from their respective governments (Mota & Moreira, 2019).

Despite governmental efforts, the "nationality" projects and achievements did not result in harmonious relationships between official institutions, bureaucrats, and intellectuals involved in their formulation and implementation (Londoño, 2017). Obviously, an artificially created "idealistic representative identity" could not incorporate all of the diversity found on the South American continent. In Brazil, for instance, only a handful of people visited the national museums, theatres, concerts, and activities promoted or supported by the State. Several were difficult to reach from major population centres, while a strict dress code excluded the poor and working class (Kraay, 2002). On the one hand, this concept of *brazilness*, to a certain extent, rendered black people more visible within the country's formation but, on the other hand, it symbolised a "co-optation" or silencing of those experiencing inequality and exploitation (Mota & Moreira, 2019). There was an attempt to create a single identity that merely pretended to incorporate the entire spectrum of Brazilian diversity. Furthermore, this identity hid a multitude of origins and pluralities:

> Therefore, the valorization of nationality as a policy of State guides government action in the cultural area by glorifying the mestizo popular culture, elevating it to a national symbol. The "popular" or folkloric, removed from its place of manufacture, masks the social relationships of which it is a product, acts in the moment of constructing "Brazilian culture", as a driving force for union between regional and class diversities. The miscegenation merged the popular types into a single being, the National Being, whose hallmarks are cordiality and pacification.
>
> (Barbalho, 2007, p.41)

The city of Buenos Aires was federalised in 1880, a landmark event in the political consolidation of the "nation state" of Argentina. However, the construction of nationality as a cultural singularity of the Argentinian people was far from consolidated at the same time (Beired & Barbosa, 2010; Escribal, this volume). An intriguing debate ensued regarding common civil interest: not all of the city's inhabitants were also considered citizens of the municipality, only those who contributed financially to the city through direct taxation (Landau, 2014). This requirement excluded a significant proportion of the county's population. The policy, therefore, recognised and addressed only one limited section of Argentinian society. The debate on nationality gradually intensified, culminating in a change in attitude towards individuals claiming Spanish heritage in Argentina due to Anglo-Saxon imperialism and political tensions reinforcing populist anti-Hispanic sentiment (Beired & Barbosa, 2010).

Understanding democracy as the management of numerous competing demands and expectations, rather than a consensal mechanism for controlling of the claims of the "majority" remains embryonic in South America. The notion of a singular national identity for a population formed by several cultures, nationalities, races, and languages is arguably no more than a power and domination-based strategy. The real nationality of South America rests on a foundation of pluralities that differs greatly between each country on the continent. The empowerment of South America, and its constituent countries, may increase when this diversity gains wider recognition, but also, importantly, becomes more stimulated and highly valued.

The magnetic compass, according to the Oxford dictionary,[1] is an instrument used for indicating direction whose needle invariably points in a direction arbitrarily referred to as "North". South American countries are bombarded by the aesthetics (music, cinema, art) of their powerful northern neighbour which influence arts production and consumption in the Southern Hemisphere (and not only in the Americas). Moreover, European institutional models influence the cultural policy development of all South American countries. International organisations such as the Organisation of Iberian American States for Education, Science and Culture (referred to by its original acronym of OEI) and the United Nations Educational, Scientific and Cultural Organisation (UNESCO) have generated data and issued statements from which governmental policy-makers in South America derive ideas relevant to the creation and development of cultural policy institutions in their respective countries (Loureiro, 2015).

Towards the end of the 1980s, a group of researchers and intellectuals[2] formed part of a group that spearheaded a questioning of cultural policy thinking exclusively produced by the State (Londoño, 2017). Even with the re-introduction of democracy in several countries, cultural policies were not developing as democratically as they should have. Decision-making was limited to a restricted number of people unrepresentative of the pluralities and diversities evident in South American countries (Loureiro, 2015). In general, it took more than two decades for South America to recognise its cultural potential and develop policies that would exploit it in favour of the wider society. Only since 2003 has Brazil rendered diversity a key guideline of its cultural policy. Up to that point, culture was understood through an identity logic paradigm, as though it were possible for a country of more than 200 million people to identify with one generally shared characteristic (Mota & Moreira, 2019). During President Lula's[3] term of office, the Ministry of Culture under Gilberto Gil[4] proposed a concept of culture termed "anthropological", the focus of which was the Brazilian society in general, rather than its cultural sources, e.g. creators, artists, and musicians (Rubim, 2007b). These cultural elements, differing from state to state and region to region, would be stimulated by, and valued for responding to, Brazil's plurality, as opposed to only one small part of the country's population. Yúdice agrees with this significative improvement in Brazilian's cultural policy:

> Brazil's cultural policy, especially during President Inácio Lula da Silva's two terms, is in a category by itself. Brazil had the good fortune of having Gilberto Gil as Minister of Culture, and of his appointment of very progressive and capable policy-makers, many from popular culture, workers' organizations, inner-city initiatives, indigenous peoples, Afro-descendant communities, regional cultures, an activist digital culture movement, and so on. For two decades, these cultural movements had transformed Brazil, and that transformation had an impact on how Brazil developed its creative economy.
>
> (2018)

After this broadening of cultural policy, significant stimulation and inclusion of popular, indigenous groups as drivers in developing an inclusive economy occurred. Indigenous groups could apply for sponsorship by submitting videos and images, rather than written applications on an official government form (Mota & Moreira, 2019). The fashion industry was encouraged to use local and sustainable resources in their products (Yúdice, 2018), while digital culture could be created and accessed in a more democratic manner. These ideas and policies adopted by governmental and national policy-makers cast popular, indigenous, traditional, contemporary, and diverse cultural influences in a pivotal synergistic role, instead of merely including them in a cultural hierarchy (Loureiro, 2015).

Clearly, cultural policies must stimulate local narratives and recognise local specificities and pluralities, rather than unsophisticatedly picking one narrative to represent all or, even worse, picking one derived from elsewhere (Loureiro, 2015; Rubim, 2007b; Yúdice, 2018).

Oceania: Not above, but adjacent

Like those of South America, the countries of Oceania were subjected to European colonisation from the 16th century onwards. Within both contexts, European settlers aimed to disseminate the Christian faith, to defend their nationality, and increase trading opportunities with Europe. Just as in the case of the indigenous populations of South America, their counterparts in Oceania were treated harshly, killed, and dispossessed of their land and culture. Often, in the name of God; an imperialist destiny; and/or trade, these colonialists felt at liberty to dominate indigenous peoples and eradicate their cultures. A curious hangover from colonialisation in both Oceania and South America is the schizophrenic manner in which Christmas is celebrated in December, the height of summer in the Southern Hemisphere, as though it were freezing cold and snowy. Traditional Christmas fare in the countries below the equator is winter food. More than five centuries have passed, and yet many in the Southern Hemisphere persist in referring to the North (like some form of cultural magnetic compass) to find their cultural way.

Making the effort to look sideways as opposed to the North may lead to an unprecedented identification of commonalities and similarities which may, in turn, inspire improvement by regarding the South as a guide to social, economic, and environmental development recognising the pluralities, and diversities of these unique southern countries. For example, Papua New Guinea is one of the most diverse countries in the world, with more than 700 indigenous groups whose members speak approximately 850 distinct languages.[5] Aotearoa (New Zealand) understands and protects its social matrix, recognising the Māoris as the traditional owners of the land and valuing their society and culture with all its richness in order to improve regional development.

The social matrix and traditional culture in Māori Aotearoa/New Zealand invoke new traditions which are continually reinvented (Memmott, 2011). This claim can be confirmed empirically: New Zealanders recognise their country as Aotearoa, which in Māori means "land of the long white cloud". Although English is the official language of New Zealand, the Māori language (legally recognised as an official language of the country since 1987) continues to be written or spoken across the national territory. It can be encountered in restaurant menus and the voice messages of several electronic services. This cultural matrix-based interaction goes beyond mere pride, also promoting the active participation of the general population in preserving, reinventing, diffusing, and developing themselves as one community.

Curiously, both Brazil and New Zealand have experienced times in their histories when culture was employed as a means of exercising power and subjugating others, and of creating an identity predominantly inspired by Europeans. Skilling explains this phenomenon at greater length:

> The Queen Elizabeth the Second Arts Council of New Zealand (QEIIACNZ) was established "as the nation's commemoration" of the Queen's visit in February 1963, and the first reading of its founding legislation described the council as "a gift" to her (NZPD, 20 August 1963). The functions of the new council were to be "to foster and encourage the arts, to maintain public interest in them, and to render them accessible to the public." Minister of Internal Affairs, Leon Gotz, claimed (NZPD, October 2, 1963) that in "the modern world there … has been a change from dancing, from music, and from acting for the sheer love of it, and now we have professional players … artists … dancers … singers etc." Art and Culture, in other words, had been subject to the same drives to efficiency and specialization that had occurred throughout modern society. Everyone, to be sure, should "retain an interest in the arts", but their participation was properly restricted to the role of educated spectator. Art, primarily, was something that was done to us; ideally, we should

appreciate the experience. The goal for the mass of the population was not to create culture but to become cultured.

(2005, p. 23)

It is clear that, at that time, no interest existed in diversity or multicultural models of arts. Not even the idea of art as an economic axis: arts funding was viewed as a subsidy or cost, rather than an investment and income generator (Skilling, 2005). From the 1990s onwards, culture in Oceanic countries faced significant changes to their policies. For example, Australian Prime Minister Paul Keating instituted a reform in his country's cultural policy that also influenced others in the region by integrating the global and regional when stimulating local production and adopting new technologies (Johanson & Rentschler, 2002, p. 175).

> One of the debates was over the introduction of new technologies to the arts, linking the global to the local, in other words, convergence. This notion was exemplified in the cultural policy document "Creative Nation" (Commonwealth of Australia, 1994). This model influenced the establishment of New Zealand's newly named arts council, Creative New Zealand, as well as the late 1990s British government's creative industries policies.

Like Oceania, South America has also changed its approach to arts and cultural policy. The primacy of *understanding* cultures has been amplified, and a wider field of vision has been applied. However, even with these improvements, much remains to be done for southern peoples in terms of promoting their equality and dignity. The Treaty of Waitangi (1840) gave the Māori peoples the same status as the British colonisers. Nevertheless, Māoris remained subject to mistreatment and discrimination. Aboriginal Australians as the original inhabitants of the land mass now constituting modern Australia, remain marginalised and treated as less significant than the majority of the country's population. As late as 1967, Australians finally voted in a referendum to allow the formal inclusion of Aborigines and First Nations within national society as people rather than fauna. This significant development also granted all Aboriginal peoples, for the first time, the right to vote, to be recognised as Australian citizens in their own right, and to participate in the census (Coddington, 2017). A cursory review of the black and indigenous peoples in South America identifies more similarities and synergies. Brazil constitutes the last country in the Americas to abolish slavery in 1888. However, even in that country today, the majority of black people are treated differently, in a discriminatory sense, to non-black peoples. This represents something of an anomaly since a significant proportion of these non-black people classify themselves as white, even if they are, in fact, of mixed race, due to the colonisation of Brazil by several countries.

Black and indigenous cultures remain marginalised in South America, and mixed-race individuals still look to the north when setting their expectations. Southern hemisphere countries still struggle to develop cultural policies that represent their own identities and pluralities; cultural policies that promote, preserve, and propagate a uniquely Southern Hemisphere identity that permits its people to recognise themselves through arts and culture produced and consumed at home. Looking at the list of 2019 number one at the box office films in Brazil[6] and Australia[7] reveals that the same film was number three in both countries: (1) *Avengers: Endgame* (2) *The Lion King* (3) *Captain Marvel*, all of which were conceptualised and produced in the North, particularly the United States.[8] It means the South looks North, consumes the production of the North, creates social expectations about the ideal of the North, and remains under the influence of the North. Again, in the same manner as the magnetic compass, the South defines itself in terms of where North lies, rather than finding its own definition.

As mentioned above, the attempt to create an identity for South America employed hallmarks of cordiality and pacification, and the image of a cordial, exotic, and peaceful country was created. In the early stage of Oceania's interaction with the "outside world", the same atmosphere was created, and people of the South were souls pacified, Christianised, colonised, and civilised living in harmony with savage nobles in beautiful nature (Hau'ofa, 1998). Unfortunately, the South remains subordinated to the North. If dangerous experiments were undertaken in southern lands in the past, nowadays the South continues to occupy a position of dependency and inferiority. The authors argue that the time has come to observe matters from our own perspective and position instead of persisting in looking to the North. It is, perhaps, time for the long-expected polar reversal to adjust our magnetic compass and aim its needle at the South where we can find our true selves. Hau'ofa proposes a process of regionalism in Oceania:

> The time has come for us to wake up to our modern history as a region. We cannot confront the issues of the Pacific Century individually as tiny countries, nor the Pacific Islands region's bogus independence. We must develop a much stronger and genuinely independent regionalism than that which exists today. A new sense of the region that is our own creation, based on our perceptions of our realities, is necessary for our survival in the dawning era.
>
> (1998, p. 5)

The authors suggest that this concept can be expanded to one of a "Global South" (De Sousa Santos, 2002; Carou and Bringel, 2010; Briceño and Simonoff, 2017). This involves not the creation of a single region, but recognition of a shared collective richness based on plurality which combines our similarities and challenges as constituent parts of the South. Such dialogue between regions demonstrating numerous social, environmental, and political similarities could represent a significant opportunity to collaborate and to re-think a novel epistemology, together with a new understanding of culture, development, and identity.

Turning monoculture into ecologies[9]

"Development is a journey with more shipwrecked individuals than sailors". This statement opens the second part of the classic *The Open Veins of Latin America* by

Eduardo Galeano (1979). It encourages reflection, through images, on the significant ideas that underpin modern "western thought". At the Economic Commission for Latin America and the Caribbean (ECLAC), economist Celso Furtado was a tireless critic of the conditions of peripheral modernisation in underdeveloped countries. In just the same way as Galeano,[10] Furtado was aware that the concepts of development that spanned the 20th century, were especially damaging to the countries of the Southern Hemisphere:

> The idea of development has only been useful in mobilizing people who are on the periphery and inducing them to accept enormous sacrifices, to legitimize the destruction of "archaic" forms of culture, to "explain" and make "understood the need" to destroy the environment, to justify forms of dependence that reinforce the predatory character of the productive system.
>
> (Furtado, 1974, p. 75)

The word "development" symbolises a great paradox in modern values. On the one hand, it produces content that induces a sense of identity and stability. On the other hand, it conceals realities and falsifies arguments in the name of a "unique and universal" epistemology. There are other words, such as "management", "consumption", "individualism", "property", "capitalism", and "globalisation", that also reinforce hegemonic values and produce semantic synergies to support them. Many of these words, defined and legitimised by modernity, based on Aristotelian and Cartesian logic, have been advanced to support the unifying values of modernity. The scientific spirit has lost its approach to the actual and observational to ignore the ambiguous dimensions of knowledge.

The rigour of a scientific concept should be measured by its ability to undergo deformation and deconstruction (Bachelard, 1967). In this sense, words require a "movement pedagogy" (Wunemburger, 2010), in order to be capable of moving ideas forward. If the last two hundred years have been marked by values of "possessive individualism" (Macpherson, 1979) and by scientific rationality, increasingly uncertain times might render urgent the deformation and re-testing of "great words" that decodes modern imaginary, much as a goldsmith carefully examines a gold bar to legitimise its intrinsic qualities. How can the "great words" that make up the rhetoric of modernity be deconstructed? How can new epistemologies capable of emancipating populations and territories from otherwise hegemonic thoughts be produced? Could culture and cultural management practices of Southern Hemisphere countries reveal emancipatory social experiences potentially essential to these novel epistemologies?

By analysing the economic, political, and institutional modernisation process that started in Brazil from the 1930s onwards, Furtado prophesised the sad reality of Southern Hemisphere countries, especially those of South America, in the 21st century: incomes and the centralisation of wealth; the erosion of social rights; the precariousness of employment; the submissiveness of a divided labour movement, and its susceptibility to international interference (Furtado, 1998). This Brazilian economist recognised the risks of a form of development that could be reduced to capitalist accumulation. In his book *Creativity and Dependence on Industrial Civilisation*,[11] Furtado went beyond mere economic analysis, bringing such words as "culture", "creativity", "philosophy", "basic science", "mystical meditation", and, finally, "the arts" into the orbit of development (2008, p. 114). By considering creativity as an invention of culture, Furtado renews and revitalises the definition of development, taking it as a basis for his analysis of southern countries.

> The challenge faced at the threshold of the 21st-century is nothing less than to change the route of civilization; it is to shift the axis from the logic of the means, in the service of accumulation in a certain time horizon, to a logic of the ends in terms of social well-being, the exercise of freedom and the cooperation between people.... The main objective of social action would stop being the reproduction of the consumption patterns of wealthy minorities in favor of satisfying the fundamental needs of the population as a whole, and education conceived as the development of human potentialities in ethical, artistic and solidarity action plans.
>
> (1998, p. 65–68)

Furtado was an unmerciful critic of capitalist societies and their sophisticated way of controlling creativity and manipulating information. He was aware of the hegemony of cultural industries that reproduced the logic of accumulation and dependence, as well as the fragility of cultural expressions in the face of the economic globalisation process experienced by South American countries. His concern regarding Brazil also extended to other Southern Hemisphere countries:

> Brazil will be marked by a whole range of imported symbol systems that often desiccate our "cultural roots" with the production of cultural goods that seek to standardize behavior patterns, the basis for creating large markets.
>
> (1984, p. 31)

However, far from being a simple process of homogenisation, globalisation represents the re-ordering of differences and inequalities between people and countries (Garcia Canclini, 2006). The globalisation process has been predicated by a universalising logic perspective which ignores the conquest and colonisation processes of the North in relation to the South. However, the bonds of dependency between these populations can no longer be understood through the traditional categories of imperialist domination (colonisers versus colonised). Global capitalism, ultra-right movements, new technologies, migration flows, nation-state decay, COVID-19, and cultural and communication industries all over the world are revealing phenomena confirming the dynamism of the subordination and dependencies between the hemispheres. Thus, novel epistemologies are required to understand these newly identified dynamics. The predominantly government policy-based cultural studies, the analysis of the differences in the production and practice of cultural management between the countries of the North and South, and the strategic construction of new epistemologies should perhaps be less grounded in the outdated consensus between nations. A more attentive analysis of stresses, cracks, deviations, and crossings between countries will be potentially more productive. Finally, the development of a new epistemology of the Global South, as though there were no Global North, could be achieved by identifying the potential elements promoting the submission of cultural management policies and practices in Latin America, Oceania, and Africa to those of European and American models. But why undertake this exercise with respect to culture?

In recent centuries, both culture and development have been considered the product of a universal form of reason.

> During the twentieth century, culture, as science, had been nourished much more by illusion than hope. It signified a universal and unique reason inherent in all people, at all times. It was also understood as a superior element, capable of defining the civilizing processes. Therefore, it has become a depressing prerogative of genocide, slavery and exclusion. As a form of scientific discourse, culture has produced masters of the universal symbols of difference (do anthropologists not epitomise such mastery?) who, in their turn, developed a kind of "humanitarian ecumenism". This movement invariably strove to negotiate solutions to conflict, to resolve disagreements, and to neutralize antagonism. Western "white" anthropology will achieve its legitimacy through a rhetoric of respect for differences and an altruistic understanding of the world. However, over time, it will not be able to hide either deep contempt for the cultures of others, or the disappointment with its own culture. According to Jean Baudrillard, Western culture will, ultimately, engender an "evil ecology" that through its development, creates excrescences. This means that apologizing for differences will neither prevent it from submerging in the industrial or urban waste that it has itself produced, nor for rendering human species (religious communities, indigenous tribes, gangs, ghetto inhabitants, deportees, migrants, under-developed populations) a waste, a worthless and meaningless residue.
>
> (Leitão, 2009, p. 19–20)

Due to an eagerness to homologate the modern values of stability and the achieving of consensus, the natural tensions inherent in culture(s) have been overlooked. From the 18th century onwards, the word "culture" came to be employed interchangeably with the word "civilisation": that is, as a set of practices (arts, sciences, techniques, philosophy, crafts) capable of evaluating and ranking the value of political regimes, according to a criterion of so-called Darwinian evolution. The progress of civilisation was evaluated by its culture, as well as the growth it promoted in civilisation (Chauí, 2009). Reflections on social changes and their cultural implications have crossed over into modern thinking, as exemplified by the works of Adam Smith, Alex de Tocqueville, and Max Weber.

In the 20th century, economists and social scientists were faced with the failure of numerous development projects in the countries of the South. They subsequently asked themselves how cultural factors created or determined obstacles to development. Throughout the 19th and the first part of the 20th century, scientific rationality legitimised hegemonic discourses commencing with a post hoc explanation of culture in which underdeveloped or peripheral countries represented an essential obstacle to their own development due to the psychosocial characteristics of their populations. The Darwinian imagery of evolution, when related to culture, creates an even deeper dependency relationship between the southern countries and their northern counterparts. The economic dependencies produced by (post-) industrial societies are symptomatic of an even greater reliance: cultural dependency. According to Furtado, in post-industrial societies, it is possible to observe the shift from the logic of ends (related to well-being, freedom, and solidarity) to the logic of means (in the service of capitalist accumulation) the effects of which will be prejudicial to creative liberties, natural resources, and put simply, the very humanity of individuals:

> Humankind struggles to gain access to its common cultural heritage, which is continuously enriching itself. It remains to be seen which peoples will continue to contribute to this enrichment and which will be relegated to the passive role of simple consumers of cultural goods acquired through the market. To have or not to have the right to creativity, that is the question.
>
> (1984, p. 25)

When referring to the cultural dimension of globalisation, this phenomenon must be analysed in relation to the roles of consumption and not only as the result of economic rationality. Rather, it should include analyses of culture as symbolic acts of communication and a place of differentiation and distinction (Bourdieu, 2009). According to Garcia Canclini (2006), consumption is a way of thinking which "represents the set of socio-cultural processes in which the appropriation and use of products take place" (Garcia Canclini, 2006, p. 60). This understanding is implicit in the semantics of consumption (Castells, 1974) that represent a space for the analysis of class conflict, a privileged locus of contests between the producers and the mode of production. In this sense, within contemporary societies, especially those of Latin America, the processes of disaggregation of traditional cultures through consumption can be observed simultaneously with innovative technological connections resulting in the hybridisation of goods and services. This reality of the growth in de-territorialised products characterises the consumption of information and entertainment arising from an "*i*nternational, relocated, cultural production system increasingly detached from the differential relationship with a territory and with the unique goods produced in it" (Garcia Canclini, 2006, p. 107). Globally, consumption between hegemonic and subordinate groups is not achieved through the simple opposition between local and imported goods, but particularly by de-territorialised products (Garcia Canclini, 2006).

Erudition and popularity, craftsmanship and industry, authenticity and imitation: each become blurred, contaminate tastes, and promote specific behaviours, particularly in populous cities. On the other hand, a combination of mainstream communication and cultural industry deprives consumption of its cognitive value, preferring its mercantile attributes. According to Gilles Lipovetsky and Jean Serroy (2014), a true "aesthetic mode of production" is generated. All sectors of human life are eventually captured by the meshes of hyper-consumption capitalism. However, the increasing desire to consume beauty leaves life apparently less beautiful; the more a cultural industry commercialises its goods and services, the less autonomy individuals enjoy in making choices; the more societies of spectacle and entertainment grow, the greater the alienation of audiences. Artistic capitalism, so jealous of the aesthetic compared to the innovative, sells lifestyles with the promise of happiness, beauty, well-being, and quality of life.

Rather than discussing the semantic variety of culture, researchers should examine the domestication of notions regarding culture. Moreover, its functional and pragmatic management that was shaped through the logic of means – serving capitalist accumulation – instead of the logic of ends – focused on well-being, freedom, and solidarity can be observed (Furtado, 1974). The logic of means produces negative impacts on creativity and freedom, on natural resources, and on the humanity of individuals. Among the range of human freedoms, creative freedom is essential to development, given that it is the greatest input supporting social transformation, especially when referring to the understanding of development as an extension of human freedom (de Sousa Santos, 2016).

In the significant discourses relating to development, Western reductionist thought obscured the possibilities, the alternatives, and the paths. De Souza Santos appeals to us to discern the invisible, to reap the discarded, to value the diversity of social, community, and intersubjective experiences, to reintroduce the unofficial, to adopt the alternative, in other words, the epistemology of the "no". Therefore, he calls for a sociology capable of facing metonymic reason, always fixed on the idea of totality in the form of order:

> The most finished form of totality for metonymic reason is the dichotomy because it combines symmetry with hierarchy in the most elegant way. The symmetry between the parts is always a horizontal relationship that hides a vertical relationship. [...] In fact, the whole is one of the parts transformed into a reference term for the others. That is why all dichotomies endured by metonymic reason contain a hierarchy: [...] scientific knowledge / traditional knowledge; men/ women; culture/nature; civilized/primitive; capital/labor, white/black; North/South.
>
> (2002, p. 242)

A critique of metonymic reason is both essential and urgent in order to recover experiences, knowledge, practices, and technologies in countries destined for exogenous development. De Sousa Santos encourages thinking beyond dichotomies and their power relations. It helps us to think of the South as if there were no North. After all, what is there in the South that escapes the North/South dichotomy? (op. cit., p. 248). The production of non-existence takes place through several logics derived from the "knowledge monoculture". This logic considers scientific knowledge and high culture as the unique criteria of truth and aesthetics.

The monoculture of linear time seeks to establish an evolutionary sense of history, led by central countries in the world-system; the monoculture of the naturalisation of differences, defining privileges based on social classifications such as race, sex, formal education, among others; the logic of the dominant scale (of the universal and the global) and, finally, the productivist logic, in which economic growth and the respective criterion of productivity are the priority and unquestionable. To face each logic, De Sousa Santos proposes a new ecology. The ecologies of knowledge, temporalities, recognitions, trans-scales, and productivity offer clear strategies for meeting hegemonic thinking in the North, contributing to the flourishing of epistemologies in the South. In Latin America and Oceania, other knowledge, temporalities, and social practices, as well as new alternative forms of economic production are beginning to gain visibility.

Contributing to the epistemologies of the Greater South: Culture as sustainable development, cultural management as a practice of social emancipation

Although culture is not explicitly mentioned in the Sustainable Development Goals for 2030 as defined by the United Nations (UN), these objectives arise in the context of a crisis of the State, a crisis of governments and institutions. From arts to cultural expressions, from copy to creativity, from segmentation to transversality, from spending to the creative economy, from quantity to quality, from products to processes, from consumption to cultural rights, from management to governance, from the will to responsibility, institutions and cultural events are put to the test.

When dealing with culture in sustainable development, declarations, conventions, and other international documents understand culture as a separate and independent aspect to different dimensions of development. This perception focuses on the protection of cultural assets, reducing culture to artistic and cultural sectors. This view disconnects the relationship between nature and culture with other social and planetary themes, finally taking culture as the fourth pillar of development.

The perception of culture for sustainable development understands culture as a mediator and facilitator, with the primary task of translating conflicts and demands between different social groups, their values, and ways of living. From this perception, culture grants sustainability to the development projects of peoples and nations, adding to them a social and human significance. However, a major challenge referred to in the most recent international documents (such as the 2030 Agenda for Sustainable Development) is to conceive of culture as sustainable development. In other words, culture creates the conditions for sustainable development on the planet. To this extent, culture is more process than product. Culture is learning, a matrix of transformation, and a foundation for the construction of new epistemologies – other forms of thinking, being, and acting in the world. Within this context, public cultural policies must increasingly commit themselves to territorial governance, governance capable of making individuals the protagonists of their own development. Thus, culture starts to mean development itself and, therefore, it needs new mental models, new public structures: new "institutionalities".

Figure 3.1 "Inverted America" (1943) by Uruguayan artist Joaquín Torres García, visually invites us to rethink the relationship between territories and hierarchies.

Despite efforts to collate data relating to the global creative economy during the last decade, the South remains largely absent from the reports produced by the United Nations Conference on Trade and Development (UNCTAD) and UNESCO. Thus, despite the cultural diversity and social technologies characteristic of its countries, their experiences remain unrecognised, while almost always being treated as aspects of management. South America and Oceania, for example, constitute strategic places in which novel epistemologies can flourish. Both utilise social technologies, especially in the areas of governance, multiculturalism, human rights, and cultural management, as well as alternative systems of production, biodiversity, and intellectual property. Despite the invisibility of these practices within the global context, they can highlight new avenues in which culture adds other meanings of development.

The challenges for cultural management in the "Global South" are compelling, but the lessons learned between Oceania and Latin America can be valuable, especially in structuring unprecedented forms of governance. It can also be valuable in tackling the cultural factors of poverty; in expanding the roles of the creative economy as a source for sustainable development; in the development of new cultural indicators; in the construction of educational programmes that contribute to overcoming all forms of discrimination against minorities; in the development of new intercultural competences; in the encouragement of cultural and creative entrepreneurship; in the recognition of cultural practices and traditional habits; and the management of cultural habits in favour of food and health. In addition, it is possible to re-think the use of clean energy by the creative industries; the creation of cultural circuits and territories; the humanisation of public spaces; the recovery, the restoration, and new uses of cultural heritage; the creative tourism and cultural tourism; and the guarantee of meaningful work for the creative sectors. Moreover, the inclusion of marginalised young people in the productive systems of the creative economy; the creation of funding conditions for small organisations; the stimulus for innovation in cultural and creative processes and products; the management of cultural rights; the protection of communities affected by violence through sustainable cultural and creative actions. All these practices are, by nature, emancipatory.

Culture as sustainable development: Thinking aesthetically

Arts and culture offer aesthetic experiences which can be triggered by different emotions including happiness, sadness, tension, or fear (Araújo et al., 2020). Aesthetic experiences also transform individuals by providing them a chance to re-consider their lives, recognise themselves, and develop a sense of belonging. Culture can be a means of ensuring sustainable development for, as previously mentioned, these ecologies can embrace several aspects of being human: harbouring desires, expectations, and needs in an inclusive, engaged, and collaborative manner. Each region produces its own culture(s), and our challenge is to use this/these culture(s) as a means of achieving at least a sense of equality within populations instead of reproducing narratives drawn from elsewhere in constructing a global identity that serves, and responds to, only one region of the world. While traditions can be reinvented, this does not mean that external influences or contributions can be avoided. Rather, instead of slavishly reproducing other "monocultures", the local and regional (whose traditions are constantly reinvented) can be prioritised to engage and include peoples in their diversity. Araújo provides an example of how external elements could be merged with regional demands:

> The manager also told a story about a Christmas event for the community. They were researching a Russian Christmas, with classical Russian waltzes. At a certain point, the design team was preparing the advertisement, using all the typical Russian outfits and the usual snow associated with European

Christmas. However, the presentation was to be performed in a tropical town with temperatures of 40 degrees Celsius and had little in common with Christmas in Russia. The team, therefore, decided to re-think the aesthetics of the show. The orchestra invited a group of young waltz dancers from the outskirts of the city to join the presentation, and even the repertoire remained as classical Russian music, some pop music was included. The audience had the chance to attend a Christmas concert that was close to their habits and culture, and at the same time, they had the opportunity to enjoy classical music that for many of them was the first experience.

(2020, p. 72)

Culture can provide a feeling of belonging, a sense of prominence. Unlike that which was proposed in the 1960s in Oceania (and all colonised territories), when the goal harboured by the majority of the population was not to create culture but to become cultured, people bring culture and arts to the centre of their lives and create an atmosphere of social development. What is development, after all? Capitalism's weaknesses and fragilities are becoming evident as a result of the COVID-19 pandemic. While capitalism is struggling with large multinational companies facing bankruptcy (without the labour and consumption it has previously taken for granted), the importance of the State and collaborative action is being confirmed and ratified. Under these circumstances, Western reductionist thought does not continue to make sense. As De Sousa Santos has claimed, it is time to render the previously invisible observable and contribute to increasing diversity and intersubjective cultural experiences in order to achieve socially shared development. Working together, the United Nations Programme for Human Settlements (UN-HABITAT) and *Complexo da Maré*[12] locate individuals suffering extreme social vulnerability in the capital of Rio de Janeiro and direct them to public services or income transfer programmes. However, these bodies face a huge challenge since not everyone has access to information. Consequently, they have organised (through cultural centres, associations, and the producing of videos, street art, banners, and images) channels to inform the population about the COVID-19 virus and access to public services. It is urgent to re-think the "unique and universal" epistemology and bring into discussion key concepts such as symbolism, emotions, beliefs, and a sense of belonging. It is compelling to evaluate and recognise the prevailing ecologies and reject the maintenance of the monocultural paradigm.

Clearly, arts and culture are directly linked with symbolic experiences that go beyond economic consumption. Aesthetic experiences are powerful ways of transformation and self-recognition, as Araújo explains:

Aesthetic experiences are full of symbolic dimensions that connect audiences and deliver experiences to them. For example, studies of symbolic, ritualistic, hedonic, and performative consumption behaviour illustrate how individuals collect past meanings, negotiate future meanings, and assemble present meanings of cultural constructs such as family, religion, gender, age, and tradition through their participation…. Human beings express the feeling of being part of a social group via aesthetic symbols.

(Araújo et al., 2020, p. 67)

Understanding culture as developmental and acknowledging aesthetic experiences as a means of transformation, self-belonging, and thought-provoking prominence could be a way of re-thinking the epistemology of the North and turning it to an epistemology of the South. Encouraging people to want to be part of creation, rather than merely passive viewers, turning communities into policy collaborators and creators, rather than simply consumers. Exploiting all the human potential inherent in each diverse element of society, and using and preserving ecologies, instead of reinforcing the imperialism of monocultures can provide a healthy, fair, egalitarian, and sustainable environment.

Notes

1 Source: https://www.lexico.com/definition/magnetic_compass (Accessed September 16, 2020).
2 Including Sérgio Miceli in Brazil, Alberto Ciria and Juan Pablo Tedesco in Argentina, José Joaquín Brunner in Chile, and Guillermo Bonfil Batalla and Néstor García Canclini in Mexico.
3 Luiz Inácio Lula da Silva, known as Lula, was President of Brazil from January 1, 2003 to December 31,2010.
4 Gilberto Gil is a Brazilian singer, guitarist, and songwriter, known for both his musical innovation and political activism. From 2003 to 2008, he served as Brazil's Minister of Culture in the administration of President Luiz Inácio Lula da Silva.
5 https://www.nationalgeographic.org/encyclopedia/oceania-physical-geography/ (Accessed July 27, 2020).
6 ANCINE – Observatório Nacional do Cinema Nacional at https://oca.ancine.gov.br/paineis-interativos?painel=viz1558970268340 (Accessed July 28, 2020).
7 Box Office MOJO at https://www.boxofficemojo.com (Accessed July 28, 2020).
8 Escribal (this volume) reports a similar situation for Argentina´s cinema consumption.
9 Concept created by Boaventura de Sousa Santos (2002).
10 The criticism of the hegemonic concept of development is intense in Latin America with different tendencies, working groups, and theories such as those proposed by Martín-Barbero (1999), Quijano (2005); Arizpe (2001); Perez de Cuéllar (1997); Cuéllar Saavedra (2009); Iglesias (2009; 2010); and Nivon Bolan (2012).
11 Criatividade e dependência na civilização industrial, 1978.
12 Available at https://nacoesunidas.org/pensando-no-coletivo-favelas-se-organizam-para-combater-o-coronavirus. (Accessed September 16, 2020). More information at https://unhabitat.org/ (Accessed September 16, 2020).

References

Araújo, B. C., de Davel, E., & Rentschler, R. (2020). Aesthetic consumption in managing art-driven organizations: an autoethnographic inquiry. *Organizational Aesthetics, Special Issue: Performing Performance*, 9(3), pp. 63–84.

Arizpe, L. (2001). *As Dimensões Culturais Da Transformação Global: Uma aborgagem antropológica*. Paris: UNESCO.

Bachelard, G. (1967). *La formation de l'esprit scientifique*. Paris: Vrin.

Barbalho, A. (2007). Políticas culturais no Brasil: Identidade e diversidade sem diferença. In: Barbalho, A. & Rubim, A. (Eds.), *Políticas culturais no Brasil*. Salvador: EDUFBA, pp. 37–60.

Beired, J. L. B. & Barbosa, C. A. S. (2010). *Política e identidade cultural na América Latina*. São Paulo: UNESP.

Berthold, M. (1972). *The History of World Theater: From the Beginnings to the Baroque*. Vol. 1. London: Continuum Intl Pub Group.

Bourdieu, P. (2009). *O poder simbólico*. Rio de Janeiro: Bertrand.

Briceño-Ruiz, J. & Simonoff, A. (2017). La Escuela de la Autonomía, América Latina y la teoría de las relaciones internacionales. *Estudios Internacionales*, 49(186), pp. 39–89. http://doi.org/10.5354/0719-3769.2017.45218.

Carou, H. C. & Bringel, B. (2010). Articulaciones del Sur Global: Afinidad cultural, internacionalismo solidario e Iberoamérica en la globalización contrahegemónica. *Geopolítica (s). Revista de estudios sobre espacio y poder*, 1(1), pp. 41–63.

Castells, M. (1974). *La questione urbana*. Vol. 24. Venecia: Marsilio Editori.

Chaui, M (2009). *Cultura e democracia*. 2 ed. Salvador: Secretaria de Cultura, Fundação Pedro Calmon.

Coddington, K. (2017). The re-emergence of wardship: Aboriginal Australians and the promise of citizenship. *Political Geography*, 61, pp. 67–76.

Cuéllar, J. P. de (1997). *Nossa diversidade criadora: Relatório da Comissão Mundial de Cultura e Desenvolvimento*. Campinas: Papirus; Brasília: Unesco.

Cuéllar Saavedra, Ó. & Moreno Armella, F. (2009). Del crecimiento económico al desarrollo humano: Los cambiantes usos del concepto de desarrollo en América Latina, 1950–2000. *Sociológica (México)*, 24(70), pp. 83–114.

De Sousa Santos, B. (2002). Para uma sociologia das ausências e uma sociologia das emergências. *Revista crítica de ciências sociais*, 63, pp. 237–280.

Furtado, C. (2008). *Criatividade e dependência na civilização industrial*. São Paulo: Companhia das Letras.

———— (1998). *O capitalismo global*. Rio de Janeiro: Paz e Terra.

———— (1984). *Cultura e desenvolvimento em época de crise*. Rio de Janeiro: Paz e Terra.

———— (1974). *O mito do desenvolvimento econômico*. Rio de Janeiro: Paz e Terra.

Galeano, E. (1979). *As Veias Abertas Da América Latina*. Rio de Janeiro: Paz e Terra.

Garcia Canclini, N. (2006). *Consumidores e Cidadãos*. Rio de Janeiro: Editora da UFRJ.

Hau'ofa, E. (1998). The Ocean in Us. *The Contemporary Pacific*, 10(2), pp. 392–410.

Iglesias, E. V. (2010). O papel do Estado e os paradigmas econômicos na América Latina. *Revista de la CEPAL, Special Issue*, 90, pp. 44–53.

Iglesias, E. (2009). Os principais eixos da política Ibero-americana. Iniciativas, Programas e Projectos Ibero-americanos. *Conference proceedings "Portugal e a Comunidade Ibero-Americana de Nações", Lisboa – UAL*, October 14, 2009.

Johanson, K. & Rentschler, R. (2002). The new arts leader: the Australia council and cultural policy change. *International Journal of Cultural Policy*, 8(2), pp. 167–180.

Kraay, H. (2002) Culture Wars in Brazil: The First Vargas Regime, 1930–1945, *History: Reviews of New Books*, 30:3, 104–104

Landau, M. (2014). La Ciudad y sus partes: Una historia de la institucionalidad local en la Ciudad de Buenos Aires. *Eure*, 40(119), pp. 151–171.

Leitão, Cláudia Sousa (2009). *Cultura e municipalização*. Salvador: Secretariat of Culture, Pedro Calmon Foundation.

Lipovetsky, G. & Serroy, J. (2014). O capitalismo estético na era da globalização. Lisboa: Edições Almedina.

Londoño, H. P. (2017). Políticas culturales: La producción historiográfica sobre América Latina en la primera mitad del Siglo XX. *Anuario Colombiano de História Social y de la Cultura*, 44(1), pp. 363–391.

Loureiro, B. P. (2015). *Néstor García Canclini and Cultural Policy in Latin America*. Birkbeck: University of London.

Macpherson, C. B. (1979). *A teoria política do individualismo possessivo: De Hobbes a Locke*. Rio de Janeiro: Paz e Terra.

Martín-Barbero, J. (1999). Globalización y Multiculturalidad: Notas para una agenda de investigación. In: Lopes de la Rocha, F. (Ed.), *Incertidumbres y possibilidades – Política, comunicación y cultura*. Bogotá: Tercer Mundo, pp. 95–122.

Memmott, P. (2011). Cultural change and tradition in *the indigenous architecture of Oceania. Architectural Theory Review*, 16(1), pp. 38–54. https://doi.org/10.1080/1 3264826.2011.560552.

Mota, T. & Moreira, O. (2019). Política cultural no Brasil: Retrocessos, resistência e reexistência. *Políticas Culturais em Revista*, 12(2), pp. 34–49.

Nivón Bolán, E. (2012). Cultura, política y Globalización. Claves para el debate contemporáneo. In: Giglia, A. & Singorelli, A. (Eds.), *Nuevas Topografías de la cultura*. México: UNAM, pp. 33–69.

Quijano, A. (2005). Colonialidad del poder, eurocentrismo y América Latina. In: Lander, E. (Ed.), *La colonialidad del saber: Eurocentrismo y ciências sociales. Perspectivas latinoamericanas*. Buenos Aires: CLACSO, pp. 227–278.

Rubim, A. A. C. (2007a). *Políticas culturais: Entre o possível e o impossível. Teorias e Políticas Da Cultura: Visões Multidisciplinares*. Salvador: EDUFBA.

——— (2007b). *Políticas culturais no Brasil: Tristes tradições, enormes desafios*. Salvador: EDUFBA, pp. 11–36.

Skilling, P. (2005). *Trajectories of arts and culture policy in* New Zealand. *Australian Journal of Public Administration*, 64(4), pp. 20–31.

Sousa, Mario Lúcio (2016). *Meu Verbo Cultura: Escritos amorosos sobre cultura e desenvolvimento*. Salvador: EDUFBA.

Williams, D. (2001). *Culture Wars in Brazil: The First Vargas Regime, 1930–1945*. Durham: Duke University Press.

Wunenburguer, J. (2012) *Gaston Bachelard. Poétique des Images*. Paris: Mimesis.

Yúdice, G. (2018). Innovations in cultural policy and development in Latin America. *International Journal of Cultural Policy*, 24(5), pp. 647–663.

4 Cultural management

The Central American perspective

Mario Hernán Mejía

Introduction

This work provides an overview of the configuration of public cultural institutions, policies, and legal frameworks in Central America and of the processes introduced for the implementation of training initiatives to strengthen the role of cultural and creative agents in each country of the region. Central America's cultural field demonstrates various levels of development and different political-institutional characteristics from one country to another. This chapter considers the meaning of culture within the region and how it is reflected in both the institutional, normative, and political structures and the theoretical-methodological approaches that inspire cultural action. In addition, this chapter reviews the background and current situation regarding cultural management training processes and the challenges posed by the emergence of new legal frameworks or the social mandate derived from cultural policies that necessitate comprehensive and systematic action with regard to professional training and applied research in this field.

Specialised training for the cultural and creative sectors is emerging as essential in view of the changes resulting from the information society, the effects of globalisation, and the challenges posed by the economic revival of these sectors in the post-Covid-19 pandemic context. Both the defence of cultural diversity and the right to participate in cultural life as a fundamental principle require the empowerment of citizens at large on an equal footing, as stipulated in the International Covenant on Economic, Social and Cultural Rights (UN, 1966). The expansion of cultural capabilities and skills, spaces, and the management of cultural life should be a strategic objective of cultural policies in Central American countries in order to exploit the potential of culture to support the fight against poverty and inequality, while promoting social cohesion, among other dimensions of development. In this regard, specialised training creates opportunities and strengthens democracy.

In the last section of this chapter, following a general review of the region, the specific characteristics of cultural management training in Honduras are identified. In addition, the initial training initiatives launched within the Ibero-American ecosystem, the internal evolution of these following their incorporation into the country's main public university, and the impetus provided to the creation of a cultural management training network and training offer resulting from inter-university cooperation appropriate to the diverse and shared contexts of the Central American and Caribbean countries receive attention.

The Central American cultural field: A brief review

Contemporary cultural processes, the emergence of new political, legal, and institutional frameworks, and international cultural cooperation initiatives in several Central American countries since the 1990s have laid the foundations for novel conceptions of culture linked to development processes and the recognition of ethnic and cultural diversity. An initial analysis indicates that the Central American cultural field is diverse in terms of its composition, levels of institutional development, and dynamism of its local agents and actors. Costa Rica, Panama, Guatemala, and El Salvador possess public bodies at the highest level of government, such as State Secretariats or Ministries of Culture. In Nicaragua, cultural affairs are the responsibility of the Nicaraguan Institute of Culture (INC), while in Honduras the Executive Directorate of Culture and the Arts is attached to the Secretariat of the Presidency of the Republic.

Guatemala's process of building both a democratic state and a multi-ethnic, multicultural, and multilingual nation began in 1996 with the signing of the Peace Accords which, following recognition of their organisations and institutions, recognised the right of indigenous peoples to participate in decision-making and national planning. One of these accords, entitled Agreement on Identity and Rights of Indigenous Peoples (AIDP), stated that cultural policies should be guided by an approach based on the recognition of, respect for, and promotion of indigenous cultural values (Bá Tiul & Rodriguez Arana, 1999, p. 77). In 2000, the Ministry of Culture and Sports of Guatemala launched its National Cultural and Sports Policies based on the Constitution of the Republic, the Universal Declaration of Human Rights, executive body regulations, and the principles and commitments established in the Peace Agreements. As a result of the participatory consultation processes established between 1999 and 2004, the Ministry of Culture and Sports of Guatemala (MCD) presented the National Plan for Long-Term Cultural Development (MCD 2005) which represents a model for development and a tool for reflection and action enabling people and their organisations to adopt the proposed methodology within the context of sustainable human development based on culture.

Costa Rica approved its first National Policy on Cultural Rights of 2014–2023. Several months later, the General Law on Cultural Rights (2014) was passed setting out a cultural rights perspective, establishing mechanisms to guarantee such rights, assigning powers and obligations to the State, rendering society responsible for creative processes, protecting and managing cultural heritage, as well as ensuring that culture contributes to the country's development (Art.1).

El Salvador strengthened its public cultural institutions in 2018 by converting the National Council for Culture and Art (CONCULTURA), in existence since 2009, into the present-day Ministry of Culture. *The Culture Act* (Decree No. 442

of 2006) aims to establish a legal framework for the development, protection, and promotion of culture, as well as the principles, definitions, institutions, and legal framework on which State policies in this field are based, with the aim of protecting those cultural rights recognised by the Constitution and international treaties currently in force (Art. 1). From 2005 onwards, Panama began reviewing and updating its cultural policies with the support of the UNESCO San José Office for the then National Institute of Culture (INAC) which, in 2019, was transformed into the contemporary Ministry of Culture.

Between 2002 and 2004, Honduras received assistance from UNESCO for the formulation of cultural policies for development and was a beneficiary of the Millennium Development Goals Achievement Fund (MDG-F) and the joint United Nations programme entitled "Creativity and Identity for Local Development (2008–2011)". It has established local and regional culture councils, strategic plans, and an updated conceptual and methodological framework to undertake reforms of its legislation and organisational structures.

This historical-institutional evolution, in addition to the legal frameworks and cultural policies established in most Central American countries, translates into a social mandate that, over time, demands specific skills and competences for pro-gramme and project execution. A contemporary vision in the relations between culture and development, in addition to an inclusive institutional articulation of civil society, is a central theme of the policies implemented that assume the partici-pation of organisations, communities, and artists as a precondition of the sustaina-bility of State-sponsored cultural plans that involve new management approaches. A series of structural conditions were identified during an initial review of the Central American cultural field, many of which constitute current challenges:

- The countries of the region are young national societies marked by ancestral foundations and cultural manifestations rooted in conditions of marginalisa-tion and poverty.
- The lack of a public cultural policies tradition and of the capacity to promote cultural activity, at a practical and material level, as either productive work or as capital/input for human development.
- Cultural sector professionals are predominantly young and demonstrate limited technical ability in the areas of cultural management and strategic planning.
- The conditions and available resources for the production and management of local cultural projects are extremely precarious, given the increasingly sophisticated standards of mass production and marketing.
- Activist cultural production sectors that, conditioned by the above factors, structure voluntarist and artisanal modes of work are poorly informed or in a very precarious condition to confront the complexity and levels of profes-sionalism attained by cultural industries in developed environments. (Durán, 2000, pp. 36–37)

The persistence, to some extent, of Central American cultural field features, including the new institutionality deployed in several countries of the region, the planning instruments developed and in force, plus the updated legal frameworks requiring greater budgetary flows and participatory implementation strategies that demand greater cultural competencies and skills for human development and economic growth. At the same time, the creative economy is expanding in the region under the leadership of the intensive capital and technology sectors. The study conducted in Guatemala – an analysis of the economic contribution of culture (Piedras, 2006) – found that the cultural industries generate a total of 7.26% of the nation's GDP. In addition, they experienced an average growth rate of 7.3% in their added value during the period 2001–2005, which is higher than many other industries within the Guatemalan economy. If the informal and illegal economy components are included, the cultural and creative sectors can be seen to account for 9.02% of Guatemala's GDP (Piedras, 2006, p. 28). The year 2015 marked the beginning of a boom in the digital animation and video game sub-sectors, while 140 audio-visual companies are reported to be currently generating 1,000 direct and indirect jobs. The country benefits from the existence of the Creative Industries Commission of the Guatemalan Exporters Association, which groups several companies in the sector and offers different services supporting their growth (AGEXPORT, 2015).

Costa Rica is the first country in Central America to implement the Culture Satellite Account (CSC), which measures the impact of both the cultural and creative sectors on national production. Figures for 2012 reveal that national cultural production amounted to US$1,045 million, which represented 2.2% of GDP, exceeding that of the computer and software industries. In the first study published by the United Nations Development Programme (UNDP), entitled *Human Development and Local Economic Dynamics: Contribution of the Cultural Economy* (2009), El Salvador demonstrated that, collectively, private sectors such as radio, television, advertising, as well as the visual arts and local gastronomy, contributed $310 million to the national economy (Tenorio, 2009, p. 99). In Honduras, cultural goods and services production activities have been partially quantified in their contribution to the national GDP. The characteristics of culture as a sector of the economy are interconnected with other creative sectors, potentially generating new dynamics within the productive sector. An initial quantification of the impact of culture on the economy carried out in Honduras in 2011 concluded that, in comparison to other sectors of Honduran economic activity, the cultural sectors selected for the study contribute 1.13% to national GDP and that their informal economy adds 50% to official figures, causing an additional contribution of 0.56% for a total contribution to the GDP of 1.69% (Gallegos et Al., 2011). In Panama, the cultural and creative sectors feature important activity and have a significant socio-economic impact by contributing 6.4% more to the GDP than other primary sectors of the economy, while the population employed in different associated professions accounts for 3.2% of total employment in the country (INDESA, 2017).

The above figures are likely to increase significantly throughout the region with the inclusion of non-traditional cultural sectors linked to tourism such as advertising, various aspects of design, and software development, among others, which have the potential to enrich and transform the Central American productive matrix.

Cultural policies and training needs in cultural management within the region

The emergence of more extensive legal and institutional frameworks within the cultural sector highlights the importance of developing systematic and comprehensive formative action. Moreover, it requires academia to train professionals in the skills and competencies to lead the processes of research, management, consultancy, administration, and implementation of programmes and cultural action projects in the public, private, and associative spheres.

Adoption of the term *cultural manager* is relatively recent within the Central American context (de la Vega Velástegui, Escribal, this volume). Many of the functions and areas of work now identified as part of this role were historically assumed by artists, pedagogues, teachers, social workers, collectives, and groups oriented towards social or community development work. In this regard, Alfons Martinell remarks,

> Despite the fact that culture has always demanded some form of communal organisation, cultural management, as we understand it today, is a very recent field of action. We could say that despite its rapid growth in recent years it is still in the structuring and definition phase.
>
> (2002, p. 267)

Cultural management has established itself as a contemporary field of interdisciplinary knowledge in countries that introduced such academic programmes in the 1990s. However, the Central American countries still have a long way to go in enhancing professionalisation of this area of activity, as only a limited number of institutions provide relevant training and education. For decades, the cultural action of Central American states has focused on the protection of the historical monumental heritage in its pre-Columbian, colonial, and republican manifestations and, to a lesser extent, on its intangible cultural heritage, which expresses the hybridity characterising the cultural expressions of the diverse communities residing within their territories.[1]

The multi-ethnic and multicultural character of societies is recognised in all countries of the region, although with different emphases and historical frameworks. Intercultural bilingual education programmes have constitutional status in the cases of Guatemala, Nicaragua, and Panama and are enforced through several special laws in the other Central American countries. For the region, the challenge lies not in the formal recognition of the diverse nature of its populations, but rather realising their full expression through political and civic participation and the enjoyment of individual and collective cultural rights. Diversity implies the recognition of multiple social actors within the public arena, the satisfaction of basic needs and services, and greater budgetary allocation for the exercise of their creative expression (Zamorano, this volume).

In the second decade of the 21st century, the challenges raised by globalisation, for example, the cultural exchanges and flows and the predominance of certain countries in audio-visual distribution, require concerted action to develop alternative spaces for distribution. These challenges go beyond the national sphere and demand an adequate response based on supranational strategies and the participation of additional stakeholders in public policy. Cultural and educational authorities from all the countries that make up the Central American Educational and Cultural Coordination (CECC-SICA) presented a first *Regional Strategic Plan for Culture 2005–2009: Culture, the Foundation of Sustainable Development in the 21st Century*. This plan sought to introduce concepts and stimulate debate around the binomial culture and development in order to satisfy strategic planning criteria during the implementation of national plans and policies.

The *Cultural Policy for Central American Integration 2012–2015* incorporates the previous debates and introduces a cultural perspective-based approach to regional cooperation. This policy has contributed to the construction of a common space that differentiates its own historical background from its diversity, while also constituting a space for confluence, a crossroads, and a means of identity appropriation as part of a strategy to face the challenges of a more inclusive form of development.

In Guatemala, since 2000, in response to both cultural and sport policies, a new approach to the nation and its society has been adopted and decentralisation plans for public services, a network of 331 sports promoters developed to serve an equal number of municipalities (one per municipality) and 22 cultural promoters (one per department) has been implemented (MCD, 2000). The promoter becomes a significant institutional figure and, therefore, a subject in need of adequate and permanent training to be able to execute the principles of the institution without restricting its creative capacity and community leadership.

Management professionalisation sets out the challenges that stakeholders themselves are addressing without the leverage of regular and organic initiatives to train and strengthen human capital. To achieve this, initiatives balanced between the recognition of endogenous capacities and methods and international dialogue on the new challenges and strategies of cultural management must be promoted.

The contexts within which cultural agents, communities, and artists undertake their activities have been transformed. New regional dynamics can be observed which are marked by a growing formalisation of associations and enterprises, the awakening of local/municipal interest, and evident tensions that must strike a balance between tourism development – a priority for Central American countries – and cultural management to ensure the sustainable use of cultural resources, among other variables.

Specialised training in cultural management initially consisted of seminars, courses, and meetings and is currently moving towards the consolidation of professional skills development through diploma courses, postgraduate courses, and international seminars. However, to date, only one official undergraduate course exists, namely the bachelor's degree in Cultural Management at the University of Costa Rica (UCR) which was launched in 2017.

In some cases, training programmes emerge from the interest of certain universities to prepare professionals to work in communities they support through third sector activities. Tertiary level institutions also train individuals from civil organisations or institutional collaborations – in particular the Spanish Cultural Centres[2] – and tend to respond to a significant independent sector demand from, for example, young visual artists who require skills in order to market their work.

A common challenge is that of recruiting lecturers with sufficient skill and expertise in the various aspects of managing the arts and culture.

The Network of Training Units in Cultural Management (IBERFORMAT) was set up in 2001 within the Organisation of Ibero-American States (OEI), in conjunction with the Interarts Foundation of Barcelona and a comprehensive network of managers, academics, and universities on both sides of the Atlantic. Numerous reflections, analyses, and training processes carried out in the region through workshops, seminars, and conferences on cultural management are the result of this network's efforts. These include "First Training of Trainers Seminar in the Field of Cultural Management" (Mexico 2003); "Training the Trainers in Cultural Management Seminar: Developing the Knowledge Base of the Cultural Sector" (Antigua Guatemala, 2006); and "Training Seminar towards the Creation of Networks in the Field of Cultural Management: The Central American Space as a Scenario for the Training of Trainers" (Antigua Guatemala, 2007).

The debates and conclusions resulting from these training experiences made evident the importance of promoting cultural management training in the different countries according to local needs, backgrounds, and realities, without losing sight of the ethos of international cooperation and experience exchange. This situation highlights the need to develop systematic and comprehensive action and requires academia to train professionals in the skills and abilities to manage the processes involved in the research, management, consultancy, administration, and execution of programmes in addition to cultural action projects in the public, private, or associative spheres. Following up on the recommendations emerging from these seminars, Costa Rica conducted a study of Training Needs in Cultural Management (2009) as a result of which the following salient objectives were identified:

- Assess the opportunities for the cultural sector and encourage the creation of programmes at the Central American level, as well as training in cultural management with governmental and international cooperation support.
- Implement UNESCO's numerous recommendations with regard to generating collaboration between different sectors to formulate cultural management training plans.
- Coordinate action with the Spanish Cooperation Training Centre, located in Antigua (Guatemala), to follow up on the initiatives undertaken at the Training Seminar for Trainers in Cultural Management "Developing the Knowledge Bases for the Cultural Sector" in 2006, and the Training Seminar "Towards the Creation of Networks in the Field of Cultural Management:

The Central American Space as a Scenario for Training Trainers" in 2007, aimed at creating a training plan in cultural management in Central America and the Dominican Republic. (Protti, 2009)

Similarly, and as a result of the implementation of the first University Diploma in Cultural Management by UNESCO and the National Autonomous University of Honduras, the study entitled "Training Needs in Cultural Management and Creative Economy in Honduras" (Mejía, 2018) was conducted. Its main purpose was to identify the cultural management competences and skills required by the agents linked to cultural goods and services production in the different branches of the Honduran creative economy. Its outcomes supported the research hypothesis that an increase in, or generation of, new capacities and competencies in cultural management and administration of the agents operating in the territory has a direct impact on the promotion of the creative economy.

As a result of recent institutional reforms, the public university of Honduras is developing a second Diploma in Cultural Management, complemented by an annual international seminar, which since 2012 has addressed specific issues. This forum for training and reflection was initially directed at university personnel (teachers and administrators) as a means of professionalising human capital. This would, in turn, facilitate the mandate enshrined in the internal university regulations through which cultural management is considered a strategic and transversal element of the substantive functions of teaching, research, and university-society linkage. At present, this course is available to local cultural agents based on local demand that is expressed through regional university centres, cultural centres, or at the express request of municipal authorities or governmental bodies. This non-formal training supports the enhancement of capacities and competencies by enriching cultural life against specific development criteria through the promotion of culture and heritage.

Cultural management training in Honduras

The different cultural agents in Honduras (civil organisations, artistic unions, organised bodies) have been requesting positive action from the Honduran State with regard to the promotion of art and culture for several decades. Public cultural institutions suffer from a series of internal limitations. For example, they operate according to their own dynamics and objectives, in many cases under precarious conditions that are uncoordinated with those of cultural agents in the various territories. Since its creation in 1975, the Secretariat of Culture, Arts and Sports has been the official body responsible for formulating policies, programmes, and strategies to guide State action in the field of cultural policies. Since 2014, this body has been reduced to a small department, the Executive Directorate for Culture and the Arts, attached to the Ministry of the Presidency of the Republic. At the local level, this Directorate of Culture has a National Network of so-called Cultural Houses, that are common in Central America, and a Network of Municipal Public Libraries, which constitute the main support for a cultural policy of spreading cultural goods and services in coordination with municipal governments and local organisations.

This process of consultation with the municipality is the first measure in terms of cultural policy that the Honduran State has adopted in order to stimulate and guide cultural development in a planned manner and with a long-term vision. Making culture a matter of public and political interest is the second policy measure necessary to guarantee the conditions and mechanisms required for participatory processes in cultural development. Among the basic conditions for the implementation of sustainable cultural policies, UNESCO's assistance mission (2002) and a study published by the same agency, "Cultural Policies in Honduras: Analysis and Perspectives for Their Development" (Mejía, 2004), made proposals and recommendations on strategic areas and innovative methodologies to foster cultural policies that promote heritage assets as resources for integral development. These cultural policy recommendations, strategies, and areas for action are structured in three domains:

A. Employment, social development, and economic growth-oriented policies.
B. Policies concerning cultural transversality and poverty eradication.
C. Heritage safeguarding and cultural diversity-oriented policies.

These recommended cultural policies require, as a precondition, the establishing by the Honduran State of a new institutional environment that enables an appropriate ecosystem for cultural development to evolve, while additionally addressing the challenges of equity in access to cultural goods and services, creativity development and the fight against poverty.

Cultural management training in Honduras is challenged by adverse conditions and a lack of appreciation by local, mostly volunteer, managers, artists, or teachers who assume leadership positions in municipal committees, independent groups, or municipal arts centre management. Training in this field, although incipient, is developing. Although non-formal education experiences are reported, it is not until the United Nations' Programme *Creativity and Identity for Local Development* of 2009, delivered in coordination with the National Autonomous University of Honduras (UNAH), that these training processes were institutionalised. The participation of the national public university filled a gap relating to the certification of training processes and the strengthening of empirical knowledge acquired in each region of the country by social agents who for decades have developed projects focused on promoting local cultural life.

Within the framework of its partnership with a UN programme, UNESCO, UNAH was responsible for the implementation of the First University Diploma in Cultural Management. Running from May 2010 to September 2011, its 40 participants were drawn from 18 cities across the country, 26 of whom had been selected by the Joint Programme and 14 through an open contest held by the university. The main objective of the diploma's curriculum was to strengthen cultural management in Honduras through the training of individuals engaged in the sector involving joint construction of knowledge, be it conceptual, procedural, and/or attitudinal. Such knowledge would allow them to approach cultural projects in a creative and systematic manner, thereby contributing to the strengthening of national identity and the country's socio-cultural development (UNAH, 2012). The exit strategy of this United Nations programme required the national public university to undertake sustainability initiatives relating to a number of the results and products of the following components: socio-cultural inclusion; cultural information systems (SIC); creative cultural enterprises; cultural policy; education programmes in culture and development; and research on cultural and artistic assets.

Beginning in 2013, the university organised higher education courses in cultural management with various foci: voluntary cultural action promotion, local cultural policies, culture and development, and cultural tourism. Such is the case of the Higher Diploma in Cultural Management for Local Development (2014) that targets municipal body officials, technicians, cultural promoters, and young entrepreneurs from the municipalities of Santa Cruz de Yojoa, Potrerillos, San Antonio de Cortés, San Francisco de Yojoa, and Las Vegas Santa Bárbara. These training programmes have been extended to other locations with the national territory where the public university has a presence and are accompanied by an international seminar that addresses a specific relevant theme each year. In regard to the theoretical and conceptual framework of these diplomas, it should be explained that cultural action in Honduras is, in principle, constituted more by empirical elements than by an academic disciplinary base such as cultural management. The training is strongly influenced by the constant exchange between theory and practice. The theoretical framework comes primarily from the social sciences, humanities, and arts and less so from management. Culture and development is one of the most central topics of courses in these academic areas. The review of development theories and their application to the cultural field constitutes an important methodological exercise to render cultural management a multidisciplinary field capable of contributing to the solving of socio-cultural problems within a specific territory. This focus on socio-cultural aspects allows the construction of a structural reference framework that gives the training meaning and relevance. It also helps to establish a set of essential operational distinctions between traditional disciplines and multidisciplinary fields (such as urbanism, peace studies, and cultural management, among others).

When it comes to the literature referenced in the training programmes, the UNDP human development reports, UNESCO publications, the OEI, and the Andrés Bello Convention on the economics of culture are important theoretical references to which the contributions of Spanish experts such as Martinell, Bonet, and Rausell can be added. Among the Latin American authors referred to in the discipline, Coelho and Ortíz from Brazil, Olmos, Santillán, and García Canclini from Argentina, as well as Nivón Bolán, Mariscal Orozco, and Jiménez from Mexico, represent the most frequent. In addition, there are also works on cultural policies and cultural management by researchers such as Yúdice and Durán who conduct regional analyses.

Towards a regional training network in cultural management and sustainable development in Central America

Between 2008 and 2012, the Spanish Fund for the Achievement of the Millennium Goals (MDG-F) implemented, through the UN, three programmes on knowledge management in culture and development in Central America, namely:

- Intercultural Policies for Inclusion and Opportunities Generation (Costa Rica).
- Creativity and Cultural Identity for Local Development (Honduras).
- Cultural Revitalisation and Creative Productive Development on The Caribbean Coast (Nicaragua).

The actions resulting from the implementation of these programmes represented a historic opportunity to enhance the value of culture as a contribution to economic and social development. The tools and knowledge developed during the execution of the programmes are collated in an online platform hosted by the Central American Educational and Cultural Coordination (CECC) website which forms part of the Central American Integration System (SICA).[3] The platform is structured from six thematic areas: Management, Policies, Creativity, Cultural Spaces, Tourism, and Revitalisation.

Notes on Culture and Development in Central America, important information about concepts linked to cultural management and advice for undertaking development-focused cultural activities can be found on the platform. It contains a wide range of materials (guides, official texts, examples of good practice, etc.) that enable cultural managers to learn about, deepen their knowledge of, and put into practice various concepts that are highly supportive of cultural development in any Ibero-American country. The platform constitutes an exercise in systematising the knowledge generated by the MDG-F in Central America. It provides access to applications facilitating the implementation and development of policies, programmes, and projects that adopt a cultural approach to development. The platform also provides a collection of three specialised guides: the *Guidebook of Community Cultural Research*; the *Guidebook of Cultural Heritage Revitalisation*, and the *Guidebook of Community Cultural Management*. These downloadable resources serve as a reference source and guide for the implementation of any cultural project with the aim of positioning the link between culture and development as a key condition for safeguarding, enhancing, and converting local cultural resources into assets for sustainable and equitable development. The platform provides users with tools and recommended practices as a means of contributing to the greater impact of future policies and programmes promoting local cultural development and the exercise of cultural rights. The guides *Learning from Practical Experiences* and *Culture and Development* were implemented by the Ibero-American Laboratory for Research and Innovation in Culture and Development (L+iD) of the UNESCO Chair of Cultural Policies and Cooperation of the University of Girona (Spain) and the Technological University of Bolivar (Colombia), commissioned by the Millennium Development Goals Achievement Fund (MDG-F).

Based on the results of the Joint Programmes of the Culture and Development Window (18 projects across four continents), the L+iD research contributed to the systematisation, storage, and transfer of knowledge and experience due to digital application formats that facilitated their access and use. Following the processes forming part of the MDG-F programmes, an initiative was launched in 2012 by the National Autonomous University of Honduras (UNAH) and the UNESCO Chair for Cultural Policies and Cooperation at the University of Girona (UdG), Spain, to set up the Regional Cooperation Network for Cultural Management Training, originally composed of Universidad de las Regiones Autónomas de la Costa Caribe Nicaragüense, URACCAN, Universidad Tecnológica de Panamá, UTP, Universidad Nacional de Agricultura de Honduras, UNA, Universidad Tecnológica de Bolívar, UTB Colombia, and the UNESCO Office for Central America in Costa Rica.

The network possessing an Ibero-American character and the goal of progressively integrating other countries and regions was proposed. Its background can be traced back to the cultural management training programmes implemented by the Central American joint programmes and the willingness to share both learning and tools. Since its first initiatives in 2012, the network has not undertaken any further activities. The initiative is being re-launched and partners gradually selected for an expansion of its scope of action, the exchange of experiences, and/or new academic offerings with specific foci. One strategy involves integrating university cultural management networks in both North and South America such as the Red Universitaria de Gestión Cultural de México[4] and the Red Latinoamericana de Gestión Cultural.[5]

In May 2017, the UNAH in collaboration with the UNESCO Chair of Cultural Policies and Cooperation of the University of Girona (Spain) agreed on a new roadmap intended to:

- Expand the network to Central American and Mexican institutions in order to strengthen cooperation through regional training activities.
- Seek alliances with the Spanish Agency for International Cooperation for Development (AECID)'s ACERCA program (Training for Development in the Cultural Sector programme) to render efforts profitable and promote new cooperation agreements.
- Propose greater regional collaboration with the Network of Spanish Cultural Centres leading to wider circulation of content and activities.
- Design strategic and action plans for the incorporation of cultural capacities into the Objectives of Sustainable Development (ODS) framework.

In order to gain an understanding of the relatively strong influence that Spanish universities enjoy in the region, it should be noted that numerous training initiatives form part of an Ibero-American ecosystem. Due to the instances of cultural cooperation promoted by the Spanish Agency for International Cooperation for Development, its network of aforementioned Cultural Centres and the agreement of the countries involved to build an Ibero-American Cultural Space (ECI), an environment facilitating the exchange of cultural goods and services and other forms of mutual support has been created.

The VI International Seminar on Cultural Management: generating academic capacity in cultural training for the Objectives of Sustainable Development (UNAH, 2018) was intended as a forum for academic and cultural cooperation bodies to raise and discuss the major training requirements of cultural management with development objectives within the framework of the new ODS in the Central American and Caribbean region. The meeting provided an opportunity to reflect on the contributions of cultural management to the objectives established in the Agenda 2030, analyse experiences from the region linked to these objectives, and to establish conceptual, methodological, operational, and regulatory elements that should be considered in the professional profiles for training in this area. The international seminar was attended by representatives of the following universities: University of Costa Rica/Campus Pacifico (Bachelor of Arts in Cultural Management); University of Guadalajara (Mexico); Technological University of Panama (UTP); University of the Arts GANEXA (Panama); Technological University of Bolivar UTB (Colombia); and the UNESCO Chair in Cultural Policies and Cooperation from the University of Girona (Spain).

The combined efforts of the Central American and Ibero-American communities with regard to training and building competencies and skills in cultural management for development will contribute to making more evident the necessary adoption of a cultural approach in the definition of policies, programmes, and projects. These indicate the cross-cutting nature of culture in other areas related to the ODS Sustainable Development Goals, while simultaneously enhancing the effectiveness of international cooperation for development. The network's vision is one of rendering Central America and the Caribbean a wide-ranging training space with a regional development approach. Meanwhile, participating organisations have consolidated their formative cultural management services in accordance with the challenges and opportunities their societies face from a dynamic situation in which their creativity, identity, dreams, and aspirations can be expressed.

In response to the crisis caused by Covid-19, UNESCO and the Central American Educational and Cultural Coordination have announced the creation of a digital culture platform for the countries of the isthmus that will allow them to share cultural content. The call to governments involves their assuming commitments in support of programmes and projects implemented by organisations, foundations, artists, and creative individuals for the sustainability of the initiative (UNESCO/CECC-SICA 2020).

Conclusions

In the Central and South American region, remarkable progress has been made in the adoption of cultural policies, laws, and plans[6] with a focus on cultural rights and sustainable human development, while public institutions at the highest level of government have been strengthened. At the same time, the cultural and creative sectors are developing important activities with measurable and increasing economic impact. This scenario calls for innovative skills and capacities linked to management, production of goods and services, innovative technologies, and the management of projects that promote the economic inclusion of individuals, groups, and emerging territories.

The vitality of cultural life in Central American countries is made possible by the efforts of content producers, companies, collectives, organised communities, artists, and foundations that deploy their own organisational structures, fundraising, and training in specific technical aspects and management skills. A key strategy for the arts and culture development is the promotion of convergence areas among the public, private, and academic sectors in order to foster positive ecosystems for social and economic development based on culture, creativity, and new technologies that cut across all sectors. This requires the revision and updating of supranational cultural policies that have an impact on integration processes and economic growth in the region. National cultural policies have the potential to provide incentives for the sustainability of cultural and creative enterprises through subsidies and training strategies that could empower them with strategic cultural management tools to ensure their viability. Regional cooperation has become supportive of local and national dynamics, enabling advancement in the consolidation of social and human capital in order to integrate cultural contributions to development and the fight against poverty.

Although cultural management training must address the context, it also has to broaden its horizons towards cultural diversity as a universal heritage and engage in dialogue with diverse cultural situations. For this reason, networking, exchange, and cooperation must strengthen academic training and positively influence the learning processes of the alumni. However, it must also have an impact on the implementers of public cultural policies. A fundamental axis in this coordination could be generated between Central American and Caribbean entities for experience, exchange, and the sharing of effective practices that could lead to joint training proposals in accordance with the regional context. This might, ultimately, turn cultural management into a disciplinary academic field with its own theoretical framework, practices, and narratives.

Notes

1 A similar observation is made by Carpio Valdeavellano in relation to Peru (this volume).
2 Spanish Cultural Centres are community spaces linked to Spanish cooperation. They currently operate in 15 Latin American countries, the United States (Miami), and Equatorial Guinea.
3 The platform is available at http://ceducar.info/cultura-y-desarrollo/page_1.html.
4 More information at https://rugcmx.org.
5 More information at https://redlgc.org.
6 Such as the National Plan for Long-term Cultural Development in Guatemala, in force since 2005, the National Policy on Cultural Rights in Costa Rica (2014–2023), and the Cuscatlán Plan by the Ministry of Culture of El Salvador (2019) are instruments that incorporate human development objectives and social inclusion with updated conceptual frameworks.

References

AGEXPORT (2015). *ICREA de AGEXPORT nuevo sector de exportación.* May 24. https ://www.perspectiva.com.gt/uncategorized/icrea-de-agexport-nuevo-sector-de-export acion/ (Accessed April 22, 2020).

Bá tiul, M. A. & Rodriguez Arana, G. (1999). *El Pueblo maya y el desarrollo sostenible.* Guatemala: FLACSO, p. 136.

Carpio Valdeavellano, P. (this volume). Cultural management in Peru: the role of the ministry of culture in challenging times. In: Henze, R. & Escribal, F. (Eds.), *Cultural Management and Policy in Latin America.* Abingdon & New York: Routledge, pp. 230–246.

de la Vega Velástegui, P. (this volume). Cultural management in Ecuador: genealogy and power relations within the constitution of a field. In: Henze, R. & Escribal, F. (Eds.), *Cultural Management and Policy in Latin America.* Abingdon & New York: Routledge, pp. 143–162.

Durán Salvatierra, S. (2000). Redes culturales e integración regional en Centroamérica: una visión del sector autónomo. In: Oyamburu, J., Visiones del Sector Cultural en Centroamérica, San José: AECI, pp. 29–62. http://bibliotecadigital.aecid.es/bibliodig/i 18n/catalogo_imagenes/gr)upo.cmd?path=1006184 (Accessed October 28, 2020).

Escribal, F. (this volume). Cultural management in Argentina: political agenda and challenges for practitioners and researchers. In: Henze, R. & Escribal, F. (Eds.), *Cultural Management and Policy in Latin America.* Abingdon & New York: Routledge, pp. 87–105.

Gallegos, C., Mejía, M. & Arteaga, H. (2011). Primera Cuantificación económica de las actividades del sector cultural en Honduras y estudio económico prospectivo sobre impactos y potencialidades del proyecto de ley general de fomento a la cultura. Tegucigalpa: PNUD. Unpublished.

INDESA (2017). *Industrias creativas culturales en Panamá: diagnóstico del sector y relevancia económica.* BID. https://publications.iadb.org/es/publications/spanish/d ocument/Industrias-creativas-culturales-en-Panamá-Diagnóstico-del-sector-y-relev ancia-económica.pdf (Accessed May 25, 2020).

Martinell Sempere, A. (2002). La gestión cultural: Singularidad profesional y perspectivas de futuro in. In: Lacarrieu, M. & Álvarez, M. (Eds.), *La (indi)gestión cultural. Una cartografía de los procesos culturales contemporáneos.* Argentina: La crujía ediciones, pp. 219–247.

Mejía, M. H. (2004). Las políticas culturales en Honduras: análisis y perspectivas para su desarrollo. San José: UNESCO. https://unesdoc.unesco.org/ark:/48223/pf0000143126 ?posInSet=2&queryId=e97e9450-7e13-47ea-9d25-9329675d215b.

Mejía, M. H. (2018). *Formación en gestión cultural y economía creativa en Honduras.* Tegucigalpa: UNAH.

MCD (2000). *Manual del Promotor Cultural.* Guatemala: Ministry of Culture and Sports of Guatemala.

MCD (2005). *La Cultura Motor del Desarrollo: Plan Nacional de Desarrollo Cultural a largo plazo.* San Salvador: Ministry of Culture and Sports of Guatemala.

Ministry of Culture of El Salvador (2019). *Plan Cuscatlán. Cultura.* https://www.plancusc atlan.com/documentos/plancuscatlan_cultura.pdf.

Piedras, E. (2006). *Guatemala: Un análisis de la contribución económica de la cultura. Informe Final.* Guatemala: Ministry of Culture and Sport.

Protti, G. (2009). *Necesidades de formación en gestión cultural en costa Rica.* San José: Spanish Cultural Centre.

UN (1966). *International Covenant on Economic, Social and Cultural Rights.* http://www
.ohchr.org/SP/ProfessionalInterest/Pages/CESCR.aspx.

UNAH (2012). Memoria Primer Diplomado Universitario en Gestión Cultural. Tegucigalpa:
UNESCO – UNAH.

UNAH/UdG (2012). Red regional de cooperación en gestión cultural para el desarrollo.
Working paper. Tegucigalpa: National Autonomous University of Honduras &
University of Girona.

UNESCO/CECC-SICA (2020). *La UNESCO se une al SICA y a la CECC en el lanzamiento
de una plataforma digital de cultura para Centroamérica.* May 20. San José: UNESCO.
https://acortar.link/3EqPe (Accessed October 28, 2020).

Tenorio, M. (2009). Desarrollo humano y dinámicas económicas locales: Contribución de
la economía de la cultura. *Cuadernos sobre Desarrollo Humano Collection*, N° 9. El
Salvador: UNPD.

Zamorano, M. (this volume). Cultural management in Paraguay since the democratic
transition: Strategies of cultural disruption in a conservative frame. In: Henze, R. &
Escribal, F. (Eds.), *Cultural Management and Policy in Latin America.* Abingdon &
New York: Routledge, pp. 106–124.

5 Managing culture in Latin America

An approach to the dimensions of a professional practice

Carlos Yáñez-Canal

Introduction

The processes of globalisation have highlighted the importance of the cultural professions and, more specifically, that of cultural management. Within this framework, the idea of resource (Yúdice, 2002) forms the basis of the instrumentalisation of culture, while also constituting a new language which, in terms of effectiveness, efficiency and profitability, represents the raw material from which meaning is produced and value is assigned to experiences, both individual and collective. Thus, culture is linked to the market and consumption, thereby indicating a close relationship between economy and culture (Jameson, 2001). As such, culture appears to be the foundation of development (Araujo & Leitao, this volume). Its relationship with the consumer is a close one which, in terms of cultural democratisation, broadens access to cultural goods and services. This, in turn, acts as an incentive to produce an enhanced offer resulting from the commercialisation of cultural and creative industry products. From a developmentalist perspective of culture, individual enjoyment of the arts and heritage is highlighted and framed as a right to culture.

Within this scenario, culture is established as a strategic facet of the contemporary economy in terms of investment, gross domestic product (GDP), employment, revenue, and exports, in addition to the administrative processes implemented which are geared to the requirements and demands of the market (global, local, regional, national).

> The sites that have been assigned value, the protected areas and the preserved intangible expressions have promoted museumification, spectacularization, the conversion of cities to theme parks, and the eradication of pre-existing groups and lifestyles. These have been replaced by uncomplicated artistic manifestations, providing tourists and real estate investors with local color. In this sense, the question of means and ends has centered on the former, in many cases obscuring or ignoring the ends, or compromising the values on which they are supposedly based. Cultural development is too often an aesthetic justification for "economic growth" divorced from the social sphere and supposedly superseded by new notions of development. The repeated

formula of "man as the means and end of development" appears to be an obfuscation of how little man is ultimately worth, at times when "culture counts" and its importance is only measured monetarily within national wealth and in the balance of payments.

(Bayardo, 2008, p. 4)

Another salient dimension of the contemporary economy is the symbolic value added to products in the form of sense formation and motivation. This added value possesses the capacity to transfer sense and meaning, thereby enabling the formulation of individual and collective statements. Within this logic, the symbolic capital of a particular product will be enhanced to the extent that the symbolic potential of the good or service is transferred to the individual. Culture appears to be not only a stimulus to consumption but also a resource which increases the value of all experiences, including consumption. Investment in culture becomes a reference point for the social responsibility of institutions and companies that contribute to the development of civil coexistence, economic development, new behaviours, and individual and collective projects.

This context of economies of signs and spaces (Lash & Urry, 1998), renders the consumption of symbolic goods an element of social distinction (Bourdieu, 1988). In other words, the products with their symbolic meanings are regarded as references for action in which borders or limits of social and cultural opposition are established. This is evidenced in the socialised character of goods, considering them a form of social power, which are discernible from "products", "objects", "goods", "artifacts" and "other kinds of things" (Appadurai, 1991, p. 17).

Focusing on the things that are exchanged, and not simply on the forms or functions of exchange, it is possible to argue that what creates the connection between exchange and value is politics, understood in a broad sense. This assertion... justifies the idea that goods, like people, have a social life.

(Appadurai, 1991, p. 17)

This last dimension includes a "culturalization of economy" movement (Jameson, 2001) in which the world of signs is framed within an aesthetisation of life. Experiences generate an aesthetic reflexivity that encompasses the economy and contributes to an understanding of both itself and implicit social practices. It is expressed in an increasing number of areas of social reality and materialises in the cultural practices that give meaning to the routine of daily life. In this process of the aestheticising of the economic cycle, culture contributes to the re-appeal of products, playing an important role in value creation. Thus, the added value of a good is not restricted to its mercantile character but provides individuals with a plus-value of meaning to configure its existence.

In other words, one does not desire the good because one likes it, but rather the good is liked as soon as it appears as absolutely desirable, and the reason for the desire consists in the promised advantage which it is possible to appropriate in the act of acquisition. It is the completion of the value chain of cultural goods and services by linking producers with consumers.

(Yáñez Canal, 2013, p. 93)

In this scenario, cultural management acquires a new meaning and the market for the profession expands hypothetically, being regarded as providing numerous opportunities which is not actually the case. When identifying the precise moment at which cultural management began to be referred to as such in Latin America, it is evident that it represents a phenomenon in which the limitations of cultural management are exposed. That is to say, an extraction process exists which relates to what is presented and whose use of administrative-economic language clearly denotes the existence of devices and technologies for governing oneself and others. Within globalisation processes, these are enshrined in neo-liberal policies that promote the instrumentalisation of culture and constitute a new discourse. In terms of effectiveness, efficiency, and profitability, this discourse constitutes a raw material through which meaning is produced and value is attributed to experiences, both individual and collective.

Alternative rationales for, and practices of, cultural management oriented towards transformational processes relating to political culture are generated. These processes result in the creation and development of meaning and significance at the community level. Within this process, both symbolic and human forms of social capital are not reduced merely to the categories established through consumption. Rather, as creators of viable forms of social fabric construction, such capital contributes to strengthening relationships of trust and solidarity between diverse groups. Precedents to such communitarian processes exist in the history of Latin America (Ochoa Gautier, 2003; Yáñez Canal, 2013).

General framework

The legal frameworks determining the economic role of culture were established by the multi-cultural constitutions of the 1980s and 1990s adopted in Latin America, such as that of 1986 in Guatemala (reformed in 1993), 1987 in Nicaragua (reformed in 1995), 1988 in Brasil, 1991 in Colombia, 1992 in Mexico (reformed in 2001), 1992 in Paraguay, 1993 in Perú, 1994 in Argentina, 1995 in Bolivia, 1996/1998 in Ecuador, and 1999 in Venezuela. The multi-cultural and multi-ethnic character of legal frameworks has, paradoxically, resulted from a series of "*i*nclusive" constitutions introduced as the Welfare State. The latter has been dismantled by a succession of neo-liberal policies:

with the end of Keynesianism, the intervention of the State was drastically reduced. With the structuring of national demand abandoned, the new model focused State action on the creation of conditions that do not hinder the free development of market forces but facilitate the participation of national economies in the global productive system. The emphasis on domestic market management and full employment shifted to supply-side restructuring. Social policies were not alien to this process. In the minimum State, social policy was subordinated to the demands of labor market flexibility and structural competitiveness. Since then, two main features have characterized the contemporary minimum State: the promotion of structural competitiveness in the field of economic policy, and flexibility and competitiveness in the field of social policy.

(Laguado Duca, 2004, p. 13)

Within this framework, a commitment to the relationship between citizenship and consumption has been established, especially in relation to representation. Cultural rights are claimed to be fundamental to a new dimension of citizenship, largely because of the composition of specific consumer audiences in which the State and the market act (UNESCO, 1982). It derives, undoubtedly, from a political strategy oriented towards the middle-class consumer to whom the promises of consumer culture privileges are made. Within this process, the Latin American countries encourage equality by establishing a formal criterion within which diversity is diminished (multi-cultural constitutions establish diversity as a form of national heritage), interpreting it differently and turning it into the country's patrimony. This process centres on the market for, and the management of, diversity within which business heterogeneity and corporate ideology are masked. Multiculturalism constitutes the power of institutions and their intermediaries to construct and interpret the representation of minorities (Yúdice, 2002).

A field of cultural policies is outlined that refers to "the dynamics of reception and distribution of culture, the latter being understood as a product to be administered through the various agencies of coordination of resources, media and people that articulate the cultural market" (Richard, 2001, p. 185). This process of governmentality (Foucault, 2006) is consolidated in Latin American countries with the creation of laws on culture and Ministries or Secretariats of Culture, in which the fusion of art and heritage in culture is clearly expressed. Similarly, the bureaucratic dynamics of cultural management in these states are consolidated through various institutions such as museums, galleries, and programmes relating to the arts, tourism, and entrepreneurship. With regard to cultural management, emphasis is placed on institutional planning and administrative cultural bodies and processes, aimed at decentralisation and participation, to the extent that a close relationship is established between development and culture based on the creation of economic and social conditions that allow communities to access cultural goods and services.

With respect to the arts, their de-aesthetisation is becoming increasingly apparent (Ochoa-Gautier, 2003),

> ... in the integration of aesthetics and narrative, ethics and creativity, in the hybridization of technology and fashion, of the commercial and the aesthetic, of marketing and meaning, of management and communication, art undergoes a profound re-definition that is not limited to the exclusivity of aesthetics. There are multiple processes that abandon the autonomy of art,

established by modernity, since it is integrated into an art market where prices are similar to the world of bonds and stock markets. Likewise, this process is the culmination of the social insertion of the artist as a creative force in fashion, technology, tourism, heritage, media, etc., establishing an interdependence with these processes. In this sense, the loss of an "aura" of symbolic distinction resulting in a restricted aesthetic objective vision can be observed in tandem with indications of the interdependence of museums, auctions, and artists with major economic, political and media actors. The art world is structured by the laws of the market. Museums and galleries are based on an administrative logic with a clear profit motive.

(Yáñez-Canal, 2013, p. 65)

In relation to heritage, the Ministries and Secretariats of Culture of Latin American States have established their respective Heritage Directorates under the aegis of UNESCO through its 2003 convention. According to Chaves (2011), a famous case occurred in Colombia where, through its Ministry of Culture, the State established both the Heritage Leadership (2003) and the Heritage Group (2005). These developments were followed by the passing of the Cultural Heritage Law (2008) and the introduction of the Cultural Interest Goods category, the Representative List of Intangible Cultural Heritage, and the Special Safekeeping Plan. Simultaneously, progress was made on the formulation of a cultural and creative industries policy, while forms of entrepreneurship and management were defined by the Heritage Law. In these terms, different cultural expressions (festivals and carnivals, etc.), while seen as productive chains, are associated with entrepreneurship and management as a means of integrating them into current economic policies. Private sector involvement in the promotion of cultural heritage has also been encouraged through multiple fiscal and tax incentives. "In this way, the possibilities of expanding cultural markets are clarified, in a dynamic moving from the culture of neo-liberalization to the neo-liberalization of culture" (Chaves, 2011, p. 22). Thus, the politics of society, in the form of public policy, is oriented to the defence of the private and the public in the limited sphere of consumption-related entertainment, without establishing clarity about the common good. This indicates a reduction in the role of the State, since it is fundamentally oriented to establishing conditions facilitating the development of the market and the participation of national economies in the global system which have been hampered by barriers, already evident at the beginning of the 21st century in the unequal relationships at a global level (CEPAL, 2005).

Within this framework, an economy of the immaterial is taking shape within which most of the added value is redirected to resources that are appreciated to the extent that they activate mental processes. Hence, three types of resources are clearly defined within this economy of the immaterial, specifically: human capital, social capital, and symbolic capital. These resources are oriented to a knowledge that reduces the terms of competition, to the capacity to activate pro-social behaviours and the capacity to associate processes of meaning and identity value with experience.

Methodology

In light of the above analysis, the main objective of the research on the professional practice of cultural management was to identify the symbolic and practical meaning of the actions of cultural managers in their workspaces through interviews with individuals whose primary occupation was in this field. To this end, the sample was selected from a group of public, private, and tertiary sector cultural institutions active in a wide range of cultural production roles, including public managers, private managers, institutional managers, project managers, business managers, cultural managers, cultural policy managers, cultural product managers, and cultural space managers. Previous research analysed what certain posts with decision-making responsibilities in public, private, and non-governmental organisation (NGO) management might represent. This clearly established that experiences alone are insufficient to develop an understanding of the new professions. Nevertheless, they constitute an adequate sample of what can be found on a larger scale.

In order to respond to the established objectives, the use of a structured questionnaire was rejected in favour of a semi-structured, interview-based approach within which cultural managers were able to freely describe their own vision of what characterises their profession, references for action, and professional capacities. It was considered important to start from the perception of the protagonists, rather than evaluating the management processes according to pre-defined parameters. Through this approach, the interviews contained various shades of meaning as they dealt with topics that included technical, organisational, and emotional factors which made it possible to address a wide array of arguments that expressed, in most cases, a search for recognition. Ultimately, it proved possible to see that a complex web of resources converges in the actions of cultural managers in which human competence, ways of relating, and individual character traits are put to the test.

Against this background, 30 interviews were conducted in public and private institutions and non-governmental organisations across various Latin American countries (Colombia, Mexico, Argentina, Chile), involving individuals of various ages and genders. This approach sought to ensure that the sample was reasonably representative of the professional work of cultural management. The interviews were conducted in different contexts over a period of approximately one year with incumbents of senior and middle management positions within the organisations they represented. Although their experiences and perceptions differed, common points were established both as a result of the description of the complex professional practice of each cultural manager, producing generalisations in various cases, and the self-reflection of each interviewee.

The quest for meaning within professional practice

The first concern emerging from the research process is related to the thought processes of cultural managers and how they define themselves through the management of processes and results, in the spaces where the praxis of production, reception, and perception of their activities takes place. Most of the interviewees sought to establish limits with respect to other cultural professions based on their experiences gained in the field. Although multiple approaches and trends can be observed in the actions of cultural managers, there was general agreement that the fundamental role of the post relates to the design and application of local projects and covers all related administrative processes, namely planning, monitoring, and evaluation. The cultural manager, through his/her immediate, medium, or long-term actions, and permanent and continuous processes, is actively involved in culture, economics, administration, and communication, through diverse agents within the pyramidal structures of the formal and informal (economy), as well as diverse resources.

The mediator represents the salient figure in a complex system of actors, institutions, practices, and policies, established on the basis of an ends-based rationality. In other words, it is a search process producing a definition of the actions necessary to achieve certain objectives. Its orientation is purely technical since, in the face of problematic and unexpected situations, it employs procedures activated through reference to a codified system of resolution strategies. It constitutes knowledge of general rules rooted in the assumption that problematic situations are characterised by deep-seated similarities facilitating the application of widely accepted practice. The high predictive power of such knowledge is capable of pre-defining the lines of action to be adopted.

In the case of this type of cultural manager, the complex web of relationships is fundamentally based on three pillars: creation, administration, and dissemination.

> The affirmation of cultural management as a professional practice comes from being efficient and effective in the capacity to unite the diverse in terms of discipline, people and institutions, in particular realities, and from expertise in the planning, accompaniment and evaluation of projects.
>
> (L. Rodríguez, Ministry of Culture, Chile.
> Personal communication, March 20, 2019)

This viewpoint is supported by another interviewee: "The cultural manager must possess a body of knowledge of a physical and dynamic nature, in order to be able to formulate the actions necessary to achieve certain objectives, for which administrative knowledge is fundamental" (L. Ríos, Ministry of Culture of Colombia, personal communication, August 10, 2018).

These positions remind us of the know-how relating to the administration of culture. The cultural manager must:

> (1) create the conditions for cultural production to happen; (2) bring the cultural producer closer to his or her audience; (3) stimulate the community to develop its own creative potential, which is achieved through audience training, discovery and preparation of professional artists. In other words,

the activities of the cultural administrator are: a) the production of works or shows; b) what has traditionally been called animation, and c) training.

(Coelho, 2009, p. 38)

As can be seen, in order to achieve the established goals, most of the interviewees attached to public and private institutions have emphasised administration which generates little recognition of the potentialities and specificities of culture. In addition to being seen in relation to art and heritage, culture is conceived instrumentally in terms of resources which highlights a certain element of culturalist reductionism (Restrepo, 2014). Thus, culture would be reduced to a commodity form that operates within complex circuits of production, distribution, and consumption (Yúdice, 2002). One of the derivations of this approach relates to displays of artistic and heritage expressions. The work of the cultural manager is fundamentally oriented towards the promotion and dissemination of the objects produced as a result of the "aura" of the artist and his creations. In this case, the aim of cultural action is the design of activities whose tools permeate administration, logistics, and operation since they are focused on cultural services. Within this view of the cultural product, the objective nature of artistic and heritage work is made evident, while its aim does not go beyond the enjoyment of, and satisfaction with, the cultural good or service: "the work of the cultural manager must be oriented towards valuing the work of the artist, who must be accompanied and supported in his production, and tends through marketing to disseminate his work according to the cultural offer" (C. Gónzalez, "The Hideout" Cultural Centre, personal communication, November 20, 2018). Thus, cultural management is the "administration of the resources of a cultural organization with the aim of offering a product or service that reaches the largest audiences or greatest number of consumers, providing them with maximum satisfaction" (Bernárdez-López, 2003, p. 3).

Another concept emphasises the role of intermediary and facilitator between cultural production (the artist's work) and cultural consumption (the public possessing the economic means to access cultural goods and services).

The fulfilment of mediation requires a focus on two main objectives. Firstly, the formation of audiences and the promotion of creation since the formation of audiences allows the recipients to have access to cultural goods, not only in a physical sense but also in terms of understanding and enjoyment through artistic or heritage education. In this sense, research tools are employed to make a diagnosis of cultural skills, habits and consumption, as well as for dissemination, promotion and even training, such as workshops, courses, conferences, and educational concerts. Secondly, the promotion of creation will allow it to diversify, expand, improve, and make available a greater number of cultural assets in context and even demanded by the public. To this end, tools such as competitions, workshops, scholarships, funding, etc., are employed.

(Mariscal Orozco, 2019, p. 33)

This position is, evidently, the basis for the market and the state, which represent the agents who establish the incentives and limits to the creation and recreation of the artist and his work:

> The cultural manager is a combination of knowledge and practice that seeks to integrate management with culture through projects that implement cultural policies established by organizations, communities and the State, and understood as tools for structuring markets in terms of cultural production and consumption.
>
> (A. Ramírez, Official of the Institute of Culture
> and Tourism of Manizales, Colombia. Personal
> communication, February 25, 2019)

There is an assumption that this vision of cultural management is based on incentives for public education and training with the clear objective of facilitating access, appropriation, and enjoyment of cultural goods and services. Cultural management is presented as a stimulus to cultural production within the limitations established by the State, under the auspices of the cultural and creative industries, which

> are those that reproduce on an industrial scale, use as raw material creations protected by copyright and produce cultural goods and services fixed on tangible or electronic supports. In each of the sub-sectors that make up these cultural industries, there are entities ranging from small businesses to large conglomerates.
>
> (CAB, 2003, p. 21)

In contrast, there are civil society organisations, consumers, and artists, collectives, and cultural activists who, through community work and social networks, challenge the cultural industries' model of copyright exploitation. Based on the acknowledgement of the right to culture, they tend towards new circuits of circulation, distribution, and socialisation through other technologies, or personal exchange, and propose an ethical and legal dimension that promotes popularisation and participation (Yúdice, 2002). "Culture belongs to everyone without restriction. The circulation of culture is collective, it is not exclusive to anyone" (M. J. Gómez, Cultural Collective, Argentina. Personal communication, October 17, 2018).

From this last perspective, there are conceptions oriented to the solution of problems that contribute to the needs of communities in the weaves and warps framework of the social fabric. As such, they form part of a long-term action with broader structures, starting from the foundations of a participatory democracy, based on diversity (resulting from cultural rights) and within the framework of social inclusion and the construction of citizenship. The projects represent the development of human resources leading to the alignment of the market, civil society, and the strategic policies of the State. To this end, unlike the other approaches focused on the techniques of codified knowledge, they appeal to a knowledge that is framed in a complex cognitive act in which the capacity of systemic and contextual reading of socio-cultural reality including cultural action is inscribed. It is not only necessary to possess certain knowledge to interpret and understand the challenges of the communities in which it operates, but also to have the capacity to assess critically the specificity of the context in which it acts in order to develop intervention strategies enabling it to initiate social transformation processes.

In terms of cultural management training, the discussion focuses on the humanistic and the administrative, giving predominance to the latter. Most of the interviewees were drawn predominantly from disciplines within the social sciences (sociology, anthropology, social work, psychology, and political science), but also economics, administration, communication, the arts, and even engineering and computer science/IT. The preparation is specialised and, in some cases, refers to the Anglo-Saxon concept of "arts management", in which marketing tools, advertising, among other forms of publicity, predominate. This situation promotes reflection on the cultural management of arts and heritage, its productivity and profitability. Cultural managers also communicate through blogs, participate in thematic social networks, and read about the history of art and artistic language and trends.

Regarding training, certain elements of culture (such as arts, theories of culture, planning, marketing, cultural research, entrepreneurship, etc.) are covered in university programmes. However, according to those interviewed, there is a question mark over heterogeneous and redundant training which fails lamentably to satisfy the requirements of the sector. With some exceptions, a contrast can be drawn between the professional profiles of individuals graduating from various educational institutions. Those who attended public institutions are largely oriented towards community cultural management, while those from private institutions tend to focus on cultural management and administration. However, this classification can be rather simplistic since there are numerous courses and diplomas that, fundamentally, develop skills in the design and setting up of projects. The logic of ongoing professional development and a strong tendency to re-engineer the operational processes of the organisations are evident from the interviews with cultural managers. During the 1980s and 1990s, the majority of cultural managers working in Latin America had been trained in Spain, the United Kingdom, France, and Canada. From the 1990s onwards, numerous seminars, courses, and specialisations were offered by universities across the globe. However, at the beginning of the 21st century, a process of consolidation of cultural management training programmes, whether at undergraduate, master's, or doctoral level, occurred. Against this background, the cultural manager role consisted not only of the design and implementation of projects and the search for resources and their distribution, but also of the contribution from, and strengthening of, local cultural dynamics and processes. These were framed within the story of nationhood formulated by the States that included decentralisation, participation, and autonomy.

Along the lines of other programmes, the aim was to consolidate a cultural sector by including different cultural agents drawn from the regions with the intention of encouraging training in tools, techniques, and concepts that would enhance their understanding in the face of cultural diversity and territorial and social contexts. Similarly, it was oriented towards the development of capacities, aptitudes, and attitudes to enable cultural managers to act as mediators of participation, cultural dialogue as a form of knowledge exchange, and the re-signification of creative and cultural memory processes. It also aimed at training audiences to value cultural diversity and intercultural relations. In many cases, the initial training processes were supported by the Organización de Estados Iberoamericanos (OEI) and the Agencia Española de Cooperación Internacional para el Desarrollo (AECID), with the result that the majority were influenced by a developmentalist vision of culture, without taking local issues into account.

The majority of interviewees subscribed to the notion that dedication to the practice of cultural management is often displayed by individuals with a deep personal vocation and powerful motivational drive. Nevertheless, many experience considerable disillusionment with regard to their work, especially in relation to the limited financial resources. Interviewees maintained that in most countries of the region, culture is not regarded as a sector worthy of investment, with the result that a passive view of culture as a resource persists.

Conclusion

The first conclusion that can be drawn from this short but comprehensive review is that the definition of the professional practice of cultural management has been arrived at in relation to the contemporary implementation of well-defined historical, social, cultural, and political processes. Associated globalising processes determine the various assumptions that culture represents a resource, but without reducing it to the status of a mere commodity since it,

> constitutes the axis of a new epistemic framework where ideology and a good part of what Foucault called the disciplinary society (for example, the inculcation of norms in institutions such as education, medicine, psychiatry, etc.) are absorbed within an economic or ecological rationality, so that within "culture" (and in its results) management, conservation, access, distribution, and investment have priority.
>
> (Yúdice, 2002, p. 13)

Following this logic, cultural policies refer to technologies and devices for governing oneself and others, which implies the cultural differentiation of populations.

This scenario determines the multiple historical perspectives of cultural management while, at the same time, highlighting the difficulty of establishing a single viewpoint from an essentialist position. Nevertheless, it can be affirmed that the cultural manager stands out as a cultural mediator whose reference to culture is taken to be an economic, political, social, and cultural resource. Three fundamental concepts have been identified within the professional practice of cultural managers, namely (1) organiser of events and performances; (2) cultural intermediary;

(3) promoter of cultural processes at the community level. In each of these cases, contrasting approaches and trends are discernible, while cross-fertilisation and cross-contamination have both been identified which could indicate differences in practices and whether they are primarily accountable to the State, civil society, or the market.

On the other hand, the multi-dimensional and multi-disciplinary role of cultural managers can be observed through their professional practice. Specialisation in culture, in the case of the majority of interviewees arose not only from their individual experience but also from a continuous education in their vocational field. In this regard, through their practice, cultural managers develop a matrix of competences tailored to the demands of their daily work. Their training emphasises the importance of administrative processes, co-existing with personal stories and experiences of deepening commitment to cultural activities, which inculcates a certain sensitivity and discernment when confronting specific challenges. A logic of self-selection seems to be imposed in which the credibility and potential of an individual's professional contribution is indicated by the richness and quality of her experiences developed in the cultural field, even though they may fall outside the strictly professional.

It could also be inferred that, within the vocational field, no adaptation of the offer to specific demands necessarily occurs. This is because an open discussion around the needs and problems of audiences or communities is evident in the conversations, which, according to some interviewees, do not clearly manifest conscious demands. This is the result, in many cases, of the continuous appeal to the personal sensibilities of cultural managers at the individual level. There is a strong tendency in this regard to interiorise the satisfaction of cultural consumers and to translate it to the logic of the project format without necessarily appealing to mental schemes. However, there is a tendency, outlined around the engineering of cultural processes in a model that elaborates techniques and tools as well as methodologies and knowledge from other disciplines, to provide solutions to cultural challenges and requirements.

Within this framework, the prevalence of an ends-based rationale contrasts with the views of some cultural managers expressed during the interviews, particularly those working at the community level or through networks as artists or activists. Their practices could be interpreted within a rationality that extols values with the intention of generating processes of social and cultural transformation. Its orientations tend to point out creativity as a reference of action of cultural managers, dissolving the idea of mediators in the questioning of the processes of production, distribution, and consumption of culture, and in its non-separation. In organisational terms, these collectives are evidently counter-cultural constituting forms of resistance since they are confronted by the symbolic production of the cultural and creative industries. There is an intertwining of the individual and collective points of view since there is no separation of the personal search and the daily affective and communicative needs of its members. On the other hand, the structure remains latent. The potential action of its members materialises depending on the activities to be implemented. Moreover, in their practices, they also

evidence an immaterial production of meaning which renders their cultural production intangible and which is indicative of an aesthetic dimension based on
affective bonds within which feeling underpins action. To this extent, a strong
sense of community predominates, with the logic of collaboration, liberation
of knowledge, and transgression of the concept of property from a political and
social character

Although its instrumental origins are evident, cultural management in Latin
America has been revealing residual practices that decentralise these approaches
and invite consideration of an alternative epistemology:

> The residual, by definition, has been effectively shaped by the past, but it's
> still active in the cultural process. It is not only an element of the past – and
> often not even that – but also an effective element of the present. Therefore,
> certain experiences, meanings, and values that cannot be expressed or sub-
> stantially verified in terms of the dominant culture, are nevertheless lived and
> practiced on the basis of a remnant – both cultural and social – of some earlier
> social and cultural formation or institution.
>
> (Williams, 2009, p. 167)

This area remains to be investigated in relation to the methods and methodologies applied by cultural managers in their work. In the recent development of
the profession, there is a need to address issues such as cultural institutions and
organisations, cultural producers, cultural activists, cultural entrepreneurs, and
the production and reproduction of knowledge in order to clearly define a conceptualisation that will allow the disciplinary construction of cultural management in
Latin America.

It should be emphasised that the professional practice of cultural managers,
whether employed by the State, civil society, or community groups, can demonstrate either continuous support for, or abandonment of, cultural policies. Even in
those organisations that declare themselves strongly independent of public power,
the possibility of an interface between the private sector, governmental entities,
and communities is not ruled out. Within this framework, the acquisition of economic and financial resources is not rejected by the idea of improving the living
conditions of less favoured or marginalised populations.

Ultimately, numerous questions remain unanswered. Firstly, there is the role of
the economic dimension, which emphasises the possibility of rendering universal
access to all cultural products effective without reducing their profitability. In this
sense, it is important to recognise that access to cultural goods and services should
be based not only on individual rights but also on collective ones, which contribute to the establishment of a participatory cultural democracy. Furthermore, it is
fundamental that social subjects participate in the planning, investigation, and
application of cultural processes, in order that social capital, both symbolic and
human, is not reduced to the categories established by consumption. Rather, as
creators of viable forms of construction of the social fabric, they contribute to the
strengthening of relationships of trust and solidarity between diverse groups and

institutions. Finally, it is necessary to question the emphasis placed on an administrative logic that is based on efficiency, efficacy, and effectiveness. Other dimensions of meaning are necessary that eschew the notion that added value consists only of the mercantile characteristics based on a certain logic of consumption as a rational response to needs. It is the capacity of symbolic capital to build and nourish our identities that assumes paramount importance.

References

Appadurai, A. (1991). *La Vida social de las cosas. Perspectiva cultural de las mercancías*. México: Editorial Grijalbo.

Araújo, B. & Leitao, C. (this volume). Thinking of the South as if there were no north: an exercise in culture-based imagination. In: Henze, R. & Escribal, F. (Eds.), *Cultural Management and Policy in Latin America*. Abingdon & New York: Routledge, pp. 34–52.

Bayardo, R. (2008). Hacia dónde van las políticas públicas culturales? *Proceedings of the First International Symposium on Cultural Public Policies in Latin America*, October 22 and 23. Córdoba: Faculty of Economic Sciences of the National University of Córdoba.

Bernárdez-López, J. (2003). La profesión de la gestión cultural: Definiciones y retos. *Boletín del PORTAL Iberoamericano de Gestión Cultural*, 4, pp. 1–10. http://www.gestioncultural.org/ficheros/BGC_AsocGC_JBernardez.pdf.

Bourdieu, P. (1988). *La distinción. Criterios y bases sociales del gusto*. Madrid: Editorial Taurus.

CAB (2003). *Impacto económico de las industrias culturales en Colombia*. Bogota: Andrés Bello Convention.

CEPAL (2005) *América Latina en el mercado global. Ganando mercados*. Caracas: Economic Commission for Latin America & the Andean Development Corporation (CAF).

Chaves, M. (Comp.) (2011). *Indígenas, afrodescendientes. La multiculturalidad estatalizada y configuraciones del Estado*. Bogotá: Colombian Institute of Anthropology and History.

Coelho, T. (2009). *Diccionario crítico de política cultural*. Barcelona: Gedisa Editorial.

Foucault, M. (2006). *Seguridad, territorio, población: Curso en el Collège de France 1977–1978*. Buenos Aires: FCE.

Jameson, F. (2001). *A cultura do dinheiro: Ensaios sobre a globalizaçao*. Petrópolis: Vozes.

Laguado Duca, A. C. (2004). La política social desde la Constitución del 91 ¿una década perdida? Bogotá: National University of Colombia, Faculty of Human Sciences.

Lash, S. & Urry, J. (1998). *Economías de signo y espacios*. Buenos Aires: Amorrortu Editores.

Mariscal Orozco, J. L. (2019). La Caja de herramientas del gestor cultural. In: Yáñez Canal, C., Mariscal Orozco, J. L. & Rucker, U. (Eds.), *Métodos y herramientas en la gestión cultural. Investigaciones y experiencias en América Latina*. Manizales: Editorial of the National University of Colombia, pp. 29–45.

Ochoa-Gautier, A. M. (2003). *Entre los deseos y los derechos. Un ensayo crítico sobre políticas culturales*. Bogota: Colombian Institute of Anthropology and History.

Restrepo, E. (2014). Interculturalidad en cuestión: Cerramientos y potencialidades. *Ámbito de Encuentros*, 7(1), pp. 9–30.

Richard, N. (2001). Globalización académica, estudios culturales y crítica latinoamericana. In: Mato, D. (Comp.), *Estudios latinoamericanos sobre cultura y transformaciones sociales en tiempos de globalización*. Buenos Aires: CLACSO, pp. 185–200.

UNESCO (1982). Informe de la Comisión I sobre cultura y desarrollo. *Statement of Mondiacult, World Conference on Cultural Policies*. México, July 26–August 6, 1982. Paris: Unesco. https://unesdoc.unesco.org/ark:/48223/pf0000052505_spa.

———— (2003). *Convención para la salvaguardia del patrimonio cultural inmaterial*. October 17. Paris: UNESCO. https://ich.unesco.org/doc/src/01852-ES.pdf.

Williams, R. (2009). *Marxismo y literatura*. Buenos Aires: Las Cuarenta.

Yáñez-Canal, C. (2013). *La identidad del gestor cultural en América Latina. Un camino en construcción*. Bogotá: National University of Colombia.

Yúdice, G. (2002). *El Recurso de la cultura. Usos de la cultura en la era global*. Barcelona: Editorial Gedisa.

Part II

Cultural management in different Latin American countries

6   Cultural management in Argentina

Political agenda and challenges for practitioners and researchers

Federico Escribal

Introduction

Despite the increasing currency of the category "cultural managers", a clear definition and discussion of the determining factors underpinning their profile and social function has yet to be produced. Cultural management has been defined as combining

> practical action with theoretical debates and ideological controversies around the concepts of culture, identity, region, territory, globalization, modernity and post-modernity, private and public sector involvement, diversity and culture, and a practice encompassing all the conflicts of the contexts within which it operates.
>
> (IBERFORMAT, 2003)

Since heterogeneity and conflict exist within this field, multiple variables are employed to define it, analogous to the vast range of perspectives regarding the definition of *culture*. In fact, the way in which cultural management is understood is determined by various core disciplines (Gray, 2010): while approaches rooted in the social sciences (anthropology, sociology, and political science) prioritise definitions that accompany, promote, or obstruct social transformation, others adopting an economic perspective tend to examine more closely the impact of the cultural dimension on development. For the purposes of this chapter, cultural management will be understood to lie "at the heart of the processes of creation, production, training and dissemination" (Orozco, 2012, p. 23) thus requiring *positions to be taken* in relation to the social and political contexts within which it operates (Olmos, 2019).

In order to explain the introduction of a domestic cultural management agenda, it will be necessary to provide certain basic information about Argentina, its cultural history, and contemporary cultural sector, in addition to the public institutions through which it has endeavoured to respond to citizens' demands in the field of culture and the arts. Against this background, the process through which cultural management has come to represent the hegemonic discipline within the cultural sector, nominally consolidating – often in a diffuse manner – other professional approaches (such as artistic production or cultural promotion) will be examined. Furthermore, the defining characteristics of cultural managers will be analysed according to their areas of operation, based on the perception that those who work in the public sector require and develop different knowledge and approaches from those employed in academia, the private sector, or the third sector (Mariscal Orozco, 2015).

Taking into account the strong link between culture and politics that runs through the region (Wortman, 2002), decolonisation constitutes the main challenge for cultural management in Argentina. The central question of national identity and its political regulation represents the distinctive feature of cultural policy in countries marked by the colonial legacy (Mulcahy, 2017). The promotion of cultural diversity having been proven as the best guarantee of the conservation of biodiversity, such activity also assumes paramount importance in a region that is particularly threatened in geopolitical terms because of its extensive reserves of natural resources (Villaseñor Anaya, 2014). Thus, the approach of this chapter assumes a de-colonisation perspective. Consequently, it ascribes the explosion of cultural management as a narrative of professionalisation within the framework of political-conceptual disputes intended to reverse inequalities in international power relations between the global North and South. Based on this understanding, the range of qualifications offered, together with their main characteristics and orientations, will be described. In addition, a reflection on the type of bibliography employed to train future professionals in this field will be undertaken. Finally, a number of challenges confronting cultural management in contemporary Argentina will be presented.

The national context

Argentina is the southernmost country in South America with a population of approximately 45 million. As a federal state consisting of 23 provinces and one autonomous city, its population is largely concentrated around the capital, Buenos Aires, which recorded 17.5 million inhabitants out of a total national population of 48.8 million in the most recent national census of 2010. In economic terms, its per capita gross domestic product (GDP) is estimated at 9,933 euros, ranking the country in 48th position on the United Nations Human Development Index. Given the country's extensive territory, featuring a multiplicity of climates, it is ideally located for food production, its primary comparative advantage. Consequently, it has historically been extremely difficult for Argentina to industrialise itself by adding value to this primary agricultural production. This situation has led to cyclical economical restrictions over the last century, causing recurrent crises aggravated by unsustainable debt management. In social terms, this situation has resulted in an increasing proportion of the population, estimated at approximately 40%, being subjected to economic exclusion, ranging from unemployment to informal employment and, therefore, dependent upon government-funded subsidies.

This phenomenon has produced a country of marked inequality and fragmentation, with geographical concentration of productive capacities and unequal decentralisation of basic public services (Steinberg, Cetrángolo, and Gatto, 2011, p. 10). As a consequence of structural inequality and inequitable distribution of national income by the end of 2019, according to UNICEF, some 7 million children were living in poverty, a figure which had increased to 8.3 million by December 2020, 62.9% of the total number of poor people as a result of the recession caused by the global COVID-19 pandemic. The Argentinian political system is based on the 1853 Constitution, reformed in 1860, 1898, 1957, and 1994, which introduced a federal republic political system. The 1949 Constitution, which incorporated substantive reforms to consolidate democracy, in addition to recognising the social function of property; the equality of men and women within family relations; and university autonomy, was revoked in 1957 by the military autocracy that had deposed Juan Peron two years earlier. The latest reform imbued cultural rights with the highest legal status by adopting international legal treaties and granting them constitutional status. It included specific rights for indigenous communities, whose ethnic and cultural pre-existence it recognised, in respect of their identity; the introduction of legally sanctioned bilingual education, communal ownership of land; and consequent participation in the management of natural resources.

How is the country constituted in cultural terms? Firstly, it is impossible to understand how shared perceptions are structured in Argentina without referring to its colonial past, and the permanence of these perceptions in terms of the *coloniality of knowledge* (Quijano, 2014). One of the main legacies of this past is the prevalence of *race* as a taxonomic category that operates both internally; building political hierarchies with social and economic implications (Margulis, 1999); and externally in the perception of the country's subordinate role in its relationship with the global powers that it must address. A political dispute over which model the country should adopt runs through Argentina's two hundred years of post-independence history, undoubtedly conditioned by the profile it was given under the colonial system. The first four decades following independence from Spain were marked by civil war between the federalist and centralist factions. The former postulated a protectionist policy aimed at industrially oriented productive development, with incentives for its equitable distribution in territorial terms. The latter was based on agriculture-focused primary production, without any interest in adding value to it or tending towards industrial development. This second opinion was mainly in the interests of the leadership of the City of Buenos Aires, whose Port Authority and Customs Service ultimately consolidated sufficient economic power to guarantee political primacy immediately after the victory of the centralist faction over its federalist counterpart at the Battle of Caseros of 1852.

The following year, with the enactment of the Constitution, the so-called *National Organisation process* commenced, which concluded with the annexation of those territories still under indigenous rule in the 1880s (Roulet and Navarro Floria, 2014). To a certain extent, this political dispute over the national model is also evident in the dynamics surrounding the inclusion/exclusion of diversity within the framework of national identity narratives. Breaks with the established liberal order occurred particularly in the framework of the majority of Peronist governments. The first occurred between 1945 and 1955; the second between 1973 and 1976, interrupted by violent military coups (the last of which left 30,000 people disappeared), and, finally, between 2003 and 2015 under Nestor Kirchner and Cristina Fernández (Grimson, 2019). These governments distinguished themselves by extending civil, social, and economic rights (including women's suffrage; nationalisation of the previously British-owned railways; free university education; and the creation of a State-owned company to exploit hydrocarbon and other natural resources). Absent from the list is the decade during which Carlos Menem governed the country (1989–1999). Initially Peronist, he shifted to become the first head of government in Argentina to implement neoliberal policies.

In 2016, the Bicentennial of Independence was celebrated. Argentina constitutes a relatively young nation, composed of diverse cultures and identities which have been historically denied in the quest to forge a commonality between national identity and culture from an assimilationist perspective (Solodkow, 2005). The political distinction between civilisation and barbarism structured the ideas of those intellectuals who supported the consolidation of a new nation-state in the first half of the 19th century (Rodriguez, 2011), Such thinkers sought to jettison the Hispanic legacy – which they considered "antiquated" – in favour of the adoption of Nordic ideals, with both the British commitment to free trade and French Enlightenment as reference points (Stavenhagen, 2002).[1] In this sense, the contributions of the so-called *Generation of 37* and *Generation of 80* are notorious. Salient among their members was Domingo Faustino Sarmiento, the "father of the Argentine School",[2] a particularly effective institution in the cultural standardisation of the diverse population of the country's vast territory (Nagy, 2013).

Argentina´s founding myth defines cultural citizenship from a white and modern perspective expressed by an urban minority, whose members resided mainly in Buenos Aires, the national capital, and who represented the incarnation of a peripheral modernity (Sarlo, 2003). Such individuals were curiously regarded as *"Europe in America"*. This constituted a "slap in the face" for the majority indigenous population whose identities, cultures, languages, and phenotypes were not taken into account when thinking about the nation (Anderson, 1993). The main identity and cultural currents excluded from this framework of cultural citizenship were precisely the indigenous (Quijada, 2000; Briones, 2004; Roulet and Navarro Floria, 2014) and Afro-Argentinian population (Maffia, Frigerio, and Lamborghini, 2011; Lamborghini, Geler, and Guzmán, 2017), to the extent that the original languages spoken in the geographical area now occupied by modern-day Argentina endure the status of 'foreign' within their own territory (da Rocha D'Angelis, 2008). The result of this process is a society that acknowledges high level of xenophobia and racism (INADI, 2005; Grimson, 2006), while simultaneously eschewing public demonstrations of these phenomena: *racism without racists* (Majfud, 2019). Within this context, the need to overcome those assimilationist patterns forged by an intercultural approach which places equal value on all identities and cultures became increasingly evident, initially in the field of education, in the early 1990s (Diez, 2004; Dietz, 2005; Walsh, 2010), and progressively in the social sciences and certain political sectors (Aguilar Idánez and Buraschi, 2012; Estermann, 2014; Guilherme and Dietz, 2014). An intercultural perspective began to be progressively incorporated into the field of the arts, while its history (Noufouri, 2017) and culture gradually came to be embraced as an approach to cultural policies (Ibañez Angulo, 2016) and cultural management (Escribal, 2017).

Contemporary Argentina is a country that continues to oscillate between economic, productive, and social models. For example, it played an active part in the early years of the 21st century in the regional "leftward shift" of governments oriented towards economic growth allied with social inclusion (Arditi, 2009) which was succeeded at the regional level by openly neoliberal administrations whose leaders were linked to financial speculation and the flight of assets, as evidenced by the so-called "Panama Papers" (*Deutsche Welle*, 2016). The assimilationist narrative relating to national identity appears a point common to such dissimilar governments as those of President Mauricio Macri (2015–2019) and his successor, Alberto Fernández (elected in 2020). Coming from opposite political viewpoints, both national leaders declared in the presence of European counterparts that Argentinians were "descended from ships", thereby rendering the founding myth of the monocultural Argentina their own (*Perfil*, 2018; Letjman, 2020).

The State began to develop public institutions to respond to the demands related to culture and the arts in the mid-20th century, particularly after assuming responsibilities in this field within the supranational system of the United Nations (Logiódice, 2012). However, it was only with the restoration of democracy in the 1980s that certain intellectual and political groups began to discuss and work on them in modern terms (Garcia Canclini, 1987; Landi, 1984). The military dictatorship wielding ultimate political power between 1976 and 1982, which was fostered by the internationally coordinated Operation Condor, was not only particularly bloody in character, but also left its mark on Argentinian culture. The disappearance of artists and intellectuals was compounded by the burning of books and censorship, introducing fear as a tactic in the dismantling of popular organisations (Romero, 2006). Against this background, a group of intellectuals, including Beatriz Sarlo and Néstor García Canclini, among others, identified culture and cultural policies as an instrument through which to consolidate democracy (1984). Public cultural management was born of the precepts of the homologation between culture and arts characteristic of the Northern European model of Enlightenment which had been embraced by the intellectuals of the 18th century.

The institutional structure of culture is based on the combination of a central point which, following the French model, has oscillated between State Secretariat and Ministry in recent years and the National Arts Fund, created in 1958, which it finances through a council of notable individuals in line with the Anglo-Saxon tradition (Chartrand and Mccaughey, 1989). Centralism is a constitutive problem within Argentinian society and has been described as tantamount to a "curse" on national culture (Bayardo, 2008). This can be seen both in terms of federal public investment in culture (Zamorano, 2016) and the location of federal cultural services. The National Museum of Fine and Decorative Arts, the National Exhibition Rooms, the National Library, and the Ministry of Culture are all located in Recoleta, a district of Buenos Aires with high real estate prices. This situation reinforces certain circuits of privilege (Olmos, 2019, p. 76), as a further expression of that enlightened perspective of culture for those cultivated people. In discursive terms, a broader view of "the cultural issue" which extends beyond the merely artistic has begun to emerge on the part of the State since the reinstitution of democracy. However, it has not been reflected in new paradigms for cultural policies, either in the last decades of the 20th century (Mendes Calado, 2015) or in the first decades of the present one, despite the introduction of certain institutional innovations such as the inclusion of the cultural diversity agenda (Zamorano, 2016).

Culture is often afforded low political priority in budgetary terms. According to the National Cultural Information System (SINCA), it accounts for 0.69% of federal public spending (with only 0.14% assigned to the MoC [Ministry of Culture]). In terms of legislation, Argentina recognised authors' rights from an early stage with the *Intellectual Property Act of 1933* but lacks a General Law on Culture, such as that adopted by Mexico in 2018 to guide and harmonise public policies and has only a handful of sector promotional laws (relating to cinema and theatre) that shape the aforementioned institutes. During the last two decades, the efforts of at least three political processes intended to culminate in the implementation of a National Culture Law which attracted widespread support from civil society organisations (Prato, Traversaro and Segura, 2015) have been frustrated. In terms of cultural policy design, the Federal Council, composed of the highest representatives of the area of each province, has been assigned wider responsibilities than those it actually exercises, and cultural policy at the municipal level remains structurally undeveloped (Abarzúa and de Sá Souza, 2005), a fact which enhances centralism. A tradition exists of holding federal meetings between public officials and cultural organisations to discuss these policies. Indeed, during this democratic period, at least five were held, an initial meeting of the Federal Council of Culture and Education held in Mar del Plata in 1984 (Chavalla, 2005), followed by four National Congresses of Culture.[3] However, since any resulting decisions are not binding, it is unusual for them to result in the implementation of specific policies.

As for its economic dimension, the cultural field represents 2.6% of Argentina's GDP, employing some 300,000 people or 1.8% of total private sector employment. This makes Argentina one of the countries in the region, together with Chile and the Dominican Republic, where this sector generates relatively higher employment (*Panorama gráfico del sector cultural iberoamericano*, 2016, p. 26). In 2019, the various activities made the following respective contributions to cultural income: audio-visual subsector 28%, digital content 17%, advertising 14%, books and publications 12%, design 10%, music 7%, performing arts 5%, and the three remaining activities (cultural training, plastic arts, and intangible cultural heritage) 2%, respectively (SINCA, 2020a). Argentina has historically contested Spain's primacy in relation to industrial cultural production aimed at the Spanish-speaking market throughout the 20th century, particularly in film and publishing production (along with Mexico in the latter case) (SCN, 2010). Argentinians are keen audiences of artistic events: 45% of the population attended at least one music event (higher regional index); 48% the cinema (second only to Costa Rica which recorded 51%), and 51% the theatre (1% lower than Uruguay's 52%) (*Panorama gráfico del sector cultural iberoamericano*, 2016, p. 38).

An early developer (the world's first animated feature film was made by Quirino Cristiani in the country in 1917), the Argentine film industry has won two Oscars, (*La historia oficial*, directed by Luis Puenzo in 1985, and 2009's *El secreto de sus ojos*, by Juan José Campanella), and accounts for a Grade A international festival in the city of Mar del Plata, founded in 1954. Argentina's middle class is composed of film enthusiasts whose consumption, however, is mainly restricted to North American output which accounted for 90% of the titles recording the highest ticket sales (the only national one occupied fifth place) in 2019 (Battle, 2019). Together with Brazil, Argentina has promoted several audio-visual coordination policies within the framework of the MERCOSUR regional integration bloc aimed at positioning itself in the face of the new features of the digital paradigm (Moguillansky and Poggi, 2017). Within the music sector, the Musicians' Union (SADEM) is the largest in Latin America. Boasting a strong tradition of popular regional festivals held throughout the country, folk and traditional music often feature prominently in this circuit. In terms of urban expressions, the largest festival is a local Lollapalooza, forming part of the global franchise, with an audience of 300,000 in 2019 (Insua Escalante, 2019). As for the theatre, its offer is more heavily centralised. According to SINCA, of the more than three million theatregoers nationwide, over two million were resident in Buenos Aires, a city with a theatre circuit which has been quantified as more extensive in terms of both venues and the number of performances staged than either Paris or New York (*La Nación*, 2008). Additionally, a very wide variety of circuits and venues generates a complex demand for professionals (Dubatti, 2013).

There are 2,256 bookstores throughout the country, 734 of them in Buenos Aires, almost 90% of which are independent (Sequeira, Arias and Arboeja, 2019, p. 18). The main national publishing sector event is the Buenos Aires International Book Fair, with a floor space in excess of 45,000 m², the participation of nearly 1,500 exhibitors drawn from approximately 50 countries, and an impressive attendance of over 1.2 million visitors.[4] In relation to the visual arts scene, a private collectors tradition has been developing in the country since the beginning of the 19th century, giving birth to the main national museums (Baldasarre, 2006). In addition to the previously mentioned National Museum of Fine Arts, the private Museum of Latin American Art of Buenos Aires (MALBA), founded in 2001, stands out as holding one of the most impressive collections in the region. Moreover, private foundations such as PROA, located in the tourist district of La Boca and Fundación Telefónica, owned by the Spanish telecommunications company, are key players in the arts sector. The most important art fair for the visual arts is ArteBA which is staged over seven days and attracts approximately 90,000 visitors. This event recorded an unprecedented sale within the domestic market when an untitled mural by Jorge de la Vega dating from 1967 was sold for U\$1.35 million in 2019 (Chatruc, 2019). One of the problems relating to both freedom of expression and the circulation of cultural content is the existence of a monopolistic media system (Becerra and Mastrini, 2011). In particular,

> The media and, subsequently, computer communication companies became stronger than the States as transnational agents of cultural exchange. Fox in the United States, Televisa in Mexico, Globo in Brazil and Clarín in Argentina do not limit themselves to retaining audiences and negotiating the orientation of citizens in exchange for economic favours (but) also selecting and managing social discontent, organising affective care communities.
>
> (Garcia Canclini, 2020, p. 46)

This scenario undoubtedly influences the cultural patterns through which societies operate.

As for community-based cultural organisations, several have become politically significant in recent years. Among their ranks is the collective Pueblo hace cultura, formed in 2010, a coalition that campaigns to guarantee the allocation of 1% of the national budget to community-oriented cultural projects. Another is Abogados culturales which has brought together lawyers who voluntarily collaborate with cultural organisations to resolve a variety of legal challenges, ranging from the need to re-habilitate spaces to the securing of legal status. The MECA (Cultural Spaces movement), founded several years ago, was entered in the Buenos Aires urban register in 2018, affiliating almost 500 community cultural centres in order to legally safeguard their operation. A national idiosyncrasy is the dynamic cultural activity and participation of trade unions, irrespective of whether they involve artistic activities. With a background in cultural promotion, active since the founding of the first worker associations at the end of the 19th century (Santillán, 1932, pp. 25–27), and a strong developer of cultural infrastructure during the second half of the 20th century, contemporary trade unions have engaged in institutional dialogue on issues related to public cultural policies, even presenting cultural bills for consideration (Escribal and Britos, 2017). Gender perspectives and issues have recently come to be included within the sector, in the framework of a large-scale and increasing social mobilisation driven by a renewed feminist movement (Pais Andrade, 2018). The *We propose* initiative, for instance, highlighted the absence of female artists from regular exhibitions staged by the major national museums.[5] Furthermore, a recent bill was passed in order to establish a female quota for participation in musical events, establishing a minimum level of 30% for events that involve more than three bands.[6] This, therefore, is the context within which contemporary cultural management is exercised in Argentina.

Cultural management in Argentina

Having described several relevant characteristics of Argentina and its cultural sector and asserted that the manner of the initial forging of the national identity constitutes a cultural policy, the emergence of cultural management will be presented as one contributory element in the modernisation of these policies (Nivón Bolán, 2005, p. 5), while acknowledging that its implementation preceded the use of the term itself (Sepúlveda and Chavarría, 2015, p. 3). In Argentina, the term "cultural management" began to be adopted in the 1990s – in a political context within which public capabilities were being weakened – as a result of intense international cooperation involving Latin America, fuelled mainly by principles imported from the University of Barcelona. These tenets underpinned the emergence of private actors who assumed those responsibilities being shed by the State. They were particularly connected to foundations able to access increasingly important Spanish capital at the time since Spain was seeking to recover its influence in the region it had dominated during the imperial era (Castiñeira de Dios, 2013, p. 86). This wave introduced new economy-based terminology into the field, such as *product* or *efficiency*, that had not previously been employed in or applied to the cultural sector (Wortman, 2009). Other currents aimed at cultural action, for example, the school of *cultural promotion*, intended to sustain traditional indigenous/peasant/popular cultures (Colombres, 2009) or socio-cultural animation aimed at community-based social development (Tabares, Truhillo and Zubiria Samper, 1998), were rendered invisible by this new narrative, resulting in "abuse" (Rius and Sánchez-Belando, 2015; de la Vega Velástegui, this volume). At the same time, in the face of the "boom" in cultural management (Wortman, 2012), the very reproduction of these cultures was interrupted by the new current subsuming the hegemony before the subjects became interested in the cultural question. The main promoters of this agenda were the Organisation of Ibero-American States (OEI), the British Council, the Alliance Française, and the three Spanish Cultural Centres. Applying for these transnational funds, the only ones available in the 1990s, meant adapting the logic and narrative of the cultural sector to the jargon and technical criteria of these cooperation bodies (Bayardo, 2018). To ensure this adaptability, cultural management was born.

New professional profiles needed to be developed through training. Therefore, an educational network began to germinate for this purpose. At the beginning of the current century, in collaboration with the University of San Martin, the OEI launched the Iberformat network uniting Ibero-American training centres on the basis of this concept of cultural management. The first public training course for cultural agents, of two years' duration, was organised by the National Institute of Public Administration in 1992. The State has provided training in cultural management in at least two areas: between 2006 and 2009 through a non-formal course focusing on the local dimension of culture (*El Ancasti*, 2008); and, since 2011, with the creation of the Institute of Public Culture (TELAM, 2013). Within the university domain, an exponential growth has occurred in the number of cultural management qualifications available over the last decade. In 2004, there were two undergraduate courses, three bachelor's courses, and seven specialisations or postgraduate courses (only one of them delivered outside Buenos Aires) (IBERFORMAT, 2005). At present, there are 20 Bachelor programmes with geographical spread covering ten provinces, in addition to 18 master's degrees and specialisations.

One deficiency of cultural management education is the absence of a comprehensive systematic mapping of the various occupational roles within the sector. This leads to the fact that anyone interested in working within the cultural sector tends to enrol on a "cultural management" course without considering the specific tools provided by the curriculum to promote the desired quantifiable performance. This leads to widespread frustration with the lack of specialised tools and overly generic training. Such disaffection is expressed in the criticism levelled at universities for seeking to "produce Ministers of Culture" (Bayardo, 2019, p. 15), although only a minority of their graduates secure employment in public administration. The inherent tension between theory and practice is evident in cultural management training. The existing curricular offerings have tended to favour the former over the latter. Unfortunately, there are no exhaustive analyses of the academic offerings within this discipline in Argentina, such as the one developed by Gonzalez Roblero through the Bachelor of Arts in Management and Promotion at the University of Sciences and Arts of Chiapas (Mexico) (2018), nor are there detailed analyses in terms of students' areas of performance, such as the one developed by Silva in relation to Brazil (this volume). In general terms, the current offer can be said to be based on an understanding of culture as an aspect of sophistication, accessible only to certain social groups (Mariscal Orozco, 2015, p. 105), and tending to experience generally low retention and graduation rates (Polo Friz and Romero, 2016). Meanwhile, career starters, differentiated by their primary interests, are divided between one group seeking technical skills linked to artistic production and another interested in the political dimension of culture. A recurrent criticism levelled by numerous defectors, particularly ones from the first group, is the lack of specific technical content. This shortcoming, already identified in 2004 in the analytical framework of the Ibero-American Directory of Cultural Management Training (IBERFORMAT, 2005, p. 22) has yet to be satisfactorily addressed. In addition, students and graduates experience considerable difficulty in securing employment within the cultural sector (Bayardo, 2019, p. 20), above and beyond the challenges resulting from the previously mentioned limited sectoral labour market. Moreover, those working in the sector regard themselves as cultural managers, having been trained as such (Fuentes Firmani, Quesada and Vovchuk, 2017).

Similarly, in order to prioritise the approach to art as a sphere separated from the social and political, in addition to the reproduction of its own circuits, the academic offer currently available in Argentina does not provide answers to those seeking to become more professional in an attempt to deepen the social dimension of cultural management. In this sense, it also underpins the over-reliance on classical European and North American theory and literature. Although regional and Spanish-based academic production on the issue is expanding, educational curricula barely incorporate that production in structural terms. Culture is still conceived of in terms of the traditional European schools of the mid-20th century, produced in response to the challenges of another era and another region. If South American authors are scarcely considered, other intellectual production of the Global South is completely ignored. No African, Asian, or Oceanian authors feature in any current curriculum. As an example of curricular Eurocentrism with regard to cultural management training in Argentina, it is worth noting the central position given by curricular programmes to the French post-war experience, and in particular the writer André Malraux and his performance as Minister of Culture. Not only relevant national antecedents are ignored – such as the impressive administration of the National Commission of Popular Libraries developed by Luis Horacio Velázquez between 1950 and 1955, that is, before Malraux (Fiorucci, 2009) – but also milestones of cultural management that occurred in Africa, where the establishment of a training school for cultural managers in Zimbabwe in 1948 is documented (Moulinier, 1984).

As for specific research on cultural management, from the perspective of practice and training it is the least developed of the three described fields in Argentina. Even those universities that train cultural managers tend to concentrate their research projects on related fields such as art history or aesthetics. Considerable work needs to be undertaken in this regard. Octavio Getino conducted pioneering research analysing cultural industries in the 1990s and early 2000s with his work culminating in two publications: the *Cultural Industries Bulletin* of the CICCUS Foundation (1996 to 1998) and the *Yearbook of Cultural Indicators* of the Nacional University of Tres de Febrero, the latter of which was launched in 2001 and remains in print. *Revista Gestión Cultural* was initially an experimental journal with only two volumes being published, one in 2004 and the other in 2009. Nevertheless, this experiment evolved into RGC Ediciones, the first publisher specifically devoted to the subject of cultural management, with 23 books by South American authors and a digital magazine published to date.[7] Actually, the project Genesis of and Advances in the Institutionalisation of Cultural Management in Argentina is currently underway at the National University of Avellaneda and aims to map the academic offer, the research process, and the articles on cultural management published in scientific journals.

Professional networking is increasingly important in the field of cultural management (Ponte; Muñoz del Campo, this volume). In terms of professional associations, Argentina lacks a consolidated national network of cultural managers. An Argentine Association of University Cultural Managers, founded in 2006, restricts its membership to graduates of the National University of Mar del Plata but has not succeeded in extending registration of new affiliates beyond the geographical confines of this touristic city.[8] In 2010, an Association of Cultural Managers of the Argentine Republic, also based on a group of university graduates, (in this case from the Universidad Nacional de Tres de Febrero) was founded (Rucker, 2012), but failed to sustain itself over time and was operational for just over a year. An Argentinian Network of Cultural Management started working with approximately 50 professionals drawn from all regions of the country in 2019 (*La Ciudad. El Diario de Avellaneda*, 2020). While yet to achieve the status of a formal institution, it brings together mainly university-affiliated members and demonstrates potential as a transcendent area for the unification of criteria and areas of operation within the framework of the profession. In 2020, it published a book, *La gestión cultural en Argentina* (*Cultural Management in Argentina*) which is the source of a number of the reflections presented in this chapter.

Ultimately, the profession appears to have embedded itself in the public consciousness. Although public recognition remains lacking in terms of occupational and tax categories, specific cultural manager job vacancies have recently begun to appear (Fuentes Firmani, 2019, p. 49). This development is reflected in the fact that, in 2016, a draft national law was presented, intended to regulate the professional practice of cultural management, following the model of a professional association, as is the case with the so-called "liberal professions" – advocacy or medicine (Alvarez Rodriguez and Mazure, 2016). Although the law has yet to be passed, the very fact that the bill has been presented is, in itself, another indication of the growing public visibility of the profession.

The main characteristics discussed above are those that distinguish the field of cultural management in contemporary Argentina.

Conclusions

This chapter, after having described the national cultural history and the political context in which cultural workers operate and the dynamics in which the discipline was introduced, has summarised the most relevant aspects of cultural management in Argentina. Certain characteristics of the training of cultural managers in Argentina, such as the scant inclusion of technical knowledge or epistemological production focused on the challenges of the region and time, were problematised. An attempt was made to explain that, in part, certain limitations in the field of cultural management are due to the imposition of categories resulting from Ibero-American cooperation at a time when there was no genuine demand for a new professional stream at the local level. From this perspective, cultural management hindered other ways of understanding the functions of professional intervention in culture that were maturing at the end of the last century. Limitations have been identified to transcending the romantic perspective that equates culture with the art and heritage of certain social groups for the purposes of both cultural policies and cultural management in Argentina. The global debates that have been taking place on the subject of cultural diversity as an imperative of cultural management have hardly been incorporated into public cultural policies in Argentina. Even when a considerable number of Argentinean identities – especially indigenous, Arab, or Afro-descendant based ones – have been traditionally invisible in national narratives, this has led different social references to "claim for a public cultural reincorporation" while "*r*esisting and challenging the continuous impoverishment of their natural/cultural environment, through reification, exhibitionism or mere folklorisation" (Chauqui in Varios, 2015, p. 52).

Within this context, the radical impact on the scenario of the COVID-19 pandemic has allowed certain discussions potentially accelerating the ongoing paradigm shift to be held. This development will, as some demand, enable the profession to address the social and political challenges of contemporary Argentina and its profound inequalities. This agenda is not limited to the acceleration of digitalisation but must also take into account the structural dimension of those conditioning factors affecting the guarantee of cultural rights of society as a whole, and especially the possibility of working in the cultural and artistic sector. In a first survey conducted during the second month of quarantine (April), 24% of workers in the sector indicated that they found migrating to the digital ecosystem impossible, while an additional 25% required support or advice on the skills that they lacked in order to do so. As for the latter, in terms of income, 66% of workers employed in the sector indicated that they require additional income from other forms of work in order to survive. Moreover, 41% had earned no income from their cultural work during the previous year (SINCA, 2020b). That is to say, they are workers in search of professional openings, forced to work in the vocational sector by the very limitations of their chosen career. Having witnessed the contribution to national income made by culture and the arts, the authors understand that both the appropriation of this income and its distribution must be called into question. In particular, the social function of art in terms of its psycho-affective benefits and promotion of mental health – within the framework of isolation – has once again been indicated. These issues constitute the list of challenges that cultural management must address in the future.

Notes

1 Moizo & Urbanavicius (this volume) describe something similar for Uruguay, which is not surprising since the two main cities of the Rio de la Plata (Buenos Aires and Montevideo) historically share a number of cultural elements.
2 *Facundo o civilización y barbarie en las pampas argentinas"* (*Facundo or Civilization and Barbarism on the Argentine Pampas*) is a book written in 1845 by Sarmiento during his second period of exile in Chile. The national canonical work that expresses the view that according to which civilisation is manifested in Europe, North America, and the cities, while barbarism is identified with Latin America, Spain, Asia, and the Middle East.
3 Organised in the cities of Mar del Plata (2006), Tucumán (2008), San Juan (2010), and Chaco (2013).
4 Data provided by https://www.el-libro.org.ar/fundacion/feria-internacional/.
5 More information at https://nosotrasproponemos.org/.
6 Law N°27.539 (available at https://inamu.musica.ar/leydecupo)
7 Available at http://rgcediciones.com.ar/revista/.
8 https://aagecu.blogspot.com/.

References

Abarzúa, G. & de Sá Souza, F. (2005). Políticas Culturales locales y su protagonismo pendiente. *Conference proceedings presented in Third Argentine Congress of Public Administration "Society, State and Administration"*. June 2–4, 2005. Tucumán.
Aguilar Idánez, M. J. & Buraschi, D. (2012). El desafío de la convivencia intercultural, *Revista Interdisciplinar da Mobilidade Humana –REMHU*, 38, pp. 27–43.
Alvarez Rodriguez, C. & Mazure, L. (2016). Proyecto de ley "Marco general para el ejercicio profesional de la Gestión cultural". Honorable Chamber of Deputies. Available at https://www.hcdn.gob.ar/proyectos/proyecto.jsp?exp=7263-D-2016 (Accessed October 14, 2020).
Anderson, B. (1993). *Comunidades imaginadas. Reflexiones sobre el origen y la difusión del nacionalismo*. Mexico: Fondo de Cultura Económica.

Arditi, B. (2009). El giro a la izquierda en América Latina: ¿una política post-liberal?, *Ciências Sociais Unisinos*, 45(3), pp. 232–246. doi: 10.4013/csu.2009.45.3.06.

Baldasarre, M. I. (2006). Sobre los inicios del coleccionismo y los museos de arte en la Argentina, *Anais do Museu Paulista: História e Cultura Material*, 14(1), pp. 293–321. doi: 10.1590/s0101-47142006000100010.

Battle, D. (2019). Taquilla: en 2019, el negocio del cine creció en la Argentina un 5.2%, *La Nación*, December 23, 2019. Available at https://www.lanacion.com.ar/especta culos/cine/taquilla-2019-negocio-del-cine-cada-vez-nid2318334 (Accessed October 14, 2020).

Bayardo, R. (2019). Algunas coordenadas de la gestión cultural en la Argentina. In: Fuentes Firmani, E. & Tasat, J. (Eds.) *La gestión cultural en la Argentina*. Buenos Aires: RGC Ediciones, p. 385.

———— (2018). Repensando la gestión cultural en Latinoamérica. In: Yañez Canal, C. (Ed.) *Praxis de la gestión cultural*. Guadalajara: Universidad de Guadalajara, pp. 17–32.

———— (2008) '¿Hacia donde van las políticas culturales?', in *1º Simposio Internacional de Políticas Públicas Culturales en Iberoamérica Facultad de Ciencias Económicas – Universidad Nacional de Córdoba Córdoba, October 22 and 23, 2008*, pp. 1–15.

Becerra, M. & Mastrini, G. (2011). Transformaciones en el sistema de medios en la Argentina del Siglo XXI, Democracia y medios de comunicación. In: Sorj, B. (Ed.) *Democracia y medios de comunciación. Más allá del Estado y el Mercado*. Buenos Aires: Edelstein Centre for Social Studies/Fernando Henrique Cardoso Institute, pp. 33–73.

Briones, C. (2004). Construcciones de aboriginalidad en Argentina, *Société Suisse des Américanistes*, 68, pp. 73–90.

Castiñeira de Dios, J. L. (2013). Critica de la gestión cultural pura, *Aportes para el Debate*, 23, pp. 79–92.

Chartrand, H. & Mccaughey, C. (1989). The arm's length principle and the arts: An international perspective. Past, present and future. In: Cummings, M. C. J. & Davidson Schuster, J. M. (Eds.) *Who's to Pay for the Arts? The International Search for Models of Support*. Nueva York: American Council for the Arts, pp. 1–10.

Chatruc, C. (2019). El misterio del De la Vega, la obra más cara de arteBA que se vendió por más de un millón de dólares, *La Nación*, April 11. Available at https://www.lan acion.com.ar/cultura/el-misterio-del-mural-de-vega-obra-nid2237380 (Accessed October 14, 2020).

Chavalla, A. (2005). La política cultural del gobierno de Alfonsín, *Pensares y Haceres*. Available at https://acortar.link/JOC5q (Accessed September 23, 2020).

Colombres, A. (2009). *Nuevo Manual Del Promotor Cultural*. México: National Council for Culture and the Arts.

de la Vega Velástegui, P. (this volume). Cultural management in Ecuador: genealogy and power relations within the constitution of a field. In: Henze, R. & Escribal, F. (Eds.) *Cultural Management and Policy in Latin America*. Abingdon & New York: Routledge, pp. 143–162.

Deutsche Welle (2016). Macri, involucrado en sociedad revelada en "Panama Papers", April 4, 2016. Available at https://www.dw.com/es/macri-involucrado-en-sociedad-rev elada-en-panama-papers/a-19162182 (Accessed October 12, 2020).

Dietz, G. (2005). *Del multiculturalismo a la interculturalidad: evolución y perspectivas, Cuadernos IAPH. Patrimonio inmaterial y gestión de la diversidad*. Sevilla:

Government of Andalusia. Department of Culture. Andalusian Institute of Historical Heritage, pp. 27–47.

Diez, M. L. (2004). Reflexiones en torno a la interculturalidad, *Cuadernos de Antropología Social*, 19, pp. 191–213.

Dubatti, J. (2013). *Cien años de teatro argentino: Desde 1910 a nuestros días.* Buenos Aires: Editorial Biblos.

El Ancasti (2008). Curso de Gestión Cultural, May 2, 2008. Available at https://www.ela ncasti.com.ar/cultura/2008/5/2/curso-gestin-cultural-46342.html (Accessed October 15, 2020).

Escribal, F. (2017). Orquestas Infanto-Juveniles suramericanas en perspectiva de Derechos Culturales, *Foro de educación musical, artes y pedagogía*, 2(2), pp. 107–127.

Escribal, F. & Britos, M. (2017). El sindicalismo argentino como efector de políticas culturales: Reflexiones sobre el colectivo Radar de los Trabajadores. In: Yañez Canal, C. (Ed.) *Politicas y derechos culturales*. Manizales: Universidad Nacional de Colombia, pp. 81–94.

Estermann, J. (2014). Colonialidad, descolonización e interculturalidad, *Polis*, 38, pp. 1–15. doi: 10.4000/polis.1064.

Fiorucci, F. (2009). La cultura, el libro y la lectura bajo el peronismo. El caso de la Comisión de Bibliotecas populares, *Desarrollo Económico*, 48(192), pp. 543–556. doi: 10.1017/CBO9781107415324.004.

Fuentes Firmani, E. (2019). ¿Y eso con qué se come? Reflexiones sobre la gestión cultural en la Argentina. In: Fuentes Firmani, E. & Tasat, J. (Eds.) *Gestión cultural en la Argentina*. Caseros: RGC Ediciones, pp. 43–62.

Fuentes Firmani, E., Quesada, J. M. & Vovchuk, L. (2017). Gestión Cultural en Argentina. Perspectivas de investigación y desarrollo. *RGC*. Available at http://rgcediciones. com.ar/y-eso-con-que-se-come-reflexiones-sobre-la-gestion-cultural-en-la-argentina/ (Accessed October 22, 2020).

Garcia Canclini, N. (2020). Ciudadanos reemplazados por algoritmos. CALAS Maria Sibylla Merian Center. Available at http://www.calas.lat/sites/default/files/garcia_ca nclini.ciudadanos_reemplazados_por_algoritmos.pdf (Accessed September 11, 2020).

——— (1987). Políticas culturales y crisis de desarrollo: Un balance lationamericano. In: Garcia Canclini, N. (Ed.) *Políticas culturales en América Latina*. Barcelona: Grijalbo, pp. 13–61.

González Roblero, V. (2018). Avatares de la gestión cultural. Acercamientos desde la licenciatura en Gestión y Promoción de las Artes de la UNICACH, *Península*, 13(2), pp. 187–212.

Gray, C. (2010). Analysing cultural policy: incorrigibly plural or ontologically incompatible?, *International Journal of Cultural Policy*, 16(2), pp. 215–230. doi: 10.1080/10286630902935160.

Grimson, A. (2019). *¿Qué es el peronismo? De Perón a los Kirchner*. Buenos Aires: Siglo XXI Editores.

——— (2006). Nuevas xenofobias, nuevas políticas étnicas en la Argentina. In: Grimson, A. & Jelin, E. (Eds.) *Migraciones regionales hacia la Argentina. Diferencia, desigualdad y derechos*. Buenos Aires: Prometeo, pp. 69–99.

Guilherme, M. & Dietz, G. (2014). Diferencia en la diversidad: Perspectivas múltiples de complejidades conceptuales multi, inter y trans-culturales, *Estudios sobre las culturas contemporáneas*, 40, pp. 13–36.

Ibáñez Angulo, M. (2016). Diversidad cultural y políticas culturales: Encuentros y desencuentros. In: Zapata-Barrero, R. & Rubio Carbonero, G. (Eds.) *Interculturalidad y políticas culturales*. Barcelona: Editorial Bellaterra, pp. 61–84.

IBERFORMAT (2005). Directorio iberoamericano de centros de formación en gestión cultural y políticas culturales. Madrid: Red Iberformat, OEI, UNESCO. Available at http://unesdoc.unesco.org/images/0013/001386/138686s.pdf (Accessed November 12, 2018).

——— (2003). In *Proceedings for the 1st Training of Trainers Seminar in the Field of Cultural Management*, June 17–19, 2003. México: IBERFORMAT.

INADI (2005). *Hacia un Plan Nacional contra la Discriminación*. Buenos Aires: National Institute against Discrimination, Xenophobia and Racism.

Insua Escalante, M. (2019). Lollapalooza 2019: 300 mil personas, más de 100 bandas y 3 días de música a pleno, en la sexta edición argentina del festival más grande, *InfoBAE*, April 1. Available at https://www.infobae.com/teleshow/infoshow/2019/04/01/lollapa looza-2019-300-mil-personas-mas-de-300-bandas-y-3-dias-de-musica-a-pleno-en-la-s exta-edicion-argentina-del-festival-mas-grande/ (Accessed October 14, 2020).

La Ciudad. El Diario de Avellaneda (2020). Nueva reunión virtual de la Red de Gestión Cultural de la Argentina, July 21. Available at https://laciudadavellaneda.com.ar/nueva-reunion-vi rtual-de-la-red-de-gestion-cultural-de-la-argentina/ (Accessed October 14, 2020).

La Nación (2008). La ciudad con más teatros del mundo, November 26. Available at https: //www.lanacion.com.ar/espectaculos/teatro/la-ciudad-con-mas-teatros-del-mundo-n id1074260/ (Accessed October 14, 2020).

Lamborghini, E., Geler, L. & Guzmán, F. (2017). Los estudios afrodescendientes en Argentina: Nuevas perspectivas y desafíos en un país "sin razas", *Tabula Rasa*, 27(27), pp. 67–101. doi: 10.25058/20112742.445.

Landi, O. (1984). Cultura y política en la transición a la democracia, *Revista Nueva Sociedad*, 32, pp. 65–78.

Letjman, R. (2020). Alberto Fernández, antes de su reunión con Francisco: "El Papa no le pertenece a nadie, ni a los peronistas ni a los no peronistas", *InfoBAE*, January 30. Available at https://www.infobae.com/politica/2020/01/30/alberto-fernandez-antes-de -su-reunion-con-francisco-el-papa-no-le-pertenece-a-nadie-ni-a-los-peronistas-ni-a-los -no-peronistas/ (Accessed October 12, 2020).

Logiódice, M. J. (2012). Políticas culturales, la conformación de un campo disciplinar. Sentidos y prácticas en las opciones de políticas, *Documentos y Aportes en Administración Pública y Gestión Estatal*, 18(18), pp. 59–87. Available at http://www. scielo.org.ar/pdf/daapge/n18/n18a03.pdf (Accessed May 28, 2017).

Maffia, M., Frigerio, A. & Lamborghini, E. (2011). *Afrodescendientes y africanos en Argentina*. Buenos Aires: United Nations Development Programme.

Majfud, J. (2019). El racismo no necesita racistas, *El correo de la UNESCO*, 2019(2). Available at https://es.unesco.org/courier/2019-2/racismo-no-necesita-racistas.

Margulis, M. (1999). La racialización de las relaciones de clase. In: Urresti, M. & Margulis, M. (Eds.). *La segregación negada. Cultura y discriminación social*. Buenos Aires: Editorial Biblos, pp. 37–62.

Mariscal Orozco, J. L. (2015). La triple construcción de la gestión cultural en Latinoamérica, *Telos*, 17(1), pp. 96–112. Available at http://publicaciones.urbe.edu/index.php/telos/ article/view/3834/4776 (Accessed October 11, 2020).

——— (2012). *Profesionalización de gestores culturales en Latinoamérica. Estado, universidades y asociaciones*. Mexico: Virtual Campus of the University of Guadalajara.

Mendes Calado, P. (2015). *Políticas culturales: Rumbo y deriva. Estudios de casos sobre la (ex) Secretaría de Cultura de la Nación.* Caseros: RGC Ediciones.

Moguillansky, M. & Poggi, M. F. (2017). ¿Hacia una política digital para el cine del Mercosur? Nuevas orientaciones en la agenda regional, *CHASQUI, Revista Latinoamericana de Comunicación*, pp. 373–389. Available at http://200.41.82.22/bitstream/10469/13225/1/REXTN-Ch134-21-Moguillansky.pdf (Accessed October 14, 2020).

Moizo, C. & Urbanavicius, D. (this volume). Cultural management in Uruguay: a country synonymous with a river. In: Henze, R. & Escribal, F. (Eds.), *Cultural Management and Policy in Latin America*. Abingdon & New York: Routledge, pp. 184–197.

Moulinier, P. (1984). La Formación de administradores culturales, *Cultural development: documentary dossier*, 28–29. Available at http://unesdoc.unesco.org/images/0006/000633/063383sb.pdf (Accessed October 29, 2017).

Mulcahy, K. V. (2017) 'Combating coloniality: the cultural policy of post-colonialism', *International Journal of Cultural Policy*, 23(3), pp. 237–253. doi: 10.1080/10286632.2015.1043292.

Muñoz del Campo, N. (this volume). Cultural management in Chile: Between professionalization and the emergence of a public intervention category. In: Henze, R. & Escribal, F. (Eds.), *Cultural Management and Policy in Latin America*. Abingdon & New York: Routledge, pp. 125–142.

Nagy, M. (2013). Una educación para el desierto argentino. Los pueblos indígenas en los planes de estudio y en los textos escolares actuales, *Espacios en Blanco. Revista de Educación*, 23, pp. 187–223.

Nivón Bolán, E. (2005). Gestión y políticas culturales en el desarrollo de los territorios, in *Seminar on Cultural Management Training*, Santiago and Valparaiso (Chile), August 9 and 10, 2005. Available at https://www.scribd.com/document/67700287/nivon (Accessed September 21, 2020).

Noufouri, H. (2017). Para una historia del arte intercultural y sin racismo, Diversidad, 8(13), pp. 148–169.

Olmos, H. (2019). Sobre cultura, política y otras yerbas. In: Fuentes Firmani, E. & Tasat, J. (Eds.) *Gestión cultural en la Argentina*. Caseros: RGC Ediciones, pp. 63–78.

Pais Andrade, M. (2018). La transversalización del enfoque de géneros en las políticas culturales públicas: El caso del Ministerio de Cultura argentino, *IdeAs y debates*, 35(35), pp. 161–180.

Panorama gráfico del sector cultural Iberoamericano (2016). Madrid: Santillana Foundation & OEI. Available at https://oibc.oei.es/otros_documentos/Estudio_CD_OEI.pdf (Accessed September 18, 2020).

Perfil (2018). Macri: En Sudamérica todos somos descendientes de europeos, January 25. Available at https://www.perfil.com/noticias/politica/macri-en-sudamerica-todos-somos-descendientes-de-europeos.phtml (Accessed October 12, 2020).

Polo Friz, E. & Romero, L. (2016). Procesos de desgranamiento y lentificación en la Educación Superior Argentina: El caso de la Tecnicatura Universitaria en Gestión Cultural, Praxis educativa, 20(3), pp. 32–37. Available at https://cerac.unlpam.edu.ar/index.php/praxis/article/view/1357/1450 (Accessed August 18, 2020).

Ponte, B. (this volume). Cultural management in Latin America and Europe: between the ashes and the flame. In: Henze, R. & Escribal, F. (Eds.), *Cultural Management and Policy in Latin America*. Abingdon & New York: Routledge, pp. 22–33.

Prato, V., Traversaro, N. & Segura, M. (2015). La sociedad civil argentina y la "batalla cultural". de la Ley de Servicios de Comunicación Audiovisual al proyecto de Ley Federal de Culturas, *Revista Estado y Políticas Públicas*, 5, pp. 81–96.

Quijada, M. (2000). Nación y territorio: la dimensión simbólica del espacio en la construcción nacional argentina. Siglo XIX, *Revista de Indias*, 60(219), pp. 373–394. doi: 10.3989/revindias.2000.i219.511.

Quijano, A. (2014). Colonialidad del poder, eurocentrismo y América Latina. In: Quijano, A. (Ed.), Cuestiones y horizontes: de la dependencia histórico-estructural a la colonialidad/descolonialidad del poder. Buenos Aires: CLACSO, pp. 777–832. Available at http://biblioteca.clacso.edu.ar/clacso/se/20140507042402/eje3-8.pdf (Accessed March 24, 2020).

Rius, J. & Sánchez-Belando, M. V. (2015). Modelo Barcelona y política cultural: Usos y abusos de la cultura por parte de un modelo emprendedor de desarrollo local, *Eure*, 41(122), pp. 103–123. doi: 10.4067/S0250-71612015000100005.

da Rocha D'Angelis, W. (2008). Lengua indígena: lengua extranjera en tierra indígena, *Avá*, 14. Available at https://acortar.link/3u3Oc (Accessed May 25, 2017).

Rodriguez, G. (2011). La raza en las narrativas fundacionales de la Nación Argentina. Sarmiento, su estigma y su legado para la politización racial de la República, *Astrolabio*, 8, pp. 61–91. doi: 10.1017/CBO9781107415324.004.

Romero, F. (2006). *Culturicidio. historia de la educación argentina*. Resistencia: Librería de la Paz.

Roulet, F. & Navarro Floria, P. (2014). De soberanos externos a rebeldes internos: la domesticación discursiva y legal de la cuestión indígena en el tránsito del siglo XVIII al XX, Revista Tefros, 3(1), pp. 6–21. Available at http://200.7.136.16/ojs/index.php/t efros/article/view/100 (Accessed April 16, 2020).

Rucker, Ú. (2012). Profesionalización y asociatividad de gestores culturales en la Argentina. In: Mariscal Orozco, J. L. (Ed.) *Profesionalización de gestores culturales en Latinoamérica. Estado, universidades y asociaciones*. Guadalajara: University of Guadalajara, pp. 143–158.

Santillán, D. (1932). *Ideologia y Trayectoria del movimiento obrero revolucionario en la Argentina: La FORA*. Buenos Aires: Ediciones HL.

Sarlo, B. (2003). *Una modernidad periférica: Buenos Aires (1920–1930)*. Buenos Aires: Ediciones Nueva Visión.

SCN (2010). Valor y símbolo. Dos siglos de industrias culturales en la Argentina. Buenos Aires: SCN. Available at http://back.sinca.gob.ar/download.aspx?id=1098 (Accessed August 9, 2020).

Sepúlveda, M. & Chavarría, R. (2015). Aproximación crítica al concepto de Gestión cultural en Chile durante la segunda mitad del siglo XX. *Proceedings for the 2nd National Meeting on Cultural Management*, October 14–17. Jalisco (México). Available at http://observatoriocultural.udgvirtual.udg.mx/repositorio/bitstream/handle/123456789/ 282/2ENGC073.pdf?sequence=1 (Accessed June 11, 2020).

Sequeira, J. M., Arias, F. & Arboeja, S. (2019). *Indicadores culturales 2017–2018. Gestión cultural. Contenidos, competencias e incumbencias*. Caseros: UNTREF.

Silva, S. (this volume). Cultural management in Brazil: Persistence in times of uncertainty. In: Henze, R. & Escribal, F. (Eds.), *Cultural Management and Policy in Latin America*. Abingdon & New York: Routledge, pp. 163–183.

SINCA (2020a). Coyuntura cultural. El valor económico de la cultura. Buenos Aires: National Cultural Information System. Available at http://back.sinca.gob.ar/download .aspx?id=3004 (Accessed September 11, 2020).

———— (2020b). *Encuesta Nacional de Cultura*. Buenos Aires: National Cultural Information System. Available at http://back.sinca.gob.ar/download.aspx?id=2947 (Accessed September 16, 2020).

Solodkow, D. (2005). Racismo y Nación: Conflictos y (des) armonías identitarias en el proyecto nacional sarmientino, *Decimonónica*, 2(1), pp. 95–121.

Stavenhagen, R. (2002). La diversidad cultural en el desarrollo de las Américas, *Serie de estudios culturales*, 9. Available at http://www.oas.org/udse/documentos/stavenhagen .doc (Accessed August 9, 2020).

Steinberg, C., Cetrángolo, O. & Gatto, F. (2011). *Desigualdades territoriales en la Argentina. Insumos para el planeamiento estratégico del sector educativo, Colección Documentos de proyecto. 9*, Santiago de Chile: CEPAL.

Tabares, M., Truhillo, I. A. & Zubiria Samper, S. (1998). El concepto de la Gestión cultural en el contexto iberoamericano, *Cuadernillos de la OEI. Conceptos básicos de administración y gestión cultural*. Madrid: OEI. Available at http://repositorio.cultur a.gob.cl/bitstream/handle/123456789/3513/CNCYA 145.pdf?sequence=1 (Accessed October 13, 2020).

TELAM (2013). Quedó inaugurado el Instituto de Cultura Pública. *TELAM Agencia de noticias*. December. Available at https://www.telam.com.ar/notas/201312/43569-q uedo-inaugurado-el-instituto-de-cultura-publica.php (Accessed October 15, 2020).

Various (2015). *#PensarLaCulturaPública. Apuntes para una cartografía nacional*. Buenos Aires: National Ministry of Culture.

Villaseñor Anaya, C. (2014). Retos para la gestión cultural en América Latina, *Periférica Internacional, Revista para el análisis de la cultura y el territorio*, 15, pp. 259–275.

Walsh, C. (2010). Interculturalidad crítica y educación intercultural, *Construyendo unterculturalidad crítica* Convention. Quito: International Institute for the Integration of the Andrés Bello, pp. 75–96.

Wortman, A. (2012). El emprendedor cultural. El auge de los posgrados sobre gestión cultural en América del sur, en particular en Argentina, *Indicadores culturales*, 2013. Caseros: EDUNTREF.

———— (2009). *Entre la política y la gestión de la cultura y el arte: Nuevos actores en la Argentina contemporánea*. Buenos Aires: EUDEBA.

———— (2002) 'Vaivenes del campo intelectual político cultural en la Argentina', in Mato, D. (ed.) *Estudios y otras prácticas intelectuales Latinoamericanas en cultura y poder*. Caracas: Universidad Central de Venezuela / CLACSO, pp. 327–338.

Zamorano, M. (2016). La transformación de las políticas culturales argentinas durante la primera década del kirchnerismo: Entre la hegemonía y la diversidad, *Aposta: Revista de ciencias sociales*, 70, pp. 53–83. Available at http://www.apostadigital.com/revist av3/hemeroteca/zamorano1pdf (Accessed May 21, 2020).

7 Cultural management in Paraguay

Emergence and development of the discipline in a conservative and restricted cultural field

Mariano Martín Zamorano

Introduction

Cultural management is becoming increasingly institutionalised across Latin America (Bayardo, 2019; Rubim et al., 2016). However, the professional management of culture remains a very challenging undertaking within the region. The literature on this topic has highlighted a set of factors influencing the orientation and scope of cultural management (DeVereaux, 2009; Dubois, 2013; Henze, 2017). These include the level of development of specific artistic sectors, such as the cultural industries, the existence of a set of organisations and resources to train managers, and the characteristics of historical or urban heritage in a defined territory. Within the Latin American framework, as mediators in charge of cultural programming and projects, cultural managers and organisations must often confront the absence of a well-established and developed market as well as a lack of public support for art and heritage (Harvey, 2014; Zamorano et al., 2014). Other variables explaining the configuration of this activity in the region include profound class and urban-rural inequality, inequitable distribution of cultural capital, and limited access to institutions or platforms distributing both popular and high culture.

This chapter aims to characterise the evolution of Paraguay's cultural management and identify the main factors explaining its distinctive configuration within the Latin American context. When examining its cultural management system, numerous determinant cultural and social factors must be considered. Firstly, the country possesses a vibrant cultural heritage, and several cultural expressions coexist in both rural and urban areas, although its artistic and institutional life is largely concentrated in Asunción (Zarza, 2007). Paraguay's historical heritage, including the Jesuit architectonic heritage or the various artistic works of the indigenous communities, significantly influences the orientation of cultural management. Furthermore, from a cultural perspective, the country is extremely heterogeneous, with 20 recognised ethnic groups and dominance of the mestizo population, who are descendants of the Spanish and indigenous Guaraní (DGEEC, 2005).[1] Paraguay's officially recognised bilingual status, incorporating the Spanish of the colonisers and the indigenous Guaraní language,[2] has evolved since the time of the Jesuit colony and survived the final period of dictatorship (1954–1989).

Secondly, Paraguay is one of the poorest Latin American nations, with 39.3% of its population living in extremely difficult circumstances with almost the same ratio (39.2%) dependant on precarious employment (OECD, 2019, p. 223). Compounding this situation, wealth is highly concentrated in the capital, Asunción, and in the hands of a limited group of families (Causarano, 2012). Since the mid-twentieth century, the country's socio-political development has been characterised as *conservative modernisation* which involves state promotion of agro-exports and the establishment of a quasi-feudal economic model (Fogel & Palau, 1989). In this manner, political power has been historically wielded by the Partido Colorado (ARN). In the last century, the ARN constituted the ruling political party except for the periods 1904–1946 and 2008–2012 and was associated with elite corporatist structures (Molinas Vega, 2001).

Thirdly, the aforementioned social framework and institutional dependencies have influenced Paraguay's cultural policies which have been characterised by their limited, patronising, and culturally restricted orientations; questioned only during certain historical periods (Moreira, 2016). At the same time, deep inequalities and the limited participation of the popular classes have been accompanied by the weak intervention of official cultural institutions and programming. The centre-periphery relationship has been crucial to defining cultural management practices within this social context. On the one hand, the productive system based on an agrarian, and increasingly automatised, economy has promoted the displacement of population to Asunción (Arditi & Rodríguez, 1987). On the other hand, rural poverty and the pre-eminence of the indigenous population in these zones (Barrios, 2006) has created specific conditions for cultural management.

Within this scenario, this chapter seeks to address the following questions: How and from which sources did cultural management develop? What are the main drivers of the cultural manager figure? What have the democratising effects of cultural initiatives implemented by private and social organisations been since the democratic transition? Furthermore, what have been the dominant philosophical grounds of bottom-up projects in the field of culture? I understand the cultural and art management system to be a network of relationships between public and private actors as proposed by Rodríguez Morató for the analysis of cultural policies (2012). Based on this approach, I intend to consider the historical and socio-institutional dynamics determining the concrete role of cultural managers and arts management institutions within the Paraguayan context. This methodological approach enables the author to venture beyond the institutional and programmatic boundaries of cultural management and locate the analysis of this discipline within a broader socio-cultural domain. Consequently, a qualitative research design involving the use of two data collection and analytical tools has been applied. First, a mapping of cultural spaces and initiatives led by social organisations which enables the analysing of their cultural projects, governance, and bottom-up strategies has been produced. Second, the content of 13 interviews conducted with relevant informants in 2010 and 2020, corresponding to a representative group of these organisations, is reviewed.[3]

Cultural management: Definition and main determining factors within Latin America

Cultural management has been defined as a profession dealing with the coordination and leadership of several activities such as the

> protection, preservation, distribution, marketing, mediation, and financial organisation of arts and cultural objects (including heritage) and experiences, such as theatre and performing arts; visual arts, including digital and installation, participatory and/or socially engaged arts, and venue and non-venue based arts and culture, including museums.
>
> (Henze, 2017, p. 34)

These institutional and mediation activities often entail the active involvement of the manager in the exhibition of disseminated artwork, which contributes to its original creative process (DeVereaux, 2011, p. 8).

Cultural and arts management was established as a specific *discipline* in Europe and some Anglo-Saxon countries after the First World War (Paquette & Redaelli, 2015). It has demonstrated high levels of institutionalisation and professionalisation in these geographical regions in recent decades. However, the existence of academic programmes or institutions legitimating these disciplines does not always go hand in hand with the daily practice of managers or art dealers who often base their work on experience (Henze, 2017; Suteu, 2006). Moreover, two deficiencies of contemporary cultural management have been identified by DeVereaux (2009). On the one hand, arts management has been framed as a reactive discipline lacking systematic prospective models, while frequently based on contextually identified needs. On the other hand, the academic and technical analysis of the discipline is frequently focused on tactics and planning techniques, frequently eschewing an analysis of the factors causing practitioners and organisations to become involved in it.

The discipline of cultural and arts management was *imported* by Latin American countries in the late 1980s through multiple channels and assumed different orientations. International organisations, such as UNESCO, and Ibero-American cultural networks linked by historical and linguistic ties (Spanish and Portuguese) were essential to the transference of these professional discourses and methods (Rodríguez Morató, Arturo, Zamorano, 2019). Spanish entities, including universities, have dominated the training of Latin American cultural managers (De la Vega, Escribal, de Britto, this volume). However, the European understanding of cultural management and its narratives did not always fit the needs of students or organisations active in the countries from which such individuals are drawn (Castineira de Dios, 2009). Moreover, while the role of cultural promoters has been relevant to the region since the independence (Bayardo, 2019), the adoption of the cultural management concept in the 1990s during the regional *neo-liberal turn* has been regarded as negative due to its depoliticising of the arts world (de la Vega, 2016).

Cultural policies in Paraguay since the democratic transition

The protracted dictatorship of Alfredo Stroessner (1954–1989), member of the Colorado Party, was initially marked by a neo-Nazi form of authoritarianism which evolved into a subsequent active anti-Communist political programme (Escobar, 2011). Within this context, governmental cultural entities were disbanded, with cultural initiatives instead focusing exclusively on the organising of national celebrations and folk festivals (Moreira, 2016). The *folklorisation* of popular elements constituted part of a model wherein *being national* included indigenous and mestizo populations. This fact, combined with the maintenance of an agrarian social model, enabled the development or in certain cases, such as ceramics, the persistence of various popular practices. By the end of the dictatorship, while the General Directorate of Cultural Assets (1983) coordinated cultural facilities and celebrations, the Commission of Morality and Public Spectacles held responsibility for surveillance and censorship. The highly centralised public promotion of culture delivered through institutions of cultural training and diffusion dealing mainly with high European culture was primarily overseen by the Culture Directorate of the Municipality of Asunción.

From the outset of the democratic transition, in 1989, the Partido Colorado continued to hold power, with Presidents Andrés Rodríguez (1989–1993), Juan Carlos Wasmosy (1993–1998), Luis González Macchi (1999–2003), and Nicanor Duarte Frutos (2003–2008). The majority of these presidential terms were marked by authoritarianism, corruption, and three military uprisings occurring in 1996, 1999, and 2000. Moreover, these decades witnessed a lack of socioeconomic development and industrialisation (Nickson, 2008). The continuity of various facets of the dictatorial model complicating the transition to democracy included "a) the pre-eminence of the Colorado Party b) the politicization of the Armed Forces c) the disarticulation and demobilization of civil society. d) prebendalism and corruption, and e) the undemocratic culture" (Barreda & Costafreda, 2002, p. 78).

Despite these negative developments, cultural policies gradually acquired formal autonomy within the state apparatus. In 1990, a new Under-secretariat for Culture was established as a body within the Ministry of Education and Culture. Although established without the resources to act (Escobar Argaña, 2007), in subsequent years it was allocated additional funding and introduced its initial programmes. Moreover, in 1992, the new National Constitution came into force integrating a novel approach to culture that established a new set of cultural rights, emphasised the multicultural character of the nation, and created the conditions necessary for public intervention in the field (Bareiro & Soro, 2008; Salerno, 2001). Subsequent successive cultural plans placed particular emphasis on the relationship between culture and the achieving of democracy, although its grounds were poorly reflected in executive actions and policy implementation (Escobar Argaña, 2007). Only in 1998, when the new Vice-Ministry of Culture was reformed and the National Foundation for the Development of Arts and Culture (FONDEC)[4] was established, did the area gain a degree of relevance. Within this weak institutional framework, the Asunción City Council continued to be one of the main public actors in the implementation of cultural policies.

Therefore, although the cultural policy was formally developed from legal and institutional standpoints at the end of the twentieth century, it has been poorly implemented during the last two decades. This is reflected in a 2007 report issued by the General Auditor's Office of the Republic on the then current state of cultural heritage which described a highly precarious scenario with missing heritage artefacts, material neglect of historical buildings and books, and an overall lack of planning (General Auditor's Office of the Republic, 2007).

However, since 2006 important changes have occurred. In that year, following promulgation of a National Culture Law (No. 3051/22/11/06), the new National Secretary of Culture (NSC) accountable to the President of Paraguay was established. This body was granted ministerial status, after having been removed from under the authority of the Ministry of Education and Culture. Moreover, this law mandated the creation of a National Council of Culture as a consulting organ responsible for liaising with other governmental bodies, social organisations, and commercial enterprises.

The new NSC was granted economic autonomy in 2008 when a leftist government assumed office. A series of social protests against Duartes Frutos' attempts to modify the Constitution in order to permit his re-election positioned Bishop Fernando Lugo as leader of a new movement. Lugo won the 2008 elections at the head of the Patriotic Alliance for Change, a coalition of left-wing political parties and organisations (Nickson, 2008). This government developed a new national plan for culture, provided greater budgetary and institutional autonomy to the sector and introduced a number of relevant initiatives in terms of cultural and territorial diversification of cultural policies (SNC, 2010; Zamorano, 2010). However, this political cycle was broken by a parliamentary coup against the Lugo government in 2012.

The contemporary public cultural policy system is integrated through the activities of the National Secretariat of Culture (SNC), the seven governorates, and the more than 250 municipalities with responsibilities in this domain. However, there is a general lack of systematic cultural action at the intermediate and local levels and very limited inter-governmental coordination within this field (Moreira, 2016; Zamorano, 2012).

Cultural management in Paraguay: Historical development, legitimate culture, and main drivers

The cultural policy of the dictatorship is one of the factors explaining the modern forms of professional cultural management in Paraguay. Given a context of minimal public support of cultural production and the repression of civil liberties, cultural management consisted primarily of isolated private initiatives. Within this scenario, various cultural collectives and actors (or exiles such as writers Augusto Roa Bastos and Gabriel Casaccia) mobilised but were repressed in the

1960s and 1970s (Nickson, 1995, p. 128). Different responses to the regime in the artistic field remained linked to high culture, while others related to popular elements, especially theatre and literature (De Los Rios, 2002). Many of these projects were implemented by subordinate actors or groups vindicating an approach towards culture and national identity that placed value on the indigenous vis-a-vis a hegemonic, traditionalist, and narrow vision of culture.

The Visual Arts Centre/*Museo del Barro* emerged from these conditions and is highly explicative of the modern forms adopted by cultural management in the country (Colombino, personal interview, 2020). Currently, it is the most prominent and recognised domestic cultural landmark and one of the most important private museums in South America. Its origins are linked to the art group *Arte Nuevo*, founded in 1954, which was faced with the prevailing academic aesthetic trend and a critical message about political life. After 1972, Olga Blinder and Carlos Colombino, artists and members of the group, developed the *Circulating Collection* project (Bello, 2004), an exhibition of graphic art that toured the country seeking to disseminate visual arts during the dictatorship era. A number of these artists and intellectuals created a valuable collection of modern and indigenous art to develop new spaces for the sector, such as the Museo del Barro. This institution was established in 1979 at the initiative of Carlos Colombino, Osvaldo Salerno, and the art collector Ysanne Gayet. Ysanne Gayet described the period that led to the creation of the museum in the following terms:

> I saw that there was a gap and a very great need to do something in crafts and the Art Gallery here. So, I launched ... my first gallery in 1976 I think it was, in Asunción, on España Avenue in front of the Asunción Tennis Club, which was a Colombino building. Because I saw a need for someone to adopt a serious attitude towards the crafts of Paraguay because there was no place where there were really good, traditional and authentic things.
>
> (Gayet, personal interview, 2010)

The museum focuses on the preservation and dissemination of the visual arts and includes indigenous, popular, and urban-contemporary art (Escobar, 2007) and has more than 4,000 art pieces dating from the seventeenth century. The initiative of Salerno (artist), Colombino (artist and architect), and Gayet (Sri Lanka-born art collector) received support from different sponsors[5] and foreign governments from its inception, including the Swedish International Development Cooperation Agency (SIDCA) and the Spanish Agency for International Development (AECID). Outstanding art and intellectual figures in the country, such as the art critic and theorist Ticio Escobar, have also been involved in the design and development of the project. Against this background, this space experienced an intense process of conceptualisation.

Despite the founding of this museum, at the time of the democratic transition, the cultural network in Paraguay was very limited (González de Bosio, 2003). It included the Municipal Theatre, closed in 1995 due to the degree of deterioration of its building and reopened ten years later, and the National Museum of Fine Arts (*Museo Nacional de Bellas Artes*) which was founded in 1909 and contained a small collection of indigenous visual arts. Another relevant cultural institution during this period was the Juan de Salazar Cultural Centre of Spain (CCEJS) established in 1975 in the centre of Asunción. This member of the network of centres promoting Spanish cultural diplomacy in Latin America has since occupied a prominent place in the cultural life of the city as a space for debate and creative activity, with a particular role in the training of individuals involved in cultural initiatives. Initially, under the influence of the then prevailing Francoist cultural diplomacy in South America, it was later integrated into the network of cultural centres coordinated by the AECID, assuming an approach more focused on local participation (Zamorano, 2012). *High culture* was predominantly centred in the capital, Asunción, although other small cities like Areguá, Ciudad del Este, Encarnación, or Villarrica launched relevant cultural initiatives, especially through institutions such as their universities.

Within this framework, many self-trained cultural managers and actors promoted the institutionalisation of cultural policies. In 1986, the group of intellectuals and artists referred to above participated in a collective known as the Workers of Culture, a broader network of cultural managers which included actors from civil society and cultural promoters (Escobar, 1995). In this manner, the emergence of a group of cultural managers from the 1970s onward seeking to develop and modernise the administration of arts and cultural heritage in Paraguay was largely related to private or non-profit initiatives by artists, curators, or experts in different cultural fields. These actors were increasingly organised and counted on the growing support of international cooperation bodies, private sponsors, and, with the return of democracy, the Asunción City Council.

Transformation of the cultural field and management system since 1989

The establishing of democracy accelerated the aforementioned transformations, facilitating the emergence of new cultural projects and actors. For instance, indigenous art gained space through the San Lorenzo-based Guido Boggiani Archaeological and Ethnographic Museum, set up in 1989 and funded by the anthropologist José Antonio Perasso (Malinowski & Baptista, 2004). Two main innovations fostered the gradual institutionalisation of cultural management during the 1990s. On the one hand, many actors who were participating in or on the periphery of the Museo del Barro project entered the capital's administration, subsequently promoting the professionalisation of the cultural field. Ticio Escobar was designated Director of Culture of the City Council for the period 1991–1996. His network introduced a plural understanding of culture into the public domain and dynamised the urban cultural field (Bogado, 1997; Zarza, 2007).

Public initiatives were promoted by cultural actors executing the role of cultural manager, such as the case of the Cinematheque Foundation established in the Asunción Municipality during the final year of the dictatorship. The cinema producer Hugo Gamarra, promoter of the project, stated:

> Then, through these situations and with the enthusiasm of the Director of Culture of the Municipality, the Cinematheque Foundation and Visual archive of Paraguay was created. The Municipality, through its Culture Directorate, becomes a founding member of that non-profit civil entity in November 1989.
>
> (Hugo Gamarra, personal interview, 2010)

On the other hand, the establishment of the UNESCO office in Asunción in 1998 (Soler, 2015), and the activities it promoted legitimised cultural management as a discipline and promoted a significant revitalisation of the cultural domain (Colombino, personal interview, 2020).

Since that time, cultural management has diversified and adopted more specialised standards. However, the socio-cultural framework posed many limitations on independent and private projects that have persisted during the last few decades. When analysing the role and characteristics of cultural managers in contemporary Paraguay, the marginalising nature of the cultural domain at the social level should be considered. According to a survey of the Organisation of Ibero-American States (OEI), less than 8% of the population confirms having gone to the theatre at least once in their lifetime (OEI, 2014, p. 23). Furthermore, only around 20% of the country's population regularly attended the cinema. Variations in access to TV and cinema among the population are high and reflected in contrasting cinema attendance between Asunción and the rest of the country (Cultural, 2011). Similarly, a digital divide has been identified (Cultural, 2011; OEI, 2014), which appears to correlate with reduced access to technology in rural areas. Moreover, 61% of the population "never or almost never" read for professional or educational reasons, while the figure for those who have not visited heritage sites during the last 12 months stood at 69% (OEI, 2014). Finally, access to the arts and cultural education remains extremely limited in the country (Lema, 2003).

Only popular events and celebrations appear to experience greater interest. For instance, 73% of surveyed individuals declared that they had attended a musical event during the previous year (OEI, 2014, p. 32), while almost 40% had participated in community or historical celebrations of cultural events at some point during the previous 12 months (OEI, 2014, p. 113).

Despite this context, the relative expansion in citizen participation and the advance of cultural policies enabled specialisation of Paraguay's cultural offer during the first two decades of the twenty-first century (Moreira, 2016; Zamorano, 2012). Examples of this phenomenon include several private and social projects such as the theatre play *Tierra sin Mal* performed by the cast of *Rocemi* from Encarnación. This independent group has staged more than 30 plays in a decade.[6] Moreover, independent galleries such as Planta Alta and Monocromo, in Asunción, have developed ambitious projects (CCEJS, 2014). The main festivals and cultural gatherings form part of the International Film Festival, a private initiative inaugurated in 1989 as the *Festival de la Capital* (Capital City Festival) and subsequently developed with the support of international sponsors and the state.[7] These include the International Theatre Festival of Encarnación, organised by the aforementioned cast of *Rocemi*, the Book Fair organised since 2014 by the non-profit association Asunción Paraguay Book Chamber (CLAP), the biennial photography exhibition *El Ojo Salvaje*, in 2011, coordinated by Jorge Sáenz, author and founding editor of the synonymous collective, and the international World Harp Festival,[8]the staging of most also drew support from public administrations. In this period, film production in Paraguay increased slightly and was internationally recognised due to films such as *Hamaca Paraguaya* (2006) and *7 cajas* (2012), both of which received support from FONDEC.

Among the interesting projects developed in the city centre is the *Puerto Abierto* (Open Harbour). Established in 2011, it constitutes a popular initiative that, promoted by activists such as María Glauser and supported by the City Council, sanctioned the development of several activities, concerts, and art craft fairs. Most of these activities are managed by artists or producers active in each domain and receive the financial support of the SNC or attract international cooperation in addition to private sponsorship.

Despite this increasing activity, the cultural system, still concentrated in Asunción, remains highly limited in terms of its offer, demand, and mechanisms for consecration. Public institutions are predominantly located in the capital. They include the Municipal Theatre under the auspices of the City Council, the Cabildo Cultural Centre (founded in 2004) which depends on the legislative body, and a limited number of museums, including the National Museum of Fine Arts (established in 1909) (González de Bosio, 2003). In addition, the National Ballet (1992), supported by the ProBallet Foundation, and the National Symphonic Orchestra (2008), both dependent on the SNC are worthy of mention. Fine Arts education largely depends on the Higher Institute of Art, forming part of the National University in Asunción, and the Higher Institute of Fine Arts, in addition to the support of the Ministry of Education, the Municipal Institute of Arts, and the Municipality of Asunción.

Turning to the private sector, the main cultural spaces include art galleries, such as the Ricardo Migliorisi Foundation, and less extensive ones such as the Centre Cultural Citibank, Itaú Cultural, and Fausto Cultural, in addition to a very limited circuit of cinemas and commercial theatres, bookstores, and libraries. The majority of these projects depend on funds provided by companies or agents possessing important economic capital which are liberal in their patronage. For instance, the Museum of Sacred Art (2010), which contains a significant collection of Hispano-Guaraní Baroque artefacts, is a personal initiative developed through the private foundation of an individual collector (Fundación Nicolás Darío Latourrette Bo).

Over the last few decades, a gradual decentralisation has occurred leading to the development of local cultural projects, even though the national circulation of assets and centre-periphery relations remain limited (Moreira, personal interview, 2020). Examples of such projects include the Centro Cultural del Lago (2010), la Casa Amarilla – a community cultural space managed by local youth, and El

Cántaro, a popular school established in Areguá that offers locals the opportunity to participate in a series of free popular creative workshops. This city, boasting a great artisanal tradition, has cemented its reputation as a bohemian and "alternative" city. The Association of Areguá Artisans numbers approximately 150 artisans from the city among its members who specialise in clay ceramics. They share installations, a kiln, and a space for advertising products, courses, and training initiatives, in addition to providing materials to their members. Numerous other potters in the region work autonomously. The city was designated a "creative city" by UNESCO in 2019 (Olmedo-Barchello et al., 2020). The application had been presented by a group of civil society organisations and cultural managers of the city, including the *Association of Areguá Artisans* in an attempt to promote the local productive fabric. Among its number is the Centro Cultural del Lago, established in 2010 which promotes craft work conceptually framed and exhibited as art, focusing on autochthonous pre-colonial artisan traditions. Its director, Ysanne Gayet, has been highly active in the promotion of this approach to artisan craft within the country and has conducted several relevant activities in this regard. Interestingly, Gayet has recently asserted that artisans may "produce fewer pieces, but of higher quality" (Diario Hoy Paraguay, 2020).

These local projects coexist with a rich set of popular celebrations and cultural events in many cities or villages, such as the Carnivals of Incarnation, Areté Guasú in Santa Teresita, Para'aná Ra'anga, Curusu Yeguia, and Tañarendy, mostly organised by local communities, in some cases, with the support of municipalities.

Public-private governance and cultural management in the 2000s

Due to the limited private investment and demand, cultural management is highly dependent on public funding. As indicated above, various socio-political transformations favoured the diversification of the cultural field from the beginning of the twentieth century. Among the limited number of incentives to the development of cultural management and cultural production, that of public instruments such as the FONDEC has been crucial (Salerno, 2001). Independent projects such as the Fundación Pro Ballet, the association Crear en Libertad, and Arlequín Teatro have received the support of FONDEC and other public institutions to develop their activities since the 1990s (Zamorano, 2012). Transformations in the public sphere were accompanied by numerous innovations concerning the projection of Paraguayan arts, such as new spaces for artists at biennial events and cultural activities in foreign countries, in addition to unprecedented demands from cultural managers.

The new cultural policy scenario of the 2000s promoted the configuration of a novel framework for the involvement of social organisations in cultural management. New public-private governance spaces and structures emerged within it. Firstly, the Paraguayan Coalition for Cultural Diversity was created in 2006. This entity is composed of ten professional cultural organisations, representatives of civil society and the performing arts, film and audio-visual, music, publishing, and cultural industry sectors. Its main objectives are the approval and ratification of the UNESCO Convention on the Protection and Promotion of the Diversity of Cultural Expressions and to work towards its fulfilment. Secondly, in 2008, with the formation of a new government, the Permanent Forum for Culture was established as a civil society initiative following the process of political change occurring in the country after decades of Colorado Party hegemony. The forum held 12 meetings in May and July of that year grouping cultural promoters, managers, and artists together with representatives of all partners across the country (Martínez, 2018). Thirdly, the Paraguayan Audio-visual Federation managed to induce the Secretary of Culture to introduce audio-visual policies in 2004 and subsequently promoted the promulgation of a Cinema Law (Hugo Gamarra, personal interview, 2010), passed in 2018, and the intervention of social organisations striving to preserve the Guaraní language, which pushed for the establishment of the post of Secretary for Language Policies in 2012 (Moreira, 2016).

The governance of cultural policies reached a new level of public-private articulation based on these bottom-up initiatives. Post 2006, institutional amendments promoted new developments regarding participation in public cultural management. As part of the National Law for Culture (2006), many of the organisations mentioned above were integrated into the public action by the SNC through the newly established *Consejo Nacional de Cultura* (CONCULTURA). By 2015, eight cultural sectors (Dance, Music, Visual Arts, Theatre, People of African Descent, Human Rights, LGTBI, Books and Literature) and more than 40 social organisations had been represented in the Council (Moreira, 2016, p. 205). Several of these associations or unions grouped several organisations together to create an extended network of actors. Mainly from 2008 onwards, the approach to cultural rights was not restricted to traditional cultural sectors, but integrated other fields related to an anthropological and political conception of cultural policies.

As occurred with the Asunción City Council during the transition to democracy, the establishment of the new government and SNC in 2008, together with the integration of the group of actors around the Museo del Barro into the institutional domain, transformed the governance of culture (Martínez, 2018). An additional element supporting a novel governance approach to cultural management was that of a certain decentralisation of public cultural action which had supported the intervention of the municipalities since 2008 (Moreira, 2016). However, several limitations on this process have been identified. On the one hand, this period was characterised by political instability and, even though resources increased significantly, the public budget remained limited and local investment extremely low. On the other hand, many restrictions on cultural participation and engagement have been recognised. For instance, indigenous organisations and any form of representation within CONCULTURA were both absent. It has already been mentioned that Western definitions of political representation at the institutional level were not compatible with the organisational forms of native communities which, consequently, limited their intervention (Moreira, 2016, p. 206). With regard to a broader understanding of the cultural sectors, restrictions on social participation have also been explained by the existence of corporate structures closely aligned with sectorial interests (Moreira, personal interview, 2020).

In this regard, the transformation of state intervention modalities within the cultural field created the conditions for the emergence of internal political tensions. Cultural sectors achieved unprecedented levels of corporate organisation and sought to enhance their negotiating capacity within a new institutional framework. Alejandra Díaz Lanz, cultural manager, dance teacher, and representative of the Paraguayan Coalition for Cultural Diversity, commented on their demands at the time:

> It's a "chicken and egg" situation. You want to stage a production, you want open cultural trade with the world, have something to show, what to produce, have new creators. Why is a new artist going to create something if he doesn't satisfy the minimum conditions? ... I practiced for six months with the dancers on the patio, under the tree, on the ground.
>
> (Alejandra Díaz, personal interview, 2010)

Besides sectorial-focused demands and corporatism, during the period 2008–2012, the cultural field also experienced confrontations due to the repositioning of culture within the political field (Martínez, 2018). For instance, the architect Alfredo Vaesken, director of the commission in charge of the Takuare'ê Festival, one of the most important in the domestic folkloric field since 1977, stated:

> I think, categorically, that even Stroessner was more supportive of folklore. This is the worst government for popular culture. In times of the Colorados if you had the political support, you received a lot of support from Itaipú.[9]
>
> (*La Nación*, 2010 p. 6)

In this way, within the context of a certain redistribution of cultural capital, cultural management was transformed due to the adoption of unprecedented mediation perspectives by the actors participating in the cultural field. In this regard, even though the Museo del Barro is said to have been very influential in the definition of cultural management discourses in Paraguay, its discourses remain disputed (Moreira, personal interview, 2020). Rather, the existence of corporate structures at the sectorial and public-private governance level, together with different types of clientele, have been underlined as factors framing these antagonisms and configuring cultural management in general. While the legitimacy of the museum is considered hegemonic, the entire cultural field would remain aligned to more conservative, folklorist, or sectorial definitions of culture (Lia Colombino,[10] personal interview, 2020).

Cultural management training in Paraguay

Until 2018, no official academic instruction in the field of cultural management was available at undergraduate or postgraduate levels in Paraguay (Lema, 2003; Moreira, 2016). Cultural management training consists predominantly of isolated public and private programmes or courses that focus on providing tools to improve the administration of concrete cultural projects or organisational policies. The interviewees stressed the lack of conceptualisation of cultural management and weak adaptability to the previously explained conditions of the cultural field as handicaps. Consequently, the "empirical" remains the primary school in a country with weak legitimacy for the role of cultural manager.

As indicated above, most of the pioneers working professionally in this domain come from other fields or disciplines, for example, Ticio Escobar – curator/lawyer, Carlos Colombino – architect/artist, or Ysanne Gayet, who started out as an art collector, despite lacking specific training in cultural management. These individuals trained and became specialised in the process of project development. A new generation of specialists such as Susana Salerno subsequently attended postgraduate courses abroad, predominantly in Spain, mainly due to their high quality and the language of instruction. In some cases, such courses are delivered online and involve work with experienced managers or in the specific spaces identified above.

It should be noted that many activities are promoted by non-governmental organisations (NGOs) or foreign institutions such as the CCEJS. The latter developed the AECID-organised ACERCA training programme which featured numerous courses on Cultural Management (CCEJS, 2014). These courses were attended by many entrepreneurs and social organisations from across the country. Foreign teachers were also delivering lectures within this scenario, thereby ensuring the continuity of Spanish cultural diplomacy in Paraguay. The seminar Espacio Crítica, founded in 2000 and coordinated at the Museo del Barro by Ticio Escobar, produced many courses each with several participants. This training was related to cultural management but has been largely aimed at framing the theoretical debate concerning the legitimising definitions of Paraguayan arts, identity, and culture. This core of critical thinking skills, associated with a new generation of intellectuals linked to the museum's network, has been crucial in the conceptualisation of culture in recent years, acting as a form of "meta-reflection" underpinning cultural management activity. For Lia Colombino, who participated in this seminar for eight years, it represents her main formal education in the field of cultural management, even though she obtained a Masters in Museology from Valladolid University (Lia Colombio, personal interview, 2020).

Other NGOs, for example, Estación A Nucleo Central, have developed courses in this area such as Systematization of the Solidarity Circuits Project (CIRSOL). This process provided mechanisms for the economic-cultural development of five artisan communities in the Central Department of Paraguay, implemented by and receiving the support of the Inter-American Foundation between 2011 and 2015.[11] As outlined by Moreira (personal interview, 2020), such activities promote concrete development and have a meaningful impact since they are irregular, often sectorial, and offer problem-oriented tools.

Civil servants have also received training in related topics through seminars or public courses, mainly during the period 2008–2012. Activities have been developed within the Centro Cultural de la República "El Cabildo" and also the

SNC with a certain degree of training for public managers at the provincial level. Each of these public and social initiatives has focused on providing instruments to managers in specific domains related to culture, thereby enabling them to further develop their projects or attend to their public duties (SNC, 2010).

At the tertiary education level, two salient experiences must be highlighted. In 2012, an inter-university project, supported by the AECID, was implemented by the Universities of Barcelona (Spain) and Asunción (Paraguay) and sought to contribute to the development of decentralised professional and institutional capacities in the cultural field through research, analysis, and training. As part of this project, academic staff from the University of Asunción were trained in cultural management, while the university itself received resources (such as books and training scholarships) to establish a postgraduate course in the subject. However, this course never materialised. In 2018, a Diploma in Cultural Management delivered by the private Universidad Autónoma del Paraguay (UAP) and the NGO Paraguay Cultural was launched. The training of university lecturers abroad was supported by the National Secretariat of Culture, and the programme was boosted by the Asociación Nacional Nosotros Somos and the World Trade Centre of Asunción. The international training of academics was heralded as an advantage of the programme.[12]

To sum up, these different training programmes and mechanisms, mostly centralised in the capital, do not treat cultural management as a comprehensive and systematic field of knowledge. Moreover, as indicated by Moreira, neither studies nor indicators concerning the impact of the above professional development programmes exist which would be crucial to identifying the role of these activities within the cultural system (Moreira, personal interview, 2020).

Discussion

The structural conditions framing cultural management in Paraguay are highly illuminating with regard to its orientation and development. The form of capitalism developed in the country, to a large extent based on extractivist and agro-export industries, has not required significant state promotion of cultural and related service sectors. However, this scenario has not facilitated private sector support of cultural development either. Within this context, a set of cultural-specific elements restricts the transformative potential of cultural management and determines the relative impact of isolated training programmes on the discipline developed during the last decade. Mediation by cultural managers is conditioned by reduced cultural consumption, sectorial corporatism, and a lack of public mechanisms for boosting both public demand and cultural production (Moreira, 2016; Zambrano, 2010; Zamorano, 2010). The feudalisation of the public field in relation to the cultural policies of many Latin American countries elucidated by Canclini (1987, p. 147) is, therefore, crucial to an understanding of the Paraguayan context within which cultural management is implemented.

The main professional pathways to cultural management in this context involve artists, collectors, politicians, or experts operating within a particular field, in addition to the representatives of cultural minorities or collectives, who become or act as cultural managers. Initially, art and cultural managers were intellectuals and artists with access to higher education in their academic disciplines who, in many cases, had lived or studied abroad. This phenomenon means that those actors leading the private cultural initiatives shared a certain economic and cultural capital. Many of these professionals also shared networks or experiences abroad and were participating in subaltern movements against the dictatorship. The survival of a subaltern popular tradition in the twentieth century was reflected in the development of movements managing culture (Escobar, 2004). Sources of legitimacy for this initial professionalisation of the activity comprised the Museo del Barro and the support of international organisations and public institutions.

A critical element in the orientation and legitimacy of cultural management as a discipline has been the vindication of popular and indigenous arts and established spaces for their promotion since the democratic transition. Different spaces and projects were proposed within a mixed approach to national identity which included elements from modern arts and a renewed understanding of popular expression. Their material basis often came from private collections such as in the cases of Yssane Gayet, Nicolás Darío Latourrette Bo, Ticio Escobar, and José Antonio Perasso, among others. The museology of these spaces reflects the deconstruction of the Western definition of arts, where indigenous art is re-inscribed and developed by a group of actors active in the cultural field (Escobar, 2004). On this philosophical basis, these spaces also identified mechanisms for establishing a successful relationship with institutions abroad and the State to promote democratisation. The political influence and quality of this project contrast sharply with the weak museological and public heritage basis of the country.

During the last few decades, innovative public policies and increasing cultural consumption, mainly in major cities, have positively influenced the diversification of cultural management. Actors have adopted its international discourse, including the establishment of the figure of the cultural manager. This process included an increase in the number of training courses or the integration of bottom-up cultural managers into the public field (Moreira, 2016). A second and third generation of managers is currently developing several projects in this diversified but limited cultural field. Moreover, as explained by Lia Colombino (personal interview, 2020), trans-generational transferences are produced through the intervention of their collaboration within public institutions, the establishment of forums such as the *Espacio Crítica*, or the direct training of new experts in the field. However, the development and formal training of cultural managers depends, to a large extent, on heritage as well as economic and social capital. Training programmes have tended to be sporadic and highly reliant on foreign investment. Furthermore, this development has often been led by international managers and institutions which are accessed by a very restricted group of actors, key sources of legitimacy, and funding for the discipline within Paraguay.

Despite these exclusionary elements and the lack of specialisation, the role of cultural managers and bottom-up organisations has been crucial for the development of the cultural system. Organised cultural managers have prompted the State to open spaces and instruments for concrete cultural sectors. Local cultural networks and self-management of artistic projects largely explain the domestic development of the discipline. Moreover, what Lia Colombino terms the "artist-etcetera", as a way of emphasising the informal character of the discipline, illustrates the general trend in this domain (Lia Colombino, personal interview, 2020).

> Here, given that you are public servant, there is no other way of practising that self-management. It is very difficult. And the self-management relates to obtaining funds, for instance, potentially dividing your activity into two strands, one that generates funding for the other that is really of primary interest, to you. And there are several individuals in this pathway
> (Lia Colombino, personal interview, 2020)

The primary sources of cultural projects that lead to the production of specific management strategies are frequently associated with the particular needs of a sector, collective, or artist. This has implications for the above-mentioned corporatist dynamics within the cultural field. As a part of these approaches, culture is often understood to constitute "the arts" and organisations striving to promote their products and open markets for their own sectors. The precariousness of most sectorial markets and lack of public support define the forms in which sector needs are framed and addressed, as well as the management of popular arts. This phenomenon can be illustrated through the case of the social organisations and cultural managers of Areguá aiming to promote local economic development based on popular traditions. As Ysanne Gayet asserts, one of the most urgent challenges is, therefore, providing added value to the craftwork production. This approach may be partially explained because, while the figure of the artisan is socially respected, his/her production is not supported economically (Lia, personal interview, 2020). The sectorial and economic focus of many cultural management projects also reveals the continuity of the above-delineated structural limitations for mediators. Within this framework, a crucial challenge for cultural management consists of not reducing the support to grassroots and popular culture, thereby fostering both the commercialisation and social appreciation of art, crafts, and the popular arts.

Notes

1 In addition, there are small colonies of immigrants from Germany, Korea, Japan, and other countries.
2 It should be noted that Paraguay constitutes the only country in South America with a constitutionally recognised bilingual status.
3 The interviewees included cultural managers (Alejandra Díaz, Beatriz Krasniansky, María Gloria González, Adelina Pusineri, Lía Colombino, José Luis Ardissone, Hugo Gamarra, and Ysanne Gayet), cultural experts (Ramiro Domínguez and Bartomeu Melià), and civil servants active in the cultural field (Ana Mello, Vladimir Velázquez Moreira, and Marcelo Acuña) (SNC).
4 Funded through a tax levied on the national lottery, this autonomous public agency represented an important instrument for supporting artistic and cultural industries projects.

 5 During its early years, the museum was sponsored by the tobacco company Benson &
   Hedges.
 6 Description of the group at http://rocemi.com.py/index.php/resena-historica/.
 7 Information available at: http://cinefestpy.org/sobre-el-festival.
 8 Further information available at: http://www.festivalmundialdelarpa.com.py/.
 9 Itaipu is a bi-national hydroelectric dam on the Paraná River located on the Brazil-
   Paraguay border.
10 Lia Colombino is cultural manager with more than 20 years of professional experience
   gained at the Museo del Barro.
11 Estación A Nucleo Central had previously developed similar projects with support
   from the European Community.
12 See: http://www.cultura.gov.py/2018/07/inician-diplomado-de-gestion-cultural/.

References

Arditi, B. & Rodríguez, J. C. (1987). *La Sociedad a pesar del Estado. Movimientos sociales y recuperación democrática en el Paraguay*. Asunción: El lector.

Bareiro, L. & Soro, L. (2008). Regulación jurídica de los partidos Políticos en Paraguay. In: Zovatto, D. (Ed.) *Regulación jurídica de los partidos políticos en América Latina*. Mexico: Legal Research Institute UNAM. pp. 739–766.

Barreda, M. & Costafreda, A. (2002). La Transición Democrática y el Sistema Político Institucional. In: Pratts & Català, J. (Ed.), *Diagnóstico Institucional de la República del Paraguay*. Asunción: IIG. pp. 71–126.

Bayardo, R. (2019). Repensando la gestión cultural en Latinoamérica. In: Yeñez Canal, C. (Ed.) *Praxis de la gestión cultura*. Bogotá: National University of Colombia. pp. 17–31.

Bello, C. A. (2004). *Somos patrimonio*. Bogotá: Andrés Bello Convention.

Bogado, V. (1997). Paraguay: Teatro y transición democrática, *Latin American Theatre Review*: 30 (2): pp. 131–138.

Castineira de Dios, J. (2009). Crítica de la Gestión Cultural pura, *Revista Aportes*, 23: pp. 79–92.

Causarano, M. (2012). Paraguay: de rural a urbano. *Revista del Bicentenario, ATLAS*.

CCEJS (2014). Centro Cultural de España Plan de Centro 2014. Asunción.

Cultural, O. (2011). *Información Estadística. Sobre Cine y TV Recopilada por el Observatorio Cultural Centro Cultural de la República El Cabildo*. Asunción.

Diario HOY Paraguay (2020). *Areguá, herencia de ancestros, donde del barro se hace arte*. Asunción.

De La Vega, P. (2016). Gestión cultural y despolitización: Cuando nos llamaron gestores, *ÍNDEX, revista de arte contemporáneo*, 2(2): pp. 96–102. https://dialnet.unirioja.es/descarga/articulo/6023734.pdf (Accessed October 29, 2020).

De Los Rios, E. (2002). *Dos caras del Teatro Paraguayo*. Alicante: Salvat.

DeVereaux, C. (2009). Practice versus a discourse of practice in cultural management, *The Journal of Arts Management, Law, and Society*, 39(1): pp. 65–72.

——— (2011). *Cultural Management and Its Boundaries: Past, Present and Future*. Helsinki: HUMAK.

DGEEC (2005). *Población indígena*. Fernando de la Mora.

Dubois, V. (2013). *Cultural Policy Regimes in Western Europe*. HAL, https://www.researchgate.net/publication/278619118_Cultural_Policy_Regimes_in_Western_Europe.

Escobar Argaña, A. (2007). Legislación Paraguaya y Normativa Internacional: Un estudio comparativo. In: *Legislaciones en el MERCOSUR relativas a las Convenciones de*

Cultura aprobadas por la UNESCO. Estudio de la situación actual en Argentina, Brasil, Paraguay y Uruguay. Montevideo: UNESCO. pp. 103–117.

Escobar, T. (1995). *Sobre cultura y mercosur.* Asunción: Ediciones Don Bosco.

—— (2004). El Mito del Arte y el Mito del Pueblo. In: Acha, J., Colombres, A. & Escobar, T. (Eds.) *Hacia una Teoría Americana del Arte.* Buenos Aires: Del Sol. pp. 85–106.

—— (2007). Los Desafíos del Museo: El caso del Museo Del Barro en Paraguay. In: Gant, M.L. (Ed.) *Aprendiendo de Latinoamérica. El Museo Como protagonista.* Gijón: Trea. pp. 55–72.

—— (2011). *Exposición de Motivos de la Ley Nacional de Cultura.* Asunción.

Fogel, R. & Palau, T. (1989). Las transformaciones en la cultura cotidiana bajo los efectos de la modernización conservadora. In: Calderón Gutiérrez, F. & dos Santos, M. (Eds.), *¿Hacia un nuevo orden estatal en América Latina? Innovación cultural y actores socio-culturales.* Buenos Aires: CLACSO. pp. 315–334.

García Canclini, N. (1987). Introducción. Políticas Culturales y crisis de desarrollo: Un balance latinoamericano. In: García Canclini, N. & Bonfil Batalla, G. (Eds.) *Políticas culturales en América Latina.* México: Grijalbo. pp. 13–61.

General Auditor's Office of the Republic. (2007). Final Report. Resolution *CGR n° 1296/06.* Asunción.

González de Bosio, B. (2003). *La cultura en el aula. Material de Apoyo Didáctico para Docentes.* Asunción: Publications Centre of the Catholic University. http://corredor delasideas.org/wp-content/uploads/2019/09/La-cultura-en-el-aula-Primera-versio%CC%81n.pdf (Accessed October 29, 2020).

Harvey, E. (2014). *Políticas culturales en America Latina.evolución histórica, instituciones públicas, experiencias.* Madrid: Iberautor.

Henze, R. (2017). *Introduction to International Arts Management.* Wiesbaden: Springer.

La nación (2010). *Este es el peor gobierno para la cultura popular.* Asunción.

Lema, G. (2003). Cultura: el derecho postergado, In Cacace, S.M. et al (Eds.), *Derechos humanos en Paraguay.* Asunción: CODEHUPY, Human Rights Coordinator of Paraguay. http://biblioteca.clacso.edu.ar/Paraguay/cde/20121001043920/culturales 2003.pdf (Accessed October 29, 2020).

Malinowski, M. I. & Baptista, S. (2004). Bartomeu Melià Jesuíta, Lingüista e Antropólogo: Os Guarani como Compromisso de Vida. *Campos,* 5(1): pp. 167–182.

Martínez, D. (2018). *Cultura Política y Política Cultural: Un acercamiento a la intervención del campo artístico en la gestión cultural pública durante el periodo de 2006–2012 en Paraguay.* Thesis for the Degree in Visual Arts at the Instituto Superior de Arte "Dra Olga. Blinder" of the National University of Asuncion – Faculty of Architecture, Design and Art. Available at https://acortar.link/WYae9 (Accessed October 29, 2020).

Molinas Vega, J. (2000). ¿Liberalización Económica con Sesgo Urbano en Paraguay? Microsimulaciones del Efecto de los Cambios en el Mercado Laboral sobre la Distribución del Ingreso y Pobreza, *Economía y sociedad,* XXII Congreso Internacional Latin American Studies Association (LASA), Miami, Florida, March 16–18.

Moreira, V. (2016). Aproximación a la g estión cultur al públic a en Paraguay. In: Rubim, A., Yañez Canal, C. & Bayardo, R. (Eds.) *Panorama Da Gestão Cultural na Ibero-América.* Salvador de Bahía: EDUFBA. pp. 199–219.

Nickson, A. (1995). Paraguay's archivos del terror, *Latin American Research Review,* 30(1): pp. 125–129.

—— (2008). Una oportunidad para Paraguay. Los desafíos de Fernando Lugo, *Nueva Sociedad,* 216: pp. 5–16.

OECD (2019). *Latin American Economic Outlook 2019: Development in Transition.* Paris: OECD Publishing.

OEI (2014). *Encuesta Latinoamericana de hábitos y prácticas culturales.* Madrid.

Olmedo-Barchello, S., Cristaldo, J. C., Rodríguez, G., da Silva, M., Acosta, A. & Barrios, O. (2020). Ciudades creativas y su aporte a la creación de un nuevo modelo de desarrollo económico, social y cultural. Una revisión de la literatura, Población y Desarrollo, 26(50): pp. 53–63.

Paquette, J. & Redaelli, E. (2015). *Arts Management and Cultural Policy Research.* London: Palgrave.

Rodríguez Morató, A. (2012). El análisis de la política cultural en perspectiva sociológica. Claves introductorias al estudio del caso español, *Revista de investigaciones políticas y sociológicas,* 11(3): pp. 15–38.

Rodríguez Morató, A. & Zamorano, M. M. (2019). *Cultural Policy in Ibero-America.* New York: Routledge.

Rubim, A., Yañez Canal, C. & Bayardo, R. (2016). *Panorama da gestão cultural na Ibero-América.* Salvador de Bahía: EDUFBA.

Salerno, S. (2001). *Gestión cultural en países en vías de desarrollo. Investigación-acción sobre Legislación cultural en Paraguay.* Madrid: Complutense University of Madrid.

Salvador Barrios, O. (2006). La experiencia paraguaya del Censo Nacional Indígena 2002. In *Pueblos indígenas y afrodescendientes de América Latina y el Caribe: información sociodemográfica para políticas y programas.* Working paper. Santiago de Chile: Naciones Unidas. https://www.cepal.org/mujer/noticias/noticias/5/27905/pueblosindi genas_afro.pdf (Accessed January 12, 2020).

SNC (2010). Mandu'a. Memoria de la Secretaria Nacional de Cultura 2009. Asunción.

Soler, L. (2015). La amistad en tiempos de guerra fría. Reconstrucción de la historia de cruzada mundial de la amistad en paraguay en las décadas de 1970 y 1980, Revista de la Red Intercátedras de Historia de América Latina Contemporánea, 2(3): pp. 75–92.

Suteu, C. (2006). *Another Brick in the Wall – A Critical Review of Cultural Management Education in Europe.* Amsterdam: Boekmanstudies.

Zambrano, L. (2010). *El Rostro vedado de la voz: (Ayvu rova ikatu'ÿva jahecha).* Zurich: University of Zurich.

Zamorano, M. M. (2010). *Paraguay, un modelo para armar: estudio histórico y diagnóstico actual de sus políticas culturales públicas.* Thesis for the Master's Degree in Cultural Management, University of Barcelona, Barcelona.

——— (2012). La evolución de las políticas culturales del Paraguay: Hegemonías y transformaciones, *Cuadernos de observación en gestión y políticas culturales,* 1(1): pp. 8–23.

Zamorano, M. M., Ulldemolins, J. R. & Klein, R. (2014). Toward a South American model of cultural policy? Singularities and convergences in the development of the cultural policies of Uruguay, Paraguay and Chile in the twenty-first century, *European Review of Latin American and Caribbean Studies,* 96pp. 5–34.

Zarza, O. (2007). Prácticas Culturales desde el Estado en la transición democrática paraguaya. El caso del Municipio de Asunción. *Lecture presented at the General Assembly of the Interlocal Network of Ibero-American Cities for Culture,* Costa Rica, November.

8 Cultural management in Chile

Between professionalisation and the emergence of a public intervention category

Norma Muñoz del Campo

Introduction

When considering the emergence of a public intervention category, in other words, a sector of public policy action, the training dynamics of a body of professionals possessing specific skills and knowledge, capable of implementing such policies must be addressed. Therefore, it is necessary to understand how, within the Chilean context, culture was transformed into a sphere of public action and to analyse the contemporary development of cultural management and the training of cultural managers.

The cultural institutionalisation process in Chile took place within the context of the democratisation, following the overthrow of Pinochet´s dictatorship in 1990, which precipitated state reform and modernisation. This process led, in 2003, to the creation of the first senior governmental institution in the field of culture in the country: The National Council for Culture and the Arts (CNCA). The creation of this institution led, at the turn of the 21st century, to what was known as a *State Cultural Policy*. The professionals employed by this institution were self-taught in an intuitive manner, learning through trial and error within a collaborative management framework, long before the inception of the CNCA. They were then confronted with a new, more technocratic perspective of cultural management upon which the CNCA itself was based.[1] The role of contemporary Chilean cultural managers is rooted in this tension that still defines the nature of their training. The second period of reform began with the debate that led to the creation of the Ministry of Cultures, Arts and Heritage in 2017, more than ten years after that of the CNCA. This period promoted an incipient professionalism due to the introduction of training focused on cultural and/or heritage management. From the moment of its founding, this ministry was composed of a body of professionals drawn from the ranks of the CNCA and of graduates of the training programmes established as a result of its creation.

The profile of the contemporary Chilean cultural manager results from inherent tensions between paradigms emerging during the period of institutionalisation culminating in the creation of the CNCA: one relating to her autodidactic and intuitive character, the other concerning her specialised knowledge. Furthermore, it is important to stress that professional training is determined by the cultural policies implemented and the nature of arts and culture-related activity funding.

This chapter addresses two main issues. The first is institutional evolution and the definitional struggles of cultural activity that stem from the different dynamics and spaces generating the two founding paradigms of cultural management. The second is the development of cultural management training, its characteristics, its central strands, and its status in Chile today. The latter allows us to observe the influence that the cultural policy funding body FONDART (*Fondo Nacional para el Desarrollo Cultural y las Artes*) possesses when it comes to defining cultural management training and curriculum planning.

The text will also identify the international, Latin American, and regional influences on the processes related to cultural policy and cultural management training. Doing so will facilitate reflection on this field of public intervention as a discipline – if it has, indeed, been constituted as such – and to undertake a review of its current challenges.

The professionalisation of cultural management: A tension between two policy paradigms

The particular forms of professionalisation recognised within the sociology of professions possess elements such as theoretical knowledge underpinning a particular competence, the development of specialised learning and training, the evaluation of skills of members of the profession through formal examinations, the establishing of a professional organisation, the emergence of a professional code, and the provision of an altruistic service (Dubois, 1999, p. 352).

The specific nature of the professionalisation of cultural management is that gaining vocational qualifications is driven more by the need to develop practical skills than obtaining theoretical or specialised knowledge. This reality is fundamental to understanding the inherent tensions within the professionalisation process. Although it would have been possible to identify examples of local cultural management, as well as emblematic cultural managers in Latin American history; for example, José Vasconcelos in Mexico, Luis Emilio Recabarren in Chile, or Mario Andrade and "*El grupo de cinco*" (The *group of five*) in Brazil (Nivón and Sánchez, 2012, pp. 7–11), the current process of professionalisation is rooted more in international relations and knowledge transfer (Ponte, this volume). In this regard, two UN meetings are regarded as milestones: Mexico (UNESCO,1982) (Mejía Arango, 2009, p. 108; García Canclini, 1987, pp. 16–17) and Stockholm (1998) (IBERFORMAT, 2004, p. 9). The former recognised culture as the axis of development processes within the region, promoting their institutionalisation, while the latter identified the need to professionalise the sector. "The confluence of the dynamism between public cultural policies, private initiative and the development of civil society organizations or the so-called third sector" (UNESCO OEI and Iberformat, 2004, p. 30) also certainly plays a role when it comes to the professionalisation of the cultural sector within the Chilean context.

As previously mentioned, contemporary dynamics in Chile that shape and constitute cultural management arise from the confluence of two mutually influencing paradigms. The first is self-taught and intuitive, building specialisation through learning based on a retrospective analysis of past experiences. This developed from a process of trial and error that emerged in the 1990s within the Culture Division, a unit of the Ministry of Education. The second involves specialised, rational, technocratic knowledge, driven by the cultural paradigm that establishes a category of public intervention as represented by the creation of the CNCA in 2003 (Muñoz, 2011).

The Culture Division: Learning by trial and error

Between the transition to democracy and 2003, when the CNCA was created, the Chilean government comprised three main services relating to cultural activity, namely the Ministry of Education, the Ministry General Secretariat of Government, and the Ministry of Foreign Affairs. Each of these public departments was composed of various culture-related sections and units. "Cultural Policies in Chile: Mapa Institucional, Legislativo y Financiero (Segegob, 1996) listed seven ministries, 11 public divisions (units, departments, and secretariats), 12 foundations, and 11 private corporations active in the late 1990s. However, the most relevant activities playing a fundamental role in the institutionalisation process created by the CNCA (1990–2003) and the ministry (2003–2017) were those delivered by this trio of ministries forming what was referred to as the "three-headed structure" of culture (Muñoz, 2012, p. 105–111).

Within this institutional mapping, two units within the Ministry of Education stand out. First, the Culture Division (with its more than 200 employees) became the basis for the creation of the CNCA, undertaking most of the cultural activities during 1990–2003. It managed private donations to cultural organisations (Valdés' Law[2]) through the Cultural Donations Committee and administered the most important financing instrument for the arts and culture up to the present, FONDART. Second, DIBAM, the Directorate of Libraries, Archives and Museums (employing in excess of 900 employees at the time) was absorbed by the Ministry of Cultures, Arts and Heritage in 2017, despite not forming part of the CNCA project. From 1997 to 2003, the division was headed by Claudio di Girólamo, a prestigious Chilean artist. The civil servants of the time were marked and trained by his form of management which led to the epithet "tribu di Girólamo" (*di Girólamo's tribe*, see Muñoz, 2011, pp. 78, 84) which conveys the concept of a team within which all members had a stake in a small horizontal structure with few resources and where the contributions of all were considered worthwhile. In the near absence of specialisation,[3] learning was based on a process defined by Peter Hall in the political science and public policy fields as the "deliberate attempt to adjust the goals and techniques of policy in response to past experience and new information" (1993, p. 278).

The division's values can be seen in the "Cabildos Culturales" (*town hall meetings*) initiated in 1999. The intention was to create a space for debate at the community level to strengthen a national proposal for cultural development as the Republic approached its bicentenary in 2010.[4] The *Cabildos* promoted a "grassroots" participatory system seeking to develop public spaces and enhance community engagement. They were guided by the concept of "cultural citizenship", introduced in Chile by a speech entitled "Cultural Citizenship, a Navigation Chart towards the Future" delivered by Claudio di Girólamo at the Intergovernmental Conference on Cultural Policies for Development, hosted by Stockholm in 1998. At that conference, both a distinct Latin American identity and citizens' cultural rights enshrined in national constitutions across the region were highlighted as mechanisms to respond to the challenges engendered by globalisation. In this manner, an understanding of cultural policy was established "from within", based on the ability of all individuals to become so-called "prosumers of culture" (di Girólamo, 2000). These values formed the cultural world of that time, while also shaping the division's staff who acted in their defence. An incipient identity had developed within this division involving participatory working practices and a concept of their attributed role, based on a shared social value: contributing to national cultural development.

From the "cultural blackout" to "culture is a task for all": A paradigm, an actor, and an instrument of public policy

Parallel to the activity of the Culture Division, an ongoing debate has existed since the transition to democracy in 1990 regarding the institutionalisation of culture in the country.[5] This process is based on the crystallisation of the paradigm "culture is a task for all", which launched the CNCA and endorsed a technocratic practice and professionalisation accompanying the legitimisation of a new actor and vehicle: the cultural manager and FONDART, respectively (Muñoz 2011, 2013, 2014, 2018). This paradigm supports public cultural policies in Chile and is of vital importance in understanding the role that the cultural manager has played in this configuration up to the present.

Looking at public policies in terms of ideas (Muller, 1995) and, more precisely, the concept of paradigm (Kuhn, 2008; Surel, 1995; Hall, 1993) requires the reviewing of milestones during a period of more than ten years (1990–2003) when the debate focused on two central questions: the importance of culture for societal development (in post-dictatorship contexts) and the type of relationship that could be established between the State and culture against a background of a novel and highly relevant factor – the market. The milestones consisted of two deliberative commissions, the Comisión Ministerial Garretón (1991) and the Comisión Presidential Ivelic (1997), together with a meeting of the National Congress, the Encuentro de Políticas Públicas, Legislación y Propuestas Culturales held in 1996.

The *Garretón Report* (1991) contains the background, analysis, and a proposal for a new Council-type cultural institutionality. It also elucidates the international context that helped to define the role of the State in cultural matters, while highlighting that it is not the State's responsibility "to direct, plan or be the fundamental actor or manager of cultural life" (Garretón, 1991, p. 7). However, the report recommends that the State play an active role at a time of economic internationalisation to "preserve and promote each country's cultural fabric, particularly with regard to heritage". This report underscores the role of UNESCO and international forums in promoting cultural policies, from EUROCULT in Helsinki (1972) to Mexico (1982), while also emphasising the definition that UNESCO coined on that occasion of the concept of culture based on both symbolic and material dimensions which would become the cornerstone of cultural institutionalisation processes in Latin America. These UN meetings and the World Decade for Cultural Development 1988–1997 sought to justify state-sponsored cultural action in collaboration with other actors since the international context showed that citizens valued the decision to create a cultural institutionality "particularly in those cases where there is a concerted action between the State, the private sector (patronage and market), and civil society organizations or associations" (Garretón, 1991, p. 9).

Diverse actors in cultural matters drew on the French model, within which the State is "the" central actor, in seeking a "facilitator" State. This classification is based *on* "the distancing of the government from direct intervention in activities, organisations, and managing the arts" (Chartrand and McCaughey 1989, p. 71) whose implementation commenced with the 1990 law governing private donations. An initiative that encouraged the involvement of private enterprise in the financing of culture culminated in 2003 with the appointment of several actors to the CNCA Board of Directors. The *Ivelic Report* (1997) declared an outstanding debt to culture towards the end of the 1990s and promoted a system of joint public-private sector financing enabling the development of culture through the greater participation by society in general and, more specifically, the private sector. At the same time, there existed the need to balance and harmonise the country's material and spiritual development in order to prevent globalisation from undermining national identity values and Chile from becoming a "large supermarket, where everything is transacted and sold without any reference to those values that are the basis of our being" (Ivelic, 1997, p. 6).

The Chilean model thus encompasses both the State's duty to build the appropriate channels for optimal cultural development and the responsibility that befalls "everyone" to drive it forward. The State should not shoulder full responsibility for cultural matters nor decide their future direction. Civil society, the cultural sector, private companies, and the market are indispensable actors in this model constructed through discourse under the adage "culture is a task for all" (Muñoz, 2011; 2012). Moreover, it is civil society that can "constitute an adequate counterweight to government action in the field of culture" (Navarro, 2006, p. 70). The dictatorship era remains at the forefront of people's minds and it was believed that a paternalistic form of intervention in the cultural field carried potential risks because the very existence of "yet another" authoritarian government could produce a further "cultural blackout" (Subercaseaux, 2006) as happened during the period of autocracy.

To establish a culture-related public action sector within which the contributions of all are valued, numerous spheres interact, and funding is derived from diverse sources. It is, consequently, essential to nominate a single actor, the cultural manager, capable of coordinating all activities.

The cultural manager's role within this configuration is that of articulator and mediator and, as such, it has become an integral part of the Chilean cultural landscape. This constitutes an entrepreneurial interpretation of cultural management resulting from the influence of new public management (NPM) on the world of culture because a successful project is defined as one that is "well-managed". This perspective is also consistent with, and simultaneously influenced by, the objectives of efficiency and effectiveness imposed by the state reform and modernisation process within which the CNCA was created, Changes resulting from this process are registered as "sectoral institutional adjustments" (Segpres, 2006, pp. 159–165).

One instrument is also central to this paradigm: FONDART, created in 1992 through a "glosa" (a budgetary line) in the national budget law. FONDART funding is based on a public tendering system whose panel is composed of artistic community members. This approach ensures a power relationship based on mediation, consultation, and exchange between the State and artists. To some degree comparable to the British arm's length principle, it ensures the legitimisation of activity by the State and actors outside the public sphere in driving cultural policy (Muñoz 2018, p. 222), rendering this instrument the central plank of public funding within the cultural sphere. As such, it both defines and restricts cultural policy in relation to its financing of arts and culture projects, structures a community, and influences the lines of training of cultural management. In other words, it develops a "savoir-faire" around the discipline and confirms its quality as a "technical and social device that organizes specific social relations" (Lascoumes & Le Galès, 2004, p. 13). In short, it organises and distributes power, giving actors outside the public sphere a role in policy formulation and implementation. Nonetheless, it must be remembered that this instrument has also been subject to a series of criticisms, intense polemics, and censorship that have marked its history.

The concepts of efficiency, efficacy, and expertise have become the benchmarks of a new cultural institutionality. These will primarily be managed by Culture Division staff who, as explained above, have a different understanding of "doing culture". There will then ensue a clash between these two intellectual practices, namely the open, participatory, and horizontal organisation of the Culture Division and that implemented through the CNCA which is marked by a technocratisation of cultural policies.

The advent of the Ministry of Cultures, Arts and Heritage almost 15 years after the creation of the CNCA introduced a chain of meanings and practices stemming from the aforementioned trajectory. The cultural manager and the technocrat coexist with a cultural mediator, a public cultural administrator, and territorial agents. The inauguration of the ministry also occurred two decades after the professionalisation of culture was initiated (the first cultural management programme having been established at the end of the 1990s) and its existence will progressively legitimise these functions. Employment within the cultural sector will no longer mean working in a minor State sector. Rather, it constitutes a role similar to any other that will be executed by appropriately trained individuals.

The artist: A Quixotic figure

Historically, the artistic community has been confronted by an extremely fragile environment riddled with gaps and highly dependent on scarce funding from
public authorities. At the time of the dictatorship's overthrow in 1990, only two
formally established groups existed: the Society of Chilean Writers (SECH), established in 1931, and the Association of Painters and Sculptors of Chile (APECH),
founded in 1940. Prior to 1990, the only protection for artistic work was provided
by the 1972 Law on Intellectual Property that had not been substantially modified
until the re-introduction of democracy. The Chilean Copyright Society (SCD) was
not created until 1987. The following professional bodies were subsequently created: the Society of Audiovisual Directors, Screenwriters and Playwrights (ATN),
founded in 1995; the Corporation of Actors (Chileactores), created in 1996; the
Audiovisual Platform, dating back to 1997; the Chilean Society of Performers
(SCI), founded in 1998; the Society of Literary Rights (SADEL), founded in
2003; and the Society of Still Image Creators (Creaimagen), created in 2003. The
formation of the Unión de Artistas de Chile (UNA) consolidated most of these
organisations. The UNA was founded in 2008 in response to the urgent need to
defend the rights of creators which were threatened by a change in the law governing intellectual property promoted by the then Minister of Culture, Paulina
Urrutia. The sector has been regulated by the Law on Workers in the Arts and
Entertainment Industry since 2003, which, despite problems in its application, has
provided a framework that defends employee rights (Negrón et al., 2010, p. 4).

Artists were fundamental actors in the process of cultural institutionalisation
and in the 1990s became judges and jury of this process which was governed by
the limited number of existing policies. At the same time, they became decision-
makers close to the seat of power. The dictatorship had been characterised by
a lack of funding for the arts and culture due to the imposition of a "cultural
blackout". During the subsequent transition to democracy, the weak three-headed
institutionality was marked by the sole availability of competitive funding such
as FONDART and, at the Latin American level, the renowned Andrés Bello
Agreement.[6] On the one hand, the limited and fragmented nature of this funding
meant that artists gained first-hand experience of negotiating and, more generally,
of the corporate world. In short, artists became cultural managers. The ineffective
defence of copyright protection forced artists to be, simultaneously, their own
agents and producers. "The processes carried out in other latitudes by screenwriters, producers and filmmakers in Chile are carried out by a single quixotic figure"
(Castillo, 2000 in Muñoz, 2012, p. 132).

On the other hand, the requirement to weave networks in order to subsist or
secure legitimacy and dialogue had promoted a rapprochement between artists
and public authorities, establishing a relationship between the former and the
wielders of power. The Garretón Commission of 1990 was formed almost entirely
by artists, and the FONDART panels were selected annually from among their
own number. There was also direct funding for certain organisations (such as
the two oldest, SECH and APECH) which continued even after the founding of

CNCA. The artists who presided over the CNCA with the rank of Minister of State, for example, the actors Paulina Urrutia and Luciano Cruz-Coke and the writer Roberto Ampuero, and the current National Deputies who included actors and musicians, should also be remembered.

Artists have embarked on several crusades culminating in victory. Iconic struggles, such as that of the Audiovisual Platform, launched to defend the arts and culture in trade negotiations with governments during the late 1990s and early 2000s are deserving of mention. Another example is the remarkable mobilisation and march from Valparaíso to the National Congress in 2003 in support of the creation of the CNCA in a second vote, following defeat in the first. Yet another struggle led to the Arts and Entertainment Workers' Law of that same year and the creation of the UNA (National Artists' Union) in 2008 when workers' rights were threatened by a modification of the then prevailing intellectual property law.

Despite these developments, insufficient autonomy has been granted to the field to engender the desired level of dynamism. Dependence on a sole funding body remains high. This combined with the close relationship between artists and the authorities could explain the near total lack of initiatives to alter the status quo. The country's artistic creation is marked by an almost complete absence of a vindicatory position and the predominance of public intervention.

The cultural manager: The hybrid of a field still being defined

Defining cultural management or the intended role of a cultural manager is a complex undertaking marked by the hybridisation, imprecision, and diversity of the concept at its core: culture. In addition, the context within which cultural managers operate in Chile has been invariably hostile, with precarious budgets and weak infrastructures. Artists and creatives have been highly dependent on FONDART for the last 30 years. The creation of the CNCA and the ministry strengthened the arts sector, although its structural weaknesses have yet to be fully addressed.

It seems that the cultural manager should combine, in the words of Bonet (1994, p. 2), "humanistic and artistic knowledge with the operational skills of management". The professionalisation of cultural management is, therefore, interdisciplinary. It considers managerial issues and involves a professional body that, while not heterogeneous, is nonetheless diverse and hybrid. Based on both general and specific knowledge and experiences, it strives to shape a professional identity (an ideal yet to be realised). The question remains of the extent to which Martinell's (2001, p. 3) statement, made almost two decades ago, that "despite its rapid growth in recent years [cultural management] is still in the structuring and definition phase" is valid.

There is no unique profile of the cultural manager encompassing, for example, individuals who manage financial and human resources in specific social and cultural realities, who teach and/or research the field, or who make decisions on cultural policy within the public or private sectors (Negrón, 2009, pp. 3–4). Administrators, producers, and planners are also identified (Schargorodsky, 2002,

p. 7). A dichotomy between management and promotion is also highlighted, which coexists with the belief that the cultural manager should be a cultural animator (UNESCO OEI Iberformat, 2004, p. 32). More recent studies refer to "cultural workers", classifying them as professional artists, cultural intermediaries, and cultural technicians (Brodsky et al., 2014, p. 14). Others refer to cultural management, emphasising its territorial and community dimensions (Bustamante et al., 2016, pp. 31–42) or the evolution of Latin American states and periods of cultural institutionalisation (Nivón & Sánchez, 2012, pp. 12–25). The previously mentioned fact that in Chile and, indeed, many other Latin American countries, artists are their own cultural managers, a fact which defines a hybrid actor: the artist-manager, should not be forgotten.

The training of artists is problematic given these different possible profiles with a strong emphasis on "managerial" aspects which are rarely community based or identitarian (Mariscal et al., 2019; Chavarría et al., 2019; Villaseñor Anaya et al., 2014; Yáñez et al., 2018). With the creation of the CNCA and the Ministry of Cultures, Arts and Heritage, a transformation and expansion of professionalisation commenced because these institutions rendered possible the creating of conditions conducive to the permanent exercise and recognition of a profession (since they required the presence of trained personnel).

A series of training courses, geared primarily towards the management of culture and heritage, were introduced. These drew on UNESCO contributions and the debates of the 1990s held in Latin America thanks to the Andrés Bello Agreement which established both the criteria and requirements of cultural management. Several salient contributions include the International Meeting on Cultural Management Training organised by the Colombian Institute of Culture (COLCULTURA) and the Executive Secretariat of the Andrés Bello Agreement in 1993, recorded in "Formación en gestión cultural" (Guédez et al., 1994); and UNESCO's publications "La gestión cultural: singularidad profesional y perspectivas de futuro" (Martinell, 2001) and "Formación en Gestión Cultural y Políticas Culturales" (UNESCO OEI Iberformat, 2004).

Training in cultural and heritage management in Chile

Incipient training in Chile was introduced towards the end of the 1990s thanks to the Postgraduate Degree in Cultural Management – Visual Arts (1995) and the Postgraduate Degree in Cultural Management – Musical Arts (1998) offered by the University of Chile, both of which led to the master's degree in Cultural Management initiated in 2007 (see Table 8.1). The first diploma course in Cultural Administration was introduced in 1997 at the Catholic University which, together with the Diploma in Cultural Management from the Universidad de San Sebastián and the Diploma in Cultural Administration and Management from the Universidad Santo Tomás, both inaugurated in 2002, were recognised as the three qualifications available in Chile by "Cultural Management: Professional Singularity and Future Prospects" in 2003 (IBERFORMAT, 2004, p. 23). Significantly, none of this trio of programmes exists today.

There are currently just over 25 training programmes in Chile, mainly diploma and master's level postgraduate courses, all of which are delivered in its capital city (RM in Table 8.1) and the V Region of Valparaíso (territorially adjacent to Santiago and the site of the CNCA headquarters until the creation of the ministry). Analysing these cultural management training course guides promotes an understanding of the perception and definition of cultural managers' actions (through the types of training), while also defining their roles and functions (through their profiles and objectives). It also enables the formalising and review of the characteristics of this practice within the country: how the inherent tensions between the paradigms are expressed and how the existence of a single funding mechanism for artistic and cultural projects (FONDART) shapes and defines the curriculum.

The various training programmes' objectives prioritise understanding and/or knowledge of the various aspects involved in cultural and/or heritage activity, the interdisciplinary nature of these fields, and the project management tools utilised therein, as well as experience-based learning with the reality of promoting network development.

The problem of defining the role of cultural manager can be clearly observed in the existing difficulty around describing both admission criteria and graduate profiles. The different training programmes focus more on entry requirements than specific profiles, even though most of the latter require applicants to be able to demonstrate previous experience in the cultural and/or heritage field without further details being provided. The various diploma programmes are aimed not only at cultural managers who work in the public or private spheres at national or local level, but also at artists, creators, technicians, social leaders, professionals, and academics from a variety of fields. Very few training courses (less than 10 %) provide a graduate profile. In those cases that do, the definitions are based on and prioritise the objectives of and skills taught through each curriculum.

The curricula of these training courses can be classified into one of three strands. The first addresses management or "culture" from the perspective of its various expressions. On the one hand, this strand proposes the study of subjects associated with cultural activity and its epistemological bases such as culture, society, and citizenship (see Table 8.1). On the other hand, it considers the areas of professional performance and its modules as potentially ranging from art history, memory and territory, and cultural mediation to the economics of culture and the creative industries. This strand exhibits the greatest differences between training courses due to factors such as where the programmes are delivered, their institutional collaborators (for example, associated faculties), and the emphasis placed on each programme.

The second curricular strand relates to the need to learn about national, local, and/or territorial institutionality. It addresses the legal and institutional aspects of these areas, while proposing the study of Chilean institutionality, the legislation associated with cultural activities, and public management, among other subjects.

The third strand provides tools for cultural management, project formulation, and implementation (or evaluation), managing and raising resources in addition

Table 8.1 Training offers in Cultural and/or Heritage Management in Chile

Bachelor's Degree in	Region	University	Department
Public and Private Cultural Management	Santiago Metropolitan Region	Alberto Hurtado University	Philosophy and Humanities Department
Cultural Management	Villarrica	Pontifical Catholic University of Chile	Institute of Aesthetics
Communication and Cultural Management	Santiago Metropolitan Region	University of Chile	Institute of Communication
Cultural Mediation and Audience Development	Santiago Metropolitan Region	University of Chile	Institute of Communication
Cultural and Territorial Management	Santiago Metropolitan Region	University of Santiago de Chile	Administration and Economics Department
Cultural Management	Temuco	Catholic University of Temuco	CEFIC Comprehensive Centre for Strengthening Local Capacities/Academic Vice-Rectory
Cultural Management	Antofagasta	Northern Catholic University	
Cultural Management	Valparaíso	Playa Ancha University	Humanities Department
Socio-cultural Management, Territory and Cultural Policies	Santiago Metropolitan Region	University Academy of Christian Humanism	
Management and Promotion of Creative and Communication Companies	Santiago Metropolitan Region	Pontifical Catholic University of Chile	Communications Department
Online course in Cultural Management	Valparaíso	Pontifical Catholic University of Valparaiso	School of Economics and Administrative Sciences PUCV/School of Journalism
Online course in Cultural Management	Online	Ministry of Culture, Arts and Heritage, MINCAP – University of Chile	
Conservation and Integrated Management of Heritage Objects	Santiago Metropolitan Region	Alberto Hurtado University	Philosophy and Humanities Department

(Continued)

Table 8.1 (*Continued*) Training offers in Cultural and/or Heritage Management in Chile

Bachelor's Degree in	Region	University	Department
Cultural Heritage Management and Research	Santiago Metropolitan Region	Alberto Hurtado University	Social Sciences Department
Sustainable Heritage	La Serena	Central University	
Management of Regional Cultural Heritage	Bio-Bio	Bio-Bio University	
Heritage, Environment and Rights of the Rapa Nui People	Valparaíso	Pontifical Catholic University Valparaiso	Law
Cultural Heritage: an Interdisciplinary Approach to Living Heritage	Santiago Metropolitan Region	Catholic University	School of Architecture
Postgraduate online Diploma in Cultural Heritage Management	Online	University of Chile	Graduate School/Faculty of Arts
Master's Degree in			
Cultural Management with Mention in Artistic Production and Socio-culture	Santiago Metropolitan Region	University Academy of Christian Humanism	Arts Department
Cultural Management	Valparaiso	Playa Ancha University	Postgraduate School
Cultural Management	Santiago Metropolitan Region	University of Chile	Art Department in collaboration with the Economics and Business Department/ Social Sciences Department
Cultural Heritage	Santiago Metropolitan Region	Pontifical Catholic University	Department of Architecture
Heritage	Valparaíso	University of Valparaiso	Department of Architecture
Arts with Mention in Heritage	Valparaiso	Playa Ancha University	Art Department
Heritage Management and Sustainable Tourism	Santiago Metropolitan Region	Autonomous University of Chile	International Graduate School
History and Management of Cultural Heritage	Santiago Metropolitan Region	University of the Andes	History Institute

Table 8.2 Three axes for training in Cultural Management in Chile

Axes	Diplomas	
	Gestión Cultural	Cultural Heritage
Culture and heritage theories	Social and Cultural Affairs	Heritage History
	Culture and the Market	Conservation and Restoration
	Postmodern Culture and Models of Cultural Development	Theory and History of Conservation and Restoration
	Chilean and Latin American Identity	Documentation, Handling and Conservation
	Contemporary Cultural Discourses	Territoriality, Cultural Identity, and Heritage
	Culture-Art-Heritage	Theoretical Approaches to the Concept of Heritage
	Cultural Policies	Arts Collections, Standards, and Protocols
	Creative Industries	Cultural Heritage
	Cultural Economy	Heritage History
	Audience Development and Mediation	
Public organisations	Public Cultural Institutions in Chile	Institutions, Regulations, and Instruments Concerning Heritage and Culture
	Cultural Regulations	Heritage Public Policies
	Public Administration	
	Public Management	
	Public Cultural Policies	
Project formulation and management	Cultural Projects Design	Project Design in Heritage
	Participatory Strategic Planning for Cultural organisations	Methodology for the Identification of Heritage Values
	Organisational Development	Heritage Communication
	Project Evaluation	Creativity and Innovation in Heritage
	Cultural Events	Environmental Assessment
	Information and Communication Technologies	Management and Elaboration of Projects
	Communication and Marketing	Heritage Action Planning
	Management of Cultural Organisations	Research-Intervention and Property Management
	Cultural Funding	Project Design in Heritage

Source: Author's own elaboration.

to communication skills applied to cultural projects. In cultural heritage training, this strand not only specifies the project design, but also identifies the values of cultural heritage, innovation, and project sustainability.

The last two strands, and above all the latter, are equally present in all the training programmes. They constitute the formative core of each programme basically oriented towards knowing how to formulate and implement a cultural and/or heritage project. The training programmes emphasise a practice-based, rather than a theory-driven pedagogy and the training courses use a *learning-to-do* methodology, in other words, mastering professional practices contained in instruction manuals that have become important reference sources. Examples include Rselló's *Manual for the Design and Evaluation of Cultural Projects* (2004), a guide for the management of cultural projects produced by the CNCA that comprises Rselló's manual and the United Nations Economic Commission for Latin America and the Caribbean (ECLAC)'s Logical Framework (which is also a reference for the formulation and evaluation of cultural policies in Chile), in addition to new publications issued on behalf of the recently instituted ministry.[7]

The first, more epistemological, strand is no less important. However, there is still no agreement as to the sensibilities or theoretical constructs that define this professional field and the actors who are active within it. The literature is as diverse as the disciplines involved and recognises UNESCO's contribution in the form of conventions, declarations, and recommendations addressing the issues of culture, heritage, identity, and cultural diversity.

Against this background, it is possible to confirm what is significant in the definition of cultural management for Chile and to what extent the Chilean cultural paradigm ("culture is a task for all") and the mechanism of cultural financing (FONDART) shape not only relevant training programmes but also the very definition of a cultural manager. Knowledge of the design and evaluation of cultural projects is also enhanced by private sector initiatives through the Law of Cultural Donations which transforms the cultural manager into a promoter of projects to companies inclined to fund cultural projects.[8]

The challenges facing cultural management and cultural policy in Chile are marked by the need to produce a definition and promote an understanding of the discipline that goes beyond mere project financing, as progressively (albeit deeply) instilled beliefs linked to technocratic practices dating from the period from 2003 to 2008 would have it. This results-oriented perspective which enables the measuring of the efficiency and effectiveness of public action has consequences for the latter because it eschews an integrated and global perspective. Furthermore, it induces organisations to meet demands rather than implement essential long-term projects. FONDART also instilled a sense of *savoir-faire* that is still highly valued in the field. Therefore, in order to limit cultural policy, the field depends exclusively on a public instrument incapable of promoting a network of cultural establishments (through subventions), supporting a diffusion network for a piece of art, or contributing to the democratisation of culture through, for instance, specific programmes. Against this background, the intervention of other actors outside the public sphere (as established for the cultural paradigm) and the diversification and enhancing of the cultural manager's field of action cannot be enabled.

The current challenge is that of enhancing current cultural policies in all these sub-sectors and improving more sensitive areas of culture such as community engagement, citizenship, territorial identities, and memory that are fundamental to the country's development. All these elements remain incipient within public programmes, yet fundamental to the development and advance of Chile's cultural and heritage sector. There is an urgent need to diversify State support and increase it beyond the current annual competition for which the prize is a single allocation of financial support. The new ministry and the artistic and cultural community shoulder a joint responsibility. Nevertheless, the world of art and culture remains closely linked to the establishment, despite achieving a certain degree of autonomy in recent years depending, as it does, on public funds to undertake projects. Greater cultural dynamism demands a more vindicatory view on the part of artists and cultural managers to open up new paths, counterbalance the influence of the State's funding mechanisms and associated dependencies, and recognise the diversity of actors and specialisations of cultural managers. This is undoubtedly a challenge for cultural policy itself and for this new field of public intervention that has emerged in the country in the first 20 years of the 21st century as an interdisciplinary, diverse, and multi-faceted discipline. An awareness of the importance of the role of culture in society is reflected in recognition of the role of the cultural manager and the varied nature of cultural management.

Notes

1 According to de la Vega Velástegui, a similar process took place in Ecuador with the creation of the Ministry of Culture (this volume).
2 The law governing donations for cultural purposes is a mechanism that encourages private intervention, both corporate and individual, in the financing of cultural, artistic, or cultural heritage projects through tax exemptions. It is important to highlight that this patronage regime has long been criticised for improper practices involving fraud and tax evasion. Substantive legislative modifications were incorporated to reduce these infractions at the turn of the century.
3 The report "Los trabajadores del sector cultural en Chile. Estudio de caracterización" (CNCA, 2004, pp. 84–87) confirmed that around the year 2000 a significant percentage of cultural workers were self-taught, recognising forms of autodidactism and informal learning.
4 The recent succession of bicentennials of the respective independences was a propitious situation to rethink the cultural and identity frameworks. Escribal (this volume) comments on this in relation to Argentina.
5 The recovery of democracy between the 1980s and early 1990s represented a turning point in thinking about the role of cultural policies and their institutions in the region (Henze & Escribal; Zamorano, this volume).
6 It is an Ibero-American organisation created by an international treaty signed in Bogotá in 1970 (supplanted by a new agreement signed in Madrid in 1990) whose purpose is the educational, scientific, technological, and cultural integration of the member states. Its name was adopted in honour of the distinguished American humanist Don Andrés Bello. Available at http://directorio.sela.org/media/26253/Convenios_Andres_Bello .pdf.
7 For example, the methodological guides for cultural or cultural heritage projects entitled *A Manual for Municipal Corporations and Cultural Foundations* and *A Guide to Funds for Cultural Projects*, available at https://www.cultura.gob.cl/publicaciones.
8 The main initiatives are from the banking, mining, and energy sector, while others are from the area of telecommunications, namely Telefónica and Entel.

References

Bonet, L. (1994). Contexto, Criterios y Necesidades de Formación del Gestor Cultural. In Guédez, V. & Menéndez, C. (Eds.). *Formación en gestión Cultural*. Bogotá: Secretariat of the Andrés Bello Agreement, pp. 20–29.

Brodsky, J., Negrón, B. & Pössel, A. (2014). *El Escenario del Trabajador Cultural en Chile*. Santiago: Proyecto Trama & UE. http://www.observatoriopoliticasculturales.cl/ OPC/wp-content/uploads/2015/01/el_escenario.compressed-1.pdf.

Bustamante, U., Mariscal Orozco, J. & Yáñez Canal, C. (2016). *Formas y configuraciones de la gestión cultural en América Latina*. National University of Colombia. http://obs ervatoriocultural.udgvirtual.udg.mx/repositorio/bitstream/handle/123456789/789/2016 %20Formas%20y%20configuraciones%20de%20la%20gestion%20cultural.pdf?seque nce=1&isAllowed=y.

Chartrand, H. & McCaughey, C. (1989). The arm's length principle and the arts: an international perspective – past, present and future. In Cummings Jr., M. & Schuster, J. M. (Eds.). *Who's to Pay for the Arts: The International Search for Models of Support*. New York: American Council for the Arts, pp. 43–80.

Chavarría, R., Fauré, D. & Yáñez Canal, C. (2019). *Conceptos claves de la gestión cultural*. Vol. I. University of Guadalajara and Ariadna Editores. http://observatoriocultural.ud gvirtual.udg.mx/contenido/conceptos-claves-de-la-gestion-cultural-vol-i.

CNCA (2004). *Los Trabajadores del Sector Cultural en Chile. Estudio de Caracterización*. Santiago de Chile: Andres Bello Convention.

de la Vega Valestegui, P. (this volume). Cultural Management in Ecuador: Genealogy and power relations within the constitution of a field. In Henze, R. & Escribal, F. (Eds.). *Cultural Management and Policy in Latin America*. Abingdon & New York: Routledge, pp. 143–162.

Di Girólamo, C. (2000). *Ciudadanía cultural, construcción del futuro*. Santiago, Chile. Unpublished.

Dubois, V. (1999). *La Politique Culturelle: genèse d'une catégorie d'intervention publique*. Paris: Belin.

Escribal, F. (this volume). Cultural management in Argentina: political agenda and challenges for practitioners and researchers. In Henze, R. & Escribal, F. (Eds.). *Cultural Management and Policy in Latin America*. Abingdon & New York: Routledge, pp. 87–105.

García Canclini, N. (Ed.) (1987). *Políticas Culturales de América Latina*. México: Grijalbo.

Garretón, M. (1991). *Propuesta para la Institucionalidad Cultural Chilena*. Report from the Advisory Committee on Culture "Garretón Commission". Santiago de Chile: Ministry of Education.

Guédez, V. & Menéndez, C. (Eds.) (1994). *Formación en gestión Cultural*. Bogotá: Executive Secretariat of the Andrés Bello Convention.

Hall, P. (1993). Policy Paradigm; Social Learning and the State. *Comparative Politics*, N°25(3), pp. 275–296.

IBERFORMAT. (2004). *Formación en Gestión Cultural y Políticas Culturales*. UNESCO, OEI. https://en.unesco.org/creativity/sites/creativity/files/training%20in%20cultural %20management_es.pdf.

Ivelic, M. (1997). *Chile está en deuda con la cultura. Informe de la Comisión Consejera Presidencial en Materias Artístico Culturales*. Santiago de Chile: Ministry of Education.

Kuhn, T. (2008). *La structure des révolutions scientifiques*. Flammarion, Champs Sciences Series, Paris, https://editions.flammarion.com/la-structure-des-revolutions-scientifi ques/9782081396012.

Lascoumes, P. & Le Galès, P. (2004). *Gouverner par les Instruments*. Paris: Presses de Sciences Po.

Mariscal, J. & Rucker, U. (2019). *Conceptos claves de la gestión cultural*. Vol. II. Guadalajara: University of Guadalajara, Ariadna Editores. http://observatoriocultural .udgvirtual.udg.mx/contenido/conceptos-claves-de-la-gestion-cultural-vol-ii

Martinell, A. (2001). *La gestión cultural: singularidad profesional y perspectivas de futuro*. Girona: UNESCO Chair in Cultural Policies and Cooperation.

Mejía Arango, J. (2009). Apuntes sobre las políticas culturales en América Latina, 1987– 2009. *Pensamiento Iberoamericano*, N°4, pp. 103–130.

Muller, P. (1995). Les Politiques Publiques comme construction d'un rapport au monde. In Faure, A. & Pollet, G. (Eds.). *La Construction du sens dans les politiques publiques; débats autour de la notion de référentiel*. Paris: L'Harmattan, pp. 152–179.

Muñoz del Campo, N. (2018). El Arte de Gobernar la Cultura. Paradigmas e Instrumentos de la Acción Pública: ¿Una verdadera participación en Chile? In Mariscal Orozco, J., Rubim, A. & Santos, F. (Eds.). *La Gestión Cultural desde Latinoamérica: Análisis de experiencias en Política Cultural*. University of Guadalajara, University of Santiago de Chile, School of Cultural Managers and Animators of Chile. http://observatoriocultural .udgvirtual.udg.mx/repositorio/handle/123456789/838.

——— (2014). Ten Years of the National Council for Culture and the Arts, CNCA from a Three-dimensional Perspective. In Rocha Lukic, Melina & Tomazini, Carla (Eds.), *Analyzing Public Policies in Latin America: A Cognitive Approach*. Newcastle upon Tyne: Cambridge Scholars Publishing, pp. 133–164.

——— (2013). La Culture au Chili: réflexions sur un processus de constitution d'une catégorie d'intervention publique. *Cahiers des Amériques Latines*, 72–73, pp. 183–199.

——— (2012). *L'État et la culture au Chili. Les enjeux et défis d'une réforme institutionnelle: Le Conseil National de la Culture et des Arts*. Éditions Universitaires Européennes EUE.

——— (2011). La Reforma Cultural: un ejemplo de polarización en la gestión de una política pública. *Estado Gobierno y Gestión Pública: Revista Chilena de Administración Pública*, N°18, pp. 61–91.

Navarro, A. (2006). *Cultura ¿Quién paga? Gestión, infraestructura y audiencias en el modelo chileno de desarrollo cultural*. Santiago de Chile: RIL Editores.

Negrón, B. (2009). *Desafíos de la Gestión Cultural en el Chile del Bicentenario*. Ibero-American Cultural Management Portal. http://www.gestioncultural.org/ficheros/BNegr on.pdf.

Negrón, B. Brodsky, R., Farías, E. & Brodsky, J. (2010). Condiciones sociales y laborales del artista en Chile. *Working documents for the National Meeting "I am an Artist" convened by the National Union of Artists*. http://www.unionnacionaldeartistas.cl/wp -content/uploads/2010/09/Descargar-Informe-derechos-laborales-y-condiciones-soci ales.pdf.

Nivón Bolan, E. & Sánchez, D. (2012). *La gestión cultural y las políticas culturales*. Santiago de Chile: University of Chile. https://www.academia.edu/10374164/Tenden cias_de_la_gestión_cultural_en_Latinoamérica.

Ponte, B. (this volume). Cultural management in Latin America and Europe: between the ashes and the flame. In Henze, R. & Escribal, F. (Eds.). *Cultural Management and Policy in Latin America*. Abingdon & New York: Routledge, pp. 22–33.

Rosselló, D. (2004). *Diseño y Evaluación de Proyectos Culturales: de la Idea a la Acción.* Barcelona: Ariel.

SEGPRES (2006). *Reforma del Estado en Chile 1990–2006.* Santiago de Chile: SEGPRES.

SEGEGOB (1996). *Políticas Culturales en Chile: Mapa Institucional, Legislativo y Financiero, 1990–1996.* Santiago de Chile: SEGEGOB Culture Department.

Schargorodsky, H. (2002). *Un perfil del gestor cultural profesional en América Latina y el Caribe: Su relación con la formación en gestión cultural.* http://www.gestioncultural .org/ficheros/BGC_AsocGC_HSchargorodsky.pdf.

Subercaseaux, B. (2006). Cultura y Democracia. In Carrasco, E. & Negrón, B. (Eds.). *La Cultura Durante el Período de Transición a la Democracia 1990–2005.* Valparaíso: CNCA, pp. 19–29.

Surel, Y. (1995). Les politiques publiques comme paradigmes. In Faure, A. & Pollet, G. (Eds.). *La Construction du sens dans les politiques publiques; débats autour de la notion de référentiel.* Paris: L'Harmattan, pp. 125–151.

UNESCO (1990). *Decenio Mundial para el Desarrollo Cultural 1988–1997.* http://une sdoc.unesco.org/images/0008/000852/085291sb.pdf.

——— (1982). *Declaración de México sobre las Políticas Culturales.* World Conference on Cultural Policies. http://portal.unesco.org/culture/es/files/35197/11919413801m exico_sp.pdf/mexico_sp.pdf.

Villaseñor Anaya, C. (2014). Retos para la Gestión Cultural en América Latina. *Revista de Análisis de la Cultura y el territorio*, N°15, pp. 259–275.

Yáñez Canal, C., Rucker, Ú. & Valenzuela, M. (2018). *La gestión cultural desde Latinoamérica: Referencias y retos del campo disciplinar.* University of Guadalajara, University of Santiago de Chile, School of Cultural Managers and Animators of Chile. http://egac.cl/2018/12/29/redlgc-presenta-libro-la-gestion-cultural-desde-latinoameri ca/.

Zamorano, M. (this volume). Cultural management in Paraguay since the democratic transition: strategies of cultural disruption in a conservative frame. In Henze, R. & Escribal, F. (Eds.). *Cultural Management and Policy in Latin America.* Abingdon & New York: Routledge, pp. 106–124.

9 Cultural management in Ecuador

Genealogy and power relations within the constitution of a field

Paola de la Vega Velástegui

Introduction

Through a series of development cooperation policies, Spain has projected a model of international culture-driven development and State modernisation in the post-Franco era, placing special emphasis on Latin American countries with the city of Barcelona as its champion (Iturrieta, 1993; Quaggio, 2014). In this chapter, cultural management is understood to constitute a category of global capitalism, inscribed in a neo-colonial model for Latin America, validated in the political-cultural structures of that region from the end of the 1980s to the first decade of the 21st century. This includes the point of return to democracy, the implementation of policies relating to the adjustment and optimisation of the State, policies pacifying armed conflicts, and, even, the emergence of progressive governments. Immersed in neo-liberalism, understood as a cultural configuration (Grimson, 2007, p. 11), management is seen as a professionalising and specialising technical tool, an instrument of the new capitalism (Garcés, 2013, p. 84). As the core of development cooperation policies, it strives through State modernisation projects to address social issues seen as constituting a technical challenge which can be solved rationally. From other perspectives, cultural management has acquired different political connotations, including the possibility of contributing to the consolidation of democratic values through the recognition of cultural diversity and rights. This view, which was expressed in new constitutions adopted in both Spain and Latin America, has its origin in a contradiction: the coincidence of the neo-liberalisation of the State with the implementation of diversity policies unprecedented in the region (Ochoa, 2003, p. 18). This emergence of cultural management – as such – in Latin America reflects a specific moment in Spain's political and economic history, the social democratic era of the 1980s, which extended to Latin America through a complex web of geopolitical power relations.

Secondly, this chapter analyses how the process was implemented in Ecuador, where cultural management emerged later in comparison with other countries of the region. Referred to for the first time in official documents issued by the Ministry of Culture – itself created in 2007 by the self-proclaimed progressive government of Rafael Correa (2007–2017) – cultural management consolidated itself in public narratives as an instrument of technical reason. The Spanish

Agency for Development Cooperation (AECID) played a decisive role in this entire process, although the category was simultaneously and rapidly appropriated by artists and creators. The process leading to the approval of a new Constitution in 2008, which incorporated the recognition of cultural rights, played a significant role in that process. This chapter will show that, within the framework of an attempt to modernise the State, this new management has rendered invisible the multiple modalities of cultural action existing within the national territory. Given that the Ecuadorian national budget is extremely dependent on oil revenues, the country experienced a boom period between 2007 and 2015, with international oil prices ranging from U$70 to U$140 per barrel. The resulting increased income both enabled significant public investment in culture, leading to an expansion of cultural bureaucracy, and facilitated an unprecedented democratic allocation of public resources for cultural projects. Faced with a lack of consolidated domestic and international markets, the cultural sector enjoyed access to public funds, demobilising and fragmenting collective organisational processes.

One of this chapter's aims is to recognise the contradictions between the Ibero-Americanist genealogy of cultural management and other modes of culture-related action rooted in our own traditions. Identifying the strategies that shaped cultural management in Ecuador, while also analysing the power relations at play, underpins an approach to answering this question by understanding the differences between the countries of the region, marked by common elements such as structural social inequalities, the colonial experience, political dictatorships, and neo-liberal reforms. This is the context within which development cooperation policies operate, confronting a tradition of cultural action rooted in community involvement and political commitment.

Cultural management emerged at a time of transformation of the global meaning assigned to culture. Its mobilisation was activated by multiple agencies (Ochoa, 2003, pp. 19–20) on the basis of transnational political identities (Segato, 2002). Within this context, diversity organisations adopted it as a sphere within which to dispute social rights, a space possessing "new ways of constructing the subjectivity of the utopian … a sphere of desire that does not always translate into mere needs" (Ochoa, 2003, p. 57). The consolidation of cultural management in Latin America involves inherent contradictions and tensions: between its instrumental use in the obtaining of rights and its political power in the production of desires (Ochoa, 2003); between the governmental rationality established by the State and development cooperation policies and the legacies aimed at social transformation (Vich, 2014); between its inclusion in neo-liberal projects of State modernisation and the strategies of cultural difference that operate within a structured system of global political economy (Escobar, 1996, p. 194). Other tensions exist between the ambition for modernity and multi-temporal heterogeneities of cultural action present in popular practices, organisational knowledge, redistributive logics of resources and care, and in autonomous projects of reproduction of life, where the cultural is not a sector but the place for political action. Still others can be observed between the forms of appropriation of corporate culture; disciplinary action; the role and rigid structures of relationships (Garcés, 2013, p. 81);

experimental and creative meanings in the exchange of knowledge; the search for the common; and the invention of new modalities of composition and organisation that are not feasible within the traditional forms of politics (Lorey, 2016, p. 24). It is precisely in these inherent contradictions that its current polysemy lies.

Ibero-American cultural management: An export model

Coinciding with the return of democracy in Latin America, Spain re-oriented its foreign policy. This coincided with the assumption of power by the government of Felipe González (1982–1996) of the Spanish Socialist Workers' Party (PSOE) when the Spanish state was established as a model of economic development that successfully overcame the crisis inherited from the Franco regime. The country became an example of economic and political modernisation based on efficient institutions. In his electoral programme, González declared himself ready to reform the state by promoting a rational structure, including culture, in pursuit of his goal to modernise Spain in order to guarantee its entry into the European Community (EC). When this was achieved in 1986, EC membership constituted a boost to its cooperation programmes, aimed at sharing its successful experience with the Latin American republics that had also endured dictatorship. Latin America also offered considerable opportunities for the internationalisation of the Spanish economy (Sanahuja, 2012, p. 107). In 1977, Spain had first embraced the notion of cooperation several decades later than other European countries which had adopted it in the immediate post-war period; "incorporating the word cooperation in the official documents of democracy, hand in hand with culture" (Estrategia Cultura y Desarrollo de la Cooperación Española 2007, p. 10). Spanish foreign policy sought to enhance the image of its international cultural policy in order to re-launch its relationship with Latin America, in support of "the reconquest of freedoms, the recovery of democratic institutions, the enforcement of human rights, and the economic and cultural development of the region" (Iturrieta, 1993, p. 193). The projection of a new international identity of democratic Spain was based on the expectations of a modern country with the democratic values of freedom and social justice incorporated in the Spanish Constitution of 1978 (Sanahuja, 2012, p. 109).

Management represented a cornerstone of this process from the mid-1980s. Its agenda includes the recognition of cultural rights, territorial decentralisation and autonomy, urban development, and the growth of cultural infrastructure and professionalisation. This canon is epitomised by the city of Barcelona. From there, a network formed by the Centre of Cultural Studies and Resources of the Barcelona Provincial Council (CERC), the University of Barcelona, and the Interarts Foundation – and later, the Cultural Policies Division of the United Nations Educational, Scientific and Cultural Organisation (UNESCO) Chair of Cultural Policies of the University of Girona – exported a particular view of cultural management to South America. Its main proponents were Eduard Delgado, Eduard Miralles, Alfons Martinell, and Lluis Bonet, leading figures of the incipient profession within the framework of international municipalism that promoted

Barcelona as a city-business from the end of the 1980s (Garcés, 2018, p. 69). Various training programmes for cultural managers were implemented in Latin America involving these expert "powerful intellectual beacons" (Bayardo, 2018, p. 21). This initiative commenced in 1991 when the Ibero-American Heads of State Summit reached a consensus on the necessity of consolidating a common geostrategic area and increased in intensity in 1992 following the celebrations of the fifth centenary of the so-called "Encounter of Two Worlds".

In 2019, Martinell commemorated the 30th anniversary of the first master's degree in Cultural Management in Spain, delivered by the CERC – University of Barcelona in 1989. At the beginning of the 1990s, the four pillars of this network were part of various cultural management training programmes in Latin America established by foundations and multilateral and intergovernmental bodies such as the Interarts Foundation, Organisation of Ibero-American States (OEI), Andrés Bello Convention (CAB), AECID, UNESCO, among others. Cultural management did not yet form part of the governmental agenda of Spanish cooperation as it was only incorporated in 2005. The Spanish Cultural Centres, dependent on the AECID and present in several Latin American cities, were also instrumental in promoting these early cultural management training programmes.

Since this work aims to identify the function of cultural management in relation to the geopolitics of knowledge (Walsh, 2001), it becomes necessary to analyse the relationship between the narratives of cultural management and those of development based on the concept of the coloniality of knowledge (Lander, 2000). This approach will enable an understanding to be developed of how cultural management in its Ibero-American form orders and legitimises numerous pre-existing forms of cultural action in Latin America – which did not define themselves as management – orienting them towards efficiency within the framework of modern scientific thought by means of technocratic tools that represent elements within neo-liberal development policies. From this perspective, management imposes measurable, and supposedly neutral, instruments based on a cognitive-instrumental rationality within which politics would appear useless; displacing political problems to a neutral field instituted by experts and specialists (Lander, 2000, p. 15). Rivera (2018, p. 38) notes that the coloniality of knowledge alludes to the intellectual colonisation of local elites, to that "blockage that prevents us from being aware of our own intellectual heritage"; hence, her invitation to work on our own genealogies. In the models envisaged within cooperation policies, signs of a regime of universality of a particular historical experience – in this case, the Spanish one – remain present from which "a lecture on the totality of time and space is produced" (Lander, 2000, p. 17). A universal vision of history is applied that classifies and hierarchises societies and determines the superiority of science and technology over all other "non-modern or traditional" knowledge which is denied the possibility of contemporaneity (op. cit., 22–26). These *geopolitics of knowledge* are set up through a "colonial policy of language" (Castro Gómez, 2005, p. 13). Thus, cooperation programmes, progressively named heterogeneous management modes of cultural action, updated colonial power relations in projects mediated by geostrategic economic and political interests of the knowledge economy. These nominating policies were also introduced as a mechanism for depoliticising the sense of culture associated with political militancy; artistic mobilisation; anti-dictatorial activism; grassroots cultural practices intertwined with critical thinking; and popular education. These were all classified by management as empirical, spontaneous, non-technical, and non-professional (De la Vega, 2016).

In political and economic terms, cultural management was part of an integration project based on a historical reconciliation between Spain and its former colonies. This was not a naïve discourse but, rather, a platform to facilitate international agreements for Spanish trade and investment relations in Latin American countries, within the framework of global financial capitalism. The constitution of economic-cultural blocks within globalisation requires consensus regarding narratives that falsify similarities while making inequalities invisible, as a necessary principle for the reconfiguration of the capitalist world order (Coronil, 2000, pp. 88–89).

The Ibero-Americanist rhetoric efficiently generated a discourse to implement an economic project focused on the agenda of emerging Spanish transnational commercial entities, including publishing and film companies. This entry of Spanish cultural industries into the regional market perpetuated colonial logic based on asymmetric conditions (De la Vega, 2019; Sanahuja, 2012; Slachevsky, 2016). In addition, major exhibitions and scholarship programmes for Latin American students have been co-financed by these corporations, increasing suspicion regarding the nature of cooperation policies (Bonet, 2012, p. 92). The educational grants provided to cultural agents from the Global South under the terms of Spanish collaboration have served inter alia as instruments of certain desires and subjectivities on the part of grant recipients who experience the miracle of Spanish cultural policy: its impressive cultural infrastructures, its museums and heritage, and its cultural industries.

The spirit of reconciliation which characterised the transition period in Spain was based on a policy of forgetting the past: it did not question or review its own legacies but took a radical turn towards a process of "cultural modernisation" (Rowan, 2016, p. 83). One of the foundations of this process was the need for technical professionalisation of cultural institutions. Thus, a large part of the political activism involved in culture was incorporated into governmental administration. The ruling Social Democratic Party believed that the interface with these socially based expressions could be addressed by the active participation in cultural policies of a substantial element of the former anti-Franco militancy which, consequently, entered these institutions (Miralles, 2014, p. 44). Committed intellectuals inserted themselves into the state apparatus in order to transform it from within. Cultural management sought to promptly shed any ideological baggage associated with its predecessor, socio-cultural animation. As a tool for socio-educational intervention, the latter focused its work on an activist perspective with an emancipatory base founded on social involvement in culture. Since the 1960s, it acted in conflicted social environments as "a line of non-formal education that promotes cultural democracy" (Úcar, 2002) with the aim of "transforming social reality in a transversal way, using cultural practices, social education and community work as tools" (Desbordar Barcelona, 2020, p. 79). As the economy of culture became the main concern for cultural politics, the epistemic framework of cultural management was impacted. Thus, "socio-cultural animation almost disappeared from cultural policies in order to be aligned with social education and free time" (Desbordar Barcelona, 2020, p. 48). For PSOE's cultural policy, socio-cultural animation constituted an obsolete tool, with no methodological background or planning capacity, defining objectives and economic indicators. With this shift, certain transformative processes of participatory democracy, activism, and community organisation, such as those closely linked to animation practices which were struggling for public facilities in popular neighbourhoods in Barcelona in the 1970s and 1980s were politically defused. One of the theorists of cultural management based in the city, Eduard Delgado (1988, p. 102), shows clearly the intimate relationship between art and communication within cultural management, initiating the "debate on audiences". Thus, he situates it as a means of mediation between audiences/consumers and artists, based on a conception of the citizenry as spectators/consumers, inactive in political-cultural decision-making.

Since at least 1984, UNESCO has recognised the concept and role of cultural administrator. However, Barcelona did not accept this approach, understanding that it "evokes the mechanical handling of procedures in bureaucracy" (Miralles, 2014, p. 45). In Martinell's opinion, administration appeals to procedures, while management goes further in executing a political role in decision-making. He adds that cultural management differs "from culture understood as the promotion of community participation, something that makes no sense from the position of a civil servant, which has nothing to do with activism" (Ibidem). Miralles (1996, p. 32) states that cultural management organises technical practices typical of a "stage of confusion" characterised by the absence of specialisation and the differentiation between artistic and cultural work, and of action resulting from "will"; all of which is "invested with a certain background, sometimes of political or social struggle".

In Spain, this process led to the formation of unions, cultural management companies, and third sector organisations that became the representatives of "civil society" ahead of the State which eschewed dialogue with grassroots social organisations. What place have experimental and transversal collective practices occupied since then in the design of democratic and participatory cultural systems? These incipient cultural management instruments that responded to the consolidation needs of the global creative economy developed, striving to balance the agency of cultural rights with the limits set by this economy. Therefore, there exists a need to review the trajectories of thinking situated within cultural management that may destabilise this paradigm and explore other politics.

Ecuador: Institutional mapping and heterogeneous grammars of cultural management

A national cultural ideology as the basis of a mestizo nation project, based on the concept of a harmonious and culturally homogeneous community that does not actually exist, was predominant in Ecuador during the 20th century. The *Casa de la Cultura Ecuatoriana* (Ecuatorian Cultural Centre) (CCEc) – an institution conceived by Benjamín Carrión (1897–1979) – was the first institution to establish a public cultural policy in 1944. It promoted the democratisation of an official culture that venerated "Hispanic cultural heritage and the elite role of intellectuals" (Grijalva, 2014, p. 12) by including mestizaje (the genetic and cultural intermixing of Spanish and American Indian people) as "an integrationist form of the ethnic minorities to the dominant nationalism" (Grijalva, 2014, p. 13). Carrión combined "a cosmopolitan yet enduringly aristocratic vision of culture with a passionate adherence to the process of forming a national-popular culture" (Rodríguez, 2015, p. 174).

The institutional weakening of the CCEc began in the 1960s – within a global context that invited changes, marked by the Cuban Revolution, Sartrean philosophy, colonial wars of independence, the dependency theory – with the emergence of the Tzantzic movement (founded in Quito in 1962 by Marco Muñoz and Ulises Estrella) that led to a peripheral Ecuadorian cultural avant-garde that assumed the role of interpreting the popular voice, using culture and art as its tools. They sought to replace the notion of disseminating culture among the people with the concept of revolutionary support: "artists were obliged by their very profession to accompany the people in their march of liberation, and to express with their voice the aspirations of the people, seeking to awaken the consciousness of the masses through poetry and theatre" (Tinajero, 2011, p. 35). They questioned the classism of intellectuals and artists of the Carrion circle, who had taken up positions in different public bodies, divorced from popular movements and seduced by the bourgeois myth of national culture. "An important sector of the movement, therefore, questioned the very institutionalisation of culture and advocated action that should be born in the street and the countryside, in the factory and the workshop" (Tinajero, 2011, p. 35). The Tzantzic movement produced a manifesto (Revista Pucuna, 2010), in which it declared its preference for reading poems and stories at trade union meetings, without publishing them, laughing at the "abysses" between writers and the people, and inviting the criticism of workers, students, and young people from the neighbourhoods. Their intervention practices within social contexts aimed at building a new hegemony that would sustain social transformation: "The demand was to speak the language of the people" (Polo, 2012, p. 69). Several of the Tzántzicos worked with the theatre director Fabio Pacchioni. With him

> one begins to investigate the surrounding reality. It is no longer a question of going and giving a show to the people and coming back. It is about a dialogue with the audience through which one investigates their problems in order to gather the dramatic material which will make possible a theatre closer to the people.
>
> (Freire, 2008, p. 57)

Experimenting with workers' theatre, drawing on Paulo Freire's pedagogy of the oppressed, the aim was to make oppression visible and to promote the liberation of the oppressed.

Believing that *intellectual* constitutes a concept rooted in bourgeois tradition, the Tzánticos used the term *cultural workers* to refer to artists occupying a place in the same hierarchy as the worker or the peasant. This definition of artistic and cultural work still involves various agents who share the same ideological Tzantzian support: develop cultural action in popular neighbourhoods and seek to break with cultural elitism, promoting action-creation at the grassroots level. This aspect of cultural management in Ecuador is part of a thought and action trend that is mobilising in Latin America and which advocates culture as an agent of social transformation (Vich, 2014, p. 85).

In the early 1970s, during the Rodriguez Lara dictatorship (1972–1976), Ecuador undertook a modernisation process funded by an oil boom. Proclaimed a nationalist revolutionary government, its project was based on developmentalism and sought to eliminate the country's economic, political, cultural, military, and ideological dependence (Cevallos, 2013, p. 50). In 1976, this administration was overthrown by a military coup that initiated a transition to democracy: Ecuador was the first Latin American country to restore a democratically elected regime with the calling of elections in 1978. During this period, the professional middle class expanded with a concomitant increase in cultural consumption. The significantly increased oil revenues also enabled the Central Bank of Ecuador (BCE) to financially support cultural policies focused on the collection of archaeology, colonial and modern art, and museums; creating a Cultural Area that during the 1970s, and especially the 1980s, overshadowed the CCEc.

The Subsecretariat of Culture within the Ministry of Education and Culture was established during Oswaldo Hurtado's presidency (1981–1984). In 1984, a Culture Law was approved, investing unprecedented authority in public cultural institutions and creating an Institutional System of Ecuadorian Culture, as well as establishing the FONCULTURA (National Culture Fund) together with the National Council of Culture, the entity responsible for its administration. This fund constituted the first reimbursable and non-reimbursable loan policy for cultural agents, popularised as *the bank of culture*. This coincided with the neo-liberal policies established by the government of León Febres Cordero (1984–1988) and was carried out with discretionary criteria: "Its real mission was to administer funds to sponsor those it considered worthy of a gift" (Tinajero, 2011, p. 37).

In parallel, from the mid-1980s to the early 1990s, the BCE's Cultural Promotion Department conducted training courses in socio-cultural animation, exclusively for the bank's employees. Meanwhile, a sector of the artistic movement in Quito perpetuated the political and creative horizons opened up by the Tzantzo movement. Two examples of this development include a street theatre supported by the Popular Artists' Coordination (1982) which functioned as "a micro space for the expression of socio-economic 'malaise' in the 1980s" (Verdesoto, 2012, p. 87), and the Theatre Workers' Association (1984) allied to the trade union movement. The second consisted of a project entitled Art in the Street, headed by the visual artist Pablo Barriga during the years 1981 and 1982, which sought to establish direct communication between artistic creators and citizens through workshops in public squares and parks, allowing members of the public to express themselves through creative expression. According to Barriga, "The only way to democratize art is to offer the possibility of artistic expression to the people themselves" (Cevallos, 2016, p. 16). In both cases, artists and cultural activists continue to define themselves as cultural workers with political commitment and a critical spirit. The management of street theatre was – and remains – closely linked to the so-called "hat economics". As the cultural work delivered in parks and squares was financially unviable, "passing the hat" was complemented by the sale of comics about the play or brochures showing how to apply make-up appropriately. Moreover, "we helped each other by putting on hall shows, selling performances, and presenting for students and social organisations who agreed to our retaining any money collected from the audience, plus receiving transport, food and accommodation expenses" (Verdesoto, 2012, p. 97). Even in the 1980s, such cultural action still represented a political vocation, close to grassroots level, in public spaces, subverting the civilising and disciplinary orders, outside the elitist institutional structures, without the productive, technical, and specialised professional pillars of management. These political and aesthetic concerns of the artistic scene were echoed in the Socio-Cultural Animation and Cultural Promotion training programmes conducted for BCE officials and promoted as official categories under the umbrella of cultural action.

The development of socio-cultural animation in Latin America was spawned by two currents (Colombres, 1999, p. 19): social work and its community-oriented vocation, of which Ezequiel Ander Egg was the major proponent, and popular education through the work of Paulo Freire:

> his ideas and pedagogical-political actions were developed in an atmosphere of lack of freedom .... The socio-cultural practices of this movement are critical and political and seek to generate consensual processes of emancipation and self-determination in the groups, communities and territories where they are produced.
>
> (Ucar 2002, p. 3)

According to Colombres (1999, p. 18), socio-cultural animation was based on the guidelines drawn up by UNESCO at the Americacult Conference held in Bogotá in 1978. Cultural promotion refers to a Mexican model and is closely linked to popular cultures: "a cultural promoter ... should be, as far as possible, a member of the community itself and not an external agent, since we believe more in the cultural self-management of popular groups than in the Redemptorist attitude of other sectors" (Colombres, 1999, p. 19). Both socio-cultural animation and cultural promotion represented institutional categories at the beginning of the 1990s in Ecuador. They were widely employed by artists and cultural workers demonstrating scarce theoretical development. During the same decade, limited numbers of civil servants drawn from public cultural institutions attended training courses on cultural management offered by the Barcelona Network. "most of these initial programs had a developmentalist vision of culture, importing methodologies and attributing little importance to cultural management practices in the region focused mainly on community work" (Mariscal Orozco, 2014, p. 216). This first wave of cultural management in Ecuador occurred at a time in which neo-liberal governmental policies were becoming more acute, institutional practices were being liberalised, and financial resources for culture were being reduced. Management was, therefore, directly associated with this programme of budget cuts; reduction of State involvement; efficiency and optimisation and the requirement for civil servants to be self-managing, i.e. able to incorporate self-sustainability tools for public cultural activity into their work (Bayardo, 2014, p. 132). Although socio-cultural animation and cultural management would seem to be antagonistic due to their connection with specific moments in Latin American political and economic history, among them were continuities and refunctionalisations (Bayardo, 2014, p. 131) that are evident in community-based movements, such as the Movimiento Cultura Viva Comunitaria, that have been in existence for more than a decade.

Cultural management was initially introduced into Ecuador by those public agents who had been trained in the above-mentioned Ibero-American programmes, with their administrative episteme and the guarantee of the individual and collective exercise of cultural rights. These were only established in Ecuador with the approval of the 2008 Constitution. Initially, the disputes between those who advocated socio-cultural animation or cultural promotion – which prioritised the relationship between education and popular-based culture – and the new cultural management – focused on the economic/cultural relationship – were recognisable (Lozano, 2014, p. 99). During a personal interview in 2018, Alfons Martinell acknowledged the presence of these tensions in both contexts (Spain and Ecuador), associating animation with a leftist position "of criticism without alternatives". Cultural management was, in his opinion, indispensable to a reform of the State's cultural policies which required a willingness to infiltrate the institutions in order to transform them. In his opinion, the need for institutional reforms was misinterpreted as *technocracy* by a more radical Latin American Left. It is essential to remember that the PSOE project in Spain (to which Martinell belonged) encouraged cultural modernisation through the construction of infrastructures and large-scale cultural activities and the promotion of industries and cultural consumption that required management as an organisational instrument. The political agenda of PSOE tended towards economic neo-liberalisation, ultimately seeking to "demonstrate the validity of a liberal economic strategy within socialism, as well as the advantages of industry and capital for the general welfare of the nation" (Quaggio, 2014, p. 333).

Cultural management as a whisper

In the 1990s, autonomous cultural action was mobilised on the basis of empathy and a commitment to eradicate inequalities. Within this framework, a series of experimental artistic practices took place in Quito that questioned the dominant narratives of culture and national identity. The transition from the modern to the contemporary in artistic languages is essential in these practices which acquire new meanings in the light of the indigenous uprising of 1990. Its greatest contribution "was to place the indigenous presence in the symbolic imagination and on the political scene" (Kingman, 2012, p. 80). While Ibero-Americanism sheltered itself in the conciliatory idea of the "Encounter of Two Worlds", around the 5th centenary of the conquest, the indigenous movement in Ecuador adopted the motto "500 years of resistance", deepening a historical dispute over access to land and intercultural education. At the same time, since the fall of the Berlin Wall, leftist narratives that had influenced cultural practices in previous decades were weakened, while a new Left arose articulating different social agendas, demands, and new political identities. Opposition to the signing of the Free Trade Agreement with the United States provided an opportunity to unite them. Between 1994 and 1997, a severe economic crisis rendered four banks and seven financial institutions bankrupt. President Jamil Mahuad (1998–2000) promoted measures to abrogate the 1994 General Law on Financial System Institutions, which had legalised self-regulation of the banking sector, expanding its power and minimising state control and supervision. The disaster resulting from the El Niño phenomenon (1997–1998) and the 1998 fall in oil prices compounded the situation. During 1999, inflation reached 52.2% and unemployment 18%. On March 8, 1999, a bank holiday was declared by the government, during which the financial assets of Ecuadorian savers were frozen. Thus,

> those affected by the banking crisis, like all Ecuadorians, had to bear the costs of an inevitable devaluation that led to the sucre losing 400 percent of its value between August 1998 and January 2000, before setting the price of the dollar at 25,000 sucres to pave the way for dollarisation. This devaluation could not be prevented in time by the State because of the huge resources it had expended on the banking sector rescue package.
>
> (Vera, 2013, p. 87)

This crisis led to population displacement with migration rates increasing sharply from 2000 onwards. In January 2001, a new indigenous uprising occurred with military participation that removed Jamil Mahuad from the presidency, demonstrating the institutional and democratic representation aspects of the crisis (Vera, 2013, p. 12). These events have given rise to a neo-liberal political subjectivity in Ecuador. Its archetypal subject is middle class, trusts private banking and his/her own self-management capabilities, within a context of declining public protection. This represented the inception of the entrepreneurial subject, which in Ecuador expressed itself through new forms of collective organisation of cultural work, based on mistrust of the State as the guarantor of rights. In the absence of public cultural policies; festivals; meetings; cultural platforms; and performing arts spaces, tactical management strategies were developed that combined domestic economy; community-based networking; international funding; and extremely sporadic public aid.

Private participation in cultural funding is traditionally marginal. In the first decade of the 21st century, Quito had an emerging rich and heterogeneous cultural scene dominated by self-managed organisations in all arts and cultural expressions:

in the visual arts, the Oído Salvaje Collective, the Al Zurich urban art meeting, the Experimentos Culturales platform; in the performing arts, the Frente de Danza Independiente, the Casa de la Danza, the Malayerba Theatre, the Festival del Sur, Arte en el Trole; in cinema, the Festival Encuentros del Otro Cine, Festival Cero Latitud, and the Ocho y Medio independent cinema, to name a few. Against the background of a weakened State, access to public cultural resources did not constitute a guaranteed right for such groups and projects. FONCULTURA and the Subsecretariat of Culture administered their funds in a discretionary manner, devoid of technical support, with allocations dependent upon the political lobby:

> The practice was to hand them over discretionally without articulating any state policy, or responding to any logic other than "eventism", that is, the production and performance of different types of acts without developing structures that would guarantee long-term continuity processes, that is, without incorporating them into the policy cycle.
>
> (Serrano, 2015, p. 67)

Discretionary and clientelist networks in Ecuador characterise the State-civil society relationship within the national political culture. The link between political culture and cultural policy is one of the most complex aspects of the latter:

> All cultural policy is mediated within society through a specific political culture, that is, through the practices that determine our way of living together in society. An innovative cultural policy, therefore, can ultimately reproduce long-standing authoritarian practices – clientelism, favouritism – or constitute new modes of exclusion, if not articulated through a renewed political culture based on a clear ethical conception of the role of social mediations in all cultural policy.
>
> (Ochoa, 2003, p. 36)

The relationship between public cultural institutions and contemporary artistic and cultural practices at that time can be characterised as non-existent.

Cultural action was forced to depend on development cooperation funding which played a predominant role from the 1990s onwards. For example, the HIVOS Fund (Humanist Institute for Cooperation and Development) was an important promoter of the performing arts in Quito: The Independent Dance Front strengthened its partnership with this fund by creating a space for training and circulation, which included the inception of the No More Moon on the Water festival. This was performed by female dancers from the Independent Dance Front, who for several years had been prevented from staging their creations by patriarchal power modalities. The Malayerba Theatre Group, again with support from HIVOS, restored a house in the city's historical centre and established it as a training and stage space. From cooperation policies, cultural management in Ecuador inherited, during this decade, project tools linked to development policy epistemes. These instruments were transferred to the design of artistic and cultural projects. Development aid was a laboratory for proposals from which the sector inherited a language and a series of tools for its organisation that must be re-thought today.

With the turn of the century, the more politicised strand – launched by cultural workers decades ago – also adopted new strategies, including union organisation. In the case of the film industry, self-managing cultural activists together with young professionals trained in the arts and related fields became "activists for cultural institutions" (Andrade, Personal Interview in 2020). Legal frameworks guaranteeing labour rights were required, in addition to renewed cultural institutions. One of their demands was the democratic, decentralised, and transparent distribution of public allocations to the field of culture. This movement placed on the agenda the concern for remuneration, labour, markets, and rights, as well as for professionalisation, which had previously been absent.

Community-based, itinerant, experimental, and territorially involved cultural action was also renewed; for example, the Asociación de Barrios del Sur, founded in the 1950s by union leaders and workers, which traditionally had an agenda focused on improving living conditions in the neighbourhoods and campaigning for public services and infrastructure. In the 1990s, at the height of the neo-liberal city model, Nelson Ullauri founded the Red Cultural del Sur (Southern Cultural Network) and invited artists to activate "dynamizing processes" (Interview, 2019). For the Tranvía Cero collective, responsible for the Al Zurich urban art meeting – close to celebrating its second decade – the involvement in this network was its first school of cultural management. During this period, as in Spain, several cultural agents also ceased working independently in order to join the institutions with the intention of transforming them.

Cultural management as a State objective

In April 2005, President Lucio Gutiérrez (2003–2005) was overthrown. Among the groups mobilised against him were "Los forajidos" (The outlaws) who, after the coup, disintegrated into a series of citizens' assemblies. Among them was the Permanent Assembly of Workers in the Arts and Cultures in which participated agents belonging to different generations drawn from diverse artistic backgrounds. This forum constituted a determining factor in the transformation of cultural institutions: for example, the Pro-Cinema Law Collective emerged which secured the approval of the Law for the Promotion of National Cinema in December 2005 during the government of Alfredo Palacio (2005–2007). This Assembly was established as a space for citizen dialogue, diagnosis, and construction concerning cultural policies and rights: the concept of a Ministry of Culture was part of its agenda in the run-up to the 2006 presidential elections.

In January 2007, Rafael Correa of the Alianza País movement – which defined itself as progressivist – assumed the presidency. The same day that he took office, through a political gesture interpreted as encouraging by those active in the cultural field, he declared the promotion of cultural development to be a state policy and created the Ministry of Culture as the institution responsible for its implementation. Antonio Preciado, an Afro-Ecuadorian poet, appointed as the first Minister of Culture of Ecuador, referred to himself as "The first black Minister of Ecuador" (Medina, 2007). Some took his appointment as an overdue recognition of diversity, specifically blackness, with its intellectual and symbolic productions. For others, it was an easy and instrumental use of difference. For those who anticipated institutional renewal, it represented continuity with the past since the poet had previously served in high positions, as President of the CECc and Director of the Cultural Branch of the BCE.

The Ministry of Culture was established within a tension that, to this day, appears irresolvable. On the one hand were the positions of the old Left whose position was one of identity-based cultural nationalism which associates itself with a clientelistic political culture. On the other hand, a reformist current existed led by cultural agents forming part of collective self-governing processes who had joined the ministerial cadre with the idea of developing renewed cultural policies in line with Correa's project for the recovery of the State. In the midst of this tension, the ministry gave the first indications of a nationalist folklorist line, based on a leftist rhetoric, which was disarticulated by contemporary narratives and problems:

> The Ministry was launched with an extremely retro-discursiveness.… We needed institutions that would render improved working conditions and a right to work in culture possible. However, the Ministry was initially excessively demagogic, employing overly simplistic rhetoric: the quaint flag, the protest song from the 60s and 70s … in 2007… The cultural scene itself had already become more complex. That was the first gap to bridge. Interesting developments had already happened to collectives, independent spaces. After 2000, something was already occurring, it was flourishing, emerging and, suddenly, that institutionality appeared which, instead of entering into a dialogue with that emergence, had disappeared forty years earlier and was incapable of responding to it.
>
> (Kueva, interview, 2018)

The first approach that the ministry adopted with regard to cultural agents was to provide resources without applying technical prerequisites, providing continuity to the prevailing political culture, "with a clear risk of sliding towards a new political clientelism" (Tinajero, 2011, p. 40). Access to resource allocation was mediated by the first cultural management tools, the adoption of which had begun to expand in the field. For its part, the section within the ministry that sought to affect an institutional renewal to support culture, even without a deep understanding of the phenomenon, imposed the role of cultural manager. The other processes of self-identification mentioned above (cultural workers, socio-cultural animators, cultural promoters, arts and community-based groups) were technified by management at the behest of the State. The category began to operate as a general umbrella term enshrined in transnational documents. Since then, defining oneself as a cultural manager enabled the establishing of a legitimate relationship with the Ministry of Culture for negotiating the allocation of funding, effectively fragmenting the sector:

> I think that for us independents the Ministry of Culture caused a breakdown. Many of the dance institutions collapsed at that time. We women saw it as a possibility to build with the support of the Ministry of Culture, to which we gave our confidence, credibility, hope and work.
>
> (Cáceres, interview, 2020)

Technical management regulation was unconcerned with the loss of singularities of the existing processes. For their part, the fragmented cultural agents, still in a state of turmoil, did not constitute a transversal set and had no common political agenda. Access to public funds produced a consensus, a single mode of relationship with the State and a dominant approach to dispute resolution which persists to the present day. The granting of resources was rapid and straightforward, without any focus on participatory processes, and directly affected the weakening of the collectives. Although financial allocation reduced their degree of discretion, the public calls for proposals made up to the present as "competitive funds", "obey a neo-liberal logic in which the State distributes resources to private subjects or organisations and, through this gesture, disengages itself from its responsibilities in the generation of integral promotional conditions" (de la Vega & Rodríguez, 2019, p. 71). Since the adoption of the 2008 Constitution, Ecuador has relied on a normative framework for the enforceability and principle of non-regression of cultural rights. It recognises itself as a plurinational, diverse, and intercultural State, with 18 ethnic groups and nationalities; and three official languages: Spanish, Kichwa, and Shua. In addition, it recognises nature as a subject of rights and indigenous territories, while proposing principles of sovereignty, self-determination, social and solidarity-based economy. It promotes a development model that would change the commodity-dependent economy into one that is knowledge based. These new recognition policies and an alleged shift in the economic model were reflected in incomplete and disparate attempts at implementing public policy, including cultural ones, because during the following decade the government did not change its orientation towards extractive activities and the dismantling of social organisations: "an archaic vision of 'development' based on large state industry as if it were an equitable alternative to the plundering of resources and the expropriation of organisational capacities and popular economic initiatives" (Rivera Cusicanqui, 2018, p. 106).

The guiding document underpinning the government's strategy for the creation of the ministry and its cultural policy at that stage was the Culture and Development Strategy (Master Plan for Spanish Cooperation 2005–2008), which was drawn up in a bilateral agreement with the AECID. It is worth noting that the nascent institution had officials who had participated in the training courses on cultural management and in the postgraduate programmes offered at the Universities of Barcelona and Girona. These were instrumental in the institutionalisation of cultural management and the consolidation of "Ibero-American" links. This strategy was implemented to achieve certain specific objectives: the training of human capital for cultural management specialising in culture and development, the consolidation of the political dimension of culture, cultural institution development, and the design of inclusive cultural policies, among others. AECI also actively collaborated in the project entitled "100 Days for Culture", consisting of working groups for the design of a Culture Law (2008–2009). This law was finally passed eight years later in December 2016, evidencing the omission of culture from the government's agenda. This caused a progressive deterioration in relations between the ministry and cultural agents and undermined confidence in the participatory instances that the former could promote on the part of the latter.

This official establishing of the discipline of cultural management laid the foundations during a new economic boom due to the State's increasing oil revenues, accompanied by the growth and the technification of its apparatus. In 2009, public expenditure on cultural sector institutions amounted to U$100,747,419.23. By 2018, it had decreased to U$2,545,013.05. In other words, national public investment in culture decreased from 0.53% to 0.11% (DISNC, 2018, p. 51). This development is partly explained by the fall in international oil prices in 2015 and its negative impact on the General State Budget.

As for the educational offer, while at the beginning of the 21st century, several universities in the country delivered relevant undergraduate courses, these no longer exist. The Ministry of Culture, in collaboration with the Latin American Faculty of Social Sciences, promoted a Diploma in Cultural Management for officials of the institution with only one intake of students in 2009. During the last three years (2018–2020), three universities in the country have launched postgraduate training courses in cultural management (Universidad Andina Simón Bolívar, Universidad Politécnica Salesiana, Universidad de las Artes), demonstrating an expansion of this academic field.

Conclusions

Cultural management – as an imperative of modernisation – has prevented Ecuador from acknowledging the heterogeneity of modalities of cultural action that currently constitute syntagma. Within this reality, spaces and times are juxtaposed, variegated complexions of the popular and multiple forms of modernity that still exist in the day-to-day fabric, non-sectored social and reproductive practices that have resisted both instrumental technification and recognition, and pledges from the capital and the State. This heterogeneity is perceptible today in cultural management in Ecuador as a practice under pressure from the contradiction between modernising aspirations and those intellectual legacies of situated thought-doing, its methodological and organisational knowledge, based on autonomy and which have been described as "empirical", "radical", and "ideologised".

The economic crisis that erupted in 2008 in Spain and, in the case of Ecuador, the fall in international oil prices from 2015 onwards, plus the end of Rafael Correa's government, led to the decline of the Welfare State model. This coupled with the permanent precariousness of the professionalised creative class, inspired a process of re-evaluation of cultural policies and cultural management. In the case of Barcelona, various actors have returned to the experiences of collective management and citizen-based movement practices reflected in works such as *Ciudad Princesa* (Marina Garcés, 2018) or *Desbordar Barcelona*, an alternative account of culture in the city (Desbordes de la Cultura 2020 Working Group), while in Ecuador processes such as the Movimiento Cultura Viva Comunitaria and the Red Comuna Kitu (a network of self-managed cultural houses in Quito) have become well established. With contributions from feminism, the cooperative and social economy, popular education, grassroots organisations, critical pedagogies, post-colonial and decolonial thinking, among others, these experiences have placed hegemonic cultural management under pressure, with principles and tools established in the late 1980s in a powerful drive towards economic growth; privatisation; the outsourcing of public management; and the neo-liberalisation of culture through globalisation and the creative industries. In short, these experiences challenge from below those problems derived from public and institutional cultural policy models that emerged from this framework, enabling the developing of a different contemporary policy for cultural management.

References

AECI (2007). *Estrategia de Cultura y Desarrollo de la Cooperación Española*. Ministry of Foreign Affairs and Cooperation, Madrid, http://bibliotecadigital.aecid.es/bibliodig/i18n/consulta/registro.cmd?id=5116.
Bayardo, R. (2018). Repensando la gestión cultural en Latinoamérica. In Yáñez Canal, C. (Ed). *Praxis de la gestión cultural*. Bogotá: Universidad Nacional de Colombia, pp. 17–32.
——— (2014). Documentos y perspectivas de la Gestión Cultural. Una mirada desde Buenos Aires. Argentina. In Yáñez Canal, C. (Ed.). *Emergencias de la gestión cultural en América Latina*. Manizales: National University of Colombia, pp. 128–140.
Bonet, L. (2012). La cooperación cultural iberoamericana en la encrucijada: papel y retos. *Cuadernos de Observación de Gestión y Políticas Culturales. Serie del Boletín de Gestión Cultural*, N°1, pp. 8–94.
Castro Gómez, S. (2005). *La hybris del punto cero. Ciencia, raza e ilustración en la Nueva Granada (1750–1816)*. Bogotá: Pontifical Javeriana University.
Cevallos, P. (2016). *Pablo Barriga. Premio a la Trayectoria 2015*. Quito: Metropolitan District Municipality-Centre for Contemporary Art.
——— (2013). *La intransigencia de los objetos. La galería Siglo XX y la Fundación Hallo en el campo del arte moderno ecuatoriano (1964–1979)*. Quito: Museos de la Ciudad Foundation.

Colombres, A. (1999). *Nuevo manual del promotor cultural*. México: National Council for Culture and the Arts of Mexico.

Coronil, F. (2000). Naturaleza del poscolonialismo: del eurocentrismo al globocentrismo. In Lander, E. (Ed). *La colonialidad del saber: eurocentrismo y ciencias sociales perspectivas latinoamericanas*. Buenos Aires: CLACSO, pp. 87–112.

De la Vega, P. (2019). Breves indicios para una gestión cultural crítica. In Yáñez Canal, C., Mariscal Orozco, J. L. & Rucker, U. (Eds.). *Métodos y herramientas en gestión cultural. Investigaciones y experiencias en América Latina*. Manizales: National University of Colombia, pp. 111–127.

——— (2019). Ecuador, entre la promesa y la decepción. *Revista Utopía*. Year 1, N°1: El dinero de la cultura. México, pp. 69–75.

——— (2016). Gestión cultural y despolitización: cuando nos llamaron gestores. *Index, Revista de Arte Contemporáneo*, N°2, pp. 96–102.

De la Vega, P. & Rodríguez, A. (2019). Ecuador, entre la promesa y la decepción. *Utopía. Revista de Crítica Cultural. El dinero de la cultura*. 1,1, pp. 69–75.

Delgado, E. (1988). La gestió cultural en els 90. *Educar*, N°13, pp. 95–103.

Desbordes de la Cultura (2020). *Desbordar Barcelona*. Barcelona: Pol Ien Edicions-LaCiutat Invisible.

DISNC (2018). *Caracterización de los sectores las industrias culturales. Diagnóstico de las principales variables socioeconómicas*. Quito: Ministry of Culture and Heritage of Ecuador – Information Directorate of the National Culture System.

Escobar, A. (1996). *La invención del Tercer Mundo. Construcción y deconstrucción del desarrollo*. Bogotá: Norma.

Freire, S. (2008). *Tzantzismo: tierno e insolente*. Quito: Libresa.

Garcés, M. (2018). *Ciudad princesa*. Barcelona: Galaxia Gutemberg.

——— (2013). *Un mundo común*. Barcelona: Bellaterra.

Grijalva, J. C. (2014). Introducción: Vasconcelos/Carrión, una democratización cultural restringida. In Grijalva, J. C. & Handelsman, M. (Eds.). *De Atahualpa a Cuauhtémoc. Los nacionalismos culturales de Benjamín Carrión y José Vasconcelos*. Quito: City Museum, International Institute of Ibero-American Literature, pp. 7–30.

Grimson, A. (2007). *Cultura y neoliberalismo*. Buenos Aires: CLACSO.

Iturrieta, A. (1993). De la transición democrática al Quinto Centenario (1975–1991). In Pérez Tabernero, P. & Tabernera, N. (Eds.). *España/América Latina: un siglo de políticas culturales*. Madrid: AIETI/OEI, pp. 181–207.

Kingman, M. (2012). *Arte contemporáneo y cultura popular: el caso de Quito*. Quito: FLACSO Ecuador.

Lander, E. (2000). Ciencias sociales: saberes coloniales y eurocéntricos. In Lander, E. (Ed.). *La colonialidad del saber: eurocentrismo y ciencias sociales perspectivas latinoamericanas*. Buenos Aires: CLACSO, pp. 1–40.

Lorey, I. (2016). *Estado de inseguridad. Gobernar la precariedad*. Madrid: Traficantes de Sueños.

Lozano, J. (2014). La vieja nueva gestión cultural y sus vínculos con la animación sociocultural y la educación. In Yáñez Canal, C. (Ed.). *Emergencias de la gestión cultural en América Latina*. Manizales: National University of Colombia, pp. 84–109.

Mariscal Orozco, J. (2014). Tendencias en la formalización de la gestión cultural en América Latina. In Yáñez Canal, C. (Ed.). *Emergencias de la gestión cultural en América Latina*. Manizales: National University of Colombia, pp. 212–225.

Martinell, A. (2019). *Gestión cultural en Iberoamérica. Una historia de éxito*. http://www
.alfonsmartinell.com/gestion-cultural-en-iberoamerica-una-historia-de-exito-y-2/
?fbclid=IwAR0orUv8j5e95rNbZkhzFjjYWit1j4toOomeHC1_FIygGvaYVm5NaNp
ZNnM.

Medina, C. (2007). Preciado, el poeta de la negritud para un ministerio de que nace.
Guayaquil: *Diario El Universo*, January 10, 2007. https://www.eluniverso.com/2007
/01/10/0001/8/584C4D3B02414CAD8AE54A9B80833EA6.html (Accessed June 2,
2020).

Miralles, E. (2014). Una conversación con Alfons Martinell. *Periférica Internacional.
Revista para el análisis de la cultura y el territorio*, N°15. https://revistas.uca.es/index.
php/periferica/article/view/2114.

———— (1996). La profesionalización en la gerencia cultural. Proceedings of the *I Curso
de Gerencia de Proyectos en las Artes Visuales*. Caracas: Polar Foundation, pp.
25–34.

Ochoa, A. M. (2003). *Entre los deseos y los derechos. Un ensayo crítico sobre políticas
culturales*. Bogotá: Colombian Institute of Anthropology and History.

Polo, R. (2012). *La crítica y sus objetos. Historia intelectual de la crítica en Ecuador
(1960–1990)*. Quito: FLACSO, pp. 33–94.

Quaggio, G. (2014). *La cultura en Transición. Reconciliación política y cultural en
España, 1976–1986*. Madrid: Alianza Editorial.

Revista Pucuna (2010). *Edición facsimilar 1962–1968*. Quito: National Council of Culture
of Ecuador.

Rivera Cusicanqui, S. (2018). *Un mundo ch'ixi es posible. Ensayos desde un presente en
crisis*. Buenos Aires: Tinta Limón.

Rodríguez, M. (2015). *Cultura y política en Ecuador: estudio sobre la creación de la Casa
de la Cultura*. Quito: FLACSO.

Rowan, J. (2016). *Cultura libre de Estado*. Madrid: Traficantes de sueños.

Sanahuja, J. A. (2012). Iberoamérica y los países andinos en la cooperación española
al desarrollo. Identidades, valores e intereses. In Verdesoto, L. (Ed.). *La Región
Andina y España: hacia una reformulación de sus relaciones*. Quito: FLACSO, pp.
107–148.

Segato, R. (2002). Identidades políticas y alteridades históricas. Una crítica a las certezas
del pluralismo global. *Revista Nueva Sociedad*, N°178, 104–125. https://www.nuso.org
/articulo/una-critica-a-las-certezas-del-pluralismo-global/.

Serrano, J. L. (2015). *Del malestar de la cultura a la enfermedad de los costos*. Thesis
for the Master's Degree in Communication with a mention in Public Opinion. Quito:
FLACSO.

Slachevsky, P. (2016). El libro y la lectura: un asunto público. *Proceedings of the XXI
CLAD International Congress on State and Public Administration Reform*. Santiago,
Chile, November 8–11, 2016. https://www.cultura.gob.cl/wp-content/uploads/2014/08
/libro-lectura-asunto-publico-paulo-slachevsky.pdf.

Tinajero, F. (2011). Las políticas culturales del Estado (1944–2010). In *Informe cero.
Ecuador 1950–2010*. Quito: Estado del país, pp. 29–42.

Úcar, X. (2002). Medio siglo de animación sociocultural en España: balance y perspectivas.
Revista Iberoamericana de Educación OEI, N°28, pp. 1–21.

Vera, M. (2013). *Más vale pájaro en mano: crisis bancaria, ahorro y clases medias*. Quito:
FLACSO.

162   *Paola de la Vega Velástegui*

Verdesoto, I. (2012). *Espacios y memoria del teatro de la calle en Quito: disputa actual por el uso del espacio público*. Master's thesis in Social Sciences, mention in Anthropology. Quito: FLACSO.

Vich, V. (2014). *Desculturizar la cultura: La gestión cultural como forma de acción política*. Buenos Aires: Siglo XXI.

Walsh, C. (2001). Las geopolíticas del conocimiento en relación a América Latina. Entrevista a Walter Mignolo. *Revista del Centro Andino de Estudios*, N°2, pp. 49–64.

10 Cultural management in Brazil

Persistence in times of uncertainty

Suelen Silva

Introduction

Cultural management is a profession developed in Brazil during the last two decades, which, as with other areas of knowledge and practice, has progressed in close relationship with various historical, economic, political, and social circumstances. This chapter provides an overview of such processes and of the emergence of cultural management within the country, while highlighting a number of its current characteristics and definitions, and suggesting references (from institutions, authors, and practices) which can be further explored by the reader.

In order to understand the development of this discipline in Brazil, and its current state, the first section reviews past events, showing how culture has constituted a disputed concept, before discussing the present context within which this new academic and professional discipline has emerged.

The second section reviews several definitions of cultural management proposed by Brazilian authors while also providing information on the profile, location, and self-image of practitioners. A list of institutions that have contributed information, discourse, research findings, and publications specifically related to the discipline of cultural management in Brazil is provided, together with a review of academic opportunities.

Finally, in linking both sections, the author explores the notion that there are two movements taking place in Brazil: one seeking to consolidate the discipline of cultural management, and another from which emerge the voices and practices of indigenous and black populations that have been historically marginalised – paradoxically so in a country renowned for its cultural diversity. It is suggested that an encounter between these two movements can broaden the discourse, references, tools, and practices within both national and international cultural management.

"Brazil has a long past ahead"[1]

The existence of what is now referred to as Brazil (and, indeed, the American continent) does not date from the arrival of Europeans. However, classifications based on opposites, for example, "cultivated versus soulless", "civilized versus savage", and "culture versus nature", were adopted in relation to the continent during the fifteenth century, following European invasion and colonisation. The colonial period, as a historical era, had largely drawn to a close in the twentieth century. Nevertheless, the colonising nations continue to benefit from its economic, social, and cultural legacies, whereas societies that were colonised remain subject to neo-colonial forms of domination and exploitation, including the prevalence of (self-) referentials, concepts, and value systems forged since coloniality (Ashcroft et al., 1995).

Within the Brazilian colonial period, from 1500/1532 to 1822, Europeans classified as "savage", "barbaric", "uncivilized", or simply "inferior" and "exotic", all those unfamiliar characteristics in the "other" that did not reflect their own values. The testimonies of those who travelled from the "Old World" to the "New World" helped to consolidate Europe's narrative of its alleged superiority over those recently contacted ("discovered", in the vocabulary of the coloniser). Within imperialist logic, this assumed superiority was also employed as justification for invading territories, plundering resources, and "civilizing", subjugating, and enslaving native indigenous populations with the intention of serving the interests of European expansion and domination. In the course of raids by various European powers, Brazil was colonised by Portugal and today, represents the only lusophone country on the continent. Following this Eurocentric colonial project, driven by a world vision centred on Europe, the Portuguese colonial legacy in Brazil included the negation of alterity, the committing of genocide [the eradication of specific populations] and epistemicide [the destruction of knowledge] of Amerindian and, subsequently, African populations (the latter of which had been forcibly transplanted from Africa and enslaved in the Americas under a colonial system).

The dehumanisation and enslavement of these populations is itself testimony to the brutal violence routinely meted out during that historical period. The symbolic control that Portugal enforced when, for example, it banned the circulation of books, the deployment of presses, and the founding of universities in Brazil is worth noting (Rubim, 2007, p. 13–14), as is the development by the metropolitan power of a specific policy intended to eradicate the use of indigenous languages in the territory (Garcia, 2007, p. 25). Portugal's intervention in what is now referred to as culture was guided, therefore, by strategic interdictions and violence intended to subjugate colonial Brazil.

During the imperial époque (1822–1889), culture was treated as an element of erudition, cultivation of the spirit, and access to literacy, forging an alleged justification for the privileges of the Portuguese royalty then resident in Brazil. In this regard, the monarchy took specific action monopolised by and aimed at a specific elite, including investment in the Academy of Fine Arts, providing patronage, and sponsoring the study of prominent artists in Europe (Schwarcz, 1998, p. 133). Thus, despite Brazil's subsequent independence, the country remained under the control of the Portuguese and culture-related activity was influenced by a preference for European values.

During the republican period (1889–1964), culture was regarded as a platform for forging the identity of a nascent nation, in a dialogue with Folklorism (a movement emerging in Europe at the close of the eighteenth century). The elite and the growing Brazilian bourgeoisie (in general, literate, nationalist, and heir to the old European aristocracy) turned their interest to the now deemed "authentic" cultural manifestations that would differentiate Brazil from other nations (Albuquerque Jr., 2007, p. 63). National institutional initiatives in the cultural field took place in São Paulo from the mid-1930s onwards. These included exploratory expeditions whose purpose was the cataloguing of artistic and cultural manifestations in the northeastern and northern regions of the country. These initiatives were located within a perspective of the São Paulo oligarchy's hegemony over the rest of Brazil, perceiving itself as playing the role of "saviour" of "exotic" cultural manifestations, purifying them of their "rusticity" (Albuquerque Jr., 2007, p. 64; Rubim, 2007, p. 15). It is significant that, during this period, cultural practices such as *Capoeira* and *Rodas de Samba* were criminalised by the Penal Code, confirmation of the drive to control cultural life. This period is also characterised by the dictatorship of Getúlio Vargas (from 1937 to 1945) which, through a combination of authoritarianism and dirigisme, began to transform the State from the ultimate patron directly sponsoring specific initiatives to a monopoliser and arbiter of culture (Albuquerque Jr, 2007, p. 68).

This political landscape intensified after a military coup installed a dictatorship (1964–1985), during which repression escalated to include censorship, kidnapping, torture, and the murder of dissidents and opponents. Against this background, the "National Integration Plan" was conceived which, in military parlance, would serve to "employ land without men", but actually served to deny indigenous populations their territorial and cultural rights and to reinforce the belief that they were an obstacle to the modernisation of Brazil (Negócio, 2017, p. 273–278; Trinidad, 2018, p. 269). On the other hand, under the pretext of guaranteeing "national security", student and popular movements opposed to the official ideology were closely monitored and persecuted, as were social and cultural events organised by the black population (Pires, 2018, p. 1068). Several artistic movements were severely marginalised with artists such as Augusto Boal, Gilberto Gil, Glauber Rocha, and Lygia Clark being forced into exile.

In addition to the violent repression of certain groups and ideas, at the other extreme of the dictatorship's course of action, several initiatives strengthening the public cultural system were inaugurated (such as the Federal Council of Culture, 1966; the National Culture Plan, 1975; and the National Arts Foundation, 1975), in certain cases, with the participation of prominent artists and intellectuals. Moreover, within the country's modernisation project, the State invested in infrastructure that served the "culture industry" (mainly broadcasting and telecommunications) concentrated in the southeastern region. Even though internal contradictions and disputes concerning these initiatives existed, cultural policy intended to build a nationalist consciousness, to depoliticise popular symbology, and to promote the existence of a supposed "social harmony" in the country (Fernandes, 2013, p. 188–189; Maia, 2012, p. 44/173; Ortiz, 2003, p. 136; Ortiz, 2001, p. 209; Pires, 2018, p. 1058). This connects with the "myth of Brazilian racial democracy" which amounts to nothing more than the denial of historical and persistent racial prejudices and inequalities imposed on indigenous and black populations.

Figure 10.1 "Natureza Morta" [Dead Nature] (2019), digital print by Denilson Baniwa (Amazonas, Brazil). Visual description: the print shows a satellite image of a forest, dissected by a few roads and minimally covered by three small clouds. There is a deforested central area, shaped like a person with a headdress. One of the hands is suspended and holds a *maracá* (musical instrument). The image resembles the outline around a corpse drawn on the ground by the police, to record the exact position in which it was discovered. The work promotes discussion of such ideas as indigenous peoples, territory, nature, deforestation, agribusiness, and death. Courtesy of the artist.

Rubim (2016a, p. 69) points out that even with the creation of culture-related structures, institutions, and public bureaucracies, work in this sector has been marked by amateurism and cronyism, there being no serious discussion on the need for professionalisation of its agents. With few exceptions, offices were assigned on the basis of personal favour or political interest. The State strove to exercise a monopoly over the organisation of culture (as during the Vargas dictatorship), reinforcing the Brazilian tradition of developing the governmental institutional cultural system during authoritarian periods (Rubim, 2007, p. 21; Vieira, 2006, p. 2).

The operating context changed during the next phase, driven by both democratic openness and neoliberalism which, according to Bayardo (2018, p. 24), was experienced more intensely in South America. As with other countries on the continent which overthrew dictatorial regimes, in Brazil democratic openness (1985) legitimately sought, on the one hand, to reverse state control over cultural and social life while, on the other, this openness was followed by a "new public management" and "minimal State" rhetoric which, in its most extreme form, attributed efficiency and rationality to the free market and inefficiency and dirigisme to State actions. In practice, this led to administrative reforms, the disintegration of public services, and reduced investment in various sectors, including culture (de la Vega Velástegui, Escribal, Carpio Valdeavellano, this volume). According to Bayardo (2018, p. 19–20), cultural management in South America developed within this context, being presented by governments, emerging markets, and international development cooperation organisations as a potential means for the sector to survive the crisis. This would be achieved by professionalising its agents, providing them with the necessary skills to make effective use of scarce resources, diversify financing sources, and profit from cultural initiatives. Bayardo (Ibid.) points out that several Latin American cultural management education initiatives were based on the transfer of knowledge, models, concepts, cases, and methodological approaches from the European and Ibero-American experience (especially that of Barcelona which invested in internationalisation strategies in the 1990s) to the Latin American reality. This process involved the support of institutions such as the Organisation of Iberic-American States (OEI), the Spanish Agency for International Cooperation and Development (AECID), and the Inter-American Development Bank (IDB) (Bayardo, 2018, p. 20–21).

Particularly in Brazil, neo-liberal influence on the sector gained strength through the promulgation of incentive laws (also known as tax exemption) as pillars of public-private cultural initiatives. Examples include the *Sarney Act* (1986), later replaced by the *Rouanet Act* (1991), in the federal sphere and several other pieces of legislation at State and local level.[2] While each of these acts (and their corresponding successors) possesses its own particularities, they all share the general goal of stimulating business sector participation in the cultural field. To this end, incentive laws allow companies that financially support artistic and cultural projects to deduct the amount in question from their fiscal liability (the level of exemption varying according to the relevant legislation). In contemporary versions of certain incentive laws, projects generally need to be first approved by the competent public agency (municipal, state, or local) and, upon approval, the proponent (an individual or a legal entity) is able to "raise funds" from companies; in other words, to convince them to financially support the project. One of the arguments used for this purpose is the subsequent tax rebate that sponsors can claim. The need for consideration, be it direct investment by the company in question or from other sources, is not a rule.[3]

The Ministry of Culture's adoption of the slogan "Culture is good business" reflected the fact that private investment in the sector has grown significantly since the mid-1990s. However, companies have perceived incentive laws less as a chance to contribute to the sociocultural fabric, and more as a form of cultural marketing (Durand et al., 1997, p. 39) which in Brazil refers to initiatives in the field of culture for the purpose of brand promotion, prioritising projects with greater potential to yield high returns and to communicate with their clientele. In this manner, the state apparatus ceased to execute the regulatory function of the cultural sector, transferring to the private sector the ultimate decision regarding those projects considered suitable for public funding, since it lacked the necessary financial resources due to unpaid taxes (Rubim, 2016a, p. 72; Vieira, 2006, p. 12).

It is within this context that the role of the "cultural producer" (sometimes the artist him/herself) has emerged in Brazil as an agent capable of developing projects and budgets; making fund-raising approaches to the private sector to raise funds; planning and executing artistic and cultural projects; in addition to dealing with the specific bureaucracies relating to incentive laws. Significantly, this context has driven the necessity for new culture professionals to not only talk and negotiate with the private sector, but also within companies, especially since such entities have started to create their own cultural projects and institutions based on current legislation (for example, the Instituto Itaú Cultural, Instituto Moreira Salles, and Centro Cultural Banco do Brasil).

This period generated a valid quest for the professionalisation and mobilisation of cultural agents, which distanced them from government interference and created new institutions and professions ("cultural producer" is an officially recognised category within the national classification of occupations issued by the Ministry of Labour). However, it also created a breeding ground for the cultural sector to advance within a neo-liberal logic of events, consumption, and marketing, where private-corporate interests are prioritised (Arruda, 2003, p. 188; Gruman, 2010, p. 151). In addition, the incentive laws further reinforced regional inequalities with the resources allocated, projects implemented, and institutions supported being concentrated in southeastern Brazil, where the bourgeoisie and financial conglomerates have historically been consolidated.

This rationale was revised in the 2000s, a decade of increasing international debate on the relationship between culture, development, and diversity, driven by the UNESCO through its Declaration on Cultural Diversity (2001) and the Convention on its Protection and Promotion (2005). In 2003, adopting the motto "Brazil, a country for all" and interacting with the international context, the new Brazilian government interpreted culture from its symbolic dimension, as a citizenship right, fundamental for both economic and social development. Finally, discussion of the defence of diversity and cultural rights and of the need to make reparations and drive systemic changes in favour of poor, indigenous, and black populations ensued. This important paradigm shift affected several sectors beyond culture enabling, for example, the adoption of affirmative action at public universities and of the Basic Income Distribution Programme (*Bolsa Família* Programme) for low-income families. Within the cultural field, public policy has focused on plurality and built on a "bottom-up" perspective, through local, state, and national conferences whose audiences were drawn from the civil, public, and private sectors. During this period, the preponderance and abuses of incentive laws were debated; statistics and research on the sector published, and both the National Culture Plan – PNC (2010–2020) and the National Culture System – SNCB (2012) introduced. The innovative programme *Cultura Viva* (2012) was also implemented which aimed to decentralise the promotion of cultural projects while, simultaneously, enhancing community protagonism. The success of this programme is clear from its adoption by other countries (Turino, 2013).

Within this process, the need to accredit professionals to act in the cultural area in various sectors (civil, public, and private) was intensified, and the debate and research relating to politics and, finally, the new profession of cultural management gained strength. The rhetoric of the time, however, was no longer limited to the neo-liberal logic of the 1990s surrounding cultural production (the basic function of which is to design projects, raise funds, manage events, and produce accounts) even though the quest for financing and sustainability of the sector is an ever-present issue. From this point on, the debate broadened, moving from the idea of cultural production to that of cultural management – the latter an area attentive to the complexity (political, sociological, anthropological, economic, etc.) and the centrality of culture to contemporary social life. Even though this distinction between cultural production and cultural management is recent (so much so that the two terms are occasionally still employed interchangeably), it is already beginning to be reflected in educational institutions (informal and formal) that have since emerged, and in which frameworks of reference, methodologies, and practices have come to be discussed, disputed, and developed between agents, researchers, and institutions dealing with the theme in Brazil.

It is true that early twenty-first-century progress in terms of public cultural policy has not overcome the sum of historical, economic, and political challenges and fragilities within the domestic sector. Nonetheless, an important drive towards (re)construction, especially with the articulation and participation of civil society, was ongoing during a period of relative economic and political stability within the country. At the dawn of this new decade, however, the emergence of populist, nationalist, and anti-democratic discourse in several countries is becoming apparent. Moreover, the Brazilian political system is in crisis, a situation exacerbated since 2019 by an ultra-right federal government whose policies, in short, threaten the 1988 Constitution, human rights, and democracy. Public agencies and cultural institutions have been ideologically co-opted and distorted from their intended social functions. Programmes and resources intended to promote science, the arts, and culture are being drastically reduced. This crisis has been deepened further by the first pandemic (COVID-19) of the current century which has radicalised embryonic historical social fragilities, injustices, and inequalities that the country was starting to confront from 2000 onwards. Only time will confirm the long-term effects of this moment on Brazilian democracy and cultural management, both of which are relatively young and still undergoing a process of consolidation.

Cultural management in Brazil: In search of definitions

In contrast to other countries, terms such as artistic management or artistic administration are infrequently employed in Brazil. Eventually, one can come across terms such as artistic group management (Valentim, 2009, p. 2; Fernandes, 2019, p. 69) and artistic career management (Carvalho, 2019, p. 13) which relate more to career plans. Within the Brazilian debate, the terms cultural management and cultural production have been adopted to refer to the field explored here. Even though they are, at times, employed interchangeably, the trend related to recent sector changes and seeks to differentiate them. When this is the case, cultural production is often assigned to actions of a more operational/specific/eventual/logistical nature relating to cultural projects, whereas cultural management would have a more strategic/generalist/regular role in programmes and institutions (Avelar, 2008, p. 50; Fernandes, 2019, pp. 56–60; Rubim, 2016b, p. 11). While cultural production, in its delimited form, would mainly react to a certain environment, cultural management being strategic would be more oriented towards proposing and creating contexts. That being said, these limits can be fluid; and functions, complementary.

Growing academic production in the field of cultural management is attempting to determine its specific objectives, as well as the skills and knowledge required by its practitioners. Among the range of ongoing developments, Rubim locates cultural management within culture organisation and considers it essential for the functioning of the cultural system at its several levels (2008, p. 10). Its practitioners must possess a multidisciplinary and generalist profile in areas such as administration, sociology, anthropology, politics, history, communication, economics, arts, and culture (2016a, p. 81). Cunha considers it a management task to qualify cultural discussions within a long-term perspective (2008, p. 14). It is, therefore, necessary for its practitioners to understand the chains of creation, production, and distribution, planning techniques, and evaluation methods, in addition to the field's symbolic, legal, political, and economic principles (2011, p. 36; 2003, p. 104). In Botelho's view (2016, p. 86), for an individual to work in cultural management, it is necessary to have an understanding of the anthropological and sociological relevance of culture and of its centrality to social and economic development. This requires diverse and transversal theoretical-conceptual competences in addition to the mastering of practical tools (such as those employed in management, financing, and planning).

In this effort to establish the field and its foundations, it can be seen that cultural management has been academically developed in Brazil as a broad and diffuse conceptual area (Amaral, 2019, p. 109). It employs administrative and technical dimensions (planning, financing, legislation, project elaboration, etc.), and moreover, it involves transversal, multidisciplinary, and generalist knowledge (humanities, arts, economics); dialoguing with diverse agents (civil, public, private), levels (local, regional, national, international), and chains (for creation, diffusion, and access); as well as understanding the different dimensions of culture (symbolic, anthropological, sociological, economic, etc.). Interdisciplinarity, sensitivity, management, and general/strategic vision are only some of the skills suggested for this profile. Perhaps unsurprisingly, the role of the cultural manager is compared to that of an orchestra conductor (Durand, 2012, p. 8; Itaú Cultural Observatory, 2008, p. 12) who, despite lacking expertise in how to play every instrument, recognises all sounds and flows, perceives and corrects dissonances, and succeeds in uniting the disparate elements effectively to achieve the desired musical effect.

The institutions' perspective

The National Culture Plan (2010–2020) requires that public sector cultural management must strive to optimise the use of public funds, complementing them with private sector investment, in order to satisfy social demands. In addition to overseeing the organisation of cultural institutions and associations, as well as the management of the National Culture System (a platform for public culture policies), the cultural management framework was intended to communicate by means of specific techniques related to heritage and artistic language, as well as through writing projects, budgets, and communication releases (Brazil, 2013).

In its MBA course proposal, the Brazilian Association of Cultural Management (ABGC[4]) suggests that cultural management is an interdisciplinary field whose professionals, in addition to possessing knowledge of culture, require competence in concepts and subjects related to administration, economics, law, and communication. The role of the manager involves planning, articulating, aggregating, mobilising, and creating a network for the various cultural agents (artists and society in general, in addition to the private and the public sectors) whose purpose is to enhance efficiency and effectiveness.

Amaral (2019, p. 119) highlights the predominance of three institutions engaged in creating references to and discourse on cultural management and production in Brazil (through research, seminars, meetings, and publications): (1) Centro de Estudos Multidisciplinares em Cultura – CULT[5] (Universidade Federal da Bahia), one of the first Brazilian institutions to discuss theoretically and conceptually the field of cultural management, with an approach based mainly on the Social Sciences. Rubim (2008; 2007; 2016a/b) and Costa (2011) are part of this group; (2) Fundação Casa de Rui Barbosa, FCRB,[6] a public institution in Rio de Janeiro which focuses predominantly on the systematisation and interpretation of data relating to cultural policy management, approaching statistical/ bureaucratic bodies and the relationship between economy and culture and which counts Calabre (2014) and Zimbrão (2013) among the researchers it employs; and (3) Instituto Itaú Cultural,[7] affiliated to one of the most profitable private banks in South America which also acts as an educational agent for culture professionals in demand in the market (Amaral, 2019, p. 131). Among its educational programmes, one specialisation (delivered in partnership with Girona University, Spain) is coordinated by Coelho (2008) and Martinell (2009).

In addition, the Observatório da Diversidade Cultural, OBDC,[8] coordinated by Barros (2014), and the Centro de Pesquisa e Formação do Serviço Social do Comércio[9] institutions, which in different ways have proposed debates, training courses, mappings, research, publications, and specialised information on cultural production and management in Brazil are both worthy of mention.

Formal education

Cultural management is a developing field in Brazil, which, at the time of writing, lacks consensus on the competences, training, methods, theories, or codes of conduct/ethics required by professionals active in the field. This poses a challenge for its consolidation within the educational system (and labour market), which has difficulty recognising the validity of hybrid programmes with inter/multi/trans/poly or post-disciplinary approaches (Durand, 2012, p. 8). Furthermore, the cultural manager can travel different paths, there being no strict monopoly on who can lay claim to this title, despite the efforts of institutions and agents in the field to establish social recognition for the profession (Cunha, 2007, p.14). This can be both advantageous, from the point of view of diversity, and negative, due to its randomness.

Academic education remains, nevertheless, one of the institutionalised means of legitimising knowledge and competence in the modern era. Therefore, as far as cultural management is concerned, both aspiring postholders and those already actively engaged in the field look to academia for opportunities to build, reflect on, and/or confirm their place. Cunha (2005), for example, found that the trajectory of practitioners in Brazil, during the 1980s and 1990s, resulted from fortuitous events leading to self-taught practice and, eventually, to training in the sector within which they were already employed. After the 1990s, cultural management and production emerged as a more deliberate choice where the search for academic qualifications preceded practical experience. This change may be correlated to the emergence, during the mid-1990s, of the first academic courses in cultural management and production in the country.

One available mapping of the creation and evolution of academic programmes in cultural management and production-related areas in Brazil was authored by Jordão, Bircce, and Allucci (2016) and covered the years from 1995 (the year of the inception of the first academic course) to 2016. The mapping shows (Table 10.1) that 90 institutions introduced 131 courses (including refresher/sequential, technical, bachelors, specialisation, masters, and doctorate programmes). Of this total, only 62 courses (47%) remained on offer in 2016 which demonstrates the volatility of the provision of academic courses. Considering the fact that a series of courses are provided by private institutions, it can be assumed that their success depends on the level of market demand.

Table 10.1 Number of courses created, active in 2016 and extinct (1995–2016)

Degree	Created		Active in 2016		Extinct	
	Freq.	*%*	*Freq.*	*%*	*Freq.*	*%*
Specialisation	87	66	37	60	50	72
Technological	13	10	4	6	9	13
Bachelor's Degree	11	8	9	15	2	3
Actualisation	7	5	0	0	7	10
Professional Master's Degree	6	5	5	8	1	1
Academic Master's Degree	4	3	4	6	0	0
Doctoral Degree	3	2	3	5	0	0
Total	131	100	62	100	69	100

Source: Mapping of cultural management and production courses in Brazil (Jordão et al., 2016).

By analysing the content of titles, pedagogical objectives, and curricula, Jordão et al. (2016, p. 15) grouped the courses into six categories, (see Table 10.2). Of the 131 courses available, 45% came under the umbrella of cultural production; 19% cultural management; 15% specific arts field production; 10% research on production, culture, and cultural fields; 6% market/creative economy; and 5% cultural policy.[10] The authors concluded that the data points to a tendency to focus on operational aspects (that is, cultural production), followed by cultural management.

This trend was confirmed by the authors in question when they analysed the content of the academic programmes through the Atlas TI software (computer-assisted qualitative data analysis). The results presented here (Table 10.3) differ from those contained in the original table produced by Jordão et al. (2016, p. 112), as the words "cultural + culture", "projects + project", and "social + society" were grouped and counted together as related terms. In this rearrangement, the concept of culture was the most frequently occurring, followed by the word "production". It is interesting to note that, although "management" is the second most frequent course category (Table 10.2), this recurrence is not reflected in the analysis of course programmes, where the ideas of "education", "communication", and "history", for example, recur more frequently than "management". The absence of "diversity", "community, "administration", and "institutions" from the most frequently mentioned words is striking.

With regard to the possible content and repertoire of training courses, it is relevant to quote Durand (2012, p. 7) who asked coordinators of academic courses in the field (participating in the International Meeting on Cultural Management Training) about the references they considered important for students of cultural management. Brazilian participants mentioned names such as Theodor Adorno, Pierre Bourdieu, Clifford Geertz, Antonio Gramsci, Jürgen Habermas, Stuart Hall, Edgar Morin, Amartya Sen, Edward Tylor, Edward Thompson, Raymond Williams, and Brazilian authors Alfredo Bosi, Marilena Chauí, Paulo Freire, Celso Furtado, Milton Santos, and Muniz Sodré. Despite the informality of such a

Table 10.2 Number of courses created, active in 2016 and extinguished (1995–2016)

Course categories	Courses created		Active in 2016		Extinguished	
	Freq.	*%*	*Freq.*	*%*	*Freq.*	*%*
Production	59	**45**	23	**37**	36	**52**
Management	25	**19**	16	**26**	9	**13**
Production in specific language	20	**15**	8	**13**	12	**17**
Research in production, culture, and languages	13	**10**	11	**18**	2	**3**
Creative economy/market-oriented	8	**6**	2	**3**	6	**9**
Cultural policy	6	**5**	2	**3**	4	**6**
Total	131	**100**	62	**100**	69	**100**

Source: Mapping of cultural management and production courses in Brazil (Jordão et al., 2016).

Table 10.3 Curriculum content analysis

#	Word	Frequency	% most frequent words
1	Culture/cultural	5289	**13**
2	Production	2162	**5**
3	Project/projects	1251	**3**
4	Art/arts	1227	**3**
5	Education	1014	**3**
6	Social/society	838	**2**
7	Communication	716	**2**
8	History	698	**2**
9	Management	607	**2**
10	Professional	555	1
11	Technology	526	1
12	Work	478	1
13	Practice	457	1
14	Relation	388	1
15	Brazilian	371	1
16	Analysis	370	1
17	Heritage	369	1
18	Policies	363	1
19	Marketing	353	1
20	Planning	322	1
Overall total (266 words)		40095	
Most frequent total		18361	

Source: Idem (rearranged by the author).

sample, it reveals a trend (in addition to the preponderance of white male authors): the weight of literature produced in the Global North (especially Europe and the United States) informing the discipline in Brazil, in comparison to literature produced in neighbouring countries, with fewer distant historical, economic, and socio-political trajectories. In this regard, it is legitimate to consider that neo-colonialism is reflected in the discipline since countries with economic privileges have greater power of circulation, recognition, and legitimation of their academic production.

With regard to academic education in the region, the mapping of Jordão et al. (2016, p. 17) pointed to the geographic concentration of relevant course provision. Considering the five Brazilian macro-regions, 58% of the 131 courses were located in the Southeast (47% in only three cities: São Paulo, Rio de Janeiro, and Belo Horizonte), 17% in the South, 16% in the Northeast, 4% in the Centre-west, and 5% in the North, relative proportions which the authors correlate with the location of business conglomerates in the country. Even though the internet is not widely accessible to all sections of the population, a digitalisation process could help to partly decentralise educational opportunities, especially in a country of continental dimensions such as Brazil. However, this remains a distant reality: according to the survey, only a small proportion of the courses (5%) were delivered online, the overwhelming majority (95%) having involved face-to-face tutoring.

In a more recent mapping by ABGC (Rodrigues and Marco, 2018), 113 courses relating to management, production, and entertainment, which were geographically concentrated in the Southeast of Brazil, were delivered in 2018. Of the courses in question, 68% were offered by private institutions and 32% by public entities. The extent to which this data influences the objectives and programme content of available courses is questionable, a point also raised by Jordão et al. (2016, p. 20) and Durand (2012, p. 15–16). This is because the private institutions[11] in which these offerings are concentrated are frequently business schools which would be more likely to navigate the operational and market-related issues (taking into account the available teaching staff), to the detriment of the more social aspects of cultural activity.

It is not possible to extract from these statistics the same degree of detail about courses focusing specifically on cultural management (classified as such). However, Jordão et al. (2016, p. 77) reported that, of the 16 courses within this category which were active in 2016, 94% were at postgraduate level and 6% were undergraduate programmes. From the mapping completed by Rodrigues and Marco (2018), it is possible to identify 13 courses specifically entitled *cultural management* of which 100% are at postgraduate level; 93% are located in the Southeast and 7% in the Northeast; while 77% are offered by private educational institutions and 23% by public organisations.

The profile of cultural management students and graduates lies outside the range of both mappings. However, considering that (a) black people are still under-represented in both public and private higher education, compared to that in Brazilian society (even though, following the introduction of affirmative policies, their access has increased since 2012);[12] (b) the courses mentioned, especially those on cultural management, are concentrated in private universities in the Southeast region; (c) on-site and full-time courses have a limited reach (Chati, 2016, p. 863); it is worth asking who in Brazil is in a position to invest in and to risk time, money, and social capital on academic courses relating to cultural management, a field within which employability is uncertain, and in a country of inequalities where problems surrounding mobility and social security intersect with variables such as gender, class, and race.

Profile, performance, and self-perception of cultural managers

The profile, performance field, and cultural practices of Brazilian practitioners who self-identified as working in cultural management and production (having received specific relevant academic training or not) were researched by Amaral (2019) through an online survey involving the participation of 517 individuals. With regard to gender, 58% of the sample declared themselves to be female and 42% male, while no one self-identified as non-binary. As far as colour is concerned, white women and men accounted for 39% and 27% of the total, respectively (a comparison: 56% of the population self-identifies as brown/black, 43%

white, and 1% indigenous, according to census data from the Brazilian Institute of Geography and Statistics (IBGE, 2019).

Turning to schooling, 83% of the sample reported having completed undergraduate courses, 31% non-degree postgraduate courses (specialisation or MBA), and 27% postgraduate degree courses (an academic or professional master's degree).[13] Recurring academic backgrounds of course participants included the arts, communication, and cultural production. Participation in informal education was also recorded, with more than half of the respondents having attended short courses as well as academic seminars. Amaral (2019, p. 175) points out that, despite the sample's high level of schooling (10% higher than the national average), this is not reflected in its economic capacity to generate personal assets (only participants aged 50 and over had asset rates similar to the national average). Amaral's research (2019, p. 193) also showed how the personal networks of respondents (who entered the field predominantly at the invitation of acquaintances) and family investment influenced the trajectory of practitioners with high qualification rates. These trends can be compared to the profiles of cultural managers in other countries with regard to, for example, the predominant participation of females and their high academic qualifications (Henze, 2018, p. 39).

As with the geographic concentration of educational offerings in the field, 70% of respondents were located in the southeastern region (46% in São Paulo alone), 12% in the South, 12% in the Northeast, 5.2% in the Centre-west, and 0.4% in the North (in comparison: 42% of the Brazilian population resides in the Southeast, 14% in the South, 27% in the Northeast, 8% in the Centre-west, and 9% in the North, according to IBGE, 2019).

From the replies collected by Amaral (2019, p. 196–198), the following map of activities can be drawn up.

- **Occupational status**: professional and voluntary (76%), solely professional (21%), solely voluntary (3%).
- **Areas of activity**: sociocultural projects (24%), cultural policy (14%), festivals (14%), art institutions (13%), artistic companies (12%), training/teaching/ research (11%), higher education (5%), cultural tourism (3%), other (3%), cultural diplomacy (2%).
- **Roles**: production (18%), project development (16%), organisation/project management (15%), artistic creation (10%), educational/training activity (9%), mobilisation with the public (9%), financial management (8%), curatorship (8%), communication advisory (7%), legal advisory (<1%), other (1%).
- **Places of employment**: association (11%), production company (10%), cultural centre (10%), artistic group (10%), artistic company (8%), collective (8%), secretariat/department of culture (8%), theatre/concert hall (7%), teaching/training institution (6%), private cultural institute (5%), museum (4%), library (3%), orchestra (2%), publishing house (2%), gallery (2%), studio (2%), other (1%), photographic studio (1%), and bookstore (1%).

- **Position**: owner/partner (22%), coordinator (17%), director (15%), regular work in cultural activities (12%), other services (10%), management (9%), consulting (9%), regular work in administrative activity (4%).

When questioned about their professional self-perception, 72% of the participants self-identified as agents of social transformation: 71% as professionals in the art world; 65% in art education or education relating to cultural issues; 62% as professionals in the public management of culture and art; 53% as agents of the preservation/protection of intangible heritage; 43% as agents for the preservation/protection of artistic and historical material heritage; 44% as artists; and 27% as professional fundraisers (Amaral, 2019, p. 207). This data can be compared with the global information reviewed by Mandel (2017, p. 60–61), with cultural managers more frequently self-identifying as "agents of social transformation" (especially in South America) and less frequently as "artists" and "fundraisers".

From an extensive list of pre-conditions for working in the sector which need to be satisfied, the sample considered it extremely important *to have an open mind* and *interest in art and culture*, as well as to undertake *training, college, and graduate studies*. In contrast to this "openness" and "interest in the field", however, their cultural practices tend to be limited to established/legitimized circuits (such as attending public cultural centres, exhibitions, biennials, and festivals). The participants acknowledged these practices, together with childhood experiences (such as receiving books as a child and visiting museums with their parents) as important conditioning factors for working in the field (Amaral, 2019, p. 209).

The sample in Amaral's research (2019, p. 208–210) considers cultural policies and the country's economic and political situation as factors influencing their work, although they do not see their own personal political experience as relevant. In general, the sample rejects associating with concrete political situations (certain types of activism were repudiated, such as participating in neighbourhood associations, local movements, and social councils), the exception being participation in conferences on culture, where norms for public policies in the field are discussed. These are regarded as extremely important. Unfortunately, there are no details as to how the interrelationship between gender and colour informs the entire range of information presented in the survey.

Final considerations or expectations

Over the brief period covered by this chapter, the author has attempted to show how the field of cultural management is being developed in Brazil. With this in mind, various notions of culture have been presented, highlighting which cultural practices were socially and institutionally validated or invalidated, in what way (by denial, subjugation, control, repression, patronage, incentive, commercialisation, departmental policy, etc.) and by which sectors (public, private, or civil). Cultural management, therefore, is not a neutral field of knowledge, education, and professional practice since it is defined by a politically, economically, and socially driven notion of culture (Fernandes, 2019, p. 44).

Only during the last two decades has cultural management gained prominence in Brazil, in a process influenced by the emergence of national and international cultural markets, by intergovernmental exchanges and conventions, and by revision of public cultural policy relating to the sector which was based on a broad process of social participation. These realities shed light on the current state of the sector in Brazil, which is undergoing consolidation and is already influenced by historical and current challenges imposed by the country's situation. In this effort to develop a distinct academic discipline and a professional field, attempts to understand the nature of cultural management in Brazil are both recent and polysemic. This polysemy is related to the complexity and dynamism of culture in the contemporary world, with the diversity of legitimacies, functions, and interests of the different sectors and agents that deal with it.

Some authors (Avelar, 2008; Botelho, 2016; Cunha, 2011; Rubim, 2016a; 2008) have claimed a differentiation between cultural producers (who came to prominence due to the demand generated by Brazilian incentive laws in the mid-1990s) and cultural managers. The latter were to be afforded not a limited place in operational matters, but a strategic and inter/multi/trans/ post-disciplinary role (Durand, 2012). The formal academic courses in cultural management and related areas appear to prioritise more operational and practical approaches (focusing on ideas surrounding production and projects), while also taking into account, although with less focus, issues such as education, art, and society (Jordão et al., 2016). Finally, the production and cultural management practised by individuals who regard themselves as active in the field (with or without specific training) have been classified from the perspective of social transformation even though, in general, they reject any association with political situations (Amaral, 2019). The work of those who perceive themselves as cultural producers and/or managers has mainly been conducted simultaneously in a professional and voluntary fashion through the production functions of third sector associations in sociocultural projects, most significantly in the Southeast of the country (especially São Paulo). These professionals are predominantly white females with a high level of education compared to the average Brazilian (Amaral, 2019).

From these definitions, it is possible to discern a movement towards the consolidation of cultural management as a novel and as yet unintegrated professional and research field in Brazil. However, this movement also operates within a context of disputes over conceptual monopolies, identities, interests, and institutional and academic safety from which it is difficult to break free. In this sense, Barros (2008, p. 28) suggests that within Brazilian cultural management a form of rhetoric was developed, rather than a new practice introduced. Amaral (2019, p. 234) sees in this development the birth of a new occupation replicating old divisions.

This brief overview, covering several definitions, profiles, and difficulties of how cultural management in Brazil has been debated, taught, and practised communicates and/or reinforces some of the challenges and conditions of Brazilian society, such as its continental size, its (neo-)colonial and neo-liberal past and present, its regional inequalities, economic concentration, and a long history of injustice, violence, silence, and racism against indigenous and black populations. If cultural diversity is often recognised as a characteristic of Brazilian society, it was only at the beginning of this century, and briefly, that it became a concrete target for public policies, the result of a peculiar political moment and also of long resistance and mobilisation by these marginalised populations.

These groups have been increasingly demanding the full exercise of their rights, including cultural rights, criticising the historical lack of representativeness in established and institutional circuits, and questioning the preponderance of theoretical and methodological references of colonial/European origin to consider their own realities. In addition, they make new offers and articulate their own networks, spaces, and artistic and cultural circuits which, with technological advances, become more widely known. Initiatives such as *Rádio Yandê*, *Festival Yby*, the *Batekoo* movement, and the tecno-brega scene in Pará are examples of new forms of association, open management models, and the (re)uses of culture in the (re)construction of identities, examples which remain to be more broadly and seriously debated and reflected within the discipline. Above all, such practices, based from the outset on uneven ground, represent a breath of fresh air within a context of breaches of systems (economic, educational, cultural, etc.).

It is worth asking if and when these two movements will meet, and the extent to which this encounter might oxygenate, expand, and create frames of reference, approaches, discourses, and innovative initiatives for Brazilian, South American, and international cultural management. If, on one hand, a far-right government and the first pandemic of the current century foreshadow a period of uncertain harvest, on the other hand, the ground for this encounter to take place seems to have been prepared.

Notes

1 Quote from the Brazilian writer Millôr Fernandes (1994, p.30).
2 A similar scheme operates in Chile through the Valdés Law, passed around the same date (Muñoz del Campo, this volume).
3 Proponents, supporting companies, and projects registered and enabled by the *Rouanet Act* can be reviewed at the Versalic Portal: http://versalic.cultura.gov.br/ (Accessed August 18, 2020).
4 More information at ww.abgc.org.br.
5 More information at www.cult.ufba.br.
6 More information at www.casaruibarbosa.gov.br.
7 More information at www.itaucultural.org.br.
8 More information at www.observatoriodadiversidade.org.br.
9 More information at https://centrodepesquisaeformacao.sescsp.org.br.
10 The categorization proposed by Jordão et al. (2016, pp. 14–15) considers the following as academic courses: (a) cultural production: training from a more operational perspective (project writing, production, post-production, and resource management); (b) cultural management: training for management positions in public or private cultural institutions; (c) specific arts field production: training for cultural production with curricula aimed at the specificities of artistic fields (such as theatre, music, or visual arts); (d) research in production, culture, and cultural fields: training which enables the

connecting of diverse cultural field knowledge and to conduct research on production chains; (e) market/creative economy: training focused on creative economy and cultural industry theories; (f) cultural policy: training courses for cultural policy managers focused on social development.
11 The main source of funding for private higher education institutions is student fees.
12 Of those entering higher education in 2012, 10.6% were brown, 2.7% black, 0.9% Asian, and 0.15% indigenous. In 2018 (six years after implementing affirmative policies at universities), the proportion shifted to 28.8% brown, 7% black, 1.7% Asian, and 0.7% indigenous (IAT, 2018).
13 In Brazil, non-degree postgraduate courses train specialists and have a minimal duration of 360 hours; at the end of the course, a certification is offered, but not a diploma. Degree postgraduate courses are masters (professional or academic) and doctorates; these award diplomas upon completion.

References

Avelar, R. (2008). *O avesso da cena: notas sobre produção e gestão cultural*. Belo Horizonte: DUO Editorial.

Albuquerque Jr., D. (2007). Gestão ou gestação pública da cultura. In Rubim, A. & Barbalho, A. (Eds.). *Políticas culturais no Brasil*. Salvador: EDUFBA, pp. 61–86.

Amaral, R. (2019). *Sob o jugo da musa: profissionalização e distinção entre produtores e gestores culturais no Brasil*. Thesis for the Doctorate in Sociology at the University of São Paulo. http://tiny.cc/7oyjsz (Accessed July 4, 2020).

Arruda, M. (2003). A política cultural: regulação estatal e mecenato privado. *Tempo social*, Vol. 15, N°2, pp. 177–193. https://bit.ly/2QQ6D8X (Accessed August 15, 2020).

Ashcroft, B., Griffiths, G. & Tiffin, H. (1995). *The post-colonial studies reader*. London: Routledge.

Barros, J. (2014). Cultura e diversidade: noções iniciais. *Textbook for the Extension Course in Public Administration of Culture*. Porto Alegre: Ministério da Cultura/UFRGS/EA. http://tiny.cc/boyjsz (Accessed June 13, 2020).

——— (2008). Os profissionais da cultura. *Revista Observatório Itaú Cultural*, N°6, pp. 21–28. Available at http://tiny.cc/3qyjsz (Accessed June 5, 2020).

Bayardo, R. (2018). Repensando la gestión cultural en Latinoamérica. In Yañez Canal, C. (Ed.). *Praxis de la gestión cultural*. Bogotá: National University of Colombia, pp. 17–32.

Botelho, I. (2016). *Dimensões da cultura: Políticas culturais e seus desafios*. São Paulo: SESC.

Brazil (2013). *As metas do Plano Nacional de Cultura*. São Paulo: Via Pública Institute; Brasília: Culture Ministry. https://bit.ly/3jqkKyJ (Accessed June 20, 2020).

Calabre, L. (2014). Estudos acadêmicos contemporâneos sobre políticas culturais no Brasil: análises e tendências. *PragMATIZES Revista Latino-Americana de Estudos em Cultura*, Vol. 7, pp. 109–129. http://tiny.cc/apyjsz (Accessed June 13, 2020).

Carpio Valdeavellano, P. (this volume). Cultural management in Peru: The role of the Ministry of culture in challenging times. In Henze, R. & Escribal, F. (Eds.). *Cultural Management and Policy in Latin America*. Abingdon & New York: Routledge, pp. 230–246.

Carvalho, A. (2019). *O papel do empresário artístico na gestão de carreiras musicais após a transformação da indústria da música*. Dissertation for the Professional Master's in Creative Economy Management of the Higher School of Advertising and Marketing, Rio de Janeiro. http://tiny.cc/epyjsz (Accessed June 10, 2020).

Chati, G. (2016). Formação em gestão cultural no Brasil. In Calabre, L. et al. (Eds.). *Anais do Seminário Internacional Políticas Culturais*. Rio de Janeiro: Casa de Rui Barbosa Foundation. http://tiny.cc/hpyjsz (Accessed Jul 13, 2020).

Coelho, T. (2008). *A cultura e seu contrário*. São Paulo: Iluminuras/Itaú Cultural.

Costa, L. (2011). *Profissionalização da organização da cultura no Brasil*. Thesis for the PhD in the Postculture Programme at the Federal University of Bahia. https://bit.ly/3juuqbx (Accessed June 6, 2007).

Cunha, M. (2011). Desafios de uma política pública para a formação de gestores culturais. In Barros, J. e Oliveira Jr., J. (Eds.). *Pensar e agir com a cultura*. Belo Horizonte: Observatory of Cultural Diversity, pp. 35–47. https://bit.ly/3ho0fRu (Accessed June 5, 2020).

——— (2008). Referências bibliográficas. *Revista Observatório Itaú Cultural*, N°6, pp. 47–56. http://tiny.cc/3qyjsz (Accessed June 5, 2020).

——— (2007). Gestão cultural: Construindo uma identidade profissional. *Proceedings of the III ENECULT – Conference of Multidisciplinary Studies in Culture*, May 23–25, Salvador de Bahia: Federal University of Bahia. http://tiny.cc/dgmosz (Accessed August 18, 2020).

——— (2005). Gestor cultural: profissão em formação. *Lecture at the Masters in Education*. Federal University of Minas Gerais. http://tiny.cc/iz1ksz (Accessed June 5, 2020).

——— (2003). Formação do profissional de cultura. In Brandt, L. (Ed.). *Políticas Culturais*. Barueri: Manole, pp. 103–116.

de la Vega Valestegui, P. (this volume). Cultural management in Ecuador: Genealogy and power relations within the constitution of a field. In Henze, R. & Escribal, F. (Eds.). *Cultural Management and Policy in Latin America*. Abingdon & New York: Routledge, pp. 143–162.

Durand, J. (2012). *Cultural manager: Official latter under construction*. International Meeting Cultural Management Training (Report). São Paulo: SESC. http://tiny.cc/lqyjsz (Accessed June 25, 2007).

Durand, J., Gouveia, M. & Berman, G. (1997). Patrocínio empresarial e incentivos fiscais à cultura: análise de uma experiência recente. *Revista de Administração de Empresas*, Vol. 37, N°4, pp. 38–44. http://tiny.cc/kqyjsz (Accessed June 25, 2020).

Escribal, F. (this volume). Cultural management in Argentina: political agenda and challenges for practitioners and researchers. In Henze, R. & Ecsribal, F. (Eds.). *Cultural Management and Policy in Latin America*. Abingdon & New York: Routledge, pp. 87–105.

Fernandes, M. (1994). *Millôr definitivo: A bíblia do caos*. São Paulo: L&PM.

Fernandes, N. (2013). A política cultural à época da ditadura militar. *Contemporânea – Revista de Sociologia da UFSCar*, Vol. 3, N°1, pp. 173–192. http://tiny.cc/rqyjsz (Accessed May 3, 2020).

Fernandes, T. (2019). Histórico da gestão cultural no Brasil. In Rubim, A. (Ed.). *Gestão cultural*. Salvador: EDUFBA. https://bit.ly/2CTNEqu (Accessed July 17, 2020).

Garcia, E. (2007). O projeto pombalino de imposição da língua portuguesa aos índios e a sua aplicação na América meridional. *Revista Tempo*, Vol. 12, N°23, pp. 23–38. http://tiny.cc/yryjsz (Accessed May 3, 2020).

Gruman, M. (2010). Nem tanto ao céu, nem tanto a terra: limites e possibilidades da lei de incentivo fiscal à cultura. *Revista Espaço Acadêmico*, Vol. 9, N°107, pp. 149–154. http://tiny.cc/4syjsz (Accessed July 9, 2020).

Henze, R. (2018). *Introduction to International Arts Management*. Wiesbaden: Springer.

IAT (2018). *Sinopses Estatísticas da Educação Superior, Anos 2012 e 2018*. Brasilia: Anísio Teixeira Institute. https://bit.ly/2Ym4Hcx (Accessed August 20, 2020).

IBGE (2019). *Pesquisa Nacional por amostra de domicílios contínua*. Brasilia: Brazilian Institute of Geography and Statistics. ftp://ftp.ibge.gov.br/Estimativas_de_Populacao/Estimativas_2019/estimativa_dou_2019.xls (Accessed July 18, 2020).

Itaú Cultural Observatory (2008). Os fazeres e os saberes dos gestores de cultura no brasil. *Revista OIC*, N°6, pp. 9–20. http://tiny.cc/243ksz (Accessed June 2, 2020).

Jordão, G., Bircce, L. & Allucci, R. (2016). *Mapeamento dos cursos de gestão e produção cultural no Brasil*: 1995–2015. São Paulo: Itaú Cultural Foundation. http://tiny.cc/ysyjsz (Accessed May 23, 2020).

Maia, T. (2012). *Os cardeais da cultura nacional: o Conselho Federal de Cultura na ditadura civil-militar (1967–1975)*. São Paulo: Itaú Cultural Foundation & Iluminuras. http://tiny.cc/gtyjsz (Accessed May 17, 2020).

Mandel, B. (2017). *Arts/Cultural Management in International Contexts*. Hildesheim: Georg Olms Verlag AG.

Martinell, A. (2009). *Las interacciones en la profesionalización en gestión cultural*. University of Girona. http://tiny.cc/0uyjsz (Accessed July 14, 2020).

Muñoz del Campo, N. (this volume). Cultural management in Chile: Between professionalization and the emergence of a public intervention category. In Henze, R. & Escribal, F. (Eds.). *Cultural Management and Policy in Latin America*. Abingdon & New York: Routledge, pp. 125–142.

Negócio, C. (2017). A violência física e cultural contra os povos indígenas durante o regime militar. *Aracê – Direitos Humanos em Revista*, Vol. 4, N°5, pp. 264–294. https://bit.ly/39sKlmp (Accessed May 3, 2020).

Ortiz, R. (2001). *A moderna tradição brasileira: cultura brasileira e indústria cultural*. São Paulo: Brasiliense.

——— (2003). *Cultura brasileira e identidade nacional*. São Paulo: Brasiliense.

Pires, T. (2018). Estruturas intocadas: Racismo e ditadura no Rio de Janeiro. *Revista Direito e Práxis*, Vol. 9, N°2, pp. 1054–1079. http://tiny.cc/fuyjsz (Accessed May 3, 2020).

Rodrigues, L. & Marco, K. (2018). *Mapeamento Nacional: formação em gestão, produção cultural e entretenimento, graduação e pós-graduação*. Brazilian Association of Cultural Management. https://bit.ly/32G970N (Accessed June 3, 2020).

Rubim, A. (2016a). Políticas e gestão cultural no Brasil. In Rubim, A. et al. (Eds.). *Panorama da gestão cultural na Ibero-américa*. Salvador: EDUFBA, pp. 59–86. https://bit.ly/2WCWsIf (Accessed May 5, 2020).

——— (2016b). Prefácio. In Costa, L. & Mello, U. (Eds.). *Formação em organização da cultura no Brasil*. Salvador: UFBA, pp. 9–12. https://bit.ly/3eLNFd3 (Accessed July 22, 2020).

——— (2008). Formação em organização da cultura no Brasil. *Revista Observatório Itaú Cultural*, N°6, pp. 47–56. http://tiny.cc/qyyjsz (Accessed July 16, 2008).

——— (2007). Políticas culturais no Brasil: Tristes tradições, enormes desafios. In: Rubim, A. & Barbalho, A. (Eds) *Políticas Culturais no Brasil*. Salvador: EDUFBA, pp. 11–36.

Schwarcz, L. (1998). *As Barbas do Imperador: D. Pedro II, um monarca nos trópicos*. São Paulo: Companhia das Letras.

Trinidad, C. (2018). A questão indígena sob a ditadura militar: do imaginar ao dominar. *Anuário Antropológico*, Vol. 4, N°1, pp. 257–284. http://tiny.cc/xzyjsz (Accessed June 9, 2020).

Turino, C. (2013). *The point of Culture: Brazil turned upside down.* Lisbon: Calouste Gulbenkian Foundation. http://tiny.cc/72kksz (Accessed July 22, 2020).

Valentim, A. (2009). Gestão como estratégia na formação de grupos artísticos. *Proceedings of the 5th Scientific Meeting of ABRACE – Brazilian Association for Research and Post-Graduate Studies in Performing Arts*, November 5th and 6th, 2009 – São Paulo. https://bit.ly/3jl9TpQ (Accessed July 16, 2020).

Vieira, M. (2006). Sintomas dos deslocamentos de poder na gestão do campo cultural no Brasil – uma leitura sobre as leis de incentivo à cultura. In Pinheiro, M. (Ed.). *Temas contemporâneos*, Vol. 1, pp. 56–62. http://tiny.cc/40zjsz (Accessed June 17, 2020).

Zimbrão, A. (2013). Políticas públicas e relações federativas: O Sistema Nacional de Cultura como arranjo institucional de coordenação e cooperação intergovernamental. *Revista do Serviço Público*, Vol. 64, N°1, pp. 31–58. https://bit.ly/2CB2XUX (Accessed July 3, 2020).

11 Cultural management in Uruguay

A country synonymous with a river

Cinthya Moizo y Danilo Urbanavicius

Introduction

Uruguay is a country located in the eastern part of South America which takes its name from that of a river. With just over three million inhabitants, it is one of the smallest countries on the continent, a situation accentuated by the fact that it borders on two behemoths: Argentina and Brazil. Uruguay can be said to be not only geographically small but, perhaps, also psychologically so. Far from regarding its condition as a privilege or an opportunity, its self-perception is one of being not only a small but, even, a "petite country".

> The Uruguayan self-portrait as the cultural champion of America is a product of its being a petite country. A country that has two giants as neighbours. A country that needs to compensate, in some way, for its inferiority complex … regarding its physical inferiority as a handicap and masking it with hubris. Curiously, this behaviour, prevalent for many decades and still evident in some sectors of Uruguayan society, has not been able to develop the idea that small is beautiful, thus regarding its own condition with pride – rather than arrogance – and without other compensatory mechanisms.
>
> (Achúgar, 1992)

Uruguayans regard themselves as supportive and relatively easy-going when it comes to lifestyle, customs, and traditions. What makes them feel even "more Uruguayan" includes mate (a traditional caffeine-rich infused drink), asado (roast meat), and the national soccer team "la Celeste" (the "Sky Blues") (Dominzain et al., 2015, p. 2). Uruguayans tend to be conservative and rooted in the past.

A meaningful summary of Uruguayan characteristics is perhaps presented in the Third National Report on Consumption and Cultural and Imaginary Behaviour from 2014, by the Humanities Faculty of the University of the Republic, which indicates that:

> Given the transformations and shifts that have occurred in recent years in the cultural sphere, a recognition map has been drawn which, at present, indicates that we have improved and greater access to culture.… We continue to be slow and questioning when faced with the possibility of change. We place

hope in the country's future while, simultaneously, accepting our limitations in the face of political, technological and cultural change, with cultural phenomena being the salient Achilles heel, given their comprehensive character within social life.... This anchoring in the past seems to be a recurrent theme with Uruguayans.... The same is not true of the future, particularly when we think of the nation, rather than ourselves. We demonstrate hope and understand that the future of the country lies in production. In other words, we continue to believe in producing and that, through individual initiative, we will come out ahead. We remain committed to solidarity, but there appears to be no clear opinion as to whether we are tolerant or racist.

(in Dominzain et al., 2015, p. 29)

A Gallicised country

Since its inception, even in times when Uruguayan territory was known as Banda Oriental, close relationships with several European nations have existed, although, for some time, that relationship existed within the context of a war of independence involving countries such as Spain, Portugal, and, later, Great Britain. At other times, Uruguay has regarded with alacrity countries across the Atlantic, particularly France. In other words, and more precisely: "Uruguayan society has traditionally been and remains a society with a need and appetite for mirrors" (Caetano, 1992, p. 78).

After a protracted series of confrontations for the Banda Oriental and a degree of internal conflict, European countries re-entered the scene, on this occasion through successive waves of immigration. According to the historians Barrán and Nahum (1970, p. 14), the demographic model of the 18th and 19th centuries emerged in a territory created from "head to toe by Europeans". Four great migratory waves emanating primarily from Europe (Spain, Italy, Lithuania, Poland, Russia, and Armenia, among others) exponentially increased the size of the Uruguayan population, which was, by no means, composed exclusively of Creoles. To be more precise, in 1843, two out of every three residents of Montevideo were foreigners, while, by 1860, 48% of the population consisted of immigrants. At the beginning of 1900, the foreigner-Montevidean ratio, although lower, was 4:1 (Barrán & Nahum, 1970, p. 90).

Other significant events influencing the course of the country in terms of its national model were the presidencies of Batlle and Ordoñez (1903–1907 and 1911–1915). Both heads of government took France as their role model when implementing various state reforms which promoted a certain degree of social, cultural, and economic and even architectural well-being that earned the country the title of Switzerland of America. It can be said, therefore, that:

just as in the ideological, cultural and educational field, the matrix of this "urban reform" was French, [nevertheless] there were many other outstanding European architects among those who built this city (Montevideo).

(Caetano, Peréz, and Tomeo, 2010, p. 27)

Within this context of nostalgia for an "idealised past" and a longing to be European, it is not surprising that, just as in the early days of cultural management, the focus has traditionally been and remains on countries like France and Spain, particularly when it comes to institution building, professionalisation and training, as well as how cultural management as a profession is defined.

The origins of cultural institutionality

If cultural institutionality were to be named after an individual, it would be the French Minister of Culture, André Malraux. As far as the year of the phenomenon's birth is concerned, this would be 1959: the year in which the first French Ministry of Education and Culture was established, an inspirational landmark of cultural institutionality not only in Uruguay but across the whole of Latin America (Escribal, this volume). For a decade, Malraux, the French novelist and politician, implemented an ambitious cultural policy, promoting a broad mobilisation of several actors: artists, local authorities, as well as national and local officials. In addition, during this first decade, a number of relevant initiatives were launched, such as the modernisation of cultural heritage policies, the popularisation of cinema through the provision of financial support, a music development policy within the 22 French regions, and the support of contemporary creators of culture (Négrier, 2003).

With regard to Uruguay's cultural institutions, in 1970, after several previous incarnations, the Ministry of Education and Culture (MEC), as it exists today, was formed. Another of the most important milestones was the founding of the Department of Culture of the Municipality of Montevideo (IMM), not only because of the institution itself but because several of the country´s pioneering cultural policies were developed there.[1] Many of these were predecessors to current ones, both at the municipal and national levels. In 1985, the IMM was created, under the directorship of Thomas Lowy and with the support of Alejandro Bluth. All cultural services dispersed throughout other departments were brought together in order to avoid even more bureaucracy. The IMM will be composed of two divisions: the Division for the Promotion of Culture and the Division for Cultural Planning and Action. The first will comprise Arts and Letters, while the latter embraces, inter alia, Municipal Theatres, Municipal Symphonic Orchestras, and Public Performances (Montevideo Intendency, 1989).

The year 1995 was highly significant for the cultural sector for various reasons. The architect Mariano Arana became Mayor of Montevideo, assigning a new institutional status to the Department of Culture, and appointing Gonzalo Carámbula as Director of Culture. His impact on cultural policies and cultural management in Uruguay remains enormous up to the present since his metaphor of understanding culture as a cultural ecosystem constitutes one of the most complete and accurate insights into the concept of culture. Significantly, Montevideo was elected Ibero-American Capital of Culture:

> Montevideo's assuming the mantle of a cultural capital city represented a starting point in re-considering the issue of culture. At that time, four axes

were proposed, namely; improvement in the quality of services, innovation in those services and activities considered necessary, investment in cultural infrastructure – Teatro Florencio Sánchez del Cerro, Mercado de la Abundancia, etc. – and the development of a cultural policies programme, including, for example, the Capital Fund.

(Pérez Mondino and Urbanavicius, 2015, p. 174)

That same year, Tomás Lowy assumed the post of Artistic Director of the MEC under the presidency of the Colorado Party member, Julio María Sanguinetti. Lowy and Carámbula rapidly reached an agreement within which the Culture Department of the City Council because of the larger budget would work, for obvious reasons, primarily in Montevideo, while the Culture Department of the MEC would operate mainly in the country's interior (Lowy, interview, 2014).

1995 represented an important year for culture in Uruguay. On July 24 and 25, the Culture Department of the Ministry of Culture and the Directors of Culture of the 19 Municipal Governments convened in San Gregorio de Polanco (Tacuarembó) and issued a number of declarations, one being that:

Culture must be seen nowadays by governments and society as being of increasing value. It is a direct generator of jobs and income, a mobilizer of resources, including those relating to tourism, a promoter of locations and activities dependent on cultural actions.

(Ministry of Culture, 1999, p. 247)

These meetings of the Directors of Culture of the 19 departments were held on four more occasions during the Lowy administration. Central issues concerning, inter alia, cultural events were discussed, and action points subsequently implemented in the following years.

The inescapable and urgent thing to do is to pave the way for the strengthening of cultural institutions, to equip municipalities with solid and versatile structures, adequate financial resources, qualified and committed personnel, and the adaptation and incorporation of technical infrastructures adequate to the requirements of the task.

(Ministry of Culture, 1999, p. 253)

Cultural policies in Uruguay

With the understanding that cultural institutions are public administrative bodies such as ministries, agencies, directorates, public services, competitive funds, libraries, and theatres, it is essential to bear in mind that the intangible dimension – regulations, laws, everything related to the legal framework – must guarantee, defend, promote, and democratise culture. Understanding that public cultural institutions are a means to an end that the State deploys in order to accomplish its duties in the most efficient way, rather than an end in themselves, means that the

State must have the capacity to adapt and change its institutions, while invariably confronting new challenges. Cultural policies represent a tool in the achieving of this objective.

García Canclini defines cultural policies as "a set of interventions by the State, civil institutions and organized community groups with the aim of guiding symbolic development, satisfying the cultural needs of the population and reaching consensus for a form of order or social transformation" (2002, p. 26).

These combine human, regulatory, natural, cultural, financial, and technological resources, considered components contributing to the creation of policies, programmes, and projects in order to address the problems of citizens, investigate their behaviour, and meet their demands in order to achieve social, cultural, political, and economic objectives. In this sense, it is essential to relate to, and update, the tangible and intangible dimensions that Canclini highlights and, therefore, have a solid platform from which to consider, design, and implement public cultural policies.

With an embryonic but well-defined national cultural institutionality, it is appropriate to describe some of the public cultural policies implemented in Uruguay in recent decades. 2005 is usually considered the year when the Left assumed control of national government, specifically with the rise of the *Frente Amplio* (Broad Front, a left-winged political movement). However, it is fair to say that from that year onwards there has been an increasing growth in cultural policies in terms of quantity, quality, and financial investment.

For example, MEC has set itself as one of its main management objectives in the field of public cultural policy, the development, circulation, and access to cultural goods and services throughout the country. To this end, it mainly manages and disperses four legally sanctioned funds supportive of long-term plans. It is relevant to mention that the organisation in charge of the dispersal of these funds was the MEC's National Direction of Culture (DNC) and these laws gave the fund a solid institutional framework.

1. In 2005, Law N°17.930 (Uruguay, 2005) created the Competitive Funds for Culture whose main objective is to democratise culture, as well as to allow access to cultural goods on an equal opportunity basis, thereby stimulating the decentralisation of cultural activities. An annual public invitation is made for artists, managers, teachers, and producers to apply for funding for artistic and/or cultural projects which together with other financial resources are evaluated by external juries.

2. The same bill created the Cultural Incentive Funds (FIC), a means of financing artistic and cultural projects throughout the country. These funds are composed of contributions from taxpaying companies and individuals that receive reciprocal tax benefits. The main objective of the FIC is to develop interaction and cooperation between the artistic-cultural sector (artists, cultural institutions, and cultural managers) and a private sector willing to contribute economic resources in order to generate inclusion, a sense of belonging, and corporate social responsibility.

3. The cultural infrastructure development funds for the interior of the country (i.e., the remaining 18 departments that constitute Uruguayan sovereign territory) were also included within Law N°17.930. These funds are primarily intended to improve the facilities of public and/or private cultural centres and/or spaces (halls, museums, libraries, theatres, among others) through the financing of building remodelling and refurbishing projects, in addition to the purchase and sale of properties which can be accessed through a public appeal for projects.
4. A few years later, under Law N°18.719 passed in December 2010, the Fund for the Promotion of Training and Artistic Creation (FEFCA) was established. This programme allocates public funds to the stimulation of artistic training and creation through competitive mechanisms. By means of an annual and public appeal addressed to artists and creators, it seeks, through a system of grants, to promote training for and the professionalisation of the artistic sector, as well as to stimulate national creators in the various targeted artistic disciplines.

After several years of implementing these policies, important steps towards a new cultural institutionality have been taken. For instance, in 2017, the Regional Competitive Fund for Culture was created, although unsupported by a law that would grant it full institutional status, to finance artistic-cultural projects (visual arts, dance, retrospectives and traditions, music, and theatre) of citizens resident in locations within the country other than Montevideo. Its objectives are to promote the democratisation of culture and equal access to the free creation and production of cultural goods within the national territory, in addition to encouraging the integration of culture into economic and social development processes.

While this initiative represents a positive starting point, it is insufficient. There remains a long way to go in terms of an equal distribution of state economic resources within the country, since within the proposed changes

> the territorial aspects of the appeal (such as obligatory geographical distribution through a certain number of public presentations) lost weight in relation to previous ones, thus undermining the concept of regionalization and the consequent allocation of specific funds. Similarly, some creators question a number of unnecessary determinisms.
>
> (Ministry of Education and Culture, 2017a)

Moreover, in 2016, the DNC of the MEC – together with the Network of Directors of Culture of Uruguay, social actors, and organisations from all over the country – elaborated a National Culture Plan (PNC) with the objective of securing input for the National Culture and Cultural Rights Law that remains in the process of promulgation by the National Congress. Several of the demands emerging from this initiative, which brought together more than two thousand cultural workers throughout the country, reflect the need of the cultural sector to secure, among other things, training in cultural management:

> During the various consultations with cultural agents, the main problems emerged ... the lack of training centres ... the strong demand across the

country for training in the artistic disciplines and cultural management, as well as for spaces for meetings and networking for dissemination and business.

(Ministry of Education and Culture, 2017b, p. 45)

In response to this request, at the end of 2017 the MEC launched an online platform – Online Culture – that enables members to familiarise themselves with the cultural scene in Uruguay. This is a collaborative space where cultural agents can register on the website.[2] At present, more than 9,600 cultural agents from across the country have joined this network. Beyond this initiative, the demand for decentralised training in cultural management has unfortunately not yet been met.

Training in cultural management

The political crisis of the 1970s, which affected both Latin America and Europe, highlighted the urgent need to consider and create cultural policies going beyond heritage and the arts. This context was favourable to the emergence of cultural management as a profession since there was an acceptance of an anthropological concept of culture, as defined by UNESCO, which was open to a dialogue with the economic sphere. A major milestone in this direction occurred when, in 1982, the international community held the World Conference on Cultural Policies in Mexico and drafted a statement on the definition of culture.

In Uruguay, while the authoritarian regime established by the civilian-military dictatorship (1973–1985) supported a rigid and exclusivist official culture, cultural manifestations gradually began to emerge as important spaces of resistance and encounter. In this regard, the activities of artists drawn from different disciplines were frequent, together with collectives and movements finding in those cultural manifestations something that transcended "the event" itself. The event also combined other factors, such as the prevailing political climate with aspirations for change. In this context, a profession of self-taught cultural managers was developed by artists and other cultural actors, after a hiatus caused by years of dispersion and setbacks imposed by the dictatorship. This was undoubtedly an extremely prolific period in which the use of cultural expressions and the generation of culture-related links inspired several individuals to seek specific tools associated with what we now call cultural management. In Uruguay, this concept started to gain currency in the mid-eighties, taking particular inspiration from Spain and France. At that time, the so-called energisers, administrators, agents, actors, or cultural workers identified the need to systematise knowledge and practice which would, in turn, allow them to create spaces for reflection and action as a means of investigating the specific processes of cultural management.

It was necessary to wait until 1996 when, with Tomás Lowy once more as protagonist, the first training courses in cultural management were initiated. An introductory course was launched, training 260 students from all parts of the country and a small contingent of Argentinians (Ministry of Culture, 1999, p.

85). Following this experience, 25 participants satisfying the criteria of academic performance and territorial diversity were selected to continue their training at the University of Barcelona (Spain). Moreover, from 1997 to 1999, various workshops were held in Montevideo, Flores, Canelones, Treinta y Tres, Colonia, Maldonado, Salto, Tacuarembó, Rivera, Durazno, Soriano, Río Negro, Artigas, San José, and Florida (Ministry of Culture, 1999, p. 86).

The former Bank of Boston Foundation – re-named the Itaú Foundation – an institution that had been and continues to be fundamental to the training of cultural managers in Uruguay, appeared on the scene in 1997. 2010 witnessed the inception of the Faculty of Culture (FC) of the Latin American Centre for Human Economy (CLAEH) offering a degree in Cultural Management which, at the time of writing, was unique in the country. In 2013, the University of the Republic launched a Diploma in Cultural Management course which, so far, has been followed by two groups of students. In 2019, the Regional University Centre of the East (CURE), forming part of the University of the Republic (UDELAR), launched its first Masters in Cultural Policy course.

Although several years have passed since the emergence of cultural management as an academic discipline, it continues to be poorly defined. This is due, in part, to its presence within the complex and changing cultural ecosystem. However, it also stems from a widely accepted incipient character which requires it to be enriched and complemented by such fields as administration, communication, marketing, anthropology, and sociology. This reliance on other disciplines causes it, in some way, to suffer from an identity crisis.

For those involved in managing culture, it is somewhat difficult and, at the same time, essential to explain both the nature of cultural management and the role and prerequisite competencies of a cultural manager. Perhaps the diffuse definition of this discipline's activities, as well as the relative youth of cultural institutions, constitute reasons why cultural managers experienced this urgent need to define their profession. While this chapter will not detail the various definitions of cultural manager, a brief review of how the role might be delineated appears prudent. In this regard, the definition proposed by Moizo and Díaz seems most apt:

> A cultural manager is a content generator, has the capacity to reflect on his or her own practice and this will provide input for decisions in a more professional manner. A mediator between theory and practice, between parties involved, [he or she] is the one who investigates, listens, plans, involves strategic partners, builds teams and motivates them.... On the other hand, he or she is a restless, curious and reflexive actor.
>
> (2015, p. 82)

This brief account of contemporary cultural management in Uruguay shows both the emerging nature of the discipline and the contexts in which it has flourished, while also outlining the perspectives that the country has adopted from across the Atlantic.

The emerging path to a national creative economy

The Culture of Work, a piece of research coordinated in 1997 by Luis Stolovich on behalf of the Department of Culture of the IMM, represented the initial investigation conducted in our country into the link between culture and economy which is still not appreciated by either society in general or the political system. For this reason, it constitutes an indispensable reference in the approach to economically evaluating the sector. Several years later, focusing on the economic dimension of culture, the MEC created the Department of Creative Industries with the aim of promoting cultural sector activities, specifically music, literature, and design, in order to develop economic activities through clusters, fairs, and national and international markets, in 2007.

At an international level, the Inter-American Development Bank states that the creative economy

> comprises the sectors in which the value of their goods and services is based on intellectual property: architecture, visual and performing arts, crafts, film, design, publishing, research and development, games and toys, fashion, music, advertising, software, TV and radio, and video games.
>
> (IDB, 2013, p. 15).

That same year, MEC, through an accord with the Faculty of Economics and Administration of the University of Uruguay (UDELAR), presented the first results of the Satellite Culture Account for Uruguay (CSCU) which, in 2009, included the audio-visual, recorded music, books and publications, performing arts (theatre, dance, and live music), plastic and visual arts, museums, libraries, and cultural training sectors.

It is estimated that in 2009 the gross added value of the cultural sector amounted to almost US$245 million, representing 0.93% of the country's gross domestic product (GDP). In 2012, the value added by the four sectors totalled US$315 million, which equated to 0.63% of GDP. This decrease in the contribution to GDP is explained by the higher growth of other more traditional sectors such as livestock and tourism during that period. In addition, the CSCU of 2012 did not include all the sectors that had been considered three years earlier. However, it is important to clarify that these statistics do not include other cultural and creative activities such as design, handcrafts, and video games. The sector generating the largest added value is the audio-visual sector at 55%, followed by the publishing sector (26%), performing arts (11%), plastic arts and photography (5%), and the museum sector (2%). Finally, music represents 1% of the GDP contribution of the creative sector. According to the findings of the 2012 study, the four sectors (i.e., audio-visual, books and publications, and music) did not register significant changes. As for the employment generated by cultural activities, it was estimated that in 2012 almost 9,250 people found work in the music, audio-visual, books and publications sectors, with the audio-visual sector being that which generated most jobs at 57% of the total. This sector was followed by those relating to publishing, books and publications, at 40%, while the music sector positions created were only marginal, at a mere 2% of the total employment in the cultural field (Achugar and Rivas, 2017).

Within this context, four aspects are important because they are both relevant and disturbing in terms of the development of the creative sector. Firstly, in Uruguay, the research investment in the vast and complex field of the creative economy was low. For example, the most recent research carried out by the MEC in this field relating to this specific South American country dates from 2012. The Faculty of Culture of the University CLAEH (UCLAEH) is currently conducting research into the impact of the creative industries on the national economy with the aim of continuing the economic measurement of cultural activity carried out under the previous CSCU. The current research not only reviews the methodology, but also introduces a survey of the seasonality of performances, specific musical genres, and the participation of women artists and technicians. In this case, 2016 represents the year of reference for the analysis which embraces the performing arts and music sectors (production of phonograms, both physical and digital, and live shows). Since this project is yet to be completed there is no available data to analyse. Nevertheless, the severity with which the cultural sector has been impacted by the current global crisis resulting from the Covid-19 pandemic can be assessed:

> The performing arts sector will be the most affected by this crisis because its nature implies the face-to-face consumption of a cultural content. This presents the challenge of reconverting different contents to a new format in an attempt to mitigate the negative impact of this situation. Effects will depend on the seasonality of the different expressions. For theatre, dance and cinema, the impossibility of putting on shows next winter will have a greater impact than for live music. In an optimistic scenario, with the return of public shows on June 1st., there will be a loss in revenue from ticket sales of 35% for music and 12% for theatre and dance. But within a pessimistic scenario, with the return of the shows on October 1st., the loss will be 55% for music and 58% for theatre and dance.
>
> (Traverso and Pienika, 2020, pp. 5–6)

Secondly, in the Uruguayan context, insecurity and informality constitutes another historical characteristic of this sector. These two characteristics apply both to the nature of job creation and to the manner in which business is conducted. Therefore, the data previously explained (GDP relating to the creative sector) excludes the data relating to a significant number of people, products, and cultural services. On the other hand, it shows that the labour rights of those working in these modalities are not respected. Although progress has been made, much remains to be done and this applies to all South American countries. The centralisation of economic resources and academic training in the country's cities is another factor that hinders the quantitative and qualitative development of the creative industries. In Uruguay, only three institutions exist that train cultural managers and confer formal qualifications: the Itaú Foundation (diploma), the UCLAEH (undergraduate, technical, and diploma), and UDELAR (postgraduate degrees). It is estimated that between 2010 and 2017 these institutions trained over 500 people, 68% of whom were female. Ultimately, in Uruguay, culture and the market are considered incompatible. In other words, as far as the artistic field is concerned, within the cultural ecosystem and, above all, with regard to cultural policies, discussions about buying, selling, supply, and demand, often result in the "reification" of culture or art. As Coelho expresses it: "a major part of cultural policy, when implemented at the State's instigation, is in conflict with the market which is supposedly the enemy of authentic culture and art" (2009, p. 208).

This perspective is shared by numerous individuals responsible for developing the sector, partly due to the profession of cultural manager being closely linked to the public sector. Most cultural managers and/or artists in the country enter into a part- or full-time relationship with the state.

> This relationship corresponds to a specific reality of our country, namely, that it has not yet found the appropriate mechanisms to enable the sustainable development of private ventures in the field of culture. Although steps have been taken in this regard, they are insignificant when considering all initiatives. This situation constitutes a notorious shortcoming that limits the sector, as well as our capacity for action.
>
> (Moizo and Díaz, 2015, p. 84)

Conclusion

"He who does not know his history is condemned to repeat it". This sentence, attributed to Napoleon Bonaparte, indicates our need to know our origins, to understand our present selves, and to endeavour to arrive with the fewest questions possible at a future which, at present, is uncertain due to the change of government of March 1, 2020.

A sequence of events in Uruguay led to the possibility of a qualitative leap in cultural management. With regard to cultural institutionality:

> it is undergoing a process of expansion and development through the implementation of various cultural policies and undertakings. In particular, since the creation of the DNC (2006) and the MEC Centres (2007), work has begun in the hinterland on issues related to cultural management at the territorial and inter-institutional level.
>
> (Caldes, Guerrero and Vezzaro, 2016, p. 11)

With regard to academic training, the emergence of the UCLAEH gave the profession a structure and legitimacy that inspired those who entered it, while simultaneously encouraging the state to create, at UDELAR, a postgraduate degree in Cultural Management and a master's degree in Cultural Policy. Another important, unprecedented milestone, and one which would suggest that, for cultural workers, cultural militancy outweighs partisan politics, is the creation of the National Network of Culture Directors. Formed by all the departmental authorities, this collective began to take shape on January 2012 and remains active today.

Thought up by a group of citizens, political actors and cultural managers who, in their role as cultural leaders in each of their departments, collectively understood that new tools were needed to implement more solid proposals in cultural matters throughout the national territory.

(Barreto, 2020, p. 10)

Understanding culture as an enforceable universal human right, ratified by the Uruguayan state through international covenants and conventions, should guarantee compliance with the right to cultures for all subjects residing in the territory. If culture is "a long conversation between all that is culture, between all those who move culture. A long and frank conversation. The best idea of freedom in culture is the idea of conversation" (Coelho, 2009, p. 84); cultural diversity then manifests itself in the dialogue between the right to identity and diversity, citizen participation, intellectual and artistic property, intellectual and artistic creation and research, cultural heritage, education, science and technology, etc.

Progress in strengthening cultural institutions, together with the professionalisation of cultural workers, are the present salient features after a lengthy process of accumulation and development These advances enabled the development of national public cultural policies which began to be professionalised (with political will, economic investment, and presence throughout the country) with the first leftist government in 2006, developing uninterruptedly until 2019.

This must be sustained and supported in the face of new challenges, both those related to the economic impact of the current global situation, as well as others related to the shift in the political orientation of the new government, whose understanding of the role of the State in these matters differs in principle from those of previous administrations.

From a liberal-conservative perspective, the current government has, to date, made explicit, not only at a discursive level but also in its actions, that it is cutting jobs and discontinuing investment in certain economic sectors of which arts and culture form a part. It is, unfortunately, still unknown whether they will prioritise the development of cultural policies and cultural rights. However, the situation does not give cause for hope.

Notes

1 Zamorano (this volume) identifies a similar situation in Paraguay with its capital, Asunción, as does Carpio Valdeavellano (this volumen) in relation to Lima in Peru.
2 Available at http://culturaenlinea.uy (Accessed October 16, 2020).

References

Achugar, H. (1992). *La balsa de la medusa: Ensayos sobre identidad, cultura y fin de siglo en Uruguay*. Montevideo: Trilce.
Achugar, H. & Rivas, L. (2017). *Tendencias y factores de cambio en la economía de la Cultura*. Montevideo: Office of Planning and Budget of the Presidency of Uruguay.

https://www.opp.gub.uy/sites/default/files/inline-files/Informe%20Econom%C3
%ADa%20de%20la%20Cultura.pdf.

Barrán, J. P. & Nahum, B. (1970). *El Uruguay del novecientos*. Montevideo: EBO.

Barreto, J. C. (2020). *Cultura en red, caminos que conectan*. Montevideo: Montevideo Intendence.

Caetano, G. (1992). Identidad nacional e imaginario colectivo en Uruguay: La síntesis perdurable del Centenario. In Achugar H. et al. (Eds.). *Identidad uruguaya ¿mito, crisis o afirmación?* Montevideo: Trilce, pp. 75–96.

Caetano, G., Peréz, C. & Tomeo, D. (2010). Baroffio, Arquitectura y primer batllismo: Las bases físicas de un modelo de ciudadanía. In Gutiérrez, R. (Ed.). *Eugenio P. Baroffio: Gestión urbana y arquitectónica, 1906–1956*. Montevideo: CEDODAL, pp. 23–38.

Caldes, L., Guerrero, S. & Vezzaro, C. (2016). *Salirse de la línea: Aportes para la reflexión en torno a la gestión cultural en Uruguay*. Montevideo: MEC.

Carpio Valdeavellano, P. (this volume). Cultural management in Peru: The role of the Ministry of Culture in challenging times. In Henze, R. & Escribal, F. (Eds.). *Cultural Management and Policy in Latin America*. Abingdon & New York: Routledge, pp. 230–246.

Coelho, J. T. (2009). *Diccionario crítico de política cultural: Cultura e imaginario*. Barcelona: Gedisa.

Dominzain, S., Radacovich, R., Duarte, D. & Castelli Rodríguez, L. (2015). *Imaginarios y consumo cultural: Tercer informe nacional sobre consumo y comportamiento cultural*. Montevideo: University of the Republic and the Ministry of Education and Culture. http://www.dedicaciontotal.udelar.edu.uy/adjuntos/produccion/1328_academicas__academicaarchivo.pdf.

García Canclini, N. (2002). *Latinoamericanos buscando lugar en este siglo*. Buenos Aires: Paidós.

IDB (2013). *La Economía Naranja. Una oportunidad infitnita*. Washington: Inter-American Development Bank. https://publications.iadb.org/publications/spanish/document/La-Econom%C3%ADa-Naranja-Una-oportunidad-infinita.pdf.

Ministry of Culture (1999). *Gestión 1995–2000*. Montevideo.

Ministry of Education and Culture (2017a). *Convocatoria 2017. Nuevas bases del Fondo Concursable para la Cultura*. Montevideo: Ministry of Education and Culture. https://fondoconcursable.mec.gub.uy/innovaportal/file/103060/1/2---nuevas-bases-convocatoria-2017.pdf.

——— (2017b). *Asistencia y asesoramiento técnico para la promoción de un diálogo nacional orientado a la elaboración del Plan Nacional de Cultura* 2017–2027. Montevideo: University of the Republic & ProFundación para las Ciencias Sociales Association.

Moizo, C. & Díaz, B. (2015). Innovar desde la Gestión. In En Caldes, L., Guerrero, S. & Vezzaro, C. (Eds.). *Salirse de la línea: Aportes para la reflexión en torno a la gestión cultural en Uruguay*. Montevideo: MEC, pp. 81–88.

Montevideo Intendency (1989). *Cultura para la ciudad de Montevideo. Estos servicios son suyos, úselos*. Montevideo: Montevideo Intendency.

Négrier, E. (2003). *Las políticas culturales en Francia y en España. Una aproximación nacional comparada*. Barcelona: Institut de Ciències Politiques y Socials. https://www.icps.cat/archivos/WorkingPapers/wp226.pdf?noga=1 (Accessed October 28, 2020).

Pérez Mondino, C. & Urbanavicius, D. (2015). Política y gestión cultural en Uruguay entre dos siglos: con Gonzalo Carámbula. *Cuadernos del Claeh*, 34(102), pp. 169–184.

Stololovich, L., Lescano, G. & Mourelle, J. (1997). *La cultura da trabajo. Entre la creación y el negocio: economía y cultura del Uruguay.* Montevideo: Fin de Siglo.

Traverso, D. & Pienika, E. (2020). *Estimación del impacto de la pandemia en las artes escénicas en Uruguay.* http://universidad.claeh.edu.uy/cultura/wp-content/uploads/sites/6/2020/04/Art_FacultaddelaCultura_202004.pdf.

Uruguay (2005). *Law N°17.930. National Salary Budget expenditures and investments.* Passed on December 23. https://www.impo.com.uy/bases/leyes/17930-2005.

Zamorano, M. (this volume). Cultural management in Paraguay since the democratic transition: strategies of cultural disruption in a conservative frame. In Henze, R. & Escribal, F. (Eds.). *Cultural Management and Policy in Latin America.* Abingdon & New York: Routledge, pp. 106–124.

12 Cultural management in Bolivia

A journey through history

Vanessa de Britto Maluf

Introduction

This chapter examines the forms, narratives, and imperatives of cultural management in Bolivia, particularly its place within a context of important political and ideological processes and developments. What is the nature of the transformations that have occurred at different points in history during which republican Bolivia has completed its transition to becoming a plurinational state? Answering this question will help to identify the point at which cultural management gained recognition within the country as a profession. In order to do this, the chapter will review political and social events that have marked Bolivia's history, exploring how, at the time of their occurrence, culture and the arts came to play a role in these ultimately conflictive developments. It will also highlight the challenges of cultural management practice within these political contexts; the operational context of cultural public institutions; and the management tools available to them.

In this context it is important, furthermore, to survey the influence and application of cultural management in recent years, in which the policies and narratives of "decolonisation" and the paradigm of "buen vivir" have been implemented against a background that the Bolivian government termed the "crisis of western civilisation". Is it, perhaps, the case that the decision to *"return to the* original path recovering values and codes" (Choquehuanca, 2006) has influenced the creative processes and practices of cultural management?

In the drive to contextualise the path that cultural management has followed, it is necessary to adopt an instrumental definition of culture, one that is consistent with the social and cultural characteristics of the country. Culture will be understood as constituting the diverse manifestations of the human spirit; the particular way of doing things; the way of viewing the life of a community; its way of thinking; forms of communicating; building a society based on a series of transcendent values; or, as UNESCO, claims:

> Culture … can be considered … as the set of distinctive, spiritual and material, intellectual and affective features that characterize a society or a social group. It includes, in addition to arts and letters, ways of life, fundamental human rights, value systems, traditions and beliefs.
>
> (2001, p. 73)

Culture has proved largely inseparable from political processes, both as an underlying cause and, frequently, in anticipating their evolution. Firstly, it is possible to affirm that during the colonial period culture was associated with a project that aimed at "ensuring the continuity of the western civilizational model" (Esterman, 2018, p. 20).

With regard to the manner in which coloniality influenced social formation in Latin America, the concept of the *coloniality of power* appeared to be a term seeking to "characterize a pattern of global domination typical of the modern/capitalist world-system originating with European colonialism in the early sixteenth century" (Quintero, 2010, p. 3).

Quijano argues that:

> The dominated populations of all the new identities were also subjected to the hegemony of Eurocentrism as a way of producing and controlling inter-subjective relationships, the imaginary, social memory and knowledge; especially to the extent that some sectors were able to learn the dominators' script. Thus, with the extended and, as yet, incomplete period of coloniality that is reinvented, the populations ("Indian" and "black") were trapped between the aboriginal epistemological and Eurocentric patterns that were, moreover, channeled as instrumental or technocrat rationality, in particular with regard to relations with the world around them.
>
> (2009, p. 7)

In order to explain how cultural management is understood in theory and practice, it is helpful to highlight the special relationship between arts and culture and its administration throughout Bolivian history.

The Republic and the revolution

Bolivia was founded as a Republic in 1825. Artistic practices continued to remain colonial, particularly in terms of their dependence on metropolitan models (Gisbert & de Mesa, 2012). Indeed,

> Colonial imposition had acted on local societies, but this particular imposition was accepted and reinterpreted in works of art.... It was about demonstrating how a whole system of mutual appropriations between different cultures went far beyond syncretism.
>
> (Bouysse-Cassagne, 2018, p. 530)

Through the exploitation of tin, the passage of the century brought the arrival of liberalism and international capitalism. This, together with the loss of the Littoral zones and the Acre (gates to the Pacific and the Atlantic, respectively), provoked a progressive reaction culminating in the expansion of cities; in road construction; in railways; in education (marked by the introduction of secular schooling); and in a powerful flowering of literature. A literature seeking to promote national reconciliation and a revolutionary attitude has yet to be conceived (Salazar Mostajo, 1989, p. 37).

At that time, a deep-seated social discontent was gathering strength against the mining oligarchy, the so-called "tin barons", who were supported by the landowners, importers, and the majority of army officers. This was capitalised on by the Nationalist Revolutionary Movement (MNR), a party founded in 1942 from a variety of social movements unifying workers, peasants, and mine workers – hitherto politically invisible social groups (Mayorga, 2003). They sought the elimination of the large monopolies in order that retail trade would remain exclusively "in the hands of the Bolivians". This was the epicentre of a fundamental transformation in Bolivia, most notably in political relations and representation, as exemplified by the Chaco War (1932–1935) between Paraguay and Bolivia.

It is only through so-called *modernism* that art in Bolivia proposed a decolonising approach involving a renewal of language through literature, understood as a rejection of imported or imposed values. That rebellious action provides us with a foretaste of what the National Revolution (RN) was to become, 30 or 40 years before 1952:

> the discourse of the indigenous ideology constituting the "national identity" that incorporated the indigenous and mestizo population into it, served as a platform for the emerging nationalism of the 1950s and [it] can be explored through pictorial art.
>
> (Rossells, 2004, p. 299)

Rossells' text: *Mirrors and Masks of Identity: The Indigenous Discourse in the Plastic Arts (1900–1950)* addresses relevant questions regarding the construction of a cultural development and the recognition of the rights of the indigenous population through the self-definition and representativeness of these artists. It investigates whether the discourse changed from the public, while also exploring which social, cultural, and political spaces indigenous plastic art occupied and whether it had any influence on and relationship with indigenous movements. During this period, subversive political movements become popular:

> the mutation of art and literature towards the figuration of the indigenous and native, as archeology, emerged within the context of a great new passion for a distant Indian past.
>
> (Prada, 2004, p. 12)

In the 1950s, on the eve of a revolution, a group of artists (Anteo) was founded by Walter Solón Romero Gonzales (1923–1999), one of the most prominent exponents of 20th-century Bolivian art. A muralist, weaver, engraver, carver, painter, and draftsman, he sought to plant the seed of a cultural movement that portrayed in its works the anguish and desires of the people, tracking the progress of the revolution at each of its stages in putting into practice the ideals of change and social justice that were fomented after the Chaco War.[1] The collective was named after the Greek god Anteon who was invincible whenever his feet were in contact with the ground. The group's message was clear: your feet must be rooted in reality in order to transform it. This movement was joined in La Paz, among others, by famous Bolivian painter Miguel Alandia Pantoja who, as Vila explains:

> [took] his inspiration from the social muralism developed in Mexico from 1921 by Diego Rivera and later by Orozco and Siqueiros.... The movement, as had happened before in Mexico, blamed the Spanish colonizers for the country's misfortunes, and proposed a return to an idyllic, pre-Hispanic, Marxist-style world.
>
> (1998, p.14)

Cecilia Lampo, contemporary visual artist, observes that,

> This era was marked by three great visual artists: painters Cecilio Guzmán de Rojas and;Miguel Alandia Pantoja as well as, José María Velasco Maidana – film director, composer, actor, painter, and dancer – who, without an explicit desire for what come to be known as cultural management, circulated and modified the expression and the understanding of art and culture in Bolivia … integrating the vast majority of the Bolivian people into a cultural community that, since the colony had been little valued, had in a certain way been denied.
>
> (Interview, 2020)[2]

The work of these three artists has continued to influence artistic and cultural work in Bolivia up to the present.

Within the framework of the congress organised by the Central Obrera Boliviana (COB) in 1970, which included art workers; peasants; miners; university federations; and high schools; as well as other unions including some from abroad; Alandia Pantoja – acting representative of both the Union of Revolutionary Artists of Bolivia and the Federation of Revolutionary Artists and Writers of Bolivia – subscribed to a manifesto on *Art and the Revolution, and a Platform for Social Claims of the Revolutionary Artist*. It is interesting to observe from this process how the cultural sector and its management sought synergy with the dynamism of the social process, in tandem with an institutional functionality attentive to guaranteeing cultural rights.

The National Revolution (RN) set the guidelines for Bolivia's entry into the 20th century, marked by a modernisation process that changed the political, economic, and social course of the nation through the promotion of citizen participation, extensive agrarian reform, and public control of natural resources. Within this process, in addition to educational reform, universal suffrage was implemented, granting suffrage to the illiterate, the indigenous, and women. During this period, society itself witnessed the emergence of a new phenomenon: that of the *avant-gardes*. This cultural insurgency proved, paradoxically, to be somewhat colonial in character, responding largely to the references established by the avant-gardes of the North which included:

> Expressionism, Fauvism, Cubism, Abstraction, Dadaism, Futurism or Surrealism. Such currents ultimately prevailed everywhere and decisively represented the artistic future up to the present, despite initial public rejection and conservative criticism. Thus, there is nothing particular or negative in the fact that, despite the country's isolation, they also found acceptance in Bolivia.
>
> (Vila, 1998, p. 13)

Even if during this period there was nothing new in the manner of managing culture and the arts, novelty consisted of the participation of indigenous people in the political and social scene, reaffirming their ancient presence (Salazar Mostajo, 1989, p. 103). In short, the Republican model adopted in Bolivia in 1825 involved the marginalisation of the original indigenous majority, and a process of centralisation that reduced a large part of national territory to a peripheral status.

Cultural institutionality between diverse forms of dictatorship and democracy

The government of the MNR was overthrown in 1964 by a military coup led by René Barrientos which presaged Bolivia's subsequent subjection to lengthy periods of dictatorship interspersed with sporadic periods of democracy. Nationalism, with fluctuations between populism and reformism, was the ideological framework of this period, in which the Banzer dictatorship is salient for its comparative longevity (1971–1978), while the dictatorship of García Meza (1980–1981) was marked by violence, intolerance, vitriol, and the misuse of power (Mesa, Gisbert & de Mesa, 1997).

In 1965, the Barrientos Government created a separate Ministry of Culture. However, after a short period, it returned to operating under the auspices of the Ministry of Education. In this regard, public cultural policies were framed by a series of institutional directives. For example, in 1970, the government of General Alfredo Ovando Candia published the Declaration of the Revolutionary Government on Educational, Cultural and Scientific Policy, whose essence was based on a search to ensure the way in which would be shaped "self-affirmation and appreciation of the spiritual legacy of the Bolivian people", through a cultural revolution aimed at "overcoming the decades of colonialist submission and alienation … by its own culture rooted in native traditions, without underestimating the common legacy of Western civilization and the energy contribution of other cultures" (Ministry of Education, 1970, p. 39). Ovando Candia left power that same year, and his declaration was archived for five years when in 1975 the government of General Hugo Banzer drew on it to justify the creation of the Bolivian Institute of Culture (IBC). Its management was entrusted to the cultural manager, researcher, and archaeologist Julia Elena Fortún (1929–2016), who was tasked with implementing the guidelines of a cultural policy in Bolivia.[3] This institute was managed by a Directive Council, an Executive Director, and an Executive Council composed of representatives of the National Institute of Archeology, the National Institute of Anthropology, the National Institute of Plastic Arts, the National Institute of History and Literature, the National Institute of Music and Dance, and the Post-Compulsory Education Division. The IBC developed the basis of Bolivian cultural policy in which it is stated that culture has a direct relationship with the individual, ethnic groups, technology, and the environment (Olivares Rodriguez, 2014, p. 6).

At the outset of the 1980s, a new national-indigenous collective identity emerged around which organisations were re-built. This process comprised three elements: the recovery of indigenous and native memories and practices to replace the class references that had dominated the initiatives of previous decades, the questioning of Eurocentrism, and the defence of diversity. This process was supported by the documenting and academic rehabilitation of the practices and institutions of indigenous communities (the *ayllu*[4]) and its wide dissemination through, for instance, research centres and community radio stations broadcasting in indigenous languages (Condori Laruta, in Wanderley, 2016, p. 60).

Democracy at last

Democracy was reinstituted in 1982, with the formation of the government of President Hernán Siles Suazo by an alliance known as the Democratic Popular Union (UDP) supported by the Left-wing Nationalist Revolutionary Movement (MNRI), the Movement of the Revolutionary Left (MIR), and the Bolivian Communist Party (PCB).

> In 1985, under the Government of the MNR, with Víctor Paz Estenssoro as president, and the support of Nationalist Democratic Action (AND), democracy was finally consolidated through what was referred to as "democracy through pacts" that closed the nationalist cycle and launched the so-called modern liberal phase, followed by a series of governments under multi-party political alliances that marked the outset of the 1990s.
> (Mercado, Leitón & Chacón, 2005, p. 42)

At present, the management of culture and the arts has been based on community organisations, political artistic activism, and the central role of the state. Although the existence of cultural management, spontaneous and self-taught, was always mentioned in historical texts, it lacked methodology and was marked by a strong orientation towards artistic dissemination.

The concept of cultural management in Bolivia, as in the rest of the region, became part of the discourse on culture towards the end of the 1980s both in government institutions and socio-cultural groups. This notion intended to introduce a new element into the discussion about cultural activities which, up to that point, had been described by the roles of cultural animators, promoters, or producers (Henze & Escribal, this volume). Since that time, cultural management has sought a re-designation of the practice, in the face of a broadening of the cultural dimension – beyond arts – which has moved the discussion about this profession on to other issues requiring greater professional capacity.

The early 1990s in Bolivia was marked by the fall of the UDP and consensus-based democracy. Internationally, events such as the fall of the Berlin Wall in 1989, heralded the beginning of a new geopolitical configuration which introduced neoliberal policies into both Bolivia and the region more generally, in addition to the concept of multiculturalism. Discussions about globalisation and its potential homogenising effect became generalised while debates about cultural industries, subsequently referred to as creative industries, were initiated.

> This same globalization process promoted the re-emergence of cultures and identities whose existence had been denied until then. This became evident when showing the historical, limited and, therefore, arbitrary character of national entities or nation-states that had been built in previous centuries on the negation of cultural plurality or with a clearly assimilationist and homogenizing national project.
>
> (Boccara, 2005)

In the present era, the *economy of culture* has become the focus: technology, particularly that relating to digitisation, and increasing mobility is now the norm, as is the loss of autonomy of the public sector. This new scenario represented a challenge for the cultural sector. Cultural actors required new skills and knowledge relevant to the concept of an empirical cultural management which needed to be professionalised in order to achieve a greater capacity for project development and management. The assumption of responsibility for the promotion of art and culture by the private sector justified, according to the new ideological framework, the withdrawal of the State from its responsibilities with regard to the production, financing, and dissemination of cultural goods, basically encouraging greater dependence on hegemonic cultures.

In October 1993, the Ministry of Education and Culture was dissolved to be succeeded by the Ministry of Human Development, which oversaw the National Secretariat of Culture (SENACULT).[5] SENACULT had a certain degree of autonomy and was charged by the Under Secretariat for Cultural Heritage with responsibility for implementing cultural heritage-related protection, conservation, preservation, and improvement policies. In August 1997, SENACULT was superseded by the Vice-Ministry of Culture (Ibid.).

The contribution of intellectuals, artists, actors, and cultural managers, in addition to the recognition of cultural assets by the State and its citizens, began to set the standard for cultural management practices, recognising the economic and symbolic value of culture. Between the 1980s and 1990s, politicians wanted to promote national culture and artistic production beyond the country's borders. This ambition triggered a certain recognition of cultural management as a practice oriented towards the promotion and safeguarding of cultural diversity, including practices in this field within the private and civil sectors. This recognition also resulted from the need to professionalise the practice of cultural managers, stimulating a type of professional practice requiring the application of new skills to initiate cultural projects and address challenges in the sector (finding resources, seeking spaces, expanding networks, strengthening circulation, and implementing promotional strategies, etc.).

From that period forward, the practice of cultural management has been based on the theories, methodologies, and narratives of international Ibero-American cooperation through virtual courses, publications, and calls for project funding. The use of these formats serves the political interests of these types of cooperation. The functions that have been assigned to cultural managers were essentially drawn from western academia, specifically sociology. Its specific and specialised roles, often far removed from Bolivian reality, tended to be adapted to authentic contemporary transformations in cultural work, a side effect of economic and social dynamics and an entrepreneurial vision of the practice. This period was also marked by the establishment of important cultural infrastructure (cultural centres, museums, libraries, etc.), the broad dissemination of Bolivian culture through participation in international events – such as music and theatre festivals and art biennials – and the strengthening of material heritage preservation projects.

The late 1990s witnessed the creation of the Cultural Foundation of the Central Bank of Bolivia, with five repositories, later expanded to the current eight. This institution became an essential instrument for the preservation of heritage and museum management within the country. It holds the most important repositories in the country[6] and constitutes:

> a model under construction for public cultural management which could shed light on the improvement in the State's institutional practices for the management of culture.
>
> (Pacheco Araoz, 2020)

Although this institution was created in the middle of the neoliberal period, its existence has set an example for the management of repositories in the country. Eventually, despite the fact that neoliberalism had strongly consolidated itself within the economic cultural, and political fields, it began to demonstrate an ideological decline. In that sense, Boron presupposes that:

> Modern political philosophy has severed its ties with the critical tradition of the social context that concerns it and has focused more on the minimization of things. It does not offer proposals for change to the social reality in which it lives.
>
> (in Domenech, 2007, p. 61)

The socio-political response to the demanding measures of turn-of-the-century neoliberalism on the part of peasants, miners, workers (including the large group of informal employees) and impoverished people resulted in the strengthening of social organisations and in large-scale protests against the socioeconomic model derived from the economic liberalism practised by the MNR government which definitively annulled its own state-socialist project, replacing it with a series of neoliberal economic measures to address the crisis.

Although the idea of the nation as a homogeneous community linked to revolutionary ideals had been the basis for the construction of the state in 1952, in fact, revolutionary nationalism (NR) did not take into account the ethnic and linguistic diversity of the Bolivian context (Mayorga, 1985, p. 12). This omission is in stark contrast to the beginning of the decentralisation process of 2003 when the lack of "a" State: "We are many States, a 'State-Kaleidoscope' [requiring a] very important challenge: a change of mentality [which must be accompanied by a] transformation of institutionalism" (Mesa Gisbert 2012, p. 13), became evident. This process was already underpinned by legislation such as the Popular Participation Law, in force since 1994, which reconfigured the administration of the territory, granting cities greater autonomy and enhancing the political action of indigenous, peasant, and urban communities in the political life of the country. These local governments assumed responsibilities both for the creation of cultural policies and for the financial support of the ensuing actions. Despite a challenging start due to lack of expertise, those municipalities with a significant native population have proved most successful in executing this cultural task.

In 1997, the "Para seguir sembrando, para soñando" (*keep on sowing, keep on dreaming movement*) emerged as the result of a symbolic seizure of Parliament, through which it sought to challenge the political-institutional system

> to sign a document placing an open debate on the public agenda regarding the urgent need for participatory design and implementation by state administrators of sustained policies in the field of cultures and communication.
>
> (Brie, 1997)

This manifesto was intended:

> to put on the table of collective debate the tasks unfulfilled by the State in the face of heritage, diversity, the essential intercultural dialogue between the tributaries of the fabric in the process of national identity, the role of cultures and arts in the construction of a better collective destiny based on inclusion, equality and participatory democracy.
>
> (Brie, 1997)

During this republican period, numerous movements of artists and managers were organised to challenge the State to promote more robust institutions and politics which supported culture (from a humanist perspective) thereby facilitating the management of cultures and the exercise of art in a more efficient manner. The "Para seguir sembrando, para soñando" movement systematised the demands of civil society before the presidential elections of 1997, questioning political parties about culture (from an anthropological perspective).

Finally, a plurinational State

In 2006, with the ascension to power of MAS-IPSP, which won 57% of the total votes cast in a disruptive political victory, a process of articulated change began within a social community with a strong union base and cultural connotations. The culmination of this process was the political recognition of an indigenous president and the construction of a plurinational State which essentially acknowledged the diversity of cultures and nations within Bolivia. This was enshrined in the Political Constitution of the State of 2009 (Plurinational State of Bolivia, 2009) which gave prominence to the identities and traditions of the different indigenous communities that inhabit the territory; granted 36 indigenous languages official status; protected sacred territories; recognised the right to collective land ownership; granted indigenous representation in the Departmental Legislative Assemblies; and recognised the right to self-determination of such communities within their territories, among other significant changes.

The political project of this new government was based on seeking "the construction of a new society in a pluri-national and community State, aimed at achieving 'Buen Vivir' within the community", registering culture as one of the transversal strategies to "contribute to a transformational process within the country that will dismantle the development model conceived by colonialism and neo-liberalism, and change the pattern of primary export development"(Ministry of Planning, 2006, p. 10.). Given the recognition of the existence of various cultures within Bolivia, the public management of culture began, on the one hand, to consolidate a narrative based on the term "cultures" that recognised the diversity and multiculturalism present in the territory and, on the other hand, to develop a cultural institutionality in accordance with the political plans of the newly installed government. In 2006, the Vice-Ministry of Culture was re-designated the Vice-Ministry of Development of Cultures and, in 2008, the first *Cultural Journeys* were held throughout the country, convening citizens in each department in an organised and institutionalised manner to discuss the orientation of cultural policies. Its main result was the establishment of the Departmental Councils of Cultures, followed by the creation of the Ministry of Cultures and Tourism of Bolivia in 2009. Strengthening the political plan to transform the country through culture as a transversal strategy, this ministry was constituted of three vice-ministries: Tourism, Decolonisation, and Interculturality. The last named promoted the search for a plurinational identity from a de-colonialisation perspective.

Important transformations in public administrative institutions have occurred over the last 60 years from state centralism to administrative decentralisation, finally resulting in an autonomous departmental administration around 2010. This development had an influence on how public cultural institutions are managed; giving departments greater capacity and more resources in order to promote the creation, dissemination, and circulation of artistic endeavours, for example, by providing funds and resources for the financing of festivals, celebrations, community groups, and gatherings, in addition to other platforms, as a response to the reduction in international cultural cooperation funds. This particular period witnessed the enacting of legislation important to the field.[7] However, there is currently no framework of national laws relating to culture, although this anomaly has been discussed by private and civil actors within the cultural sector for more than ten years. Nevertheless, the Autonomous Municipal Government of La Paz passed a cultural law and continues to be the leader in cultural public policies.

The cultural stance of the current Political Constitution of the State (Plurinational State of Bolivia, 2009) is crucial as it established certain guidelines among which are those relating to the cultural plurality of Bolivia:

> Article 1: [...] it is constituted in a Unitary Social State of Pluri-national Community Law, free, independent, sovereign, democratic, intercultural, decentralized, and with political constituted autonomies. Bolivia is founded on plurality and political, economic, legal, cultural and linguistic pluralism, within the country's integration process.

> Article 2: Given the pre-colonial existence of the indigenous peasant nations and indigenous peoples and their ancestral dominance over their territories, their self-determination is guaranteed within the framework of the unity of the State, which consists of their right to autonomy, self-government, and culture; and the recognition of its institutions and the consolidation of its territorial entities, in accordance with this Constitution and the law.

These guidelines operate both for public management of culture, and for civic and private cultural management initiatives. Although Bolivia has several regulations currently in force (among the most recent: the Book and Reading Law, Heritage Law, and legislation governing cinematographic activity and the audiovisual arts), it should be noted that the law on Bolivian audiovisuals,[8] for instance, has been marked by years of debate and conflict within the sector, which led in 2019 to its revision and enactment, including the creation of a Cinema Agency (ADECINE) with autonomous administration depending on the Ministry of Culture and Tourism (MCT).

On the other hand, in 2012, the Ministry of Culture and Tourism launched an important project to collect data about the impact of cultural expression on the country's economy. This work, carried out in collaboration with the National Statistics Institute, gathered initial information, analysing some of the scattered indicators of diverse sectors. However, the continuity of the aforementioned project or its progress in establishing a national cultural information system has not been reported. That same year, a *Plurinational Registry of Artists* was established which sought to accredit the status of *Bolivian Artists* recognised by the Ministry of Cultures in order to grant artists both a health insurance service as well as retirement pensions. It also allowed them to circulate in the General Personal Identification Service database (SEGIP), enabling artists to classify their work as a profession on their identity card. Individual and collective registrations are both allowed.[9]

That year, the Ministry of Cultures, with the support of the Organisation of Ibero-American States, promoted a programme called "Strengthening the

Arts – Recovery and Awareness of Intercultural Values", which essentially sought to promote cultural public policies that facilitate a process of structural change in the development of formal artistic training. This first initiative consisted of scholarships for stage artists.

Training in cultural management

With regard to the provision of cultural management training, considering its increasing recognition in recent years as an emerging profession, several important initiatives have been launched. Nevertheless, there is still no formal or continuous training in this field. In the 1990s and 2000s, a number of online training programmes were established, setting guidelines for action, which provided some cultural managers with useful orientation:

> Commencing with the Stockholm Conference, organized by UNESCO in November 2000, the training and establishment of cultural managers in Latin America and the Caribbean has been promoted. As of 2003, this institution, in coordination with the Organization of Ibero-American States (OEI) and the IBERFORMAT network of Cultural Management Training Centers and Units, has held courses for the training of cultural managers in Ibero-American countries, with the aim of solving social problems and satisfying culture-related needs.
>
> (Gonzalez, 2019)

Important initiatives came from private institutions such as Vision Cultural, Foundation Cajías, and cultural cooperation centres (AECID) or foreign cultural diplomacy organisations such as the Goethe-Institut. The effective use of specific tools for the administration and organisation of cultural projects, artistic and cultural production, fundraising, and cultural tourism was imparted. Unfortunately, neither other minor initiatives, nor postgraduate university programmes such as Masters in Cultural Management, Heritage Management, or Territorial Development enjoyed any continuity.

Nevertheless, in order to encourage artistic production, the work of cultural management and artistic production has been recognised for more than 20 years by the National Culture Award, considered the highest that the Bolivian State grants to outstanding personalities active in the cultural field. This award was instituted in 1969 with the aim of stimulating artistic, literary, and scientific production. A National Novel Award introduced in 1998 also exists, with the intention of promoting the dissemination of Bolivian literature. In 2001, the Yolanda Bedregal National Poetry Award was instituted in homage to one of the most prominent figures in Bolivian literature. Since that time, there has been a flood of national awards for children's and youth literature, comic production, and other narrative forms. In 2011, the first prize for Original Languages "Guamán Poma de Ayala" was awarded, seeking to re-value the oral and written tradition of the indigenous, peasant, and Afro-Bolivian peoples and nations of the Plurinational

State of Bolivia. In 2011, the Fund for the Promotion of Patriotic Civic Education was created with the objective of promoting and strengthening patriotic civic education.

In 2018, the La Paz autonomous local government launched the FOCUART–Development Fund, with significant and consistently increasing investment, for the following areas: arts and new technologies, municipality-based audiovisual projects, the development of networks, mobility, and cultural circulation, the development of community living culture, research and training, and the strengthening of cultural spaces and cultural heritage. In 2019, the Urban Interventions Programme (PIU) was launched by the national government aimed at artists, cultural managers, filmmakers, technological innovators, agents of social change, and athletes who could apply for funds divided into four large categories: film and audiovisual, cultural industries, social and technological innovation, and sport. These grants might cover airfare, travel expenses, and daily subsistence for individuals representing the country abroad, thus covering costs that had generally been the most challenging to meet. These new funds promoted the emergence of novel cultural projects but also new promoters of such initiatives (which almost always combined the roles of artist/cultural manager). At the time of writing, this programme is on standby.

Despite the inequitable access to financial support offered by the State at different levels (recognising again the extremely important role in cultural policies and public cultural management of La Paz autonomous government), cultural management projects in both the private and civil sectors have proliferated and encompassed a wider variety of subjects in recent years. The actors are generally private institutions (less representative) and foundations (certain among them are affiliated with companies). Many are simultaneously supported by both public and private organisations. Among the institutions with an important trajectory, it is worth mentioning the Simón I. Patiño Foundation which implements policies related to the authentication of heritage through research and dissemination of the sculptural and musical heritage of Bolivia; the dissemination of contemporary art and comics; in addition to the provision of important library services in its three national headquarters. The Pro Art and Culture Association of Santa Cruz, responsible for the organisation of the music festivals in Chiquitos and other provinces, has achieved significant national and international recognition. Among the private enterprises active in the different areas of artistic and patrimonial expression, a major player is Cultural Vision that organises international meetings on the baroque, with the participation of national and international cultural managers.

Several independently managed collectives promoting community-based action have emerged in recent years, networking with cultural workers' movements, including the We Are All Culture movement. These practices established around the management of culture have generally emerged in conventional, self-management circuits, and appear to be oriented towards pre-determined methods and systems, functional to a globalised world view. Cultural managers have convened in several national and international meetings in recent years in order to discuss the formal recognition of the practice. They are seeking to encourage the creation of an association of cultural managers which is lacking in the country and the entire region.

Where we are today

In November 2019, following a complex electoral process, a new demonstration of social discontent took to the streets, convulsing the country. Collective action of the so-called "pititas" or "new resistance against the MAS" caused the resignation of President Morales and his cabinet. They were succeeded by a transitory government which, due to the effects of the COVID pandemic, failed to comply with its mandate to call elections, instead postponing the polls until at least September 2020 when this chapter was written. Meanwhile, the Morales administration introduced structural changes such as the abolition of the MCT, again subsumed within the Ministry of Education. At the time that this chapter was written, there is neither an authority in place nor a government capable of introducing mechanisms for new institutions and policies to reactivate the sector.

Cultural management in the public sphere in Bolivia has recorded a series of achievements continually instigated by the collective action of cultural workers, through mobilisation, congresses, manifestos, and cultural conferences. Despite the arduous road travelled in the construction of a Bolivian brand of cultural institutionalism in both the public and private sectors, cultural management is confronted by the discontinuation of projects and plans with each change of government and authorities at various State levels, in addition to other as yet unresolved challenges.

The Bolivian cultural manager still strives to go beyond the empirical: the recognition of cultural practices, the generation of new narratives, and the preservation of a social memory, while the promotion of plural and diverse cultural rights remains one of its goals. Managing culture in Bolivia involves considering the diversity of the country's cultural expressions (folkloric, artistic, heritage-related, etc.) from different perspectives based on the particular understanding of one's own culture which bears a significant ideological load within a still-disputed territory.

The public cultural institutionalism of the last 20 years was founded on exactly this philosophy yet provided only sporadic and insufficiently specialised training in the duties and responsibilities of a cultural manager within this diverse context. Professional practice continued to have a strong autodidactic element linked to the urgent requirements of the sector, including; the production of artistic proposals and their distribution, the sustainability of artistic projects, the preservation of heritage and memory, and the valuing of cultural diversity through community-based expressions. Moreover, there exists the challenge of understanding the transformations in the country's social organisations and the imperative to pay special attention to human and cultural rights.

Because of that diversity, together with the profound social and economic contrasts evident in the country – rich in history, heritage, social memory, and artistic expression – it can be assumed that cultural managers should bear the responsibility for fostering critical thinking, establishing independent criteria, broadening knowledge of traditions and narratives and, simultaneously, promoting the desire to look beyond one's own space. The challenge confronting cultural management is that of developing the necessary skills to bring together and mobilise cultural actors, cultural managers, and artists from various social spheres; to inhabit the here and now while utilising historical tools and their processes; updating these in order to prevent artistic and cultural sector professionals from repeating themselves; generating new spaces of knowledge; and understanding new forms of expression.

Notes

1 More information on Solon´s work can be traced at Fundación Solón (2015).
2 Guzmán de Rojas (1899–1950) recognised the importance of the Indians and their forms of expression incorporating them into his paintings. Alandia Pantoja (1914–1975) saw in the proletariat the possibility of finding freedom and progress and portraying the reality of its world – in the tradition of Mexican muralism – with the intention of claiming it. Velasco Maidana (1899–1989) glimpsed the importance of multiculturalism and included indigenous aesthetics in his films *Amanecer Indio* and *Wara Wara* (Lampo, interview, 2020).
3 Fortún's administration created more than 30 institutions, organizations, and cultural programmes in Bolivia such as the National Institute of Linguistic Studies (INEL), the Bolivian Institute of Culture (IBC), 55 rural and Houses of Culture (endorsing an intercultural perspective), the National Folkloric Ballet, the National Museum of Popular Art (the present-day MUSEF), and the National Theatre Workshops, among others.
4 Ayllu constitutes an Aymara and Quechua social technology that can be understood as forming the basis for community organisation within Andean societies, founded on social reciprocity. In-depth anthropological studies (Platt, 1982) and others focusing on the economic sphere (Murra, 1975) report that *ayllu* represents ancestral Andean economic and political formations. In other words, the forms and ways of relating to space and the ecosystem. The ayllu has endured to the present in modern Andean communities, maintaining a remarkable continuity with the preconquest period.
5 The institutional history can be found at https://www.bolivia.com/empresas/cultura/Breve_historia/.
6 The Casa de la Libertad, the National Archive and Library of Bolivia, the National Museum of Ethnography and Folklore, the Mint, the National Museum of Art, the Centre for Plurinational Culture, Museum Fernando Montes, and the Centre for the Cultural Revolution.
7 General Law on Autonomy and Decentralisation "Andrés Ibáñez". N°31 (adopted July 19, 2003); Law against Racism and all forms of Discrimination. N°45 (adopted October 8, 2010); General Law of Rights and Linguistic Policies, N°269 (adopted August 2, 2012); Law for the Promotion and Development of Crafts, N°306 (adopted November 8, 2012); Law on Books and Reading "Oscar Alfaro", N°366 (adopted April 29, 2013); Bolivian Cultural Heritage Law, N°530 (adopted May 23, 2014).
8 Law of Bolivian Cinema and Audiovisual Arts, N°1134 (adopted December 20, 2018).
9 During the COVID-19 pandemic, foreign artists residing and acting in Bolivia launched a campaign to be recognised by this registry which is under the management of the Ministry of Cultures and Tourism and the Cultural Foundation of the Central Bank of Bolivia (FCBCB), because "they revealed that without such accreditation they are not entitled to health benefits during the current national health crisis" (Huaranca, 2020).

References

Boccara, G. (2005). Antropología diacrónica. Dinámicas culturales, procesos históricos, y poder político. Nuevo Mundo Mundos Nuevos (online). https://journals.openedition .org/nuevomundo/589 (Accessed October 29, 2020).

Bouysse-Cassagne, T. (2018). *Historia del arte en Bolivia*. La Paz: Editorial Gisbert.

Brie, C. (1997). Manifiesto para seguir sembrando, para seguir soñando. *Revista El tonto del pueblo*, 2, pp. 77–80.

Chavarría Contreras, R. (2019). *Conceptos clave de la gestión cultural: enfoques desde Latinoamérica.* Volume I: Cultural administration. Santiago de Chile: Ariadna Ediciones.

Choquehuanca, D. (2006). Hemos decidido volver a nuestro camino, recuperar nuestros valores, recuperar nuestros códigos. *Intervention at the Continental Meeting of Indigenous Peoples and Nationalities of the Abya Yala*. La Paz, 9 de octubre de 2006. La Paz: Ministry of Foreign Affairs, pp. 49–62. http://www.planificacion.gob.bo/upl oads/Vivir_bien.pdf.

Domenech, E. (2007). El Banco Mundial en el país de la desigualdad: políticas y discursos neoliberales sobre diversidad cultural y educación en América Latina. In Grimson, A. (Ed.) *Cultura y neoliberalismo*. Buenos Aires: CLACSO, pp. 61–89. .

Estermann, J. (2018). Interculturalidad y conocimiento andino: reflexiones acerca de la monocultura Epistemológica. *Revista Kawsaypacha: Sociedad y Medio Ambiente*, 2, pp. 11–32. https://doi.org/10.18800/kawsaypacha.201801.001 (Accessed July 16, 2020).

Fundación Solón (2015). *Solón: El retrato de un Pueblo.* June 10. https://fundacionsolon .org/2015/06/10/solon-el-retrato-de-un-pueblo/#more-1325.

Gisbert, T. & de Mesa, J. (2012). *Historia del Arte en Bolivia. Periodo Prehispánico, periodo Virreinal, periodo Republicano (three volumes)*. La Paz: Editorial Gisbert.

Gonzalez, D. (2019). Gestionar cultura en Bolivia. *Diario Opinión*. April 14. https:// www.opinion.com.bo/articulo/ramona/gestionar-cultura-bolivia/2019041400000067 9669.amp.html (Accessed October 28, 2020).

——— (2019b). Gestionar cultura en Bolivia. *Diario Opinión*. April, 14. https:// www.opinion.com.bo/articulo/ramona/gestionar-cultura-bolivia/2019041400000067 9669.html (Accessed August 9, 2020).

Henze, R. & Escribal, F. (this volume). Introduction. In Henze, R. & Escribal, F. (Eds.). *Cultural Management and Policy in Latin America*. Routledge, pp. xvi–xxvi.

Huaranca, L. (2020). Artistas de 11 países piden ser incluidos en Registro Plurinacional y una reunión con autoridades. *Diario Opinión*. May 14. https://www.opinion.com.bo/ articulo/cultura/artistas-11-paises-piden-ser-incluidos-registro-plurinacional-reunion-a utoridades/20200514110221767658.html (Accessed September 21, 2020).

Mayorga, F. (1985). Discurso del nacionalismo revolucionario: Centro de Información y Documentación para el Desarrollo Regional, Cochabamba, Bolivia.

Mayorga, F. (2003). La revolución boliviana y la participación política. *Proceedings of the International Conference on 20th Century Revolutions – 50 Years of the Bolivian Revolution*. Cochabamba, October 7–9, 2002. La Paz: PNUD. http://www.pieb.com.bo /blogs/mayorga/archivos/revolucion_mayorga.pdf (Accessed October 22, 2020).

Mercado, A., Leitón, J. & Chacón, M. (2005). El crecimiento económico en Bolivia (1952–2003). *Revista latinoamericana de desarrollo económico*, 5, pp. 9–42.

Mesa Gisbert, C. (2012). Gestión cultural. Retos y buenas prácticas. *Proceedings of the Bolivian Meeting of Cultural Managers*, La Paz, Bolivia, October 24–26, 2012.

Ministry of Education (1970). *Declaración del Gobierno Revolucionario sobre política educacional, cultural y científica*. La Paz: Ministry of Education of Bolivia.

Ministry of Planning (2006). *Plan Nacional de Desarrollo 2006–2010. Bolivia digna, soberana, productiva y democrática para Vivir Bien*. La Paz: Ministry of Development Planning.

Murra, J. (1975). *Formaciones económicas y políticas del mundo andino*. Lima: Peruvian Studies Institute.

Olivares Rodríguez, L. F. (2014). *Desenvolvimiento histórico de la gestión cultural en Bolivia y la formación de sus actores culturales. Caso: gestión cultural con sede en La Paz 1975–2005*. Doctoral Thesis for the Doctorate in Higher Education from the Universidad Mayor de San Andrés. La Paz, Bolivia.

Pacheco Araoz, C. (2020). La fundación en retroceso. *Diario Los Tiempos*. June 26. https://www.lostiempos.com/doble-click/cultura/20200626/fundacion-retroceso (Accessed October 28, 2020).

Platt, T. (1982). *Estado boliviano y ayllu andino: tierra y tributo en el norte de Potosí*. Lima: Peruvian Studies Institute.

Plurinational State of Bolivia (2009). *Constitución Política del Estado*. Adopted February 7. La Paz: Official State Bulletin of Bolivia.

Prada, M. (Ed.) (2004). *Revista de estudios bolivianos 12. La cultura del pre 52*. La Paz: Institute of Bolivian Studies/CIMA.

Quijano, A. (2009). Colonialidad del poder y subjetividad en América Latina. In Pimentel, C. (Comp.). *Poder, ciudadanía, derechos humanos y salud mental en el Perú*. Lima: Cecosam.

Quintero, P. (2010). *Notas sobre la teoría de la colonialidad del poder y la estructuración de la sociedad en América Latina*. Working Paper N°19. June. 2010. Lima: Centre for Interdisciplinary Studies in Ethnolinguistics and Socio-Cultural Anthropology. https://core.ac.uk/download/pdf/61698027.pdf.

Rossells, B. (2004). Espejos y máscaras de la identidad: el discurso indigenista en las artes plásticas (1900–1950). In Prada, A. R. (Ed.). *Estudios bolivianos 12: La cultura del pre-52*. La Paz: Institute of Bolivian Studies/CIMA, pp. 297–368.

Salazar Mostajo, C. (1989). *La pintura contemporánea de Bolivia. Ensayo histórico-crítico*. Lima: Librería Editorial Juventud.

UNESCO (2001). *Universal Declaration on Cultural Diversity*. United Nations Educational. Adopted by the 31st Session of the General Conference of UNESCO, Paris, November 2. http://unesdoc.unesco.org/images/0018/00 1803/180303m.pdf.

Vila, M. (1998). La influencia de las vanguardias en el arte boliviano del siglo XX. *Revista Ciencia y Cultura*, 4, pp. 11–21.

Wanderley, F. (2016). La economía solidaria y comunitaria en Bolivia. *Revista de la Academia*, 21(Autumn), pp. 57–75.

13 Cultural management in Mexico

From precariousness to development

Cristina Peregrina Leyva and Aarón Hernández Farfán

Historical context

Mexico is the product of a colonial process. Research on the prehispanic era has disseminated information about the existence of various cultures that demonstrated certain similarities expressed through their religions, traditions, and even their cultivation of particular crops, namely green pumpkins, chilis, beans, and, more importantly, corn, throughout an extensive region known as Mesoamerica. This region encompassed the geographical area extending from the centre of present-day Mexico (around the actual States of Sinaloa, Jalisco, Guanajuato, Zacatecas, and Veracruz) to Central America on the current borders of Honduras and Costa Rica.

The agricultural techniques involved in corn production have cemented cultural structures that evolved through religious expression, traditions, and culture. Therefore, the different civilisations shared certain common ground, the most relevant being the Olmecs, Teotihuacan, Toltec, Zapotec, Mixtecs, Mayas, and Mexicas (also known as Aztecs, a term which has fallen out of favour within contemporary academic circles). It is important to take account of this period in order to understand current cultural diversity, united through corn as the most important product that shapes the majority of cultural elements, but also to appreciate that numerous differences exist between the regions that constitute modern Mexico.

When in 1521, the Spanish empire conquered Tenochtitlan (present-day Mexico City) and founded the viceroyalty of New Spain, a process combining elements of Spanish and indigenous cultures commenced. The development of mining and the applications of other technologies enabled the Spanish empire to enforce its hegemony in Europe, but at the cost of exploitation and discrimination (both expressed and enforced by a caste system established throughout the colonial era) in the American colonies (Israel, 1980) that still resonates today. Among the changes in Europe under Bourbon leadership during the 17th century, social tensions in New Spain led to the war of independence culminating in 1821, with the founding of Mexico as a modern nation state. It would, however, endure almost 50 years of both internal conflict and military invasions by France and the United States before finally achieving stability and reinstitution as a republic, with the Porfirio Díaz presidency commencing in 1877. Social inequality persists to the present day and continues to prevent Mexico's membership from joining the ranks of the so-called developed nations.

The first initiatives on the part of the Mexican government with regard to cultural activities were launched in 1905 (UNAM, 2019). Since then, as in many other Latin American countries, cultural management in Mexico has adopted the French model of taxpayer-funded public administration dependent on governmental ideas and visions (Nivón Bolan, 2006). The Mexican Revolution of 1910 to 1917 precipitated a reorganisation of public institutions. The Ministry of Public Education (SEP) was founded in 1921 by José Vasconcelos, an important historical figure in the field of education, arts, and culture in Mexico. The SEP has, up to the present, been primarily responsible for the administration of all resources and policies concerning education and culture (Brambila, 2015). Vasconcelos undertook what he termed "Cultural Missions " (1923), a crusade "to incorporate indigenous people and peasants into the project of a civilized nation and inculcate in them rational and practical thinking in order to eradicate religious fanaticism and violent tendencies as a means of achieving physical and domestic health" (Gamboa Herrera, 2007). Furthermore, he supported the production of mural paintings, the construction of libraries, the development of the media, education in rural areas, educational and cultural exchanges which incentivised international artists and intellectuals to relocate to Mexico. Culture, as promoted by Vasconcelos, always had an overwhelming propaganda purpose (Brambila, 2015), while also being strongly influenced by a Eurocentric educational model which pretended to adapt itself to the Mexican context by omitting its own cultural characteristics. In 1934, Narciso Bassols, head of the SEP, created the Department of Fine Arts that, five years later, evolved into the National Institute of Anthropology and History (INAH). This institute focused on heritage, history, and archaeology to the exclusion of artistic disciplines. In order to include the latter, the National Institute of Fine Arts and Literature (INBA) was created in 1946 to foster and invigorate a professionalised artistic movement and new generation, thereby creating the roots of the prevailing artistic and cultural environment throughout the 1950s and up to the 1970s.

In Mexico, what came to be known as cultural management, has been developing since the 1980s. It is important to emphasise that although, in theory, the governmental model of the primary public cultural institution in Mexico was a council, the political reality was that it operated in the same manner as the French model (UNAM, 2019). This was due to the fact that it was oriented to public subsidy, rather than promoting the independence of the artistic sector. In 1988, a new attempt to modify the institutional cultural management model was made in order to promote artistic creation and achieve autonomy from the SEP. For this purpose, the National Council for Culture and the Arts (CONACULTA) was created, based on the British model, in an effort to introduce a greater degree of autonomy. Unfortunately, such autonomy was never achieved and CONACULTA remained under the tutelage of the SEP.

CONACULTA: An institution intended to politically control the artistic sector by centralising cultural management

Carlos Salinas de Gortari, a Mexican politician from the Institutional Revolutionary Party (PRI), who served former President Miguel de la Madrid Hurtado as Head of the Programming and Budgetary Ministry (a form of Ministry of Finance), became president in December 1988. The creation of CONACULTA was published in the Official Register of the Federation in the same month. For this reason, the creation of this council was perceived by Salinas' critics as representing a strategic element of his political project and vision, particularly since he had only been in power for a week when this decision was announced. On paper, the mission of the institution was one of "promoting strategies enabling the continued promotion, preservation, and development of all cultural areas of the nation" (Cultural Ministry, 2015). However, in practice, it constituted a means of maintaining political control over the artistic sector, while simultaneously encouraging its development, provided that precise rules and guidelines were followed in order to obtain support.

The "Ateneo del Angangueo" meetings (Garza Orellana, 2017) led to speculation that those intellectuals involved in the formation of CONACULTA had forged a close relationship with the former president and saw their loyalty rewarded with the establishing of the institution. At that time, Sergio Garza Orellana highlighted three perspectives regarding the creation of CONACULTA: (a) the institutional position emphasising its role as an autonomous and democratising promoter of culture, (b) a means of liberalising the culture sector, and (c) merely a political ploy by Salinas to legitimise his highly questionable appointment as president under the shadow of electoral fraud. During this period, a process was implemented that Ejea Mendoza (2011) refers to as *liberalisation* – rather than democratisation – although the government identified the foundation of CONACULTA as a democratising agent. Liberalisation is understood to constitute "a survival strategy of the authoritarian regime: to open up spaces of participation, of free expression or extension of rights, to politically 'decompress' a critical situation" (Camou, 2000). The highly strained relationship with the artistic sector that Gortari experienced due to his highly questionable presidential victory (marked by all manner of irregularities, found in CONACULTA a means of *removing* the pressure through a system of financial support for artists who ran the risk of being co-opted.

Although it represented a step forward in institutional terms, the creation of CONACULTA – by means of a presidential decree – did not interrupt the discretionary trend for the administration of funding for culture. Nor did it succeed in guaranteeing a truly democratic and participatory state policy on culture (Ejea, 2011). Due to its vertical operational structure, with a director appointed by the Executive, who simultaneously officiated as President of the Council, it tended to concentrate power around this figure in personalistic terms. This frustrated the objective of democratising cultural management and artistic development. During Gortari's presidency, the organisation had two presidents: the first one was Victor Flores Olea (1988 to 1992), a career diplomat and active member of the PRI, the political party that had governed for nearly 70 years (beyond doing so in a democracy, it was ironically named the "perfect dictatorship"). In 1989, under the management of Flores Olea, the National Fund for Culture and the Arts (FONCA) was created, the most important fund for artists depending on CONACULTA (Vargas, 2020). According to Ejea, Salinas de Gortari sought with his cultural policy to achieve minimum consensus with some sectors of the left in order to advance his right-wing economic programme. In that register, the FONCA was conceived as an instrument of co-optation of artists and cultural groups, in which the officials would act as mediators (Ejea, 2011).

In 1992, Flores Olea was succeeded by Rafael Tovar y de Teresa, who continued to preside over the organisation during the six-year term of Ernesto Zedillo from 1994 to 2000. During Tovar y de Teresa's first term, artistic production and dissemination were prioritised (Cuevas Villanueva, 2009). The artistic sector saw an opportunity to develop, seeing its necessary prerequisites mostly satisfied, and the inception of an invigorated artistic movement oriented to the creation of an *haute culture* system. During the years since the founding of CONACULTA and FONCA, multiple critics have raised their voices criticising the formation of an artistic elite which reserves all financial support for a selected and restricted group. This then indicated the need to democratise FONCA's regulations, rendering possible the appointing of expert juries to analyse artistic projects requesting funding. These juries were also formed from current or former FONCA beneficiaries. Artists, then, were judging artists through the various programmes funded by the council.

During the Vicente Fox presidency (2000–2006), the Mexican Federal Institute of Access to Information and Data Protection (IFAI) was created to monitor and regulate the internal transparency of public institution procedures. Consequently, it also reformed several of the guidelines governing CONACULTA and FONCA with the intention of further democratising these institutions. At the same time, substantial budget reductions were implemented, negatively impacting their ability to access a wider population consisting of both artists and audiences, a policy that continued and was strengthened with the subsequent government of Felipe Calderón, whose victory was similarly tainted by rumours of electoral fraud. Further budget cuts were introduced in order to channel the resulting available resources into the so-called war against the drug cartels, a strategy also actively pursued by Calderón to legitimise his presidency, and one that reaped the most terrible of results.

Ministry of Culture

In Enrique Peña Nieto's presidency (2012–2018) the highest public institution promoting culture finally achieved a Ministry status, following Chile, Colombia, Venezuela, Brazil, and Argentina (Ramírez Cuevas, 2009). Created from the residual structure of CONACULTA it was, once again, headed by Rafael Tovar y de Teresa, who was charged with overseeing the effective transition of the former council, building on the autonomy and independence of SEP, providing the newly established Ministry with the necessary tools for a new era, one of important structural constitutional reforms (a package of new and energetic educational and financial policies intended to constitute Peña Nieto's legacy). Tovar y De Teresa passed away while in office, leaving the process incomplete. This development caused the Secretariat to continue to implement the existing cultural policies. María Cristina García Cepeda took charge of the Ministry from 2017 to 2018, assuming the task of continuing the policies and management style of her predecessor.

The current government led by Andrés Manuel López Obrador is characterised as one of transition and change under a *Fourth Transformation* banner. This draws its inspiration from the historical power of three previous structural transformations experienced by Mexico: (1) The War of Independence from Spain (1810–1821); (2) The War of Reform (1858–1861); and (3) The Mexican Revolutionary War (1910–1917). The present-day war is one against corruption, marked by austerity in public administration, while focusing new policies on supporting, developing, and benefitting the most vulnerable groups through promotion of the common good.

Several administrations have reduced the funding for culture. The current one proposed cutting approximately one billion Mexican pesos from the Federal Budget for 2019, with the film industry being one of the most affected sectors (Gutierrez, 2018). In 2019, the budget allocation of the Ministry of Culture was 3.9% lower than that of the previous year (AFP, 2019) and according to a special programme broadcast by Rompeviento TV more than a thousand employees of the National Institute of Anthropology and History, the Ministry of Culture, and National Institute of Fine Arts and Literature (INBAL) were made redundant during the first few months of this six-year period. Alejandra Frausto has been designated as the new Minister of Culture, reorienting its policies in order to prioritise indigenous communities and transforming its artistic programmes in order to achieve the objective of caring for so-called "vulnerable groups". This has created a perception of an almost populist orientation that runs the risk of diluting the artistic sector, one that is accused by the current government of being an elitist and privileged group of the rich. This perception does not correspond to the reality and challenges facing the average artist who struggles to make a living under precarious conditions without social care alternatives, facing a violent and opaque (personally and collectively) development panorama.

Cultural rights in a context of violence

The cultural sector suffers from a highly precarious employment context. The artists' campaign for entitlement to social security is ongoing, even within an industry that makes a significant contribution to the nation's gross domestic product. In this regard, the Chamber of Deputies published a document which posited that

> an essential element within the analysis of this issue is to highlight that, in a habitual and recurrent manner, independent cultural workers are contracted verbally or through outsourcing or subcontracting schemes. Such recruitment processes are subject to countless abuses such as the failure to honour the

agreed salary, the cancellation of contracts or the lack of social security provision, among others.

(González Rodríguez, 2020)

The same document mentions the "Recommendation concerning the Status of
the Artist" and the "Social Rights of Artists", both of which were adopted by
UNESCO, of which Mexico is a member. Affiliated countries are evaluated
according to the parameters set out in the second document mentioned. In the
Latin American region, countries such as Chile, Colombia, Paraguay, Brazil,
Costa Rica, Peru, Uruguay, and Cuba have a dedicated social security scheme for
artists (González Rodriguez, 2020).

On the one hand, the cultural sector in general and various CONACULTA
and Ministry of Culture administrations have identified the need for social security provision relating to independent workers. This is the reason why González
mentions that the Senate in Mexico approved the 2011 law governing the so-
called Support Fund for Access of artists, creators, and cultural managers to
Social Security which, unfortunately, was subsequently rejected by the Chamber
of Deputies in 2016. On the other hand, access to culture is an important subject
particularly within a context of extreme and systemic violence that influences
both communal and personal situations in Mexico. Fundamental human rights
are undermined by the corruption and drug trafficking endemic across the entire
national territory. Cultural management must be considered and implemented
against the background of this social context, although both Mexico's governmental model and academic institutions draw on a European heritage against
which the country's socioeconomic context differs considerably.

Art, as an instrument of peace building, has been widely debated (Evron,
2007; Baily, 2019), and is also considered an important component of governmental strategies for violence prevention. Within the Mexican context, examples
such as RedesArte Peace Culture exist which deliver arts education in neighbourhoods with high rates of both crime and poverty. The context of violence
affects all sectors which, furthermore, are not exempt from the political logic
of the parties in power, resulting in cases of corruption in these spaces, such
as occurred with a youth orchestra programme promoted by Fundación Azteca
(García Bermejo, 2018), an NGO founded by Grupo Salinas (which controls one
of the main television networks, TV Azteca), securing financial support from
the public purse for media coverage and other political benefits during election
campaigns.

The issue of cultural rights has become fundamental: Jiménez writes about the
importance of culture from a transversal perspective applied to those development
policies demanded by the violent context which Mexicans are experiencing. She
also states that cultural policies must be reformulated taking citizenship based on
cultural rights and human rights into account:

the basis for the exercise of cultural rights is access to training, to intercultural
and artistic education, not only to dialogue with ethnic and linguistic diversity,

but also to be able to interact with the set of diversities that characterize cultural life today.

(UNESCO, 2018)

Anyway, this perspective of cultural rights and democratisation is not necessarily one that prevails in all initiatives within the cultural sector. In an extremely unequal society such as Mexico's, it is important to consider the characteristics and attributes of this type of work. As Jiménez points out, "the right to participate in cultural life, as a key concept of cultural rights, implies giving an essential change to the bases on which modernity was built, in relation to artistic creation and its relationship with society merely as spectators" (UNESCO, 2018).

Mapping of Mexico's cultural sector

The National Institute of Statistics and Geography issues the National Survey of Cultural Consumption in Mexico (INEGI, 2012). Expenditure on cultural and artistic activities by Mexicans is around 3.8% of total household expenditure. This seems relatively low, but according to the National Council for the Evaluation of Social Development Policy, 41.9% of the Mexican population lives in poverty (CONEVAL, 2018). Access to culture within this socioeconomic context is undoubtedly a challenge. Furthermore, it is not only the economic level that plays a role when it comes to access, but also the place that an individual inhabits. Not all areas provide a fruitful ecosystem supportive of artistic production. Another factor to consider in terms of access is the concentration of cultural spaces in urban areas where Spanish is predominantly spoken. Content produced in indigenous languages, especially in a country of 68 languages (Milenio, 2020) with Nahuatl being the most widely spoken after Spanish with 725,000 speakers (El Universal, 2019), must be taken into consideration.

The Atlas of Cultural Infrastructure (CONACULTA, 2003) contains references to the importance of developing a superior infrastructure in order, for instance, to allow equal access to goods and services and a balanced regional development. In fact, a centralist tradition of production and access to art and culture – especially in the capital – has always been criticised throughout the country (Ejea Mendoza, 2011; Alvarez Sánchez, 2002). The same CONACULTA document explains that geographical proximity represents a fundamental condition in relation to infrastructure and that an individual's approach to cultural infrastructure also depends on a range of factors. These include the costs, the availability of programming information, the reduction of psychosocial barriers to approaching certain spaces, as well as the individual's cultural habits and practices which constitute the product of multiple conditions. Problems in accessing the available information on infrastructure have been cited as an obstacle for many years.

The country has approximately 119,938,473 inhabitants (INEGI, 2015) that are catered for by 6,610 public libraries; 3,797 lecture rooms; 2,823 movie theatres;

1,592 houses of culture and cultural centres; 1,146 bookstores; 1,058 museums; and 544 theatres (Cultural Infrastructure Atlas, 2003). There is undoubtedly a historical debt concerning the general marginalisation of indigenous peoples for which the cultural sector must assume responsibility. Consequently, much remains to be done in terms of generating accessible content in other languages and also for rural areas.

While the sector suffers from a number of shortcomings in terms of fundamental rights, its considerable economic value is increasingly recognised. One conception of the *Orange Economy* outlined by the Inter-American Development Bank (IDB) in 2013 is that proposed by John Howkins:

> It comprises the sectors in which the value of their goods and services is based on intellectual property: architecture, visual and performing arts, crafts, film, design, publishing, research and development, games and toys, fashion, music, advertising, software, TV and radio, and video games.
>
> (quoted in Buitrago & Duque, 2013)

According to another study subsequently published by the IDB, the exports of Mexican creative industries totalled U$4,651.88 million in 2012 (Rodriguez Oliva, 2018). The same document cites Ernesto Piedras, economist specialising in this topic as it relates to Mexico, who posits a contribution of 7.4% to the country's gross domestic product (GDP) in 2017. Undoubtedly, the creative industries and specifically those relating to the cultural sphere are important to the national economy, so its workers' rights should be prioritised not only for its economic impact but also the social benefits it entails such as "the regeneration of the social ecosystem, the empowerment of women, the participation of youth and their economic and financial Independence" (Rodríguez Oliva, 2016)

Academic training for cultural managers

Since the creation of the SEP, the government has identified the need to professionalise cultural workers (Brambila, 2015). In the absence of specific postgraduate programmes for cultural managers, many practitioners decided to study in Spain from the 1990s on (Mariscal Orozco, 2009). The term *cultural management* was introduced in an attempt to standardise the nomenclature of the work of those "dedicated to study and employment in the world of cultural meanings of social groups, starting with the development of projects linked to the arts, heritage, and creativity" (Hernández et al., 2017) and to differentiate it inter alia from cultural promotion (Henze & Escribal, this volume) and the work of those participating in formal processes of education within an institution. It is assumed that this taxonomy affects the manner in which agents intervene. They systematise and reflect training processes that equip them with planning, design, systematisation, and evaluation of practices; with knowledge and analysis of a theoretical and methodological framework and, therefore, with the capacity to reflect on intervention models, as well as an ethical framework that regulates their actions

(MacGregor, 2008). In the face of this global trend towards cultural management, public cultural institutions recognised the necessity of professionalising their personnel drawn from a variety of backgrounds. Both public and private universities across the country began to offer postgraduate degrees which were strongly influenced by governmental institutions as well as the development of cultural management as seen in countries such as Spain, Argentina, and Colombia.

In the 1990s, during the six-year term of President Vicente Fox, more training programmes for cultural professionals were established. Through the former CONACULTA, the Personnel Training Program for Cultural Development in Mexico was launched, and agreements were entered into with universities to develop degree programmes (Brambila, 2015). At this point, Mexico possessed a well-functioning infrastructure and significant cultural offers which necessitated the training of cultural agents. A group of universities introduced cultural management programmes, many of which recruited teachers and participants from the CONACULTA training programme because they not only had relevant experience but had also undergone theoretical and methodological training in order to design and teach programmes at undergraduate level (Hernández et. al., 2017). Most notable among these were University of the Cloister of Sor Juana, University of Guadalajara, and the Development and Intercultural Management programme at the National Autonomous University of Mexico. The private and public university degree programmes in Mexico range from undergraduate to doctoral, delivered through both face-to-face and distance learning modes. In 2014, there were 62 Bachelor's degrees, 11 specialisations, 80 Master's degrees, and 17 doctoral programmes (Salas, 2014). The range of undergraduate options continues to expand. However, some regions of the country, being rural or developing, lack higher education programmes in cultural management, marking a tendency to centralise education provision in the national capital, Mexico City, and some other major conurbations such as Guadalajara and Monterrey.

The local Mexico City Culture Department has established the *Imaginación en movimiento* ("Imagination Moving") programme which provides artists and cultural managers with the prerequisite knowledge and technical tools to establish their own cultural companies, in keeping with the stipulations of the Orange Economy that participants have to produce their own business plans. However, the economic environment has not supported the development of financial products that take the cultural sector's particularities and needs into account. Consequently, there is a significant gap between the private sector and emerging cultural companies. Therefore, only those companies that offer profitable products (e.g. videogames, apps, video or film production) are proving themselves to be commercially dynamic, although they are far from consolidating themselves as an industry. Visual artists regard galleries and management agencies as an effective means of internationalising their work, while simultaneously rendering it profitable. Artists or cultural managers who focus on the performing arts, particularly the younger and emerging ones, still struggle to consolidate their initiatives due to a lack of financial support.

Cultural management in Mexico

In Mexico, cultural management was developed in conjunction with education processes and the development of the idea of *nation* and progress (Molina, 2011). This process involved moving from the concept of cultural promotion to one of sociocultural animation (Henze & Escribal, this volume), based on a social development approach (Molina, 2011) involving multidisciplinary social functions: education, community development, and health, in addition to artisanal and agricultural production (Nivón & Sánchez, 2012). There is no single underlying concept of cultural management in Mexico, leading to its exercise according to the needs of institutions and agents, their knowledge, and their backgrounds. As Eduardo Nivón explains (2016), in Latin America, four distinct approaches towards cultural management can be identified: (a) the first focuses on the fine arts, heritage, and popular expression (mainly urban, such as graffiti and street art); (b) the second is more oriented to the study of traditions, customs, and lifestyles; (c) the third regards culture as "what gives meaning to social life, political action, and all communication efforts", while (d) the fourth, and most recent, views culture as a human right.

A relatively recent constitutional reform, in 2009, rendered possible the inclusion of access to cultural goods and services as a right as mentioned in Article 4 of the Mexican Constitution. Nevertheless, it remains a diffuse right due to the complexity of Mexican society. Precarious conditions render it unaffordable for the majority and thus restrict access to culture. Culture is both an individual and collective right but defining the limits that can legally guarantee its free exercise remains problematic. It is also difficult to regulate these limits without considering the multicultural characteristics of the population. Consider, for example, the fact that the national territory of Mexico is sufficiently large as to accommodate almost 24 European countries, while its population possesses various ethnic roots and expresses numerous different needs. It is for this reason that cultural rights encapsulate the following typology: (a) right to creation, (b) right to the protection and dissemination of cultural heritage, and (c) the right of access to cultural goods and services. (Dorantes Díaz, 2013), while striving to create a coherent legal basis through which to promote cultural policies.

Fortunately, despite the political functions giving rise to CONACULTA and the present Ministry of Culture, FONCA being the nodal structure which activates cultural management, the reformed defined legal context is provided by this institution. FONCA enables artists and emerging cultural managers to work in parallel (one group, obeying government requirements and policies, the other driving forward artistic and social interests). This provides both with access to financial support for creation, personal development and implementing an artistic environment, utilising government resources to create their own infrastructure, as well as generating their own income through their art, staging arts events, and networking with NGOs, especially those addressing social development issues. This framework enables the artistic sector to ground its projects according to the activated programmes resulting from civil society initiatives.

Without disregarding the risk of cooptation when accessing state funds, both artists and cultural managers have been sufficiently adroit at working together in executing their artistic and social responsibilities. A number of individual artists or groups had been able to formalise their legal structure as independent NGOs (*Triciclo Rojo Danza Clown* and *Lagartijas Tiradas Al Sol* being two examples). Others, after consolidation, have combined government funding with their own resources, even building or renting their own venues (as in the examples of *Producciones El Milagro* or *Compañía de Teatro Los Endebles*), as well as collaborating with private funding bodies such as *Fundación BBVA* or *Fundación Jumex*.

Contemporary challenges appear even greater considering the global changes that the Covid-19 pandemic has induced. With the current government headed by Andrés Manuel López Obrador, which is focused on austerity and transparency, NGOs run the risk of being stigmatised as mechanisms that facilitate corruption and the misappropriation of funds, an unfortunate generalisation that ignores the work and contributions of those who legitimately promote social and cultural development. Various trust funds that managed federal resources have been cancelled, FONCA included, in order to transfer the financial resources to priority programmes. In the face of present-day adversity, the health sector is prioritised, at the expense of social programmes that benefit the economically disadvantaged, while also representing electoral and political dividends for President Obrador and his MORENA party.

During the period in which this chapter was written, the designated budget for Culture was approximately €535,675,169.13, a minimal increase compared to the 2020 budget of €511,850,360.03. Approximately 25% of this first figure, some €134,368,859, will be applied to the megaproject entitled *Complejo Cultural Bosque de Chapultepec*, transforming the former presidential residence known as *Los Pinos* into a new cultural complex. In order to achieve this, most of the core institutes and departments that form the actual cultural infrastructure will experience financial stagnation (this is the case for INAH, INBAL, and IMCINE). Within this scenario, recently introduced tax policies are blocking the creation or operation of new NGOs, directly affecting the civil initiatives supposedly in order to guarantee transparency and the effective allocation of public funds, creating an extremely challenging environment for the artistic sector's financial sustainability and independence.

Conclusions

Cultural management in contemporary Mexico seeks to address the complexity that defines the country's society, wrestling with historical inequality, precarious conditions, and undeveloped social infrastructure. Moreover, the political and partisan interests pursued by every government struggling to democratise its institutions are accommodated.

The artistic and cultural management sector has adapted itself to work in a parallel system that creates, finances, collaborates with, and attempts to develop its initiatives. This involves combining federal funding for the arts and culture with private sources of support, and especially, active and consistent networking ini-tiatives. Mexico possesses a cultural management system that assimilates North American and European approaches, striving to achieve its impact through social development action, despite legal and operational ambiguity resulting from this combination. This leaves the average artist highly unprotected, without access to Social Security infrastructure and, currently, at significant risk of being stigma-tised as part of an elite that, in fact, struggles to make a living; a reality underlined by the recent Covid-19 pandemic that is revealing the precariousness that the sec-tor has faced during the last two decades.

Among the global challenges that a *new normality* represents, the Mexican artistic and cultural management sector faces that of creating alternatives which promote its sustainability, perpetuate its capacity to operate in parallel ways, and, given unprecedented possibilities, to update study programmes and continue to provide education. It aims to be as independent as possible from political inter-ests, transparent, and vibrantly creative, contributing to social stability and peace as it has been doing, despite not being justly recognised as a fundamental means of reducing violence. This and extreme poverty represent the main challenges to be overcome by Mexican society.

Bibliography

AFP (2020). La otra epidemia que golpea al país: México tuvo el domingo su día más violento del año. *Animal Político*. April 20, 2020. https://www.animalpolitico.com /2020/04/mexico-violento-dia-mas-asesinatos/ (Accessed June 6, 2020).

———— (2019). Sector cultural está inconforme por recortes del gobierno y la falta de un plan de trabajo. *Animal Político*, June 24, 2019. https://www.animalpolitico.com /2019/06/sector-cultural-inconforme-recortes-gobierno-amlo/ (Accessed April 17, 2020).

Alvarez Sánchez, S. (2002). Approach to a hypothesis on cultural policy in Mexico in the 20th century. *Context*, N°4, pp. 36–38.

Amparo Casar, C. (2015). *Anatomía de la corrupción en México*. Center for Economic Research and Teaching (CIDE) and Mexican Institute for Competitiveness (IMCO). N°28. June 2015. http://www.pudh.unam.mx/perseo/category/la-corrupcion-en-mex ico/ (Accessed May 20, 2020).

Animal Político (2019). Pobreza en México solo ha reducido 2.5% en 10 años; en Chiapas, Guerrero, Oaxaca y Veracruz aumentó. *Animal Político*. August 5, 2019. https://www .animalpolitico.com/2019/08/pobreza-mexico-reduccion-anos-chiapas-guerrero-oaxa ca-veracruz/.

Baily, A. (2019). *The art of peace: The value of culture in post-conflict recovery*. British Council, https://www.britishcouncil.org/sites/default/files/the_art_of_peace_0419 .pdf.

Brambrila, B. (2015). *Formación profesional de gestores culturales en México. El caso de tres programas universitarios*. Mexico: University of Guadalajara.

Buitrago, F. & Duque, I. (2013). *Economía Naranja: una oportunidad infinita*. Inter-American Development Bank. https://publications.iadb.org/publications/spanish/docu ment/La-Econom%C3%ADa-Naranja-Una-oportunidad-infinita.pdf.

Camou, A. (2000). Democratic transition and governability in Mexico: a look from the Latin American mirror. In Labastida Martín del Campo, J., Camou, A. & Luján Ponce, N. (Eds.), *Transición democrática y gobernabilidad. México y América Latina*. Mexico: Institute of Social Research (IIS-UNAM). 219–246

Campuzano Montoya, I. (2002) Las elecciones de 1988. *Estudios de historia moderna y contemporánea de México*, Vol. 23, N°286, pp. 207–241. http://www.historicas.unam .mx/moderna/ehmc/ehmc23/286.html (Accessed March 19, 2020).

CONACULTA (2003) *Atlas of Cultural Infrastructure in Mexico by the National Council for Culture and the Arts*.

CONEVAL (2019). *10 años de medición de la pobreza en México: avances y retos en política social*. Mexico: National Council for the Evaluation of Social Policy. https ://www.coneval.org.mx/SalaPrensa/Comunicadosprensa/Documents/2019/COMU NICADO_10_MEDICION_POBREZA_2008_2018.pdf (Accessed March 11, 2020).

——— (2018). *Medición de la pobreza*. Mexico: National Council for the Evaluation of Social Policy. https://www.coneval.org.mx/Medicion/MP/Paginas/Pobreza-2018.aspx (Accessed May 20, 2020).

Cortés, J. (2019). The 10 most widely spoken indigenous languages in the country. El Universal. August 9. https://www.eluniversal.com.mx/nacion/sociedad/las-diez-leng uas-indigenas-que-mas-se-hablan-en-el-pais (Accessed May 20, 2020).

Cuevas Villanueva, J. (2009). Las Políticas culturales institucionales en México: el círculo vicioso aparentemente sin fin. *Folios*, N°13, pp. 22–29.

Dorantes Díaz, F. (2013). Derecho a la cultura en México. Su constitucionalización, sus características, alcances y limitaciones. *Alegatos*, N°85, September–December 2013. https://www.corteidh.or.cr/tablas/r32205.pdf.

Ejea Mendoza, T. (2011). *Poder y creación artística en México. Un análisis del Fondo Nacional para la Cultura y las Artes*. México: UAM Azcapotzalco.

——— (2009). La liberalización de la política cultural en México: el caso del fomento a la creación artística. *Sociológica*, N°71, pp. 17–46.

Evron, N. C. (2007). Conflict and peace: Challenges for arts educators. In Bresler, L. (Ed.). *Springer International Handbook of Research in Arts Education*, Vol. 16. https://doi .org/10.1007/978-1-4020-3052-9_71.

Galindo Cáceres, J. (2015). Prólogo. In Brambila, B. (Ed.). *Formación profesional de gestores culturales en México. El caso de tres programas universitarios*. Mexico: University of Guadalajara, pp. 11–23.

Gamboa Herrera, J. (2007). Las misiones culturales entre 1922 y 1927. *Proceedings for the IX National Congress on Educational Research. Mexican Council for Educational Research*. November 5–9, Merida, Mexico. http://www.comie.org.mx/congreso/me moriaelectronica/v09/ponencias/at09/PRE1178909741.pdf (Accessed May 8, 2020).

García Bermejo, C. (2018). El fraude de TV Azteca: no da casi nada para sus orquestas. *Animal Político*. June 19, 2018. https://www.animalpolitico.com/2018/06/fraude-orqu estas-tv-azteca/.

García Canclini, N. (2004). *La cultura extraviada en sus definiciones*. Barcelona: Editorial Gedisa.

Garza Orellana, S. (2017). *Modernización, liberalización, legitimación e interculturalidad en las políticas culturales de CONACULTA (1988–1994)*. Thesis for the Master's Degree in Socio-Cultural Management at the Iberoamerican University of Torreón. https://acortar.link/jICwN (Accessed June 2, 2020).

González Rodríguez, J. (2020). *En contexto. La seguridad social de los trabajadores de la cultura en México*. Mexico: Chamber of Deputies. http://www5.diputados.gob.mx

/index.php/esl/content/download/170557/849698/file/CESOP-IL-72-14-SegSocTrabC
ultura-20200228.pdf (Accessed May 21, 2020).

Gutiérrez, V. (2018). *AMLO propone 1000 millones menos a Cultura*. El Economista. December 16, 2018. https://www.eleconomista.com.mx/arteseideas/AMLO-propone -1000-millones-menos-a-Cultura-20181216-0038.html (Accessed May 4, 2020).

Hernández, A., Nuñez, F., Pantoja, A. & Ruth, R. (2017). La Licenciatura en Gestión Cultural del ITESO: contexto, actualidad y retos. In Bernal Loaiza, G. (Ed.). *50 años en la formación universitaria de comunicadores*. Mexico: ITESO, pp. 237–248.

INAH (2011). *INAH estrena nuevo sistema de registro de bienes culturales*. Mexico: National Institute of Anthropology and History. https://www.inah.gob.mx/boletines/786 -inah-estrena-nuevo-sistema-de-registro-de-bienes-culturales (Accessed March 3, 2020).

INEGI (2015). *Poblacion*. México: National Institute of Statistics and Geography. https:// www.inegi.org.mx/temas/estructura/ (Accessed March 3, 2020).

——— (2012). *Encuesta Nacional de Consumos culturales en México*. Mexico: National Institute of Statistics and Geography. http://internet.contenidos.inegi.org.mx/conte nidos/Productos/prod_serv/contenidos/espanol/bvinegi/productos/encuestas/hogares/ encc/2012/ENCCUM2012.pdf (Accessed May 20, 2020).

Israel, J. (1980). *Razas, clases sociales y vida política en el México colonial*. Mexico: Fondo de Cultura Económica.

JaliscoTV (2016). *Interview with Lázaro Israel Rodríguez Oliva, International Consultant on Cultural Policy*. https://www.youtube.com/watch?v=ACCdgBrKHYc.

Kroeber, A. L. & Kluckhohn, C. (1952). *Culture: a critical review of concepts and definitionsPapers. Peabody Museum of Archaeology & Ethnology, Harvard University Press, Cambridge, 47*(1), viii, 223.

Mariscal Orozco, J. (2009). *Educación y gestión cultural: experiencias de acciones culturales en practicas culturales*. Guadalajara: University of Guadalajara.

Martinell, A. (2007). *La Gestión cultural. Singularidad professional y perspectivas de futuro*. UNESCO. https://oibc.oei.es/uploads/attachments/75/La_Gestion_Cultural_-_ Singularidad_profesional_y_perspectivas_de_futuro.pdf (Accessed February 7, 2020).

McGregor, J. (2008). La profesionalización del gestor cultural en México. In Mac Gregor, J. A. & Ruiz Razura, A. (Eds.). *Gestión cultural: una visión desde la diversidad*. Girona: University of Girona, pp. 17–30.

MENR (2018). *Mexico, biodiversidad que asombra*. Mexico: Ministry of Environment and Natural Resources. https://www.gob.mx/semarnat/articulos/mexico-biodiversidad-que -asombra (Accessed May 22, 2020).

MFA (2014). *Bienvenida*. Mexico: Ministry of Foreign Affairs. https://consulmex.sre.gob .mx/sanpedrosula/index.php/bienvenida-y-directorio/34 (Accessed May 22, 2020).

Ministry of Government (2015). *Sistematización de la práctica RedeseArte Cultura de Paz: desarrollada por el Consorcio Internacional Arte y Escuela*. http://www.mercops.org /Vigentes/150.RedeseArte_Cultura_de_Paz_ConArte.pdf (Accessed August 8, 2020).

Milenio (2020). Conoce las 68 lenguas indígenas de México. February 2. https://www .milenio.com/cultura/conoce-las-68-lenguas-indigenas-de-mexico (Accessed May 30, 2020).

Molina, A. (2011). La gestión cultural en América Latina. Motivos y realidades. In Negrón, B. & Silva, M. (Eds.). *Políticas Culturales, Contingencia y Desafíos*. Santiago de Chile: LOM Ediciones. https://www.academia.edu/617468/La_Gesti%C3%B3n_Cu ltural_en_Am%C3%A9rica_Latina_motivos_y_realidades (Accessed June 2, 2020).

Molinar, J. & Weldon, J. (2014). 1988 Elections in Mexico: Crisis of Authoritarianism. *Mexican Journal of Public Opinion*, N°17, pp. 165–191.

Nivón Bolán, E. (2016). Derechos culturales y ciudadanía. Una reflexión desde la condición mexicana. *Periférica Internacional. Revista para el análisis de la cultura y el territorio*, N°17, pp. 251–258. Cádiz: University of Cádiz. https://revistas.uca.es/index.php/perife rica/article/view/3280/3082.

———— (2006). *La política cultural. Temas, problemas y oportunidades.* Intersecciones Collection N°16. México: CONACULTA.

Nivón Bolan, E. & Sánchez, D. (2012) *La gestión cultural y las políticas culturales.* Santiago: University of Chile. http://rubi.casaruibarbosa.gov.br/bitstream/20.500.1199 7/16605/1/NIVON_SANCHEZ_La-gestion-cultural-y-las-politicas-culturales%20%2 81%29.pdf (Accessed March 11, 2020).

Piñon, A. (2020). Artistas cierran instalaciones de SC y piden pagos. El Universal. January 16, 2020. https://www.eluniversal.com.mx/cultura/artistas-cierran-instalaciones-de-se cretaria-de-cultura-y-piden-pagos (Accessed June 5, 2020).

Ramírez Cuevas, J. (2009). Las políticas culturales institucionales en México: el círculo vicioso aparentemente sin fin. *Revista Folios: publicacion de discusión y análisis*, N°13, pp. 24–31. http://www.revistafolios.mx/dossier/las-politicas-culturales-instituci onales-en-mexico-el-circulo-vicioso-aparentemente-sin-fin.

Rodríguez Oliva, L. (2018). *Economía Creativa en América Latina y el Caribe. Mediciones y desafíos.* Inter-American Development Bank. https://publications.iadb.org/publicatio ns/spanish/document/Econom%C3%ADa-creativa-en-Am%C3%A9rica-Latina-y-el -Caribe-Mediciones-y-desaf%C3%ADos.pdf (Accessed February 22, 2020).

Román García, L. (2011). A theoretical review of cultural management. *Digital Journal of Cultural Management*, N°1, pp. 7–8.

Rompeviento (2019). *Budget cuts to the cultural sector.* June 26, 2019. https://www.you tube.com/watch?v=6VA2gS9x09A.

Salas, V. (Comp.) (2014). *Oferta educative en gestión cultural y afín. Catálogo 2014.* Mexico: Gestores Culturales Universitarios México. https://gcumexico.ucoz.com/_ld/0 /59_Estudios_gestin.pdf (Accessed February 13, 2020).

Sánchez Ambriz, M. (2018). La cultura en el sexenio de EPN y lo que viene. *Nexos*. November 23, 2018. https://cultura.nexos.com.mx/?p=17075 (Accessed May 20, 2020).

Sepúlveda Contreras, M. (2019). Saberes y conocimientos. Aproximaciones desde la gestión cultural en América Latina. In Mariscal Orozco, J. & Rucker, U. (Eds.). *Conceptos clave de la gestión cultural. Enfoques desde Latinoamérica (Vol. II).* Santiago: Ariadna Ediciones. pp. 78–92.

TV UNAM (2019). *What model of cultural management does Mexico need?* September 20, 2019. https://www.youtube.com/watch?v=EBatZgK5_i0&t=1080s.

UNESCO (2018). *Derechos culturales y Derechos Humanos.* UNESCO Mexico Office and National Human Rights Commission of Mexico. http://appweb.cndh.org.mx/bibl ioteca/archivos/pdfs/Derechos_Culturales.pdf (Accessed May 20, 2020).

Vargas, A. (2020). Rechaza Flores Olea que el Fonca se creara para "acallar voces". *La Jornada.* April 20, 2020. https://www.jornada.com.mx/2020/04/20/cultura/a07n1cul (Accessed May 6, 2020).

Zong, J. & Batalova, J. (2018). *Mexican Inmigrants in the United States.* Migration Policy Institute. October 11, 2018. s://www.migrationpolicy.org/article/mexican-immigrants -united-states (Accessed April 2, 2020).

Zubiría Samper, Abello Trujillo, I. & Tabares, M. (1998). *Conceptos básicos de Administraión y Gestión cultural.* Organization of Ibero-American States for Education, Science and Culture. http://www.cba.gov.ar/wp-content/4p96humuzp/2015/07/Con ceptos-b%C3%A1sicos-de-administraci%C3%B3n-y-gesti%C3%B3n-cultural.pdf.

14 Cultural management in Peru

The role of the Ministry of Culture in challenging times

Paloma Carpio Valdeavellano

Introduction

This text identifies the common ground between those cultural managers who have been making significant contributions to the debate on certain key aspects of the public management of culture. It also seeks to evaluate the Peruvian Ministry of Culture's decade-long existence, a particular challenge given the bicentennial national independence celebrations. Decentralisation, the intercultural approach adopted, information management, and communication strategies have all been identified as salient themes when discussing current challenges facing the sector.

The raison d'etre of this work is the combining of the various voices within the ongoing dialogue. The individuals interviewed in the course of the research for this chapter have specific perspectives and experiences resulting from their involvement with the Ministry of Culture. The interviewees include Juan Carlos Adrianzen, who was responsible for establishing the programming guidelines of the *Gran Teatro Nacional*, a major cultural institution created by the Peruvian Government at the same time as the Ministry of Culture; Diana Guerra, a cultural manager specialising in heritage and tourism; Gloria Lescano of the UNESCO office in Peru who specialises in cultural promotion and local government; and Ingrid Cafferata, Director of the Decentralised Culture Office in Tacna and a specialist in public policy. The questions asked should serve to identify and analyse the factors determining the role played by the Ministry of Culture in its ten years of existence. This should, in turn, help to formulate alternative strategies in addressing the main challenges faced by this institution, among others, that have clearly emerged within the context of the COVID-19-engendered crisis. In order to do so, the characteristics of contemporary Peruvian society require detailed description.

Cultural management in Peru

Discussing cultural management within the Peruvian context requires an understanding of its various contradictions and complexities. In Peru, the narratives, epistemologies, customs, and traditions of the native peoples of the Andes and the Amazon coexist with those from Europe, Asia, and Africa together with those introduced into daily life as a result of globalisation. The country faces the challenge of preserving its collective memory and ancestral knowledge, while simultaneously protecting its biodiversity and natural resources. In order to understand the scope of cultural management in this South American country – beyond the models that focus purely on tangible heritage and cultural industries – it is necessary to take into account the historical events that have shaped it.

Before describing the historical elements conditioning Peru's current challenges which necessitate cultural management solutions, it is important to emphasise that, although cultural diversity's status as an academic subject has been comprehensively addressed within the social sciences (Mariategui, 1928; Arguedas, 1964; Degregori, 2009), it has been included in neither the theoretical reflection on cultural management nor its practice.

This apparent anomaly is partly due to cultural management training programmes having emerged over the past 15 years, in most cases delivered by private institutions. The only Peruvian tertiary education institution outside the capital offering undergraduate Cultural Management courses is the University of Piura. The number of individuals trained as cultural managers in Peru, and who define themselves as such, remains extremely low. Beyond the small number of specialists possibly trained at the University of Piura, or through academic courses abroad, the majority of the Peruvian cultural managers have a background in various fields such as anthropology, archaeology, history, sociology, communications, and languages related to art.

It remains a challenge to ensure that more professionals possess the capacity to generate projects through which knowledge of indigenous peoples and the influence of the diverse cultures that coexist in this country (due to the effects of migration) can be combined with the creative capacity of our artists. Due to the low institutionality of culture, its limited areas of specialised training, and the broad spectrum of cultural manifestations that coexist in a territory as diverse and full of contrasts as Peru, it is necessary to evaluate the role played by the Ministry of Culture in the management and promotion of cultural diversity, as the governing body within this field.

Cultural heritage in Peru

Since the discovery of and research into the Caral archaeological site, Peru has been considered the "cradle of civilisation". Located on the coast, to the north of Lima, the Caral civilisation, the oldest known in the Americas, developed between 3000 and 1500 BC. Diverse cultures originating around the millennium became established along the coast and Andean region of contemporary Peru until the *Tawantinsuyo* (or "Inca Empire") was unified between 1200 and 1532 AD. With Cusco as its centrepiece, its territory extended to the present-day area occupied by Colombia, Ecuador, Bolivia, Chile, and Argentina.

After the arrival of the Spanish and their conquest of this geographical region, the Viceroyalty of Peru was established. Due to the Spanish influence on the political administration, Peru was the last country in the region to achieve its

independence which, although declared on July 28, 1821, was not sealed definitively until 1824, resulting in the separation of Alto Peru after the formation of
Bolivia as an independent republic in 1825. However, to this day, Peruvians shoulder what the sociologist Julio Cotler terms the *colonial heritage* (1977) meaning
that, at a cultural level, the racism, classism, authoritarianism, and patriarchy displayed in colonial times continue to manifest themselves in contemporary Peru.
These vestiges of the colonial system also manifest themselves in the perception
held by a majority of the populace of their distance from those in power seeking
to impose a vision of the Western world based on the natural resource exploitation
which threatens native peoples' lifestyles.

The effect of this colonial legacy has, since its inception, caused Republican
Peru to oscillate between warlords, military coups, and the resignation and flight
of its governors, among other political acts, that highlight the fragility of its
democracy. As of 2000, following two decades marked by violence and political
crisis – whose most infamous agents were the terrorist groups Sendero Luminoso
(Shining Path) and MRTA (Tupac Amaru Revolutionary Movement), as well as
the government of the dictator Alberto Fujimori – Peru entered a period of greater
stability. During the last 20 years, democratically elected governments have continuously held office. By mid-2010, the last year of Alan García's presidency, the
Ministry of Culture (based upon the former National Institute of Culture) was
created by Law No. 29565.

What were the decisive factors that led to its creation? Historian Antonio
Zapata pointed out in an interview that the creation of this ministry consisted
of "those measures adopted to close one government, gaining some prominence
and transferring the responsibility to the next" (Escribano, 2010). The statements
made by President Garcia at the official public presentation of this new institution
showed a staggering lack of awareness of the significance and direction of this
institution. "The Ministry aims to raise to the level of national policy this concept
of representation, of creation, of what constitutes culture, and what differentiates
the product from cultural creation" (Escribano, 2010). In other words, it is created
through high-brow discourse lacking an in-depth analysis, rather than as the more
appropriate result of a public debate on its relevance and social function. The
creation of the Ministry of Culture was preceded by one of the most painful social
conflicts in the history of Peru; the so-called "Baguazo", an incident in which the
clashes between the police and members of the indigenous Awajún community
culminated in 33 deaths.

Native communities settled in the territories of Bagua province resisted the
implementation of legislative decrees that – under the pretext of implementation of the Free Trade Agreement with the United States – violated the agreements established by Convention 169 of the International Labour Organisation
(ILO). This convention protects indigenous peoples with regard to those activities permitted in their territories and requires a process of consultation which
was not carried out (Peña, 2019). This episode highlights the inherent tensions between different perspectives of development that coexist in Peru; one
of which seeks to preserve a harmonious relationship between the national

territory and natural resources, while the other supports the exploitation of natural resources by private companies. Given that Peru is a country the economic management of whose government is based mainly on extractive industries, these perspectives are in permanent conflict due to the prioritising of private sector interests.

Having said that, it is worth asking which role the Ministry of Culture should play in managing these conflicts and harmonising political agendas. Ironically, the creation of the Ministry of Culture, even though it occurred only a year after the events in Bagua, did not stimulate a debate on the challenges of interculturalism. Within the context of post-colonial societies such as Peru such a debate should raise the issue of how to ensure that indigenous inhabitants are not subjected to the unrealistic processes of forced acculturation, culminating in their expulsion from ancestral territories and the denial of their fundamental rights. In other words, the issue centres on how to conceive and generate forms of political organisation and coexistence based on the recognition of diversity, socio-economic inclusion, and political participation of the original cultural groups that have been secularly neglected (Tubino, 2003).

This necessary debate regarding the challenges of interculturality had been inadequately conducted in Peru before the creation of the Ministry of Culture. On the contrary, the simultaneous creation of this ministry and the Grand National Theatre led to the strengthening of the ongoing association of the word "culture" with "high culture", "elites", and "fine arts". In spite of these developments, just one year after the creation of the ministry, when the Grand National Theatre was nearing completion, a change of government resulted in the ascendency to the presidency of Ollanta Humala. The centre-left government he headed allowed certain topics – such as intercultural citizenship, grassroots culture, social inclusion, and social appropriation of heritage, among others – to be included within the remit of the newly created office. A number of achievements were realised during its first decade, such as the passing of the Puntos de Cultura, a policy that seeks to recognise, articulate, promote, and strengthen organisations whose work in the fields of art and culture, has a favourable influence on the community and a positive impact on citizens (Congress of the Republic, 2016)[1] or the implementation of a programme for the economic promotion of the cultural sector (Ministry of Culture, 2018). Nevertheless, the institutional weakness of the Ministry of Culture leaves cultural agents in a situation of vulnerability exacerbated within the context of the current pandemic.

This vulnerability of the sector is enhanced by another crucial feature of the Peruvian society, namely informality. According to a recent report by the Peruvian Ombudsman's Office, Peru is the Latin American country with the highest rates of insecurity. According to the National Institute of Statistics and Information Technology, by 2018, the economically active population consisted of 16,776,500 individuals, of which 72% were employed in the informal sector. This insecurity primarily affects women, 75% of whom work in this sector. In the cultural sector, the rate of informal employment is even higher. A recent survey conducted by the Municipality of Lima in cooperation with the Ministry of Culture tried to measure the impact on the sector of the crisis unleashed by the pandemic. Of a total of 10,452 respondents, 72% (7,530) categorised themselves as an employee (non-business owner) or as self-employed, 10% (1,011) declared themselves to be a legally registered business owner, and 10% (998) classified themselves as working in the non-formal economy, living a hand-to-mouth existence. In other words, 82% of those surveyed lack a stable job guaranteeing social and labour rights that would allow them to weather this crisis without being severely affected. 56% of participants are not enrolled in any public or private health care system.

The performance of the Ministry of Culture will be evaluated against this background, seeking to identify possible courses of action to strengthen its governance and, consequently, to provide a vision of development and cultural democracy that could contribute to overcoming the inequalities and social conflicts that persist in Peru. The first decade of the Peruvian Ministry of Culture coincided with the global health crisis caused by the COVID-19 virus, as well as the occasion of the bicentennial of national independence (BBC, 2020). Within this context of crisis, hopelessness, and death, in which Peru "celebrates" 200 years of existence as a republic, it is necessary to examine the role an institution such as the Ministry of Culture should play in formulating strategies to overcome the crisis and carve out a desirable future for the country.

In order to identify the variables that impact the Ministry of Culture's performance – and affect its outcomes – four cultural managers experienced in public management and with different perspectives responded individually to the following two questions: Which structural factors are decisive in the governance of the ministry? What are the challenges and transformations that can be expected a decade after its establishment? The respondents' answers have been categorised, analysed, and compared with institutional documents that provide an overview of the Ministry of Culture structures.

The organic structure of the Ministry of Culture

It is worthwhile collecting references from its own institutional bases that contribute to an evaluation of the Ministry of Culture's functioning. With regard to programmes, the law that created the ministry states the following:

> Article 4. – Programme action areas: these are domains in which the Ministry of Culture exercises its competencies, functions and attributes for the achievement of the objectives and goals of the State. a) National Cultural Heritage (Tangible and Intangible). b) Contemporary cultural creation and living arts. c) Cultural management and cultural industries. d) Ethnic and cultural plurality of the nation.

In order to attend to these areas, the Ministry of Culture maintains an organic structure incorporating two vice-ministries: the Vice-Ministry of Cultural Heritage and Cultural Industries and the Vice-Ministry of Interculturality. Each office contains general directorates and directorates covering the four programme areas established by its founding law.

Of the seven constituent departments of the ministry, four are devoted to heritage issues. Only one is responsible for the cultural industries and the arts, while two are devoted to interculturality. A major challenge highlighted is that, by focusing exclusively on indigenous peoples, interculturality may be misunderstood as leading not to integration, but to segregation. The National Policy for the Transversalization of the Intercultural Approach, approved in 2015, states that a primary objective is to promote a state that operates with cultural relevance and thus contributes to the "elimination of discrimination, respect for cultural differences, social inclusion and national integration" (Ministry of Culture, 2015). However, the organisational structure of the Ministry of Culture itself does not encourage the integration of specialists drawn from different disciplines and backgrounds. Consequently, its actions do not always promote the integration of different ways of experiencing culture.

This is mainly due to the fact that the functional structure of the Ministry of Culture was based off that of the former National Institute of Culture, an institution whose primary mission was the preservation of material heritage. With the creation of the Ministry of Culture, the functions of the National Institute of Culture (INC) and the National Institute for the Development of the Andean, Amazonian and Afro-Peruvian Peoples (INDEPA) were subsumed by this new institution.

Therefore, the Ministry of Culture's organisational structure has two distinctive focuses: one dealing with heritage and the other with indigenous peoples. Everything related to the arts and cultural industries, the aims of community-level cultural development, information systems, and networking with other governmental levels are fairly recently identified issues, scarcely represented in the activity of the ministry. As a result, these interactions and common goals between tangible and intangible heritage policies, contemporary creation, and grassroots culture, are supported by private organisations that undertake huge fund-raising campaigns to sustain their work.

The Decentralised Cultural Departments need to be mentioned at this point. They report to the Lima-based Ministry of Culture headquarters in their capacity as regional-level representatives of this institution. The resources allocated to these offices are minimal and their main role is limited to issuing Certificates of Non-existence of Archaeological Remains (CIRAS), possession of which constitutes a pre-condition for proposed real-estate projects slated for implementation within a defined territory.

The political role of the Ministry of Culture

As indicated in an EFE Agency article published in 2010, the Ministry of Culture is

one of the ministries with the broadest responsibilities of the entire Peruvian Government since it must not only take charge of the investigation and conservation of the incalculable cultural heritage and archaeological sites of the country, but also has significant indigenous policies to implement.

However, if its extremely limited annually assigned budget is taken into account, it is evident that no correspondence exists between the importance of this institution and its prioritisation within public administration.

The scant appreciation of the Ministry of Culture's role within successive governments during these ten years is evident in the high turnover of ministers, 14 in total, who have headed it. Recently, Alejandro Neyra, very briefly Minister of Culture at the beginning of 2018, has returned to confront the COVID-19-related crisis in the midst of a general malaise affecting the cultural sector due to the inaction of the ministry at this juncture. On average, Ministers of Culture in Peru serve for a period approaching nine months. Predictably, this high turnover of incumbents of the post generates instability. As Victor Vich points out, 14 Ministers of Culture in little more than nine years of operation "gives a perfect account of the absolute disinterest that the political class has in cultural policies in Peru". As this scholar states,

> What is questioned is the lack of leadership with a specialized vision; leaders possessing not only experience and knowledge of the sector's heterogeneity, but also demonstrating an outlook that can position culture as a meaningful factor in the design of different national public policies.
>
> (2020)

The lack of continuity and leadership has resulted in a weak connection between the Ministry of Culture and other ministries at the intra-governmental level. This reinforces the perception of culture as divorced from the problems of citizens' daily lives. By directing scarce financial and institutional resources to heritage protection and indigenous peoples' preservation (both of which are undoubtedly fundamental tasks), the engagement with other ministries (such as Education, Development and Social Inclusion, Women and Vulnerable Populations, Health, Environment, Justice and Human Rights, to mention only a few) has been minimal. The only ministry with which there is an asymmetric level of dependence is the Ministry of Foreign Trade and Tourism since the latter's activity is closely linked to archaeological sites and gastronomy. Minimal indispensable dialogue exists between the two ministries, but it is the Ministry of Foreign Trade and Tourism that takes the lead and imposes its agenda. This illustrates the fact that public cultural policies are targeted at an elite (in this case, foreign tourists), while the right of the inhabitants themselves to participate in the cultural life of their community continues to be limited. The exploitation of Peruvian culture by the tourism industry leads to the instrumentalisation and exoticisation of the lifestyles of native peoples and minorities. It could be affirmed, according to George Yúdice's analysis of "culture as a resource" (2003), that the images and products of these peoples have been used to give "value" to the "country brand", without any concomitant expansion of the rights and concrete opportunities of their communities.

Budget and social gaps

According to information presented to Congress at the end of 2019 by the former Minister of Culture, Luis Jaime Castillo, the ministry's annual budget has never exceeded 0.42% of the National Public Budget. This percentage was reached during its first year (2011), given the high costs of the construction of the National Grand Theatre. During the subsequent years, this percentage has never exceeded 0.38%. This is despite the fact that – according to the National Institute of Statistics and Information Technology (INEI, 2017) – cultural activities (audiovisual, books and publications, design, music, cultural training, plastic and visual arts, performing arts, games and toys) account for 1.2% of the country's gross domestic product, a figure higher than activities such as fishing or financial services.

The low budget allocation (the annual budget of the Ministry of Culture is limited to two hundred million dollars) also gives cause for concern if we examine its distribution within this government department. As much as 33% of the Ministry of Culture's budget is allocated to the "Enhancement and Social Use of Cultural Heritage"; another 33% is accounted for by "Budgetary allocations that do not result in outputs"; 24% to "Central Actions", and 10% to "Development of the Arts and Cultural Industries". "Central Actions" are those oriented to guaranteeing "the management of its human, material and financial resources, which contribute in a transversal and indivisible way to the achievement of Budget Programs targets" (MEF, 2016). Those budgetary allocations that do not produce an output are the ones aimed at "attracting attention to a specific purpose of the entity, which does not result in the delivery of an output to a specific population" (Ibid.). According to these figures, which formed part of a presentation to the Congressional Culture and Heritage Commission, less than 2% of the resources allocated to the Ministry of Culture are directed to the main projects of the Vice-Ministry of Interculturality and are regarded as constituting part of the percentage relating to "Central Actions". Most of the Ministry of Culture's expenditure is devoted to covering its operational costs and to funding the management of tangible heritage.

In addition, according to the National Survey of Budget Programmes (INEI, 2017), the citizenry's participation in cultural activities demonstrated deficiencies that need to be addressed. 48% of the population declared that its main cultural activity consists of participation in traditional festivals. 26% of those individuals surveyed attended at least one craft fair every year, while 34% watched films. Alternative cultural activities fell far below these levels. Only 10% of the population attend theatre, circus, and dance performances. Therefore, it can be said that the main activities mobilising cultural participation are oriented towards intangible heritage and activities associated with local or community culture. However, the relationship with respect to public investment in these activities does not correspond to their importance for Peruvians. This reaffirms that investment in culture has an economic focus and is not oriented towards human development.

Given that most of the resources allocated annually to the Ministry of Culture correspond to "Directly Collected Revenue", which are generated, to a considerable extent, by activities associated with Machu Picchu and tourism, the redistribution within the Ministry of Culture tends to be directed towards the enhancement of the most important archaeological sites within the country.

Discussion

Taking the performance of the Ministry of Culture within the context of the pandemic crisis and the evaluation of its administration over its ten years of existence as well as the contributions of the cultural managers interviewed for this text into account, it is possible to categorise the challenges facing the Ministry of Culture as one of three decisive factors. (1) poor task definition, (2) institutional weakness, and (3) scant acknowledgement of the relevance of the cultural sector by both the state and citizenry. In the following section, these three categories will be examined more closely.

•   Lack of definition and orientation

As mentioned above, the creation of the Ministry of Culture was not the result of a public debate or consensus within the cultural sector that would have enabled it to focus its actions. It was, rather, the result of the personal ego of a president who wished to be remembered for the creation of the Grand National Theatre. Although a large number of cultural managers, who met in the course of the Spanish Agency for International Cooperation (AECID) funded "Project to Promote Cultural Policies", which recommended the drafting of a founding document, their proposals and recommendations were not, to any great extent, incorporated into the vision and operational structure of the ministry. As Juan Carlos Adrianzen mentions in relation to the role of the Ministry of Culture:

> The reason for the creation of this ministry is insufficiently clear, not for its own agents, for the rest of the public sector, or for the citizenry. A fundamental flaw exists in that it has not been part of a broad debate defining its mission. Is it an agent of cultural promotion? Is it a regulatory body? Is it a producer of events? During these years, people have been both inefficient and ineffective because of this complex origin that prevents anyone having a clear idea of its role.
>
> (Interview, 2020)

It is this inability to establish a clear function that undermines every attempt to strengthen its institutional framework. As cultural manager Diana Guerra explains:

> I think both internal and external factors are involved. Internal ones concern the professional team employed, its cohesion and capacity to lead participatory cultural policy design processes, manage conflicts, co-opt various

stakeholders, reach agreements, consolidate cultural institutions, etc. As for internal factors, it is also important how the ministry is organised, how information flows between areas, how decisions are made, and how tasks are prioritised and communicated.

(Interview, 2020)

As previously noted, the lack of orientation, the fragmentation as well as disarticulation of the various directorates of the Ministry of Culture led to the institutional weaknesses that Guerra identifies, as well as to the fact that the prioritised initiatives are not always strategic but, rather, limited in scope. There is no strategy for promoting citizen participation. Each department determines, according to its own criteria, the manner of its relations with cultural organisations and agents. The ministry itself does not encourage the exchange of perspectives, information, and experiences of its own specialists. Along the same lines, Ingrid Cafferata, Director of the Decentralised Culture Directorate in Tacna (a region on the southern border of the country), observes the following:

The Ministry of Culture has not been able, so far, to define the main axes of a national cultural policy and, as a consequence, inconsistencies are perceived in the administrations, since each of them tries to prioritise the issue that it considers most relevant.

(Interview, 2020)

• Institutional weaknesses

As already pointed out, all these problems are interconnected. There are several contributory factors to the Ministry of Culture's failure to achieve the necessary institutional building, and – consequently – ensure greater priority being assigned to culture within the government's overall political agenda. In order for the Ministry of Culture to have greater social impact and thus help to address the country's structural problems, which feature aspects associated with the aforementioned "colonial heritage" (racism, classism, authoritarianism, among others) – it is necessary to overcome those factors limiting its management's effectiveness.

Limited budget: as mentioned above, the culture sector's budget does not match the magnitude of its tasks. According to Ingrid Cafferata, this

reveals the degree of interest that we, as a country, have regarding the importance of cultural development, on the one hand, and the limited value placed on the cultural legacy expressed in the materiality and immateriality of the country's cultural heritage on the other.

(Interview, 2020)

In other words, budgetary allocations reflect the degree of previously mentioned attention and priority assigned to culture at the national level. In addition to the modest annual budget allocated to the Ministry of Culture, there is no patronage system or incentives for private investment to supplement the resources available for the development of cultural projects.

Centralism: the manner in which the Ministry of Culture is managed reflects the centralism that characterises the country. The distribution of resources prevents a more prominent role for the Decentralised Directorates of Culture which have no alternative but to function as the reception desk for the central headquarters. Associating this aspect with the budgetary dimension, Guerra states that "the funds needed to operate and the modernisation of its structure (which also includes the decentralisation of its work at the national level) are also crucial" (Interview, 2020). Similarly, Gloria Lescano points out that there is little autonomy (administrative, strategic, partnership, and planning) in the regions (Interview, 2020). As a result, power is concentrated in the capital culminating in widening disparities and limited representation and protagonism of cultural expressions from the country's diverse regions. The strengthening of the Decentralised Directorates of Culture will be fundamental. As Cafferata stated, one challenge that must be tackled in order to promote equity is the promotion of:

> the administrative decentralisation and empowerment of the Decentralised Directorates of Culture, which should have the autonomy to provide culturally relevant services with adequate budgets in order to become genuine promoters of cultural activity in each region, as well as to strengthen the social fabric around arts groups, cultural industries, bearers of intangible heritage, museums, libraries among others.
>
> (Interview, 2020)

Lack of sustained leadership: frequent ministerial changes have prevented the consolidation and deepening of a clear cultural management vision. As Cafferata suggests, "the volatility of and, in many cases, improvisation by the main authorities (ministers, vice-ministers, general secretaries, etc.) has not allowed the implementation of a cultural project at the national level" (Interview 2020).

This instability has resulted in the weakening of the cultural sector's influence within the Council of Ministers with the result that intergovernmental and intersectoral work is almost non-existent. Moreover, the ministry's day-to-day management is limited to responding to requests and emergencies on an ad hoc basis. In addition, there are still some regulatory gaps that complicate the work of cultural managers and cultural institutions.

Limited recognition of the cultural sector by the State and citizenry

This third challenge is closely related to the two previous ones. The communication and distribution of information represent central points worthy of closer inspection. As emphasised by Cafferata:

> the insufficient information (statistical data) available to the Ministry of Culture makes it difficult to secure higher budgets for the sector.... This

influences the public's perception of the role of the Ministry of Culture, the social valorisation of heritage, the appreciation of the relevance of art as an element that can transform reality, and the recognition of diversity.

(Interview, 2020)

This scarcity of data is also referred to by Gloria Lescano who indicates that it is necessary to have an information system that provides records, mappings, inventories, and multidimensional research on the impact of the sector, among other data, that would enable evidence-based decision-making. In this regard, a degree of progress has been accomplished through the implementation of a Culture Satellite Account, although it is limited to measuring the contribution to culture within the country's gross domestic product. The statistical model known as the Satellite Account refers to a series of analytical instruments that allow a detailed study of a particular economic sector, examining its relationship with some of the main macroeconomic variables such as its contribution to gross domestic product (Piedras, 2015). These types of mechanisms (in addition to the implementation of information systems and/or cultural observatories) allow states to develop data and evidence-based policies. This is essential in the case of the cultural sector, since it bears enormous responsibilities associated with the quality of people's lives, but whose relationship has been inadequately studied. To this end, not only is it necessary to work with institutions such as the National Institute of Statistics and Information Technology, but also to form alliances with universities and research centres that render possible the quantitative and qualitative measuring of the impact of culture on such important elements as education, gender equality, and health, among others. Progress has been made in this regard by the Peruvian participation in the "UNESCO Culture for Development Indicators" project (UNESCO, 2014). However, the launching of this initiative has not achieved the expected scope since it has not involved the implementation of concrete measures, either at the national or local government level.

This poor valuation of culture and, particularly, the ministry's role in its promotion is partly due to inadequate communication strategies and promotion of citizen participation. Only a few institutional-level initiatives are based on a close and proactive dialogue with and between cultural agents. Among them, it is worth mentioning the *Puntos de Cultura* Programme, which has a legal framework (Law 30487, Law for the Promotion of Points of Culture) that was the result of collaboration between mid-ranking officials within the Ministry of Culture and community-based cultural organisations. Another noteworthy initiative is that of the Intangible Heritage Directorate which has worked with artisans from all regions of Peru who participate in creating a platform for exhibiting their work called *Ruraq Maki*. At the level of the Vice-Ministry of Interculturality, it is appropriate to highlight the efforts that have been made to preserve and promote indigenous languages, as well as measures to reduce ethnic and racial discrimination. These initiatives include approval of the regulations for Law No. 29735, on the regulation of the use, preservation, development, recovery, promotion, and dissemination of native languages, as well as the "Anti-Racism Alert" initiative.[2]

Communication is of central importance when addressing the above-mentioned challenges. Without adequate dissemination, it is not possible to communicate, promote, and emphasise the value of cultural management to the public. The current situation leads to low investment in the sector and, consequently, to significant challenges in strengthening its institutions. Within the context of the current pandemic, communication has a fundamental role to play because citizens need to recognise the relationship between culture and the "new social coexistence" that these times demand. This is what the government calls the transition period towards new habits that citizens must, supposedly, adopt in order to get through the COVID-19 crisis. These measures imply, in the short term, the implementation of physical distancing, repeated washing of hands, consistent use of face masks, as well as the avoidance of crowds. In the medium term, they highlight public priorities such as protecting the elderly and people at risk, promoting mental health, strengthening health services, using open data and recording information, fighting misinformation and corruption, among others (PCM, 2020). Promoting these transformations implies understanding the cultural dimension as that in which "imaginaries" are built, transformed, and established. Therefore, in the current debate on new forms of coexistence, public institutions with competences in culture should play a greater role. As Victor Vich states,

> If culture is a "way of life" and every way of life is a way of apprehending the world, we citizens can appeal to culture to reconfigure common meanings and establish a set of demands that begin to put into practice new types of social relations.
>
> (2005, p. 275)

Within a context characterised by the reorientation of economic and social activities as a result of the pandemic – in addition to revisiting the country's 200 years as a republic – it is essential to discuss the role of the Ministry of Culture, which should be more prominent. Collective exercises involving discussion of this situation and the future should be encouraged. Unfortunately, since the Ministry of Culture does not adequately execute this role, the collective common sense of citizens continues to assert that cultural activities are merely supplementary and dispensable, even more so at times of crisis such as the one currently being experienced.

This inability of the Ministry of Culture to adequately communicate its role engenders potential conflict situations. In the present pandemic context, it aims to develop content and services potentially contributing to the economic reactivation of the sector. Meanwhile, cultural workers have been experiencing the cessation of their activities and the concrete expression of enormous inconsistencies in access to technology which are critical at this time of crisis. In addition, one section of the population expresses its opposition to the decision to redirect approximately US$15 million in order to address the impact of the pandemic on the culture sector. While for a large percentage of citizens there is no justification for directing resources to a sector not regarded as playing a significant role within the country, for cultural workers this level of funding is inadequate.

Considering the Ministry of Culture's institutional weakness, the political instability that has characterised its governance, the lack of a meaningful communication strategy to publicise its role, and its inadequate political weight within the strategic policies of the state; it is not surprising that this institution is the object of continual proposals that it be abolished or merged with another entity. In fact, a congressman has recently presented a bill for the "strengthening of the Culture and Tourism sector through its integration into the Ministry of Culture and Tourism". This proposal intends to locate this ministry's headquarters in the city of Cusco, home to major national tourist attractions. Once again, culture is only valued as a resource contributing to the growth of the gross domestic product.

Conclusions

In light of the combination of the COVID-19-induced global crisis, the bicentennial celebrations, and the first decade of the Ministry of Culture's existence, it is worth examining the appropriate role of this institution within the new social scenario and the adjustments necessary for its administration to command greater political and societal support. In order to achieve this, more extensive interaction between each of its composite parts must be ensured in order that its governance responds in a transdisciplinary manner, not to isolated initiatives but, rather, to shared purposes and goals. Consequently, it will be necessary for the Ministry of Culture to overcome its bureaucratic mindset in order to implement procedures marrying its work more closely with that of various cultural actors. As Guerra suggests, it is essential:

> to work on national cultural agreements, national and regional cultural policies, and integrated management plans (for heritage, cultural industry, traditional arts), in addition to fostering decentralisation processes relating to cultural governance…. Moreover, an invitation must be issued and the openness exist for civil society and private enterprise to participate in heritage management, for example, by establishing clear rules for care and protection, but also for jointly managed wealth generation. Culture is not, and cannot be, the exclusive preserve of the state. Finally, in order to strengthen its relationship with other state entities such as those of the tourism sector, (and, of course, all stakeholders), the formation of technical committees to work specifically on joint culture and tourism policies (and, similarly, on education, health, environmental issues, etc) is recommended.
>
> (Interview, 2020)

The generation and management of information is key to improving the functioning of the Ministry of Culture. In this context of crisis, the lack of updated statistics regarding the situation of creators and cultural agents in this country has constituted a serious problem.

Furthermore, in a country with Peru's archaeological wealth, promoting the social appropriation of heritage is fundamental. To this end, it is necessary to strengthen community initiatives that expand citizens' capacity for participation, expression, and organisation. It is from these interactions between an appreciation of ancestral knowledge and contemporary forms of expression that the acknowledgement by new generations of their role as cultural agents will be possible. In addition to the promotion of citizen participation and the transparent and accountable administration that it requires, it is essential to intensify coordinated efforts at the intersectoral and intergovernmental levels.

The recent approval of a National Policy on Culture to be implemented until 2030 should lead to a broad debate that will position the Ministry of Culture as a key agent of national development. Within a context such as that currently prevailing, it will be vital to establish links with other ministries in order that the structural problems highlighted by the current crisis resulting from the need to transform the imaginaries[3] that condition human coexistence are addressed. Peru is a country where racism and discrimination undermine relationships, where the value of the public sphere and the role of the state as a rights guarantor has been lost. The prioritisation over the last 30 years of a model of public management that subordinates all dimensions of life to the economic dimension has created profound social inequalities within the country. As long as indigenous peoples are forced to resist the occupation of their territories by private interests for the exploitation of their resources, as has been ongoing since colonisation, and as long as the authorities consider that economic capital should take priority over people's rights, overcoming the conflicts that characterise Peru will prove extremely challenging.

Against this background, strengthening the Ministry of Culture's role within the cultural dimension will prove the only possible means of transforming the colonial and patriarchal structures of our society. In the medium term, Peruvians can recognise themselves in a country where the lifestyles of our native peoples are respected, and where creativity and symbolic expression are promoted as the means of understanding our relationship with the past, present, and future, as well as integrating Peru with the rest of the world.

The COVID-19 crisis has indicated the precariousness of public systems and citizens' behaviour. In the latter case, it can be seen in the continuous forms of transgressing norms and citizens prioritising the exercise of their individual liberties over that of the common good. This is why, ten years after the creation of the Ministry of Culture and with two hundred years of existence as a republic behind us, this could be the appropriate moment to generate a debate that the very creation of this ministry should have triggered. Such discourse would enable public institutions and citizens to discuss the orientation of a development model in line with Peru's cultural diversity. Moreover, it would enable the country to rise to the challenge of seeking forms of intercultural dialogue as the basis for defining policies that contribute to overcoming the structural inequalities that affect governance and coexistence within the country.

Notes

1 Puntos de Cultura is a policy initiated in Brazil in 2004 that completely changed the manner in which grassroots cultural organisations are subsidized, recognising certain types of organisations that were previously considered unsuitable for support by the Ministry of Culture, and removing certain bureaucratic restrictions with which these groups were never able to comply. As part of the Cultura Viva policy, the programme created an unprecedented category of benefitting organisations through a variety of networks. Its regional prestige was such that in 2011 the MERCOSUR Cultural recommended its adoption as a policy by other countries in the region, precipitating the implementation of similar programmes in Argentina, Peru, and Bolivia, among other countries. For more information, see Barbosa. & Calabre (2011).
2 Available at www.alertacontraelracismo.pe (accessed August 24, 2020).
3 "Social imaginary" is a concept frequently used in Latin American social sciences and relates to the Greek philosopher Cornelius Castoriadis. It refers to the social representations embodied in institutions. It is usually used as a synonym for mentality, cosmovision, collective consciousness, or ideology, but it specifically seeks to relativise the influence that the material and productive/economic dimension has on social life.

References

Arguedas, J. M. (1964). *Todas las sangres*. Buenos Aires: Losada.

BBC News (2020). *Coronavirus: Peru economy sinks 40% in April amid lockdown*. https://www.bbc.com/news/world-latin-america-53051157 (Accessed June 26, 2020).

Castillo, L. J. (2019). *Proyecto de Presupuesto para el Año Fiscal 2020 – Sector Cultura*. Congress of the Republic of Peru. http://www.congreso.gob.pe/Docs/comisiones2019/Presupuesto/files/exposiciones/ppt_cultura_2020.pdf.

Congress of the Republic of Peru (2016). *Ley 30487 Ley de Promoción de los Puntos de Cultura*. https://busquedas.elperuano.pe/normaslegales/ley-de-promocion-de-los-puntos-de-cultura-ley-n-30487-1404903-1/.

Cotler, J. (1977). Clases, estado y nación en el Perú. Perú Problema Series, N°17 Lima: Instituto de Estudios Peruanos.

Degregori, C. I. (2009). *No hay país más diverso. Compendio de antropología peruana*. Lima: IEP.

Escribano, P. (2010). Se creó el Ministerio de Cultura. *Diario La República*. July 22, 2010. https://larepublica.pe/tendencias/475821-se-creo-el-ministerio-de-cultura/.

INEI (2017). *Encuesta Nacional de Programas Presupuestales*. National Institute of Statistics and Information. https://www.inei.gob.pe/media/MenuRecursivo/publicaciones_digitales/Est/Lib1442/libro.pdf.

Mariategui, J. C. (1928). *Siete ensayos de interpretación de la realidad peruana*. Lima: Editorial Minerva.

Ministry of Culture (2018). *Estímulos Económicos Para la Cultura*. https://estimuloseconomicos.cultura.gob.pe/.

——— (2015). *Política Nacional de Transversalización del Enfoque Intercultural*. https://acortar.link/OLxxh.

MEF (2016). *Directiva para los programas presupuestales en el marco del presupuesto por resultados*. Lima: Ministry of Economy and Finance. https://acortar.link/eXWPk.

PCM (2020). *Decreto Supremo 094–2020*. Lima: Presidency of the Council of Ministers. https://acortar.link/1p5i.

Peña Jumpe, A. (2019). El Baguazo en sus 10 años: el Perú sin integración. PuntoEdu. Lima: Pontifical Catholic University of Peru. https://puntoedu.pucp.edu.pe/opinion/el-baguazo-en-sus-10-anos-el-peru-sin-integracion/.

Piedras, E. (2015). *Nociones y Definición de la Cuenta Satélite de la Cultura. https://acortar.link/v8ldm.*

Tubino, F. (2003). Del interculturalismo funcional al interculturalismo crítico. *Rostros y fronteras de la identidad.* https://red.pucp.edu.pe/ridei/wp-content/uploads/biblioteca/inter_funcional.pdf.

UNESCO (2014). *Culture for Development Indicators: Methodology Manual.* https://es.unesco.org/creativity/sites/creativity/files/iucd_manual_metodologico_1.pdf.

Vich, V. (2020). La última rueda del coche: sobre el Ministerio de Cultura. *La Mula.* May 30. https://victorvich.lamula.pe/2020/05/30/la-ultima-rueda-del-coche-sobre-el-ministerio-de-cultura/victorvich/.

———— (2005). Las políticas culturales en debate: lo intercultural, lo subalterno y la dimensión universalista. In Vich, V. (Ed.). *El Estado está de vuelta: desigualdad, diversidad y democracia.* Lima: Institute of Peruvian Studies, pp. 265–278.

Yúdice, G. (2003). *El recurso de la cultura. Usos de la cultura en la era global.* Barcelona: Grijalbo.

Index

For Product Safety Concerns and Information please contact our EU
representative GPSR@taylorandfrancis.com
Taylor & Francis Verlag GmbH, Kaufingerstraße 24, 80331 München, Germany